THE COMPLETE JULIAN
OF NORWICH

PARACLETE
GIANTS

ABOUT THIS SERIES:

Each Paraclete Giant presents collected works of one of Christianity's greatest writers—"giants" of the faith. These essential volumes share the pivotal teachings of leading Christian figures throughout history with today's theological students and all people seeking spiritual wisdom.

Forthcoming in This Series...

THE COMPLETE THÉRÈSE OF LISIEUX
Edited with translations by Robert J. Edmonson, CJ
Fall 2009

For more information, visit www.paracletepress.com.

PARACLETE
GIANTS

The COMPLETE

Julian

OF NORWICH

Father John-Julian, OJN

PARACLETE PRESS BREWSTER, MASSACHUSETTS

DEDICATED WITH GRATITUDE TO

ROBERT LLEWELYN, MICHAEL MCLEAN,
VALERIE LAGORIO, AND BRANT PELPHREY

WHO SHOWED ME THE WAY.

The Complete Julian of Norwich

2009 First and Second Printing

Copyright © 2009 by The Order of Julian of Norwich

ISBN 978-1-55725-639-3

The map on page vii was drawn by Sister Thérèse, OJN.

Library of Congress Cataloging-in-Publication Data
John-Julian, Father, O.J.N.
  The complete Julian of Norwich / Father John-Julian.
    p. cm.
  ISBN 978-1-55725-639-3
  1. Julian, of Norwich, b. 1343. 2. Mysticism. I. Julian, of Norwich, b. 1343. Works.
English. II. Title.
  BV5095.J84J64 2009
  242--dc22
                                    2009000267
10 9 8 7 6 5 4 3 2

Published by Paraclete Press
Brewster, Massachusetts
www.paracletepress.com

Printed in the United States of America

CONTENTS

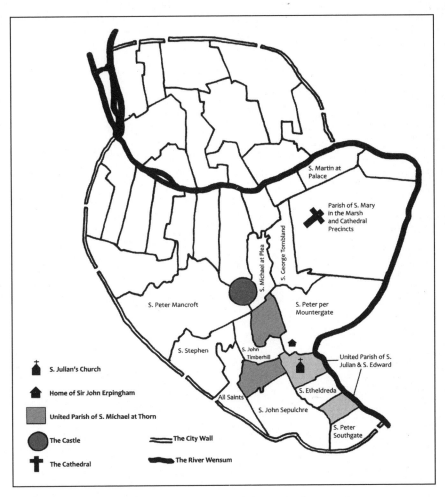

S. Martin at Palace

Parish of S. Mary in the Marsh and Cathedral Precincts

S. Michael at Plea

S. George Tombland

S. Peter Mancroft

S. Peter per Mountergate

S. Stephen

S. John Timberhill

United Parish of S. Julian & S. Edward

S. Etheldreda

All Saints

S. John Sepulchre

S. Peter Southgate

✝ S. Julian's Church

⌂ Home of Sir John Erpingham

▢ United Parish of S. Michael at Thorn

● The Castle

✝ The Cathedral

━━ The City Wall

━━ The River Wensum

The Medieval Parishes of the City of Norwich
Based on information from the Norfolk Family History Society

PART
ONE

INTRODUCTION AND MAJOR THEMES

INTRODUCTION AND MAJOR THEMES

Christopher Ricks has defined a great work of art as "one that continues to repay attention."[1] As one who has translated *The Revelations of Julian of Norwich* and who has read, studied, and reflected daily on the book for over a quarter of a century, I can unmistakably assert that, in the sense of Ricks's definition, Julian's book wholly qualifies as at the very least "a great work of art." In all these years, I have never picked up her book for a serious read when I have not discovered some previously undiscerned insight: like Holy Scripture itself, *The Revelations* clearly "repay attention."

Thomas Merton once wrote: "Julian is without doubt one of the most wonderful of all Christian voices. She gets greater and greater in my eyes as I grow older and whereas in the old days I used to be crazy about St. John of the Cross, I would not exchange him now for Julian if you gave me the world and the Indies and all the Spanish mystics rolled up in one bundle. I think that Julian of Norwich is with Newman the greatest English theologian."[2]

Recently, the Archbishop of Canterbury has characterized Julian's book as "what may well be the most important work of Christian reflection in the English language."[3] Even the *Encyclopedia Britannica*—not known for its editorializing—declares that Julian's book "is generally considered one of the most remarkable documents of medieval religious experience."[4]

What is it about this retiring, obscure, fourteenth-century English anchoress that stirs the hearts and minds of some of the greatest spiritual leaders of our time? What is it that has motivated scores of books to be published about Julian in the last thirty years after over 600 years of silence? What spark has she struck in the imaginations and in the souls of moderns that has brought her finally into the very forefront of contemporary spirituality?

The answer is to be discovered in the pages of her book—in her own account of the miraculous revelations granted her during a

seemingly mortal illness, and her long-awaited and carefully considered understandings of the meaning and implication of those
visions.

However, since my primary goal in this work is to increase Julian's
accessibility to contemporary readers, it might be helpful to suggest
some of the themes and patterns of thought and theology that spring
from her insights. I do not pretend to speak *for* Julian—she speaks too
well for herself—but I want to point out some of Julian's primary
lines of thought so that readers may be sensitive to the uniqueness of
her understandings and to their amazing relevance to our lives today.

1. Optimism

First, Julian is a theological optimist. Standing over against the pessimism and sin-absorption of the theology of much of the Middle Ages—and in spite of living in the midst of devastating cultural upheaval and the collapse of centuries-old institutions and patterns of life on which entire cultures had been based—Julian stands forward as a primary voice of clarity and hope.

When we consider what happened during her life in England, the parallels with our own time present themselves with awesome clarity. She saw the assassination of a king and an archbishop; she saw the nation-wide rioting of the Peasants' Rebellion (and the harsh suppression of that movement—especially by her own military bishop Henry le Despenser of Norwich). In her lifetime, she lived through at least three sieges of the massive Pestilence that struck East Anglia and killed over half of the population. She saw the beginning of what came to be called the Hundred Years' War between England and France. She saw the firm rock of the papacy come crashing down—crumbling, first, in the Babylonian Captivity at Avignon, and then collapsing entirely in the Great Schism, when for a time there were three men who claimed to be the true Pope. She watched the continuing degeneration of the monasteries from centers of the highest sacrifice and devotion to England's most self-aggrandizing landlords. She saw the results of the moral collapse of the Franciscan movement in which so many in England had placed high hopes. And she lived during the rise of England's first heretics in the persons of Oxford's John Wycliff and his later Lollard followers. (And, if my tentative identification of her has any accuracy, she even saw the murder of her own young husband.)

The fourteenth century was the mad, crumbling, convulsive world in which this exceptional woman lived, and it was in this world that, astoundingly, she was able to accept and articulate those most famous words: "All shall be well, and all shall be well, and all manner of thing shall be well."

But there is in Julian's optimism nothing of the self-blinding "make believer" who simply converts pain, suffering, and sin into fictions and pretends they are not real. Julian's "all shall be well" does *not* suggest that "tomorrow things will be better," but that in that final Great Day, God's will *shall* ultimately be worked in all of God's creation, and that even now, "the sweet eye of pity and of love never departs from us, and the working of mercy ceases not." Her optimism is one of solid faith and absolute conviction, and the refusal to believe that the muddle and violence of earth is the final and exhaustive expression of reality.

I like to describe Julian as an "originist"—one who bears witness against our own inclinations to think that what a thing *does* is always what it *is*. If Julian were asked, "What is a human being?" she would not base her answer merely on observations of the activities of humans, but she would answer first by describing human origins: the gift of humanity by the Father to the Son before all time (the "first creation" of our human "essence" by God in heaven), then God's bonding of that human essence with our "soul" and our "fleshliness" in our birth, and then our being "bought again" by God's incarnation in Christ and re-incorporated utterly into him.

And Julian's conclusion would be that humanity is of utmost value and worth: humanity is the final and supreme creation of God, the gift of the divine Father to the divine Son, possessed of a "divine will that never consents to sin, nor ever will," participating in the divinity of the Trinity itself. Julian would follow the now-unpopular Scholastic traditions of differentiating clearly between action or function, on the one hand, and essence or being, on the other. Regardless of what humans *do,* Julian knows what they *are*—and even in God's own eyes, they are "very good."

2. TRANSCENDENCE OF HISTORY

There is not a single specific mention of any of her world's turmoil in Julian's writings. The reason is what we would describe as Julian's "transcendence of events." Any specific historical occurrence is of relative unimportance to one who does not worry over and has no anxiety about those events.

Julian's transcendence is not a repudiation of pain, suffering, and turmoil (for we see, even in the examples she uses, that she knew those things well), but it is a "passing beyond" those earthly things, a refusal to be trapped by the existential, in the quiet confidence that "truly He does and causes every thing that is done." There is, for Julian, no need to complain about circumstances and historical events, because whatever those circumstances or whatever those events, they are there at the will of God and "our heavenly Mother Jesus cannot allow us that are His children to perish."

There is also in her work no diversion of devotion or compromise of commitment to what was an increasingly corrupt institutional Church. There is in Julian not a shred of anti-clericalism or anti-institutionalism. Although some critics have striven to "modernize" Julian by dressing her in the garb of crypto-Protestantism or anti-clericalism, they are dead wrong. Time and time again, she deeply honors and unquestionably respects the systematized teachings and practices of Holy Church—while recognizing that those truths may have been at times misused or misapplied.

Julian was able to do what any Christian person today longs to do: to transcend the madness of the world, to see through its insanity, and to pass beyond it to the eternal verities, to live *sub specie æternitatis* in the midst of worldly rot, death, and collapse. It is my conviction that this offering of a mystical transcendence (which allows one to make sense of external madness) is a major element that draws us to this woman. When circumstances of the world are no longer sane, and when they have moved beyond one's personal power to change, one either leaps into the madness oneself, or finds the route through and past it to the planes of reality, sanity, and order. And that Julian offers us.

3. No Wrath in God

Julian's uncompromising proposition that "our Lord was never angry, nor ever shall be" speaks to the guilt-ridden Christian of today. Julian is blatant (almost a little short with potential opponents): "[God] cannot be angry. It would be impossible." For Julian, God is never a judgmental Daddy-writ-large. And with a psychological acumen far in advance of her time, she declares that the reason we tend to see wrath in God is that wrath is in us, and in our own blindness, we project and attribute that same wrath to God. She has a unique certainty in holding to this conviction even in the face of countless biblical metaphors that speak directly of the wrath of God.

Julian teaches a classical Christian theology that God is impassible, unassailable by any passion (such as anger), and ever unchangeable (not subject, for instance, to a beginning and/or ending of "wrath"). The familiar "wrathful God" is an Old Testament God and not the God of perfect Love manifested at Bethlehem and on Calvary. In a time when "God's Judgment" is often preached from pulpits, Julian's assurance that wrath is contrary to the entire character and nature of God is a splendid balance and reminder of him who said, "I came not to judge the world, but to save the world."[5] Julian's revelations are, in fact, chiefly concerned with that divine love.

4. Sin Has No Substance

In her own discomfort with an apparently over-simplified view of the place and power of sin, Julian faced the terrible paradox of God's goodness with evidence of the world's evil and the damnation of souls. Uniquely, she was led to a way of living *within that paradox*.

How in the face of God's apparent total goodness and power could there continue to be sin and damnation? This was a contradiction that Julian longed to resolve—and that she finally brought to resolution in her own mystical and unique way. Once again, in Merton's words: "This is, for her, the heart of theology: *not solving the contradiction, but remaining in the midst of it,* in peace, knowing that it *is* fully solved, but that the solution is secret [in God], and will never be guessed until it is revealed."[6]

One catches a flavor of this in her simple statement that "God cannot forgive"[7]—because God has *already* forgiven! That forgiveness was already offered on the Cross. Julian was not trapped by appearances or circumstances, but based her convictions on faith.

In consciousness of a Higher Reality, Julian could declare that "I believe [sin] has no manner of essence nor any portion of being";[8] that it is nothing, it is "no deed";[9] that all of us carry within our souls a "divine will," which *imago Dei* (image of God) "never consented to sin nor ever shall" and "is so good that it can never will evil, but always good";[10] that we are enclosed and enfolded constantly in God; that at all times God is "nearer to us than our own soul"; that God is with us in our spiritual flights and our physical needs (surely no conceit could be more powerful or graphic—or even shocking— to a modern mind than Julian's declaration of God's presence with us even in the process of bodily elimination).[11] Sin is known only by the pain it produces, and even in the face of that pain we are protected in our Friend's hand.

To those of us who blanch at the sin of human beings, and who can find no comfort or hope in a punishing God, Julian introduces the power of faith. "Look," she would say, "you have faith in the immeasurable goodness and power of God, but in the face of that you can't understand the existence and power of sin and its resulting pain—so forget trying to 'understand' it. Trust that faith of yours, and leave the understanding of the paradox to God's revelation in God's own time. God knows all that you know, and God has it all under control."

5. GOD WILL WORK HIS WILL

Julian's understanding of the spiritual challenge of evil in the world is the clear awareness and belief that all that is done on earth is done or allowed by God, that God shall not fail to work his will, and that "God's word shall be preserved in all things."[12]

It seems that Julian's awareness goes beyond the classical concept of the "permissive will of God" (which *allows* evil to happen rather than compromise human free will) to an even more positive sense that whatever we perceive as evil in the world has already, by the time we perceive it, been converted by God in his foreseeing wisdom and power into an outright good. In that commitment of faith, one can say that at a mystical level, the only true evil in the world is our own choice to be separated from God.

Many commentators on Julian (who supposedly respect her) apparently do not take her seriously when they foolishly and pointlessly try to guess what the "Great Deed" is that Julian alludes to, when she says that God shall do a "Secret Deed" and all will ultimately be well. We are cautioned by Julian several times not to try to find it out, but these commentators theorize that it may be "universal salvation" or "a new creation."[13] I suspect that Julian's answer to those queries would simply be the "Great Deed" is God's business and not ours, and that is more than enough for a person of faith to know. For Julian, the knowledge that what God wills *will* finally come about is comfort enough.

6. MYSTICISM WITHOUT HISTRIONICS

In our dilemma, Julian doesn't offer us a sociological, psychological, political, religious, or theological solution, but a *mystical* solution.

She guides us back to our forgotten spiritual roots, to the transcendence that is ours by virtue of our creation by the Father and our spiritual re-creation in the Son, back to the vision of reality we have almost lost in the thickets of technology and rationalism. She calls us to look beyond the misery and sin to the divine frame in which these evil displays are seen—the frame of God's creation, God's love, and God's constant protection. He is *always* "our Maker, our Keeper, our Lover." She speaks for us in saying that there is no solution to the hellish experience of our world in any terms in which we have learned to seek solutions—but only in the rediscovery of the transcendent love of God. The wrath is not in God, but in us; the blindness is not divine, but human; the judgment is not heavenly, but earthly.

For this holy woman there are no rolled-back eyeballs; writhing on flagstone floors; dubious analogues of divine sexual intercourse; induced trances, levitations, or bilocations; and no denials of *any* aspect of humanity or human experience. She does not display or ask us to participate in any extremes or ascetics. Her understanding is sharp, orderly, and clear, and her spirituality works by transcending, not by denying, the daily reality—and of waiting, praying, and contemplating for some twenty years (as she did) before venturing to express everything in words.

7. Blindness

"Blindness" is Julian's favorite characterization of our failings and our sins—and it is an important one for a modern Christian. We have a hard time thinking of God as a Being whom we simply do not generally experience. Instead, we seem to demand God's manifestation to us *on our terms*, and have forgotten that for at least 1500 years of Christian history, the experience of the "Absence of God" (or the lack of experience of the Presence) would be attributed not to a failure on God's part, but to a failure on the part of humankind. It is that "failure," from Julian's point of view, that is our *blindness*.

God surrounds and encloses us—and most of the time we do not know it because we are not looking or seeing the Divine Reality on whom we are grounded. There has been no wrathful withdrawing on God's part; there is only sinful myopia on our parts. God is not dead and not "gone" for Julian: for her God is utterly present in our nature and soul, but often invisible because of our own inadequate sight.

Julian would have a word for the Death-of-God theorists, and it would be that it is only the shadow of our own mortality with its present shallowness and ridiculous pride that "requires" that God prove himself to us on nonspiritual terms. We, on the one hand, are concerned by what we think about God; on the other hand, Julian *knows* what God thinks about us, and that far outshines our self-centered presumption.

8. PRAYER

True prayer, in Julian's words, is usually and predictably "barren and dry."[14] Julian surely honors the presence of "devout intention and wise effort" in our prayer, but the eighteenth/nineteenth-century idea (springing originally from the followers of the Wesleys) that unless prayer is constantly "heartfelt" it is invalid, would have made her smile. God is much more pleased, according to Julian, when our prayer is *unrewarding* to us but is centered on God, rather than on our self-oriented personal "experience." "Praying," she declares, "is a true, gracious, lasting intention of the soul one-ed and made fast to the will of our Lord by the sweet, secret working of the Holy Spirit"[15]—a simple act of faithful and trust-filled *willing*.

She attributes "failure" in prayer to "our feeling, our foolishness,"[16] not to an inadequate method or insufficient emotions. Julian delivers us from the guilt of not *feeling* prayerful. In a direct analogy, one may often not *feel* like going home to one's spouse, but one goes home nevertheless out of faithfulness, and thereby demonstrates a love that transcends the myth of romance and the sentimentality of emotions. Good Thomist that she is, Julian knows that loving and praying are both done with the will, not the emotions.

9. JULIAN'S AIMS, COMPARED TO THOSE OF HER CONTEMPORARIES

In thirteenth- and fourteenth-century Western Christendom, the single most powerful spiritual impact on the Church was made by the development and proliferation of Franciscan spirituality. This involved an affective approach to the human life of Jesus, and significant efforts to identify with that Jesus personally and individually—notably in a realm beyond (although not opposing) the corporate spirituality of the Church and its sacramentalism.

The early fourteenth-century *Meditations on the Life of Christ*—long attributed to St. Bonaventure—was composed by an Italian Franciscan, John de Caulibus, from San Gimignano, for the use of a Poor Clare for whom he was a spiritual director; it became widely popular.[17] It called for an intentional, in-depth meditation on certain events in the life of Christ, with the goal of experiencing one's spiritual presence at those events—or, even more powerful, of identifying oneself *with Jesus* in those circumstances. Caulibus wrote:

> . . . to make yourself more deeply compassionate and nourish yourself at the same time, turn your eyes away from his divinity for a little while and consider [Jesus] purely as a man. You will see a fine youth, most noble and most innocent and most lovable, cruelly beaten and covered with blood and wounds. . . . Imagine yourself present and consider diligently everything done against your Lord and all that is said and done by him and regarding him. . . . With your mind's eye, see some thrusting the cross into the earth, others equipped with nails and hammers, others with the ladder and other instruments, others giving orders about what should be done, and others stripping him.[18]

Saint Bonaventure's own thirteenth-century writings—notably *Lignum Vitae* and *Vitis Mystica*—called for the same approach to spirituality.

The early fourteenth-century German mystic (and protégé of Meister Eckhart) Henry Suso identified in the same way with the suffering Jesus when he identified with Christ in the first person in his *Little Book of Truth*:

> See, my right hand was pierced by a nail, my left hand was transfixed. My right arm was stretched out, and my left most painfully twisted. My right foot was cut, and my left cruelly hacked through. I hung impotently, and my divine legs were most weary. All my tender limbs were immovably riveted to the narrow halter. My hot blood burst out copiously through many a wound, in my anguish, so that my dying body was covered with blood, which was a distressful sight. Behold, a lamentable thing: my young, fair healthy body began to grow grey, to dry up and wither. The gentle weary back leant painfully on the rough cross. My heavy body sank down, my whole frame was bruised, wounded and cut through and through—and yet my loving heart bore all this lovingly.[19]

So Julian's graphic writings about the Crucifixion did not break any "new ground" in their graphic depiction of an experiential, affective, and visceral encounter with the passion of Jesus. As a literate and devout woman in the fourteenth century, she would probably have been aware of writings such as these, and the broad popularity of these forms of spirituality would assuredly have made her less hesitant about recording her own experience.

However, Julian did not merely accept the words of "the experts," but had much that is unique about her experience and her record of it.

First, Julian's *Revelations* were not "induced." Virtually all the writers who extol a personal "experience" of elements of Jesus' life recommend (and even *direct*) that a practitioner set out intentionally to meditate affectively on the human Jesus and his travails. For Julian the revelations may have been broadly hoped for, but were basically unexpected, and certainly did not derive from any deliberate program of intentional meditation on her part. She did not set out a priori to see the visions!

Second, the purposes for such programs of meditation given by the writers of her time were four:

1. Conversion,
2. Penitence,
3. Self-Revelation,
4. Didacticism.

But Julian's unique experience and her record of it do not fit the same pattern:

1. It is plain that for Julian no conversion to a devout life was needed. It seems clear that she had lived a singularly devout life long before her revelations.

2. There is very little of the bitter breast-beating, denigration, and vilification of self so characteristic of the other writers of her day. While Julian did not hesitate to recognize her own sins and share them with her readers, this was not done with the malignant masochism of the other writers. Personal penitence is not a major motive for Julian's writings.

3. There is certainly at least some *minor* dimension of self-revelation in Julian's visions. She did not hesitate to reveal her inadequacies. It is true that she probably knew more about herself when the revelations were finished than she did before they had begun, but she did not see increased self-knowledge as central to her mystical experience. There is virtually nothing in her book of a personal testimony to a life-changing experience.

4. It seems clear that for Julian the purpose of her visions was primarily didactic: that is, to reinforce and expand *her own* understandings of the nature of the Atonement and the relationship between God and God's creation. In this way, her reflections on her visions are somewhat uncharacteristic of the spiritual thinkers of her age, since she did not record her experiences in order to provide a model for the practice of prayer or for living a Christian life. She wished to share the insights she had been given into the ineffable and universal love of God for us, but she did not intend her *Revelations* as primarily *moral* teachings or *practical* instructions (like, for instance, *The Cloud of Unknowing* or the writings of Richard Rolle). The other title for her work,

Showings is highly accurate in that in Julian's revelations God's spiritual activity serves mainly to reveal deeper truths about divine and human nature and their relations with each other. If one were able to express God's motive in showing the revelations, it would be to give Julian (and, through her, her fellow Christians) confidence in metaphysical realities that were little appreciated by most other writers of her age. It may be said simply that Julian's revelations had little or no *practical* application.

In summary, a comparative reading of Julian's *Revelations* with the works of other spiritual and mystical writers of the fourteenth century (both in England and on the Continent) indicates that while Julian's experience and graphic descriptions of the Crucifixion were characteristic of many mystical writers of her day, a radical distinction must be made between her mystical, theological, and didactic writings on the basis of their motive and style. While virtually all other writers intend for their audience to feel horrendous guilt, shameful culpability, and degrading ignominy over the Passion, Julian, uniquely and brilliantly, turns her vision of the suffering humanity of Jesus into a matter for gratitude and joy. Exactly like her vision of the face of her suffering Savior, Julian recognizes the pain but uniquely sees it transformed into bliss.

It is time to turn to this astounding woman herself—whose work has been called the quintessence of English spirituality. She has lain quiet and still for 600 years, contemplatively awaiting the moment when the world's needs would call her again from her anchorhold cell—that tiny cell that contains the cosmos.

10. TEXTS AND ABBREVIATIONS

While Julian of Norwich wrote her important work in the late fourteenth or early fifteenth century, no original manuscripts survive. The manuscript copy of her writing generally accepted as the oldest is "The Short Version" (3, below). For many years, Julian scholars believed this to have been a later abbreviated version of the longer manuscripts (1 and 2, below), but more recent scholarship tends to agree that this "Short Version" was an initial manuscript, written relatively soon after Julian experienced her revelations, and enlarged later in "The Long Version" after many years of contemplation and reflection on those revelations.

Manuscripts 1 and 2 contain virtually the same material. They are of approximately the same length and have relatively few variations between them. It is likely that these are both copies of a (possibly common) now-lost manuscript, and Julian scholars do not agree on which of these two may be the older. I have used manuscript 1 as the basis of my translation, occasionally adding some additional clarifying material from manuscript 2.

The other manuscripts (4–7 below) include only fragments of the work, often bound together with other spiritual writings.

11. SURVIVING MANUSCRIPTS

1. British Library, Sloane Manuscript No. 2499. Probably copied in approximately 1650, apparently by English Benedictine nuns in Paris. [The Long Version]
2. Paris, Bibliothèque Nationale, Fonds Anglais No. 40. Probably copied in the seventeenth century imitating a script of around 1500. [The Long Version]
3. British Library, Additional Manuscript No. 37790. Probably copied in mid-fifteenth century in a monastic setting. Likely the oldest surviving manuscript copy. [The Short Version]

4. British Library, Sloane Manuscript No. 3705. Probably copied in the eighteenth century by an unknown hand.

5. St. Joseph's College, Upholland (Lancashire, England). Probably copied around 1650, apparently by English Benedictine nuns in Cambrai, France.

6. Westminster Archdiocesan Archives, London. Probably from the late fifteenth or early sixteenth century.

7. Cressy Text: First printed version. Published by R.F.S. Cressy in 1652, probably in England.

12. ABBREVIATIONS USED IN THIS BOOK

BCP = *The Book of Common Prayer, According to the Use of the Episcopal Church* (1979 edition).

BV = British Version (British Library, Sloane Manuscript No. 2499).

C&W = Edmund Colledge and James Walsh, eds., *A Book of Showings to the Anchoress Julian of Norwich,* vols. 1 & 2 (Toronto: Pontifical Institute of Medieval Studies, 1978) or (when indicated) *Julian of Norwich: Showings* (New York: Paulist Press, 1978).

LV = Long Version (Integrated BV and PV).

ME = Middle English.

OED = The Compact Edition of the *Oxford English Dictionary* (Oxford, UK: OUP, 1971).

PV = Paris Version (Paris, Bibliothèque Nationale, Fonds Anglais No. 40).

SV = Short Version (British Library, Additional Manuscript No. 33790).

W&J = Nicholas Watson and Jacqueline Jenkins, eds., *The Writings of Julian of Norwich* (University Park, PA: Pennsylvania State University Press, 2005).

WM = Westminster Manuscript (Westminster Cathedral Treasury 4).

PART TWO

ALL ABOUT JULIAN

1
JULIAN'S IDENTITY

One of the problems a historian faces is a matter of undiscriminating habit. For instance, we know for certain that from at least the thirteenth century (until the modern day) it has been common practice of monks, friars, sisters, and nuns to change their names to the name of a saint when they take religious vows.

Probably based on that monastic practice, somewhere in the early years of research on the identity of Dame Julian of Norwich, some commentator wrote, "Since it was common practice for an anchorite of her day, it is *possible* that Julian took her name from the patron saint of St. Julian's Church." A little later some other commentator wrote: "Since it was common practice for an anchorite, it is *probable* that Julian took her name from the patron saint of St. Julian's Church." And later still some other commentator wrote: "We do not know her real identity because Julian *took* the name of the patron saint of St. Julian's Church as was common practice for an anchorite." Thus, the *possibility* became a *probability,* and the *probability* became a *fact.* And so came into being the legend that Julian took the name of St. Julian himself when she became an anchorite at St. Julian's Church—and virtually every commentator since then has repeated that story without checking the facts.

In my research, I have examined primary and secondary sources for every one of the 789 known English hermitages and anchorholds and their inhabitants for the eleventh through the fifteenth centuries. (In some cases, historians and archaeologists know that a hermitage or anchorhold existed at a particular location, but records do not reveal the name of the inhabitant.) In most instances, the names of the hermits or recluses are known, and in several instances (including Julian's own) as many as five or six of them may have serially occupied the same site. However, in all of this research there is no evidence of any kind that *any* English anchorite *ever* took a new "name-in-religion," to say nothing of taking the name of the patron saint of the church to which his or her cell was attached or affiliated. Historical records show that it was certainly *not* a "common practice" as is so often erroneously maintained. In fact, quite the opposite is true: in a great many instances, the places or churches that sheltered well-known hermits or anchorites actually assumed the name of the recluses who dwelt there.

Even if this renaming were probable and actual practice, it is unlikely that a *female* anchorite such as our Julian would take or be given the name of a *male* saint—St. Julien of le Mans, the patron saint of St. Julian's Church. Even though there were women in fourteenth-century England whose baptismal name was "Julian" (or "Juliana"), it remains unlikely that a religious woman would actually assume the name of a male saint.

Blomefield,[20] Collins,[21] and Fosbrooke[22] all refer to Julian of Norwich as "Lady Julian." Since "Dame" (English for the Latin *domina*) was the appropriate and common title for a Benedictine nun or anchoress in the fourteenth century, the fact that Julian may have been referred to as "Lady" suggests that the title *may just possibly* have been a secular title properly owed to an aristocratic woman rather than an ecclesiastical honorific.[23]

All of this at the very least strongly suggests that Julian of Norwich—like all other known anchorites in English history—probably used her own baptismal name both before and after her enclosure.

But the question remains: Who, then, was this Julian of Norwich? And the question is certainly not as simple as it sounds, nor is it easily answered, because no incontrovertible evidence of Julian's identity can be found anywhere outside of her own writing, and she gives precious little information about herself in her book. However, there are a few matters we can assume, and a few more we can speculate about.

It is fairly certain that at the time of her enclosure Julian was a member of the aristocracy (or at least, the gentry) and that she therefore had available considerable means to provide financially for her own support. One of the major issues a bishop had to face when deciding to enclose a recluse or an anchorite in the fourteenth century was assurance that the means to support the anchorite for the remainder of his or her life were available (since if this were not so, the costs of that support would fall upon the bishop himself). There were anchorites whose regular income was guaranteed by the crown, a parish church, a bishop, friends, or by the anchorite's own holdings, but most commonly by the property of the anchorite's family. In the absence of any records to the contrary, it is likely that Julian fell in one of the two last groups—especially if our suggested identification of her with Julian Erpingham (see below) is true.

In 1951, Mr. J.F. Chaplin (who, along with A.G. Berry, was the architect responsible for the rebuilding of Saint Julian's Church in 1951–53) was also an antiquarian, and, indulging in his avocation, he scoured all the local histories and registries, tracing every Norwich "Julian" whose dates seemed consistent with our Julian's life. He discovered in Francis Blomefield's extensive history of Norfolk a prominent Julian whose records seemed to come to an unusually abrupt end (in most cases the deaths of prominent people were recorded)—especially as she was a woman of considerable rank. That person is the Lady Julian Erpingham, elder sister of the famous Norfolk knight banneret Sir Thomas Erpingham (who fought at Agincourt, was a Lord Warden of the Cinque Ports, and a close personal friend of the King).[24] This Julian, it is recorded, married a Roger Hauteyn, and, childless, was widowed in 1373 (the same year as our Julian's *Revelations!*) when her husband was killed (presumably in a duel) by a Sir John Colesby.[25]

Since I was obviously interested in this possibility, I undertook further research and discovered that Julian Erpingham married again after she was widowed, this time to Sir John Phelip (I) of Dennington, Suffolk,[26] and she bore him three children: Rose, William, and John (II). Her last child (John) was born in 1389, the same year her second husband died.[27]

Since children of the higher social classes in medieval England were virtually always "fostered out" at an early age and sent to be raised and taught manners by another high-born family,[28] it is at least *possible* that if Julian Erpingham were "our Julian" she had her illness and famous visions in the same year as the traumatic and unexpected death of her first husband (1373), probably having moved back to her family home (two blocks from St. Julian's Church). Then in 1376 she may have married again—this time to a Suffolk man—and borne three children, been widowed a second time in the year her youngest child was born (1389), and with the death of her second husband and the fostering of her youngest, dictated the Long Version of her book (c. 1393) and entered the anchorhold.[29] Her daughter, Rose, married John Glenham (c. 1393); her sons would certainly have been fostered; and she could then have been free to become an anchoress.[30]

There is much to support this thesis: if Julian were born in 1342–43 as she claimed, she would have been twice widowed by the age of forty-seven. She would have been a wealthy woman, with a legacy from her first husband[31] and the returned dower and a third of the estate from her second husband. Julian was in the enviable position of being a very wealthy widow with no apparent motivation for a third marriage. But it is strongly unlikely that she could have remained simply a wealthy widow, since the king had the power to *require* that a widow under sixty marry (in order to keep her wealth in circulation). In fourteenth-century England Julian faced four choices: a third marriage, the position of a secular "vowess" (under vows of chastity but living in the world), entering a convent, or being enclosed as an anchorite. Given her experience with the revelations and her obvious personal religious devotion, it would seem that anchorite status would have been the most attractive alternative.

Further, the widely popular *Ancrene Wisse* (which gave directions for the anchoritic life—and which Julian almost certainly knew) declares that a recluse is to "regard any vision [she] may see, whether in dreams or waking, as mere delusion, for it is nothing but [the devil's] guile."[32] This would make it further unlikely that Julian's visions were received *while she was an anchoress.*

Julian Erpingham Phelip died in 1414, and would then have been an anchorite for up to twenty-one years.[33] This could mean that when (in

1373) she wrote, "I desired to know of a certain creature that I loved if it would continue in good living (which I hoped by the grace of God was begun)," she could have been speaking of one of her children.

The Erpinghams were a notably devout family. Sir Thomas (as well as taking as his first wife the daughter of a man who had joined a religious order) gave a great deal of money to ecclesiastical foundations and also built—notably not long after the death of his sister, Lady Julian—a number of monuments in churches and elsewhere. He built the Dominican Church in Norwich (where his and Julian's brother Robert was a Dominican friar) and the excellent Erpingham Gate that is still the major arched entry into the Norwich Cathedral close.

Also, Sir John Erpingham (Father of Thomas and Julian) had his townhouse at 60 King Street, about two blocks from Saint Julian's Church—the townhouse where Julian would have been raised as a child and to which she probably returned after losing her first husband—and made substantial donations to Carrow Abbey (which at the time held the title to Saint Julian's Church).[34]

It seems at least possible that the widowed Julian Erpingham, having returned to her family home in Norwich (her mother was present on her supposed deathbed), received the revelations as a relatively new and grieving widow, then, three years later, remarried, bore three children, and when widowed a second time became an anchorite.

Further, Julian may have chosen not to remarry as a promise to her second husband (with whom by every account she had a loving relationship). Sir John Phelip's will has not survived, but in a later (unrelated) will we find an admonition that occurs in more than one surviving testament: "And wife, that you remember your promise to me that you take the order of widowhood."[35] Julian's husband could have included such a fairly common admonition in his will, with the agreement of his wife.

Although early scholars thought for some time that Julian may have been a nun at Carrow Abbey (she is portrayed as a nun in the "Benedictine" window in Norwich Cathedral), the evidence seems strongly to point away from that conclusion: (a) Julian never even hinted about convent life; (b) her mother and apparently several others were present at what they believed to be her deathbed, and that is unlikely in the case of an enclosed nun; (c) Julian said that her "curate" came to her with the crucifix, and that word indicates a secular and parochial priest, *not* the chaplain of a convent; (d) Julian twice (Chapters 4 and 8) used Latin—in both cases it was grammatically incorrect. Her phrase (if the British Manuscript reports accurately) was *Benedicite Domine*. It is derived from the closing words of the Monastic Office of Prime in the Sarum rite and from the traditional greeting of the monk or nun who awakens the others in the morning and the response of the awakened one: ℣. *Benedicite* ℟. *Domino*. If Julian had been a nun, this phrase above all others would have been fixed firmly in her memory and she would not have made the error.[36]

In sixteenth-century use, the words "young" or "in youth" (which Julian uses at least five times to refer to herself at the time of her revelations) when applied to a *man* may have meant that he was unmarried. However, I have the assurance of Professor John Burrow[37] that it would not carry that implication for an English woman in the fourteenth century. Apparently the word "youth" had many interpretations, and there are a great many historical paradigms defining the duration and end of "youth" (for instance, Saint Isidore of Seville declared that "youth" lasted until the fiftieth year). So Julian's referring to herself as "in youth" at the age of thirty is neither revealing nor inappropriate—especially if when she wrote it she had been living in recent widowhood and had borne no children.

Several commentators have suggested that if Julian herself had been a mother, many of her comments on the motherhood of Christ and God makes more poignant sense in that she would have experienced motherhood firsthand.

It should be noted that among the various legacies left to the anchoress Julian, the *earliest* one is from Roger Reed in March of 1393–94. It would seem curious that if she were enclosed as long as twenty years before that date, no legacy would have been left to her during those first years of her enclosure.[38]

Finally, in the 1845 restoration of St. Julian's church, a portion of an ancient pavement was discovered about eighteen inches below the chancel floor level on the south side of the church. The coat of arms appearing on one of those tiles is of the Stanhow family.[39] The arms were assumed by Sir John Calthorpe (c. 1379–1421) when he married Ela Stanhow. His manor of Calthorpe was directly next to Erpingham Village (and a part of Erpingham Hundred). Since church donors almost universally included a sign of their name, family crest, or figure, it is therefore *possible* that this tiling *may* have been part of the floor of Julian's original cell, and the cell *may* have been constructed (or at least tiled) by Sir John as a pious gift to his family friend, Julian Erpingham Phelip, when she decided to become an anchoress.

It is, of course, a practical impossibility without as-yet-undiscovered evidence to prove beyond any doubt that Julian of Norwich was, in fact, Julian Erpingham Phelip. Indeed, one of the other birth dates found in other records (1339 or 1360) might be accurate and would preclude this identity, but it can at least be said that this identification with Lady Julian Erpingham is well within the realm of possibility.

⇒ 2
JULIAN'S EDUCATION

There are as many opinions about Julian's education as there are commentators, some of which are so fanciful as to be almost humorous. Julia Holloway thinks Julian knew English, Latin, *and* possibly even Hebrew! She also believes that Julian was crippled and had been a nun of Carrow Priory before her enclosure.[40] Colledge and Walsh have suggested that Julian not only knew Latin but also had serious literary training and became "a master of rhetorical art as to merit comparison with Geoffrey Chaucer." They also conclude that she obtained her education in a religious order she had joined in her youth before entering the anchorhold in 1393.[41] Denys Turner makes the offhand comment, "We do not know what Julian read—and for that matter we do not know for certain that she could read at all."[42] Wolfgang Riehle believes that Julian's claim to be unlettered "almost certainly means knowing no Latin and probably also no French."[43] Sister Anna Maria Reynolds seemed to hold that Julian's protestations of being unlettered probably meant simply "that she was no 'scholar' . . . interpreting 'unlettered' as meaning 'ignorant of *Latin*' " but that there are pieces of evidence "which seem to suggest that the anchoress had at least mastered the art of reading."[44]

In the booklet published by the Celebration Committee for the six-hundredth anniversary of Julian's *Revelations* in 1973, it was pointed out that "Julian's claim to be unlettered might mean only that she had not learned to write Latin or even French."[45] A.C. Spearing wrote, "She may have had little or no Latin (to know 'no letter' could well mean that) and nothing is known for certain of her reading."[46]

The highly perceptive Grace Jantzen wrote, "It is likely, therefore, that her comments about not being a teacher and being an ignorant unlettered woman, should be taken in the context of her time to indicate the lack of formal education such as would have been available to men in monastic and cathedral schools and universities. . . . It is possible that Julian, though formally without the sort of education available to men in her time, either knew Latin already or, more plausibly, learned it in the fifteen years between the two versions of her book."[47]

Watson and Jenkins (with true sensitivity to Julian's style) make the best case: "These self-characterizations [unlettered, etc.] are more than gestures of modesty. In the visionary genre it is such individuals, helpless in their untutored createdness, not the educated, who experience visions: chosen individuals, to be sure, but more importantly representatives of everyone."[48]

With a similar sensitivity, Marion Glascoe wrote, "Julian talks of herself as: *a simple creature that cowde no letter.* It is very probable that her account of the revelations was dictated to an amanuensis. Certainly the rhythms and inflexions of her use of language are often those of the speaking voice."[49]

A number of commentators suggest that Julian may have had an education as a girl at Carrow Priory. However, while the Carrow nuns *may* have run a school for girls from leading families in the mid-fifteenth century (the accuracy of those records is at least dubious) there is no evidence that such a school existed in the four-teenth century.[50] There is, therefore, no evidence that Julian could have been educated in a school at Carrow Priory. Also, although few commentators make note of it, it is entirely possible that, like many a high-born woman in fourteenth-century England, Julian was able to read, but did not know how to write.[51]

It is virtually certain that Julian dictated her texts to a professional scribe or amanuensis. There is even evidence of small errors or adjust-ments in the text apparently made by a scribe or copyist. Even if Julian had been able to write well enough for her own *personal* use, it is exceedingly unlikely that she would have been able to manage the more formal script required for any writing intended for public exhibition.

It is my opinion, then, that when Julian received her initial visions, she was truly and literally "unlettered," knowing verbal Middle English, and possibly able to *read* English, but unable to write it. Her seeming familiarity with earlier spiritual writers and with Holy Scriptures in no way required her ability to read those sources herself.[52] It seems that small inaccuracies suggest that if she knew these other works, she probably knew them by memory. The common practice—especially for a noblewoman—would be to remember sermons well[53] and to have other matters read to her. It seems likely that during the twenty years between her vision and the final long version of her book, as a noblewoman, Julian may have become truly literate—at least in Middle English, and possibly in Norman French.

⤚ 3
TESTIMONIAL EVIDENCE OF JULIAN'S EXISTENCE

(1) From a will of Roger Reed, vicar of St. Michael's, Coslany, in Norwich, who on 20 March 1393–4 bequeathed two shillings to "Juliane anachorite apud ecclesiam St Juliane in Norwico" ["Julian anchorite at church of St. Julian in Norwich"].[54]

(2) 19 May 1404: Thomas Emund, chantry priest of Aylesham, bequeaths "Item Iuliane anachorita apud ecclesiam sancti Iuliani in Norvico xii idem sar, commoranti eum eadem viijd" ["Likewise, to Julian anchoress at St. Julian's Church Norwich 12 pence, likewise to Sara living with her 8d"].[55]

(3) In approximately 1413, Margery Kempe wrote, "And than sche was bodyn be owyr Lord for to gon to anankres in the same cyté whych hyte Dame Jelyan" ["And then she (Margery) was bidden by our Lord to go to an anchoress in the same city who was called Dame Julian"].[56]

(4) The author of the preface to the (Amherst) Short Text wrote: "Here es a visionn schewed be the goodenes of god to a deuoute womann, and hir name es Julyan, that is recluse atte Norwyche and yitt ys onn lyfe, anno domini millesimo CCCC xiij" ["Here is a vision shown by the goodness of God to a devout woman, and her name is Julian, who is a recluse at Norwich and is still alive, AD 1413"].

(5) In a 1415 will of merchant John Plumpton of Conesford at Norwich: "Item lefo le ankeres in ecclesia sancti Juliani de Conesford in Norwice xvd et ancille sue xijd Item lefo Alicie quondam ancille sue xijd" ["Likewise, I leave to the anchoress in the Church of St. Julian at Conesford in Norwich, 40d, and to her maid 12d. Likewise, I leave to Alice her former maid 12d"].[57]

(6) A will of Countess Isabel Ufford (née Beauchamp and widow of Sir William Ufford, Second Earl of Suffolk) for 1416: "Item jeo devyse a Julian recluz a Norwich xxs" ["Likewise, I distribute to Julian recluse at Norwich 20s"].[58]

> Given the inexactitude of late medieval language (Latin or Anglo Norman), Countess Ufford's will could be accurately translated, ". . . I distribute to THE Julian recluse at Norwich . . . ," that is, to the person who was a recluse at St. Julian's Church in 1416.

(7) A will of 1429, wherein Robert Baxster bequeathed three shillings and four pence to "the anchorite in the churchyard of St. Julian's, Conesford in Norwich."[59]

ADDITIONAL TESTIMONIALS

In Norwich, there were several anchoresses, and we know that two of them were named "Julian." Early in the research on Julian of Norwich, there was serious confusion between our anchoress Julian at St. Julian's Church and the anchoress Dame Julian Lampett at Carrow Priory. Julian Lampett was enclosed in an anchorhold *at the Priory* between 1426 and 1481. This second Julian (Lampett) was apparently a woman of some stature, since she received specific bequests in the wills of some sixty-seven persons during her fifty-six years as a recluse. Because of their common name, some early commentators assumed these two anchoresses were one and the same, and concluded that Julian of Norwich had lived to be over a hundred years old!

More modern scholarship has finally distinguished clearly between these two Julians, but information concerning legacies to Julian Lampett still may have an impact on our understandings of the identity of Julian of Norwich.

(1) In his will, probated at his death in 1428, Sir Thomas Erpingham (brother of Julian Erpingham Phelip) granted five marks for distribution among the recluses of Norwich, and an *additional* grant of 23s. 4d. specifically to Julian Lampett (whom he mentions by name).[60]

(2) In 1438, Sir William Phelip of Suffolk granted ten marks to be distributed to the poor of Norwich according to the "assignment, will and discretion" of Julian Lampett.[61] (In her 1477 will Lady Bardolf [Sir William's widow] included similar dispositions.)[62]

The scholar must ask about these apparent coincidences: Why would Julian Erpingham Phelip's brother specifically designate the anchoress Julian Lampett by name for his bequest when all other Norwich recluses in his will were covered in an anonymous distribution? Why would both Julian Erpingham Phelip's eldest son (who lived in Dennington, Suffolk, not in Norwich) and his widow take the step (unparalleled, to my knowledge) of appointing the anchoress Julian Lampett to serve as distributor of his alms to the poor? It certainly appears that the Erpingham/Phelip family had some quite significant relationship with Dame Julian Lampett, and we should consider that they saw her as the successor to their own sister/mother, Julian of Norwich.

4
JULIAN AND MARGERY KEMPE

Margery Kempe was born in 1373, the year in which Julian experienced her revelations. This is not the place to provide a full account of Margery's peculiar and bizarre life. Suffice it to say that she was the daughter of the Mayor of King's Lynn in Norfolk (about forty miles from Norwich). She mothered fourteen children before persuading her husband to a mutual vow of chastity, and spent most of the rest of her life on pilgrimage: to the Holy Land, to Rome, and to various devotional shrines in England and on the Continent. She was given to visions and dreams and the gift of voluble and vociferous tears of devotion (which her fellow travelers often scorned and derided). At one point, she was even formally charged with the Lollard heresy, but was acquitted.

Margery visited Julian in her anchorhold—probably about 1413—and in her book (written c. 1430), Margery wrote of the meeting (providing one of the few external evidences of Julian's existence and state of life):

And then she [that is, Margery] was bidden by our Lord to go to an anchoress in the same city who was called Dame Julian. And so she did, and showed her the grace that God put in her soul of compunction, contrition, sweetness, and emotion, compassion with holy meditation and high contemplation, and full many holy words and conversations that our Lord spoke to her soul, and many wonderful revelations which she showed to the anchoress to know if there were any deceit in them, for the anchoress was expert in such things and good counsel could give.

The anchoress, hearing the marvelous goodness of our Lord, highly thanked God with all her heart for his visitation, counseling this creature to be obedient to the will of our Lord God and fulfill with all her might whatever he put in her soul if it were not against the honor of God and the benefit of her fellow Christian, for if it were then it were not the moving of a good spirit, but rather of an evil spirit.

"The Holy Spirit moves never a thing against love, and, if he did, he would be contrary to his own self, for he is all love. Also he moves a soul to all chastity, for chaste lovers are called the temple of the Holy Spirit, and the Holy Spirit makes a soul stable and steadfast in the right faith and the right belief. And a man double-in-soul is ever unstable and unsteadfast in all his ways. He that is evermore doubting is like to the flood of the sea, which is moved and borne about with the wind, and that man is not likely to receive the gifts of God. Whatever creature has these tokens, he must steadfastly believe that the Holy Spirit dwells in his soul.

And much more, when God visits a creature with tears of contrition, devotion, or compassion, he can and ought to believe that the Holy Spirit is in his soul. Saint Paul says that the Holy Spirit prays with mournings and weepings unspeakable *[Rom. 8:26]*, that is, today he makes us ask and pray with mournings and weepings so plenteously that the tears cannot be numbered.

There can no evil spirit give these tokens, for Jerome says that tears torment the devil more than do the pains of hell. God and the devil are evermore opposites, and they shall never dwell together in one place, and the devil has no power in a man's soul. Holy Writ says that the soul of a rightful man is the seat of God.[63] And so I trust, sister, that you are. I pray God grant you perseverance. Set all your trust on God and fear not the language of the world, for the more despite, shame, and reproof that you have in the world, the more is your merit in the sight of God. Patience is necessary to you for in that you shall keep your soul."

Much was the holy conversation that the anchoress and this creature had by communing in the love of our Lord Jesus Christ many days that they were together.[64]

It is amazing that Margery's extended visit with Julian and recounting of Julian's words to her are entirely consistent with Julian's own writings and patterns of thought. In other words, there is very little in Margery's account of Julian's advice that we cannot find in some form in Julian's own work, either directly or by implication. This is particularly poignant given the fact that Julian's own life was so diametrically different from the peripatetic, emotion-wrought life of Margery. Indeed, it may be said that Julian's spiritual insight and intellectual vitality, her face-to-face apparently sympathetic (if cautious) reactions to Margery, may give some legitimacy to Margery's idiosyncratic spirituality.

It is important to note that Margery's account of her visit to Dame Julian and the several legacies left to the anchoress are the only *external* evidence of Julian's very existence.

⮑ 5
DATE AND TIME OF JULIAN'S VISIONS

Julian dated her illness and the revelations as follows:

In Chapter 3 she wrote of:

> a bodily sickness in which I *lay three days and three nights; And on the fourth night* I received all my rites of Holy Church and expected not to have lived till day. After this I lay *two days and two nights*, and on *the third night* I expected often to have passed away (and so expected those who were with me). . . . Thus I endured *till day*. My curate was sent for to be at my ending. . . .
>
> After this my sight began to fail, and it grew all dark about me in the chamber *as if it had been night.*

And in Chapter 66 she wrote:

> After this, the good Lord showed the 16th showing *on the following night*, as I shall say later, and the 16th showing was the conclusion and confirmation of all 15.

It becomes apparent that Julian's "three days and three nights" is a literary convention which reverses "night" and "day"—that is, chronologically it would need to be "three nights and three days," her sickness beginning in the first night.

The *actual* date of the beginning of the Showings is not altogether clear because the two major manuscripts disagree: the Sloane Manuscript says in Chapter 2 that the Showings took place on the *"viiith day of May"* ["the 8th day of May"] while the Paris Manuscript reads *"the xiij daie of May"* ["the thirteenth day of May"]. One of the scribes made an error in transcribing an "x" for a "v" or vice versa.

Since the Sloane Manuscript was the most popular and most familiar in the 1970s, it was the decision of both the Church of England and the Episcopal Church in the United States to include the commemoration of Dame Julian in the ecclesiastical kalendars on

May 8. More recent research (including that of Colledge & Walsh and of Julia Holloway), however, has tended to favor the later date.

I have reconstructed the calendar for the days of Julian's sickness and the timing of the Showings, and I find that it works out as follows:

Illness begins on Night 1			Last Rites received on Night 4			Showings 4 AM on Day 7 to 3 PM on Day 8	16th Showing during Night 8
Night 1	Night 2	Night 3	Night 4	Night 5	Night 6	Night 7	Night 8
Day 1	Day 2	Day 3	Day 4	Day 5	Day 6	Day 7	Day 8
May 7	May 8	May 9	May 10	May 11	May 12	May 13	May 14
Thursday *Feast of St. John of Beverley*	Friday	Saturday	Sunday *3rd Sunday after Easter*	Monday	Tuesday	Wednesday	Thursday

It should be noted that in the England of Julian's day the "Last Rites" were usually administered in two parts: the Confession and Communion would be administered when the person was apparently terminally ill, but still conscious and at least potentially capable of recovery. The second part—the anointing with holy oils in the Sacrament of Extreme Unction—was usually postponed until the very moment of death (or even up to several minutes *after* bodily death since it was believed that the soul did not leave the body immediately). The reason for this postponement of the second half of the Viaticum was the common belief that once one had received the Sacrament of Extreme Unction (considered to be one of the "indelible" sacraments) and the person happened to recover, he or she was expected to live a life of total, unalloyed purity and sinlessness, usually even renouncing all meat and (in some instances) all sexual intercourse. Consequently, Julian's Confession and Communion could have taken place on Night 4 (May 10), and the priest could then have returned on Night 7 (May 13) for the final anointing and brought the crucifix that became the focus of Julian's visions.[65]

If the date of the onset of the Showings were May 13, then it is likely that the last liturgy a pious Lady Julian would have experienced before her illness would have been the commemoration of the feast day of Saint John of Beverley (which fell on May 7). This might suggest why she called to mind the somewhat obscure St. John of Beverley in Chapter 38 of her book.

So my conclusion is that the evidence seems strongly weighted in favor of the May 13 date for her visions.

And, what time of day?

In Chapter 65 Julian wrote:

> Of these 15 showings the first began early in the morning, about the hour of four, and they lasted, appearing in a most beautiful order and solemnly, each following the other, until *it was past three in the afternoon* or later. [Original Middle English: *till it was none of the day overpassid*]

What specific hour Julian refers to here can be something of a conundrum depending on one's understanding and translation of the Middle English word *none*. It has been translated in other places as either "nine" or "noon." However, since Julian would not have had access to a clock,[66] I am quite certain that Julian would have followed the common practice of telling the hour from the bells of the monasteries that rang for the monks' daily Offices: Prime (at the "first hour"—6 AM), Terce (at the "third hour"—9 AM), Sext (at the "sixth hour"—12 noon), and None (at the "ninth hour"—3 PM). Thus Julian's "none" would very likely refer to the monastic Office of None, which, if a mechanical clock were used at Norwich Cathedral, was recited at approximately three in the afternoon.[67]

However, a problem arises when we understand that originally monastic time was kept on a "clepsydra," a water-clock device in which water dripped through a narrow aperture. In monastic use, a day-and-night was not divided into twenty-four equal hours: rather, *daylight* was divided into twelve parts, and these varied in length according to the season of the year. Consequently, as daylight grew longer and longer during summer seasons, the time for the Office of None (ordinarily kept at the ninth hour, that is, 3 PM) would fall earlier and earlier until it could come to fall very near to our present hour of noon.[68] So, at midsummer, "None" could fall near "noon-time." Therefore, Julian's "none" in early May, depending upon what time-keeping method was in force in Norwich at that time, could refer to an hour at three PM, or in the earlier afternoon, or quite near noontime.[69]

ᔕ 6
JULIAN'S CELL
AND DOMESTIC HABITS

While the foundations of Julian's cell had been found earlier, they were clearly seen when St. Julian's Church was rebuilt in 1953 and it was clear that the cell in which she lived would have been approximately nine and a half feet by eleven and a half feet.[70] As an ecclesiastical structure (and in the pattern of other surviving medieval anchorholds in Norfolk), the walls would most likely have been built of flint with stone quoins or corners, and with plaster covering the walls on the interior. It is very likely that the roof was thatched, although as an ecclesiastical building it was possible that tiles were used for roofing.[71]

The floor was probably tamped earth (even the cathedral and most churches had earthen floors in Julian's day), but it *may* have been flag-stoned or tiled. It would have been covered with rushes that would probably be changed twice annually and amid which scented herbs might occasionally be strewn. (Bay leaves were favorites since they repelled insects as well as providing a pleasant odor.)[72]

The cell would have had three windows: a small "squint" window[73] opening into the church so the anchorite could see the church altar with the pyx (where the Sacrament was reserved) hanging over it,[74] and also receive Holy Communion;[75] a second window would have opened into a kind of lean-to room where the lay sisters or servants[76] could prepare the food, do laundry, and deliver such things as books or vestments to be embroidered;[77] a third narrow window[78] would open onto the public way.[79] This third window would have been covered with a curtain made of a piece of white cloth sandwiched between two pieces of black cloth, and a cross cut in the middle of the black cloths so that a white cross showed through in the center. This curtain was *never* to be pulled aside, so the anchorite was never actually to see the face of anyone who came to speak with him or her, and no one (except the servants) was actually to see the anchorite's face.[80] It is possible that the outside window may have been glazed either with thin horn or with leaded "whorl glass" (what we now call "bottle glass") in a metal frame since plate glass would not have been generally available.

There was only one door to the cell, and at the ceremony of enclosure, the door would have been locked and sealed *permanently* with the bishop's wax seal. An anchorite was not free to change his or her mind about enclosure if it became "uncomfortable"—at least not without the danger of excommunication. In fact, there was more than one anchorhold in England where the anchorite was literally *walled in* with mortared stonework filling the entryway. There were also anchorholds in England that, unlike Julian's, included two to four rooms, or that were two storeys high, or that included a walled garden in the enclosure.[81] There was apparently a common temptation for people to use the enclosed recluse's cell as a safety deposit box for valuables or money—a practice warned against in the *Ancrene Wisse*.

It is possible that Julian's anchorhold was not heated. (In medieval monasteries, it was customary to have only one common room warmed by a fire—the "calefactory"—and all individual cells remained unheated.) It was ordinary for the halls of larger houses to be heated only by a central raised hearth with a smoke hole in the roof. However, in Julian's century, fireplaces with chimneys had begun to come into use in England, and the anchorhold may well have had a small corner fireplace[82] that would probably have burned peat since wood was already far too rare and precious in Norfolk to burn.[83] The room would be lit by pricket candles, cresset lamps,[84] and/or rush lights.[85] There would probably be a candle lantern (a box with thinned horn panels on the sides and a handle at the top—a "lant-horn") to avoid drafts.

The furnishings would have included: (1) a box bed[86] with a straw-filled mattress, linen sheets, pillows, and quilts or woolen blankets ("ruggs"); (2) a trestle-style table and stool; (3) a "press" (or chest) for storage; (4) a wooden "necessaries bucket"; (5) an "altar"—likely a shelf with a crucifix and candles and possibly a reliquary or a small statue (some cells had a full "rood," that is, a crucifix with pictures or statues of St. Mary on Christ's right side and St. John on the left) with probably a prie-dieu before it; and (6) a collection of small things: precious sewing needles and thread or floss; goose (or swan, raven, or crow) quill pens[87] for writing and a small "penknife" (for sharpening the quill); an inkwell probably made of horn (and called an "inkhorn") or leather, the ink made from oak galls or blackthorn bark; a bag of pumice powder (used to smooth the surface of parchment and to dry the ink); a wash basin; towels; dishes (of pottery or wood); green or yellow glazed cups and pitchers; eating utensils. She would have probably had two or three leather costrels (bottles/jugs) or pottery pitchers for beer and/or water for washing. (7) There certainly would have been a Book of Hours of some sort and probably one or two other devotional books.[88]

Julian's clothing would have looked very much like a traditional nun's habit of today, but it would have been what *any* gentlewoman wore in her day, without the bright colors, ribbons, and hairdress-ings that would have been common among the aristocrats. In the fourteenth century, a gentlewoman showed her hair publicly only if she was young and unmarried (or a "loose woman"), so all married or widowed women wore a linen wimple (usually of two pieces: one from the chin over the head—if pointed at the chin, it was called a "chin-barbe"—and the other around the forehead, framing the face) and a dark-colored simple veil over it.

The ordinary straight-sided tunic was common wear for both men and women; the older or more aristocratic the person, the longer the garment.[89] The tunic would be bound with a girdle or belt and covered with a scapular (which served as an apron to spare the tunic—which was probably worn year-round—from soil). There would also have been a warm, hooded cloak of some kind. All of an anchorite's clothing would be undecorated and of subdued colors, probably natural, black, or dark brown, and would be woolen (except for linen undergarments and wimple)—even burial shrouds were, by British law, required to be of wool.[90] Julian would also have worn a "fob" (a small purse, usually of leather) suspended from the girdle or belt, and a small wooden- or horn-handled knife in a leather sheath (called a *hauschnitte* or "house knife"). She would have had a pair of leather gloves and would have worn either somewhat pointed leather shoes made of soft goatskin or, as an ascetic, perhaps *galoches* with wooden soles.[91] It is conceivable (but unlikely) that she would have been barefooted. It is of course possible (but unlikely) that she would have worn a hair shirt or girdle made of rough goat's hair beneath her habit.[92]

What would Mother Julian's diet have been like? That is a difficult question because it would depend to some extent on the degree to which Julian's secular tastes and practices would have been carried over into her anchorhold. It is unlikely that as a gentlewoman she would have lived on a strictly "peasant" diet, but it is also likely that she would have followed general monastic practices regarding her menu. It would have been her practice to eat two meals a day from Easter through Holy Cross Day (September 14) and probably only one meal a day during the rest of the year.[93]

This would mean a reduction in meat dishes (pork, mutton, venison, rabbit, etc.), which would probably be available only on high feast days (and would usually be boiled or stewed),[94] and an increase in seafood (salt herring, flounder, trout, eels, mussels, etc.), poultry (cranes, herons, geese, ducks, swans, quails, pigeons, woodcocks, snipe, etc.), dairy products, and porridge. Bread and cheese would be a common meal, and there were no distinctions in the menus among breakfast, dinner, or supper, except that it was unlikely Julian would have had cooked breakfasts, or that she had more than two meals a day even on festive occasions. Onions, leeks, beans, peas, mushrooms, and turnips were commonplace. Butter was almost never used, but both cow's milk and goat's milk (much preferred) would have been fairly common. (It was usual for a farmer to lead his goat or cow through the city, milking her at the door of each customer.) Berries, raisins, honey, and a small bit of sugar would have been available.

And because it was never reliably pure, Julian would virtually *never* have drunk plain water, but at all meals would have slaked her thirst with up to three pints of "small beer" a day ("small beer" was actually a weak homemade ale [about three percent alcohol] made from barley malt, wheat meal, oatmeal, and water—since during Julian's lifetime hops had not yet been added to ale—which would have made it "beer"). This "small beer" was the common drink, and was served to children as well as adults. Red and white wine would have been available, but their use was limited to the gentry, and Julian probably would have chosen to abstain from them. Her Lenten menus would have included only fish, bread, and vegetables, since no meat or animal products were allowed.[95]

Waste, untidiness, and neglect of household duties were forbidden an anchoress. The category of faults to be confessed includes these: "Dropping crumbs, or spilling ale, or letting a thing grow mouldy, or rusty, or rotten; clothes not sewed, wet with rain, or unwashen; a cup or dish broken, or anything carelessly looked after."[96]

Since the *Ancrene Wisse* forbids anchorites to have any animals except a cat, it has already become traditional hagiography to show Mother Julian with a cat (indeed, there is a pleasant children's book called *Julian's Cat*). Of course, the cat had a practical use in keeping down the mouse and rat population. The thirteenth-century Bartholomaeus

Anglicus wrote of the cat: "He is a full lecherous beast in youth, swift, pliant and merry, and leapeth and reseth on everything that is to fore him: and is led by a straw, and playeth therewith: and is a right heavy beast in age and full sleepy, and lieth slyly in wait for mice: and is aware where they be more by smell than by sight, and hunteth and reseth on them in privy places: and when he taketh a mouse, he playeth therewith, and eateth him after the play."[97]

It is also likely that once in the anchorhold, Mother Julian would never have taken a bath! This practice, unsavory as it seems to modern minds, would have had two motives: first, in the medieval world "fasting" from bathing was a widely accepted sign of sanctity—especially among religious women under vows. Bathing was thought to be a "luxury" that was selflessly surrendered by the true ascetic. Not bathing was seen as a kind of penance voluntarily undertaken. Second, it would have been virtually impossible to move a large medieval wooden bathtub into the cell, and the anchorite could not go outside to bathe (which was a frequent secular practice in her day).[98] Undoubtedly, the "sponge bath" would have been common, and general cleanliness maintained as far as possible, but a full bath was extremely unlikely.

Medical practice was poor in the fourteenth century. There were basically four kinds of practitioners: physicians, barber-surgeons, "cunning folk," and pharmacists. The physicians were university-trained doctors, basing virtually all their knowledge and practice on the works of Galen (d. 203), whose medical teachings were followed by virtually all European physicians for over 1400 years, with little or no improvement during that time. In *Piers Plowman*, William Langland attacked the wealth of fourteenth-century doctors and went on to say: "for these doctors are mostly murderers, God help them!—their medicines kill thousands before their time."[99] The barber-surgeons, on the other hand, were self-trained or came up through an apprenticeship. Their numbers in fourteenth-century England vastly outnumbered all other practitioners. They practiced phlebotomy, dentistry, shaving, and barbering. The "cunning folk," including midwives and "wise women," were local practitioners mainly working with herbology and magic. For the majority of the population of England, especially those living in small villages and towns, these "cunning folk" were the only medical personnel available. However, in view of the fact that Dame Julian mentions no medical ministrations to her in her illness, it is likely that the general low regard in which the medical professions were held may have meant that she simply did not choose to endure such ministrations. Julian may well have followed the monastic pattern of having regular "bleedings," but there is no evidence of any other medical intervention.

It was also the custom for an anchorite to be buried beneath the floor of his or her anchorhold.[100] No such burial for Julian is recorded nor was one discovered during reconstruction of St. Julian's Church in the 1950s. The location of Julian's relics is, therefore, unfortunately totally unknown. (If she were, in fact, Julian Erpingham Phelip, her remains may have been interred with her second husband's in Dennington, Suffolk, but, again, there are no records or clear evidence to support that possibility.)

Many commentators suggest that Julian's cell was destroyed in the sixteenth-century dissolution of the monasteries under Henry VIII. However, Blomefield mentions that the cell still existed when he wrote (1768). Others have perhaps more accurately asserted that the cell simply fell into disrepair and dilapidation and was pulled down during the 1845 reconstruction of the church. Blomefield writes that the cell was used by other anchorites after Julian's death: "In 1472 Dame Agnes was recluse here [at St. Julian's Church]; in 1481 Dame Elizabeth Scott; in 1510 Lady Elizabeth; in 1524 Dame Agnes Edrygge."

Finally, romantic commentators on Julian love to point out that her cell was only a half mile from the notorious "Lollard's Pit" of Norwich where Lollard heretics were burned at the stake, and that Julian would have known of such executions. However, the first burning in Lollard's Pit (an old, abandoned chalk pit) did not take place until September 1428 when the priest, William White, gained the dubious honor of beng its first victim—at least several years after Julian's death.

⤳ 7
JULIAN'S CHURCH

THE NAME

In many accounts, one will read that St. Julian's Church in Norwich was named after St. Julian the Hospitaller. This is usually suggested because St. Julian the Hospitaller had the strange circumstance of having murdered his parents by mistake, and in reparation gave the remainder of his life as a ferryman at a dangerous river crossing—and St. Julian's Church was very near a major ferry landing on the Wensum River.

However, Alban Butler disagreed. He was a Roman Catholic priest and famous hagiographer, born in Appletree in Northamptonshire in 1710. He was ordained priest on Easter Day in 1734 and became a Professor of Philosophy (and later, of Theology) at the English College in Douai, France, where he began the composition of what later became his enormous and exhaustive work on the lives of the Saints: *The Lives of the Fathers, Martyrs and Other Principal Saints.*[101] In 1749 he was sent back to England, and he hoped to be located in London where he could find resources to complete his work. However, he was sent instead to a parish in Staffordshire, and, shortly thereafter, to Norwich to serve as Chaplain to the Duke of Norfolk and tutor to the Duke's young nephew and heir.

Father Butler spent close to eight years in Norwich, and he wrote the following in 1757 in his article on St. Julien of Le Mans of France:

> [St. Julien] was much honored in France, and many churches built during the Norman succession in England, especially about the reign of Henry II[102] who was baptized in the church of St. Julien, at Mans, bear his name: one in particular at Norwich, which the people by mistake imagine to have been dedicated under the title of the venerable Juliana, a Benedictine nun at Norwich, who died in the odor of sanctity, but never was publicly invoked as a saint.

It is quite obvious that Fr. Butler knew what he was talking about from firsthand experience during his many years in Norwich. He was certainly the person in England in his day most informed regarding the lives of saints and the dedications of churches, and his opinion holds a validity that other conjectures and speculations do not have.

In addition, the Norfolk historian Blomefield (1739) wrote about a funeral at St. Julian's:

> Nic. son of *John Page* and *Christian* his wife, was buried in the churchyard of ST. JULIAN, the *King* and *Confessor* [which shows that it was not dedicated to St. *Julian* the *Bishop*, nor St. *Julian* the *Virgin*].[103]

Blomefield's error came from the fact that there was originally a church of "St. Edward, King and Confessor" situated between St. Julian's and St. Etheldreda's parishes. St. Edward's was closed between 1269 and 1305,[104] and the parish was united with St. Julian's, so the resulting dedication was "St. Julian and St. Edward, King and Confessor." Blomefield mistakenly conflated the titles.

Following the reconstruction of the building in 1953, controversies were set aside and the church was clearly rededicated to St. Julian of Le Mans, and a splendid, large iconic portrayal of him holds place of honor in the church.

THE BUILDING

In Julian's day, what is now "King Street" was still known by its older name of "Southgate," and St. Julian's Church stood just off Southgate between two small (no longer existing) cross-streets which ran west from Southgate to Ber Street: Sandgate to the north and Skeythgate to the south. In addition, there was a narrow short lane called "Freway" (later known as "Horn's Lane") running north from Skeythgate to the south side of St. Julian's Church[105]—directly to what was then the main door of the church and to Dame Julian's cell.

Immediately to the south and southeast of St. Julian's Church stood the Priory of Friars of Our Lady. The Priory was founded in 1290, and the members were "begging friars," living under the rule of St. Augustine, wearing white habits with black cloak and cowl. In the great pestilence of 1348–49 all the friars died of the plague and their house fell into private hands. (Some old walls and reused materials can still be seen on the site.)[106]

Across Southgate from St. Julian's Church in the fourteenth century stood the huge Augustine Friary that was known throughout England for its outstanding library. It is likely that one of the Augustinian Canons may have served as Confessor for Dame Julian, and it is also possible that the Friary library may have loaned books to the anchoress.

The original round tower of Saint Julian's Church may be one of the (if not *the*) oldest church structures in Norwich. It was very probably of Saxon origin, and may have been built in the tenth century. The Saxons built towers that could provide a relatively safe refuge when the Vikings attacked, and since St. Julian's tower was originally crenellated, this may have been its purpose. It is also known that in 937 the Saxon King Athelstan (grandson of Alfred the Great) issued a law laying down what was needed for a local leader to claim the status of *thegn* (a minor nobleman). One requirement was that the thegn's land had to have a bell tower on it. St. Julian's tower may have been built as a result of this royal decree.

It is also possible that an original (wooden) St. Julian's had been destroyed when Sweyn Forkbeard burned Norwich in 1004. And the church was almost certainly one of the "new" churches listed in the 1086 Domesday Book. Alan Ellis's record lists the present St. Julian's Church as having been built in 1254.[107]

St. Julian's Church was part of a large beneficence given to the nuns of the nearby Benedictine Carrow Priory by King Stephen in 1135, and the Priory still held the advowson in Julian's day[108]—which is a reason why some early scholars suspected that Julian may have been a nun at Carrow before she entered the anchorhold. However, virtually all modern scholars doubt (for good reasons) that Julian had ever been a Carrow nun. (See the earlier discussion on Julian's Identity.)

According to Abbot Butler, in 1750 the outside flint walls of the church had been plastered over and were smooth. That plaster was removed in the 1845 reconstruction. However, the decision was made to repair the church, and during the reconstruction, the blocked-up priest door (on the south side) was flinted over; all niches in the church were blocked up; the wall paintings and Scripture texts on the interior walls were obliterated; all memorials were removed from walls and floor; the rood screen, the Laudian altar rails, the pulpit, and the box pews were all removed. A small vestry was built on the south side of the church, and the ruinous top of the tower removed, lowering it by five to seven feet.

THE BOMBING

"During the early hours of Saturday morning, 27th June 1942, German raiders flew over the city and caused widespread damage, mainly by fire, particularly in the St Stephen's Street and Ber Street area. In King Street high-explosive bombs caused the destruction of St Julian's. A shapeless heap of rubble was all that was left of the tower; of the remainder of the church only the north and east walls were left standing."

"Thus did it remain until nearly ten years later, when work was put in hand to clear away the rubble and rebuild the church, especially at the instigation of the Sisters of the Community of All Hallows, Ditchingham. As much as possible of the surviving fabric was retained, in particular the north wall of the nave with its circular Norman (sic) window. A fifteenth-century font brought from the redundant All Saints' Church took the place of that which had been broken beyond repair, while a Norman doorway from the neighbouring Church of St Michael-at-Thorn, gutted during the same raid, replaced one of similar date, which had been sketched and etched by John Sell Cotman. This now gives access from the nave to a sacristy built on foundations, laid bare in 1906, of what was thought at the time to have been the cell of Dame Julian, the fourteenth-century anchoress or religious recluse."[109]

THE REBUILDING
The reconstruction of St. Julian's in 1953 was accomplished mainly through the good offices of the then-rector Father Raybould and the Community of All Hallows Sisters of Ditchingham who were mainly responsible for raising the considerable funds for the reconstruction.

8
JULIAN'S PAPACY

When Barbara Tuchman wrote her classic European history *A Distant Mirror*, she subtitled it *The Calamitous Fourteenth Century*,[110] and "calamitous" is almost an understatement in describing the massive and widespread sociological, ecclesiastical, economic, literary, and political upheavals of those hundred years in Europe. This was particularly true in England: from the famines of 1315–17 (which may even have prompted cannibalism in England), to the almost immeasurable destruction of repeated bouts of the Black Death, the rise of Lollardy as England's first heresy, the vast political and economic disruption of the Peasants' Rebellion, the murder of an archbishop, the assassination of two kings, the momentary triumph of Agincourt followed by the loss of the vast English possessions in France, the beginning of the Hundred Years' War, and the unexpected early death of the idolized Black Prince. But perhaps more disruptive than any of these was the collapse and disintegration of the one primary center of European civilization and Christendom: the papacy.

In 1305, Clement V was elected pope. He was, at the time, the Archbishop of Bordeaux, and his major concern was that the papacy had developed very poor relations with the powerful French throne. As a Frenchman, he looked for ways to improve that relationship. Since the city of Rome had physically and socially degenerated to a great degree and the infighting of the Colonna and Orsini families in Rome made the city literally unsafe, Clement first considered moving the papal throne to Spain or Austria, but decided the best political move would be to find a site under the protection of France. He hit upon Avignon, in the independent province of Arles (but actually under the control of the French King). At the insistence of the French king, Clement was crowned at Lyons rather than Rome, and then began to construct the papal court at Avignon, where it eventually became a sumptuous and opulent palace. Curiously, Pope Clement—presumably the heir to St. Peter as bishop of Rome—never set foot in the city of Rome in his entire life.[111]

To seal the French control of the papacy, Clement appointed a large number of cardinals (that is, the papal electors), almost all of whom were French. Consequently, the next six popes were all French and maintained the papal court at Avignon. However, spurred by his own sense of guilt, considerable personal pressure from St. Birgitta of Sweden and St. Catherine of Siena (both of whom were very highly regarded), and his concern about losing control of the Papal Lands in Italy, Gregory XI decided to return the papal court to Rome.[112] It took him nearly four years to work out the plans, but in 1377, just a year before his death, the papacy returned to the Holy City.[113]

Predictably, the predominately French College of Cardinals did not approve of the move, and when Gregory died, they hoped to elect a Frenchman and return the papal court to Avignon. However, they were perforce located in Rome, and during the Conclave for election, the people of Rome rioted, broke into the Vatican, and demanded an Italian pope! Intimidated by the violence, the Cardinals unanimously elected Urban VI, a Neapolitan by birth, and the Archbishop of Bari—notably the last pope elected who was not a cardinal himself.

However, during his first five months as pope, Urban showed a side of his personality unrecognized till then. He set out to make serious reforms, including serious limitations on the privileges of the cardinals,[114] and he did this so arrogantly and imprudently that it was thought by some that he had actually become insane. The cardinal electors slipped surreptitiously out of Rome and met secretly again in the Italian city of Anagni. Although there was no precedent for it, they declared the previous election invalid and elected Robert of Geneva (another Frenchman) as Pope Clement VII, who was soon enthroned at the old papal court in Avignon.

Excommunications flew back and forth between the papal camps,[115] armed groups clashed, and even crusades were mounted against each other by the two competing popes. Each of them appointed more cardinals who would support him. Europe's foremost doctors of law were consulted and generally found for the Roman pope, but the theologians were divided. France, Spain, Cyprus, Naples, and Scotland supported the Avignon pope, while England, Flanders, Denmark, Norway, Poland, and Sweden and most of the Italian and German states sided with the Roman pope.

When the Roman Pope Urban VI died,[116] his cardinals elected Boniface IX, who was in turn succeeded by Innocent VII and then Gregory XII. And when the Avignon pope Clement VII died, his cardinals elected Benedict XIII.

In 1409 the Council of Pisa met and, in an effort to solve the standoff, elected a third pope, Alexander V, and when he died ten months after election (possibly poisoned), the Council chose John XXIII. However, instead of solving the problem, this simply added a third pope to the stew.

The major political struggle that subsequently arose was between the scholars and theologians who believed that a true Ecumenical Council (that is, with representatives from the entire Catholic Church) had authority and power over the pope (Conciliarism), and others who maintained the supremacy of the papacy over any Council.

However, in 1414, the Council of Constance met, deposed John XXIII, accepted the abdication of Gregory XII, and denied the validity of Benedict XIII. In 1417, the council elected Martin V. In spite of scattered opposition, the wider Church's fatigue and exasperation with the disputes of the past four decades made the solution generally acceptable, and the Great Schism came to a spluttering end. Curiously, one of Pope Martin V's first papal actions was to betray his Conciliarist electors and repudiate the principle that any Council could hold authority over the papacy.

While the Great Schism probably had relatively little *practical* effect on the local Christian in England, it was certainly part of the broad perception that the Church and her powers over the people were weakening. Add to this the general moral degeneration of English religious orders, the prevalence of uneducated and inadequate parish clergy, the overwhelming engagement of bishops and archbishops in secular political life, the unrest of popular Lollardy, and the gradual escalation of religious texts available in the vernacular. The result was an almost unconscious (but widespread) movement that began to give significant validation to a serious spirituality that depended less and less on formal ecclesiastical or clerical sources of approval, and more on personal experience and sanctity—such as the devout writings of Julian of Norwich and her fellow English mystics.

⤜ 9
JULIAN'S BIBLE

There is no Julian scholar to my knowledge who contests the proposition that Julian demonstrates a familiarity with the Holy Scriptures. Some (notably Colledge & Walsh) believe that she was educated (probably, they believe, she spent time in a convent) and that she could read the Latin Vulgate text of the Bible, doing her own translations. Another Julian scholar actually makes the improbably extravagant claim that Julian knew Hebrew.

During Julian's lifetime, the Latin Vulgate of St. Jerome was the only "authorized" version of Scripture in general use throughout the Church. Contrary to what Colledge & Walsh maintain, I believe that it is both culturally and literarily extremely unlikely that Julian knew Latin—at least not at the time of the first record of her revelations. Indeed, had she been conversant in Latin, there would have been much less reason for her to have written her book in English. Virtually all other Julian scholars now accept that it is unlikely that Julian had been a nun in a religious community previous to or at the time of her visions.

Consequently, since Julian seems to demonstrate familiarity with the Bible, it is likely that she knew an English translation, rather than the Latin Vulgate. If so, what translation?

Julian describes herself as *lewde* (Middle English for "unlettered"), as a "simple creature"—one who at the time of her writing *cowde no letter.*[117]

McGrath describes the language problem in fourteenth-century England:

> [T]here was a more complex anxiety within English academia concerning the very nature of the English language itself. To its Latin- and French-speaking critics, English was a barbarous language, lacking any real grammatical structure, incapable of expressing the deep and nuanced truths of the Bible in particular, and the Christian faith in general. This complaint, which had been implicit in much fourteenth-century dismissal of English as a serious language of faith, became explicit in an important debate at Oxford in 1401. Richard Ullerston defended English against its critics valiantly, but ultimately in vain. The debate concluded that English was not an appropriate language for the translation of the Bible. It was but a small step from this literary judgment to the essentially political decision to ban English language altogether from every aspect of English church life. This decision, taken in 1407–9 by Thomas Arundel, archbishop of Canterbury, had special relevance for the issue of biblical translation. . . . English thus became the language of the religious underground. To write in English was tantamount to holding heretical views. Even as late as 1513, John Colet—then dean of St. Paul's Cathedral, London—was suspended from his position for translating the Lord's Prayer into English.[118]

But, if that is the case, to what version of the Bible could Julian possibly have had access? The only complete English translations of the Bible that would have been generally available in fourteenth-century England are those of and related to John Wycliffe (1380–88).

Master John Wycliffe was the fourteenth-century Oxford professor who was the inspiration for the ecclesiastical reform movement
that came to be called "Lollardy." He published dozens of pamphlets
and treatises and was the first declared "heretic" in English church
history, but sometimes called by supporters "the Morning Star of the
Reformation" since many of his criticisms of the Church were later
echoed by the sixteenth-century reformers. He was a voluble and
vociferous advocate of making the Scriptures available in the vernacular
tongue. Eventually dismissed from his position at Oxford, he retired to
his parish at Lutterworth, was declared a heretic by an English Church
Convocation, was condemned by six Papal bulls, and, after his death,
was condemned by the Council of Constance.

For our purposes, we can set aside the controversies over whether
John Wycliff himself participated in the translations that his followers
promulgated, and simply leave it that he may possibly have had a hand
in the first version (completed in 1382, two years before his death),
but he was far too old and far too ill to have contributed to the
later version (which was not completed until at least 1388, four years
after Wycliff's death).[119] The first version was a perfectly literal, word-
for-word translation, following the Latin word order. This meant that
some passages were almost unreadable in English; indeed, some were
nonsensical or with the meaning actually inverted. Some examples:
The Latin Vulgate had "*Dominum formidabunt adversarii eius.*" The first
Wycliffe translation, following the Latin word order, translated this
as "The Lord his adversaries shall dread." This can give the opposite
sense of its proper translation: "His adversaries shall fear the Lord."
Other constructions were simply awkward.

Almost immediately work began on a "second edition" that would
correct some of the literalism in the first, and obviously showed a
commitment to translate the *meaning*, rather than the literal words
or word order. Consequently, that later edition was fairly readable.
However, in some editions of the book the biblical text was preceded
by a prologue or preface that not only explained the principles on
which the translation was made, but also promulgated some core

aspects of the Wycliffite heresy—particularly an attack on sacramental theology. In some copies, there were also printed marginal comments—some of a virulent quality—that were strongly offensive to English orthodoxy.

In 1407–8 Thomas Arundel, Archbishop of Canterbury, convened an ecclesiastical Synod to purge the Church of Lollard influence. Among other constitutions of the Synod, one related to Bible translation:

> We therefore decree and ordain that no man shall, hereafter, by his own authority, translate any text of the scripture into English, or any other tongue, by way of a book, libel, or treatise, now lately set forth in the time of John Wyckliff, or since, or hereafter to be set forth, in part or in whole, privily or apertly, upon pain of greater excommunication, until the said translation be allowed by the ordinary of the place, or, if the case so require, by the council provincial.[120]

It has often and commonly been claimed either that (a) Julian could not have used a Wycliffe translation, because those translations were formally condemned and severe punishments instituted for those who owned or read them; or (b) that Julian was a radical scofflaw and crypto-Protestant who, in order to thumb her nose at the authorities, would have used a Wycliffe translation even at great risk to herself.

However, neither of these claims is true. Even in the Synod Constitutions, the vernacular Scriptures were not *absolutely* prohibited. Nor was even the Wycliffe translation in itself declared heretical: it was for the most part a faithful rendering of the Latin Vulgate. Its only plainly heretical material appeared in the so-called "General Preface." But of the more than 200 surviving copies, the offensive preface is found in only 11 of those copies.

Among known owners of Wycliffe Bibles were the royal family, Duke Humphrey of Gloucester, the Carthusian Priory of Sheen (whose copy had been a gift from the King himself),[121] Fotheringale College, Sir William Weston (last prior of the Knights of St. John), John Lacy (a Newcastle Dominican), the Dominican Priory at

Cambridge, Roger Walton (an early sixteenth-century parish priest), and even the unquestionably orthodox Brigittine convent of Syon.[122] Further, the fact is that over 200 copies of the Wycliffe translation survive[123] and from inscriptions in these surviving copies and records of them in wills, legacies, and benefactions, we know that many were in the possession of priests, nuns, and prominent laity. Clearly, the translation, *apart from the prologue*, was not prohibited, and could easily be possessed with episcopal approval and license—and was apparently widely read.[124]

In fact, in 1394 Archbishop Arundel himself preached at the funeral of Anne of Bohemia (Richard II's queen) and noted that "notwithstanding that she was an alien born she had in English all the four gospellers with the doctors upon them." And she had submitted these translations to Arundel for his inspection, and he found them "good and true."[125] Here was very clear evidence that Wycliffe translations were acceptable (even to Archbishop Arundel, the very composer of the condemnatory Constitutions of the Oxford Synod) as long as those translations had been approved by ecclesiastical authorities.

It is almost certain that Julian knew at least what we call the later editions of Wycliffe. It has been suggested that Julian sympathized with the Lollards. However, the most common targets of Lollard attacks on the Church establishment were monasteries, convents, and specifically anchorites.[126] It is highly unlikely that Julian would have been in sympathy with a religious movement that so powerfully repudiated her chosen way of life.

A more practical question is also raised when we consider that paper had only just begun to be used in fourteenth-century England,[127] and the printing press had not yet been invented. Consequently, the cost of a fourteenth-century handwritten Bible—probably still on parchment—was more than a priest's annual stipend (about $6,000 modern). To own such a volume one would have to be very wealthy, but it is possible that Dame Julian could have afforded such a precious volume or borrowed it from one of the religious houses in Norwich—notably from the Austin Friars, who had one of the greatest libraries in England and whose Friary was virtually across the street from St. Julian's Church.[128]

I think it can be safely assumed that Julian had access to the Bible associated with the name of Wycliffe, either owning one herself (with ecclesiastical approval) or borrowing one. It might also be noted that in Chapter 4, Julian quotes of the words of the Blessed Virgin: "Lo me, Gods handmayd" (Luke 1:38), and it may be interesting to notice that *only* Wycliffe translates this word (Greek: *idou*; Latin: *ecce*) as "Lo. . . ." *All* others have translated the word as "Behold . . ." or omitted it altogether.

PART THREE

THE *REVELATIONS*, WITH ANNOTATIONS

ollowing are translated portions of Julian's *Revelations* and my comments on the text. They are designed on facing pages, with Julian's on the right and the comments on the left. Superscript numbers set in boldface type in the *Revelations* correspond to the comments on the left. Superscript numbers set in standard type in the comments refer to endnotes. Underlined text indicates a phrase or word specifically explained or referred to in the accompanying note. For the sake of clarity, all pronouns referring to God or Christ have been capitalized. All translations of medieval texts are mine, unless otherwise indicated.

COMMENTS ON CHAPTER 1

1. Many commentators and scholars agree that this disclaimer may be nothing more than a literary convention or, at most, an admission that Julian did not know Latin (a claim I support). On the other hand, there are those who claim that she could read and write not only Middle English and Latin, but even (in one case) that she knew Hebrew. It seems entirely unlikely that she could have been that well educated. In the SV, the scribe notes that Julian is *yit on life, anno domini 1413*. This tells us that there must have been a copy of the SV written in that year—presumably copied twenty years after it had been written.

2. This "catalog" or "index" of Julian's Showings does not appear in the SV—another indication that this LV was thought out in detail by Julian before it was set to paper. It is an indication of how her long years of thought and contemplation made her revelations—clearer than ever to her. W&J tell us that the word "revelation" was a new word in 1380, replacing the more ancient "shewing."

3. *Dearworthy* is one of the wonderful Middle English words that I have chosen to retain without translation. Strictly speaking, it means "valued" or "precious" ("of dear worth") but it has an engaging quality and it "sounds" like Julian to me.

4. See Appendix 14, "The Holy Trinity."

5. The Middle English is *worshipful thankeing*. *Worshippe* in ME does not usually mean the same as our modern word. It means "honor." (When someone was referred to as "Your Worship" it meant exactly the same as our "Your Honor.")

6. *Well and woe* is another ME phrase I retained for its poetic and winsome quality, especially as a keynote of Julian's theology: that God's love never departs from us, no matter our "spiritual condition."

REVELATIONS
shown to one who could not read a letter.[1]
ANNO DOMINI, 1373

≈ 1

[2]This is a revelation of love that Jesus Christ, our endless joy, made in sixteen showings or revelations, in detail, of which

The first is concerning His precious crowning with thorns; and therewith was included and described in detail the Trinity with the Incarnation and the unity between God and man's soul, with many beautiful showings of endless wisdom and teachings of love in which all the showings that follow are based and united. [Chapters 4–9]

The second showing is the discoloring of His fair face in symbolizing His dearworthy[3] passion. [Chapter 10]

The third showing is that our Lord God—all Power, all Wisdom, all Love[4]—just as truly as He has made every thing that is, also truly He does and causes every thing that is done. [Chapter 11]

The fourth showing is the scourging of His frail body with abundant shedding of His blood. [Chapter 12]

The fifth showing is that the Fiend is overcome by the precious Passion of Christ. [Chapter 13]

The sixth showing is the honor-filled favor[5] of our Lord God with which He rewards all His blessed servants in heaven [Chapter 14]. The seventh showing is a frequent experience of well and woe[6]—the experience of "well" is grace-filled touching and enlightening, with true certainty of endless joy; the experience of "woe" is temptation by sadness and annoyance of our fleshly life—with spiritual understanding that even so we are protected safely in love—in woe as in well—by the goodness of God. [Chapter 15]

The eighth showing is the last pains of Christ and His cruel dying. [Chapters 16–21]

7. Julian was one of a handful of mystics (among them, St. Francis of Assisi) who showed devotion to the Sacred Heart before its explosion of popularity in the seventeenth and eighteenth centuries.

8. See Part One where I have described Julian as an "origin-ist." It is telling, I think, that Julian perceives the *redemptive* "power, wisdom, and goodness" (her three analogies for the Holy Trinity) as identical with the *creative* power, wisdom, and goodness. Julian has the deep insight that redemption is mystically related to the very act of creation itself. (Note that for clarity, to delineate which words are the Lord's and which are Julian's in this translation, all statements of direct address are put in Elizabethan/Jacobean language.)

9. This is a considerable over-simplification of the thirteenth showing.

10. This admonition to "keep us in the Faith and truth of Holy Church" is repeated in several forms throughout the book. In spite of the wishes of some modern interpreters (who would like to portray her as an ecclesiastical revolutionary), Julian never belittles or replaces the Catholic Faith of the Church. She is not a crypto-Protestant.

11. Julian's ME here is *that our lord is ground of our beseekeing*—perhaps "beseeching" may be a more powerful and engaging translation than simply "prayer."

12. Julian's ME here is *and be fulfilled of joy and blisse in hevyn*—a suggestion that joy itself is true human fulfillment.

The ninth showing is about the delight which is in the blessed Trinity because of the cruel Passion of Christ and His regretful dying; in this joy and delight He wills we be comforted and made happy with Him until when we come to the fullness in heaven. [Chapters 22–23]

The tenth showing is that our Lord Jesus shows his blessed heart cloven in two in love.[7] [Chapter 24]

The eleventh showing is a noble, spiritual showing of His dearworthy Mother. [Chapter 25]

The twelfth showing is that our Lord is all supreme Being. [Chapter 26]

The thirteenth showing is that our Lord God wills that we have great regard for all the deeds that He has done in the great splendor of creating all things, and of the excellency of creating man (who is above all His other works),[8] and of the precious amends that He has made for man's sin, turning all our blame into endless honor, and here also our Lord says: "Behold and see; for by the same Power, Wisdom, and Goodness that I have done all this, by that same Power, Wisdom, and Goodness I shall make well all that is not well, and thou thyself shalt see it."[9]

And in this showing He wills that we keep us in the Faith and truth of Holy Church,[10] not wishing to be aware of His secrets now, except as is proper for us in this life. [Chapters 27–40]

The fourteenth showing is that our Lord is the foundation of our prayer.[11] Herein were seen two elements that He wills both be equally great: the one is righteous prayer, the other is sure trust; and in these ways our prayer delights Him, and He of His goodness fulfills it. [Chapters 41–43]

The fifteenth showing is that we shall without delay be taken from all our pain and from all our woe and, of His goodness, we shall come up above where we shall have our Lord Jesus for our recompense, and be filled with joy[12] and bliss in heaven. [Chapters 64–65]

The sixteenth showing is that the blessed Trinity our Creator, in Christ Jesus our Savior, endlessly dwells in our soul, honorably

COMMENTS ON CHAPTER 2

1. See comment 1 for Chapter 1.
2. See Part Two, section 5, "Date and Time of Julian's Visions," for a discussion of this date.
3. ME has *mende of his passion* ("mind of his passion") which carries a stronger sense of consciousness than simply the word "memory."
4. See Part Two, section 1, "Julian's Identity," for a discussion on "youth."
5. The fourteenth-century *Meditationes Vitae Christi* stressed mental imaging of the Passion, for anyone to "make hymselfe present in his thoghte as if he sawe fully and with his bodily eghe all the thyngys that be-fell abowte the crosse and the glorious passione of our Lorde Ihesu." (C. Horstmann, ed., *Yorkshire Writers*, 1895. I. p. 198.)
6. C&W point out a possible textual flaw here which may originally have read "all his true lovers that were living at that time and saw his pains," and since then believed in his pains, referring both to immediate witnesses and later followers. (See Appendix 13, "The Stabat Mater.")
7. The word *rites* here could as well be replaced by the original word *rights* because "taking one's rights" in the fourteenth century meant "receiving Communion." One can also see here an early hint of Julian's willingness to turn aside from the relative luxury of earthly life to the hardship of the life of a recluse.
8. Here, again, is a ME word which I have chosen to leave in its original form rather than translate it as "departing." To my mind words such as *outpassing* give us an endearing flavor of Julian's own gentle style.

governing and controlling all things, powerfully and wisely saving and protecting us for the sake of love; and that we shall not be overcome by our Enemy. [Chapters 66–68]

⇌ 2

These revelations were shown to a simple creature that had learned no letter,[1] in the year of our Lord, 1373, the 8th day of May.[2] This creature had previously desired three gifts from God: the first was memory of His passion;[3] the second was bodily sickness in youth at thirty years of age;[4] the third was to have from God's gift three wounds.

As for the first, which came to my mind with devotion, I thought I had some sense of the passion of Christ, but still I desired more by the grace of God. I thought that I wished to have been at that time with Mary Magdalene and with the others who were Christ's lovers, and therefore I desired a bodily sight wherein I could have more knowledge of the bodily pains of our Savior,[5] and of the compassion of Our Lady and of all His true lovers who at that time saw His pains, for I wished to be one of them and to suffer with them.[6] I never desired any other sight or showing of God until the soul was departed from the body (for I believed to be saved by the mercy of God).

The purpose for this petition was so that after the showing I would have a more true consciousness of the Passion of Christ.

The second gift came to my mind with contrition, freely without any effort: a willing desire to have from God's gift a bodily sickness.

I wished that the sickness would be so severe as to seem mortal so that I could, in that sickness, receive all my rites of Holy Church, myself expecting that I should die, and that all creatures who saw me could suppose the same (for I wished to have no kind of comfort from earthly life).[7]

In this sickness, I desired to have all the kinds of pains, bodily and spiritual, that I would have if I were to die, with all the fears and temptations of the fiends—except the outpassing[8] of the soul.

9. The ME word I translated as "benefit" is *speede*, which carries the sense of "fortune" or "luck." (The modern use of the ancient phrase "God speed" is actually a leftover relic in ME: it literally translates to modern English as "Good luck" or "Good fortune," and has nothing to do with going fast.)

10. This phrase "for it seemed to me this was not the common custom of prayer" exists only in the PV.

11. These three words appear in the SV only.

12. Here is Julian's deeply personal version of Christ's cry to God in Gethsemane: "Yet not my will but yours" (Matthew 26:39), and it is the coda all Christians must add to any prayer of petition, lest prayer be made against the will of God.

13. In the SV, Julian explained the "three wounds" metaphor when she wrote: "I heard a man of Holy Church tell of the story of Saint Cecilia in which telling I understood that she had three wounds of a sword in the neck with which she suffered death. By this inspiration, I conceived a mighty desire, praying our Lord that he would grant me three wounds in my lifetime." Paintings of St. Cecilia were very common on rood screens in East Anglia churches.

COMMENTS ON CHAPTER 3

1. Since the revelations took place in May of 1373, this means that Julian was born near the end (November or December) of AD 1342.

2. See Part Two, section 5, "Date and Time of Julian's Visions," for a discussion of the dating of the revelations.

3. See Part Two, section 1, "Julian's Identity," for a discussion on "youth."

4. There is a hint here that Julian believed one's heavenly state was "improved" by the degree in which one had lived a life of deep devotion. This may be related to her later idea that the sins and pains of earthly life were transformed into rewards in heaven. (See Chapter 38.)

(And this I intended so that I would be purged by the mercy of God and afterward live more to the honor of God because of that sickness, for I hoped that it could be to my benefit[9] when I would have died, for I desired to be soon with my God and Maker.)

These two desires for the Passion and the sickness I desired of Him with a condition (for it seemed to me this was not the common custom of prayer[10]) saying thus: "Lord, Thou knowest what I wish—if it be Thy will that I have it, grant it me;[11] and if it be not Thy will, Good Lord, be not displeased, for I want nothing except what Thou wilt."[12]

For the third gift, by the grace of God and teaching of Holy Church, I conceived a mighty desire to receive three wounds while I was alive;[13] that is to say, the wound of true contrition, the wound of kind compassion, and the wound of wish-filled yearning for God.

And, just as I asked the other two with a condition, so all this last petition I asked mightily without any condition.

The first two desires passed from my memory, but the third dwelled with me constantly.

⇒ 3

When I was thirty years old and a half,[1] God sent me a bodily sickness in which I lay three days and three nights; and on the fourth night, I received all my rites of Holy Church and expected not to have lived till day.

After this I lay two days and two nights.[2]

And on the third night I expected often to have passed away (and so expected they that were with me).

And being still in youth,[3] I thought it a great sadness to die—not for anything that was on earth that pleased me to live for, nor for any pain that I was afraid of (for I trusted in God of His mercy), but because I would have liked to have lived so that I could have loved God better and for a longer time, so that I could have more knowledge and love of God in the bliss of heaven.[4]

5. Psalm 39:6 (BCP), "You have given me a mere handful of days, and my lifetime is as nothing in your sight; truly, even those who stand erect are but a puff of wind."

6. The fact that Julian refers to her priest as "my curate" means that he was a secular, parish priest, rather than a monk or chaplain of a convent. This is a good indication that Julian was *not* a nun in a convent or in an anchorhold at the time of the revelations.

7. In the SV, the text reads: "The parson [the ME word is *persone*] set the cross before my face"—another evidence that the attending priest was a secular parish priest. (Note: In the Middle Ages, the parish priest was called "the person" since he was usually the only one in the community who could read and write, prepare wills, etc.) In parallel modern colloquial English he might be called "the Man."

8. We need to understand that it was only in the fourteenth century—during Julian's own time—that the "suffering crucifix" came to be the normal portrayal of the Crucifixion. Previous to that all crucifixes portrayed the body of Christ virtually resting and reclining on the cross, relaxed, with only a garland or a crown around his head (no thorns), and in no way a body realistically twisted in pain. Consequently, the "image" the priest brought may well have been a "suffering crucifix," which could have been uncommon in Julian's experience and might itself have helped to initiate the revelations. (Indeed, just such a small brass crucifix was discovered hidden beneath the floor of St. George's Church, Norwich—probably to hide it from the pillaging Puritans.)

9. Julian had previously mentioned in the fourth paragraph above that it was daylight, so this darkening can be seen as part of God's action in preparing for the revelations.

For it seemed to me that all the time I had lived here—so little and so short in comparison to that endless bliss—I thought of as nothing.[5]

Wherefore I thought: "Good Lord, could my living no longer be to Thine honor?"

And I understood by my reason and by the experience of my pains that I would die.

And I assented fully with all the will of my heart, to be at God's will.

Thus I endured till day, and by then my body was dead from the midst downward as regards my feeling.

Then was I aided to be set upright, supported with help, in order to have more freedom for my heart to be at God's will, and thinking of God while my life should last.

My curate[6] was sent for to be at my ending, and by the time he came I had cast my eyes upward and could not speak. He[7] placed the cross before my face and said: "I have brought thee the image of thy Maker and Savior. Look thereupon and comfort thyself with it."[8]

It seemed to me that I was all right, for my eyes were set upward to heaven (where I trusted to come by the mercy of God) but nevertheless I consented to fix my eyes on the face of the crucifix if I could, and so I did (for it seemed to me that I might longer endure to look straight forward than straight up).

After this my sight began to fail, and it grew all dark about me in the chamber as if it had been night,[9] except on the image of the cross on which I beheld an ordinary light, and I know not how.

Everything except the cross became ugly to me as if it had been much possessed by the fiends.

And after this the upper part of my body began to die so noticeably that scarcely had I any feeling—my worst pain was shortness of breath and waning of life. And then I expected truly to have passed away.

But, in the midst of this, suddenly all my pain was taken from me and I was as whole (especially in the upper part of my body) as ever I had been before.

10. There is some confusion here between "wounds" and "gifts." The experiencing of Christ's pains was part of the first "gift" Julian had requested. But "compassion" (which means "feeling with") was the second wound she requested. It seems that her request for "compassion" referred to her wish to "feel with" Christ in his pains.

11. This is an important disclaimer: Julian wishes her readers to know that she had not requested or even expected any visions from God. She wants her visions to be seen as having their origin entirely in God and in God's actions. She wants us to know that the Showings were a surprise to her.

12. The mystical idea of suffering with Christ was a common one in the late Middle Ages, and was the idea that lay behind some of the more extreme ascetical practices of the day.

COMMENTS ON CHAPTER 4

1. It is important to realize that in all of the Showings, Julian is given a kind of "supplement" to Holy Scripture. Most of the details she sees in her visions do not appear explicitly in the Gospel accounts, but were a very important part of the Church's devotional and ascetical traditions of her day.

2. On many occasions, Julian makes it clear that the Showings were directly from the Lord, not the product of prayers to the saints or prophets. (See Chapter 6, where Julian discusses intermediaries.)

3. Reference the end of the consecration prayer in the Eucharist: "Through Christ, and with Christ, and in Christ. . . ."

I marveled at this sudden change (for it seemed to me that it was a mysterious act of God and not of nature), but even with the feeling of this comfort, I trusted never the more to live; and the feeling of this comfort was no full ease to me, for it seemed to me I would rather have been delivered from this world, for my heart was wishfully set on that.

Then came suddenly to my memory that I should desire the second wound[10] of our Lord's gracious gift: that my body could be filled with the memory and feeling of His blessed Passion, as I had prayed before (for I had wished that His pains were my pains with compassion, and, afterward, yearning for God). Thus I thought I could with His grace have the wounds that I had desired before.

However, in this I never desired any bodily sight nor any kind of showing from God[11] (except compassion, such as a natural soul could have with our Lord Jesus, who for the sake of love willed to be a mortal man). And therefore I desired to suffer with Him, while living in my mortal body, as God would give me grace.[12]

4

[1]In this showing suddenly I saw the red blood trickling down from under the garland, hot and freshly and most plenteously, just as it was at the time of His Passion when the garland of thorns was pressed onto His blessed head.

Just so, I conceived truly and powerfully that it was He Himself (both God and man, the Same who suffered thus for me) who showed it to me without any go-between.[2]

And in the same showing suddenly the Trinity almost filled my heart with joy. (And I understood it shall be like that in heaven without end for all that shall come there.)

For the Trinity is God, God is the Trinity; the Trinity is our Maker, the Trinity is our Keeper, the Trinity is our everlasting Lover, the Trinity is our endless Joy and Bliss, through our Lord Jesus Christ and in our Lord Jesus Christ.[3]

4. All of Julian's Showings are powerfully and consistently Trinitarian. She refers to the Trinity almost fifty times in the showings.

5. See Part Two, section 1, on Julian's identity. There it is explained that the Latin given here (from BV) is wrong, and should be *Benedicite Domino*. (It is given properly in the PV.)

6. In Julian's ME, the word is *homely*, which means "home-like" or "informal." For Julian, it is often set up as a contrast to the word *courteous*, which means "courtly" or "formal."

7. The idea of end-of-life temptation was common in Church teaching. (Note the modern translation of the Lord's Prayer: "Save us from the time of trial. . . .") At this point, Julian still expects to die.

8. Julian speaks of two of her three kinds of Showings: (1) *bodily sight* of the Passion and (2) *in my understanding*. There was more to the visions than just what Julian saw with her eyes. She believed also that her mind was also being "shown" meanings.

9. Notice Julian's unconscious parallel between her sense of herself (in the fourth paragraph above) with that of the Blessed Virgin Mary.

10. In her ME, Julian uses the word *Lo* (translated here as *Behold*), which of all translated Scriptures of her day, occurs only in the later translations attributed to Wycliffe. This suggests that she knew that Bible, although she may have simply heard the passage translated in sermons.

11. We see here a devotion to the Blessed Virgin Mary that was entirely typical of Julian's day, but she carefully makes a distinction between the *veneration* due to Mary and the *worship* due Christ. There is much honor, but no hint of the idea of Mary as co-redemptrix here.

(And this was shown in the first revelation and in all of them, for whenever Jesus appears, the blessed Trinity is understood, as I see it.)[4]

And I said: "Benedicite domine!"[5] (This I said, for reverence in my meaning, with a powerful voice, and full greatly astonished because of the wonder and amazement that I had that He who is so respected and awesome wished to be so <u>familiar</u>[6] with a sinful creature living in this miserable flesh.)

Thus I understood that at that time our Lord Jesus out of His gracious love wished to show me comfort before the time of my temptation (for it seemed to me that it could well be that I would—by the permission of God and with His protection—be tempted by fiends before I died).[7]

With this sight of His blessed Passion along with the Godhead that I saw in my understanding,[8] I knew well that it was strength enough for me (yea, and for all creatures living that would be saved) against all the fiends of hell and spiritual temptation.

In this showing He brought Our Blessed Lady Saint Mary to my mind. I saw her spiritually in bodily likeness, a simple maid and humble, young of age and little grown beyond childhood, in the stature that she was when she conceived with child.

Also God showed in part the wisdom and the truth of her soul wherein I understood the reverent contemplation with which she beheld her God and Maker, marveling with great reverence that He wished to be born of her who was a simple creature of His own creation.[9]

And this wisdom and truth (knowing the greatness of her Creator and the littleness of herself who is created) caused her to say full humbly to Gabriel: "Behold[10] me here, God's handmaiden."

In this sight I understood truly that she is higher in worthiness and grace than all that God made beneath her, for nothing that is created is greater than she, except the blessed Manhood of Christ, as I see it.[11]

COMMENTS ON CHAPTER 5

1. The second of Julian's three ways of "seeing": by "bodily sight," by "spiritual sight," and by "word formed in my understand-ing." We might call these: vision, insight, and comprehension.

2. The image of God's *enfolding* us is a frequent analogy Julian uses to describe the indescribable spiritual intimacy between God and created human beings.

3. Here is an example of Julian's understanding of God's presence as universal. It is a kind of orthodox version of pantheism: wherever anything "good" is, there is God. One is reminded of the traditional Anglican Antiphon for Maundy Thursday: "Where true charity and love are, God himself is there." (See the Episcopal Hymnal 1982, #606.)

4. Here is a minor example of the mystical term *deification*: creation lies poetically in the hand of God, and yet here it is shown in the hand of Julian. She is shown creation *sub specie aeternitatis*, from God's point of view.

5. Certainly the most popular of all Julian's images, and shown in several iconic portrayals of her. "The size of a hazel nut" was, in fact, a term used in cooking (and still in use in Europe): "Take a bit of butter the size of a hazel nut . . ." (or a walnut or a pecan). What is emphasized is its diminutiveness. (An interesting note: When the Globe Theater was rebuilt on its original site in London in the twentieth century, excavators found thousands and thousands of hazel nut shells at the site of the ancient theater: apparently the hazel nut had been like our modern popcorn.)

6. Another example of Julian's own interpreting of what she has been given as a vision. She doesn't merely "accept" the vision, but strives to understand its implications.

7. Julian is not a dualist who sees material reality as evil, but here she points out the priority of the uncreated over the created (which latter must be *set at naught* or put aside so it won't come between us and God).

⤚ 5

At this same time that I saw this sight of the head bleeding, our good Lord showed to me a spiritual vision[1] of His simple loving. I saw which He is to us everything that is good and comfortable for us. He is our clothing that for love enwraps us, holds us, and all encloses us because of His tender love, so that He may never leave us.[2]

And so in this showing I saw that He is to us everything that is good, as I understood it.[3]

Also in this revelation He showed a little thing, the size of a hazel nut in the palm of my hand,[4] and it was as round as a ball. I looked at it with the eye of my understanding and thought: "What can this be?" And it was generally answered thus: "It is all that is made."[5]

I marveled how it could continue, because it seemed to me it could suddenly have sunk into nothingness because of its littleness. And I was answered in my understanding: "It continueth and always shall, because God loveth it; and in this way everything hath its being by the love of God."

In this little thing I saw three characteristics: the first is that God made it, the second is that God loves it, the third, that God keeps it.

But what did I observe in that?[6] Truly the Maker, the Lover, and the Keeper, for, until I am in essence one-ed to Him, I can never have full rest nor true joy (that is to say, until I am made so fast to Him that there is absolutely nothing that is created separating my God and myself).

It is necessary for us to have awareness of the littleness of created things and to set at naught everything that is created, in order to love and have God who is uncreated.[7]

8. This is a subtle reference to the Holy Trinity, since in several places Julian describes the Father as all power, the Son as all wisdom, and the Holy Spirit as all goodness.

9. Note that the *deus absconditus*, the "hidden God," wishes to be known. And note this phrase by way of introduction to Julian's perfect prayer three paragraphs later.

10. This is pure Scholasticism: St. Thomas Aquinas teaches that the soul naturally seeks the Good, but is diverted by not perceiving the *true* Good, and settling for less.

11. Once more, Julian shares her "understanding" or her interpretation, which she believes is also of divine origin.

12. Here we are given what to my mind is (the Lord's Prayer alone excepted) the finest prayer in the entire Christian tradition. It is in fact a Prayer of Total Oblation, masquerading as a Prayer of Petition. If the divinely intended goal of human existence is union with God, this prayer is absolutely seminal! If no other Christian prayer were ever prayed, this would suffice. Note that Julian declares that these words "most nearly touch upon the will of God and His goodness."

13. An Episcopalian will recognize the beginning of the Consecration Prayer in Rite II: "In your infinite love you made us for yourself . . ." (BCP, 362).

For this is the reason why we are not fully at ease in heart and soul: because here we seek rest in these things that are so little, in which there is no rest, and we recognize not our God who is all powerful, all wise, all good,[8] for He is the true rest.

God wishes to be known, and He delights that we remain in Him, because all that is less than He is not enough for us.[9]

And this is the reason why no soul is at rest until it is emptied of everything that is created.

When the soul is willingly emptied for love in order to have Him who is all, then is it able to receive spiritual rest.

Also our Lord God showed that it is full great pleasure to Him that an innocent soul come to Him nakedly and plainly and simply. For this is the natural yearning[10] of the soul, thanks to the touching of the Holy Spirit, according to the understanding that I have[11] in this showing—

> God, of Thy goodness, give me Thyself;
> for Thou art enough to me,
> and I can ask nothing that is less
> that can be full honor to Thee.
> And if I ask anything that is less,
> ever shall I be in want,
> for only in Thee have I all.[12]

These words are full lovely to the soul and most nearly touch upon the will of God and His goodness, for His goodness fills all His creatures and all His blessed works, and surpasses them without end, for He is the endlessness.

And He has made us only for Himself[13] and restored us by His blessed passion and ever keeps us in His blessed love.

And all this is from His goodness.

COMMENTS ON CHAPTER 6

1. The ME has *for unknowing of love.*
2. In the fifteenth-century *Commonplace Book* of Robert Reynes there is a section that speaks of those who have wounded Christ in swearing by parts of his body, and "in wall-paintings and stained glass were pictures of Christ's bleeding and dismembered body surrounded by people who had sworn on the afflicted part" (Duffy, 72).
3. It is quite amazing for a fourteenth-century woman to see through the universally practiced (but theologically indefensible) invocation of saints to work miracles, etc. In the following paragraphs she justifies prayers to the saints as long as one understands that it is actually the goodness of God that is being recognized and appealed to.
4. Julian does not repudiate intermediaries (as some commentators hold), but she absolutely refuses to accept the use of "intermediaries" *unless one understands that the source of the goodness is in God*, not in the intermediaries themselves.

⇌ 6

This showing was made to teach our soul wisely to cleave to the goodness of God.

At that time the custom of our praying was brought to mind: how for <u>lack of understanding and recognition</u>[1] of love, we are used to creating many intermediaries.

Then saw I truly that it is more honor to God and more true delight that we faithfully pray to Himself out of His goodness, and cleave to that goodness by His grace with true understanding and steadfast belief, than if we created all the intermediaries that heart can think of.

For if we create all these intermediaries, it is too little, and not complete honor to God, whereas all the whole of it is in His goodness, and there absolutely nothing fails.

For this, as I shall say, came to my mind at the same time: we pray to God by His Holy Flesh and by His Precious Blood, His Holy Passion, His dearworthy Death and Wounds, by all His blessed Human Nature, but the endless life that we have from all this is from His goodness.[2]

And we pray to Him by His sweet Mother's love who bore Him, but all the help we have from her is of His goodness.

And we pray by His Holy Cross that He died on, but all the strength and the help that we have from the cross is from His goodness.

And in the same way, all the help that we have from special saints and all the blessed company of heaven[3]—the dearworthy love and endless friendship that we have from them—it is from His goodness.

For God of His goodness has ordained intermediaries to help us, all fair and many, of which the chief and principal intermediary is the blessed Human Nature that He took from the Maid, with all the intermediaries that go before and come after which are part of our redemption and our endless salvation.

Wherefore it pleases Him that we seek Him and worship Him by intermediaries, understanding and recognizing that He is the goodness of all.[4]

5. Note that Julian describes prayer as changing the one who prays; it doesn't change God (who is already all goodness) but gives life to the soul and makes it grow in grace and strength.

6. A controversial passage, and does not appear in the British BV but only in the PV. The word translated as "food" is Julian's ME *soule*, and some scholars translate it as *soul*, but others claim that the word is *saule*, which comes from an Old English word, *sufol*, that means "cooked or digested food" and was nearly obsolete even in Julian's day (C&W II, 306). With our modern sense of propriety it may seem odd or even offensive for a spiritual writer to use so earthy an image as the elimination of human excrement for an analogy of God's presence in "the lowest part of our need," but Julian wrote in a less prudish age and, remarkably, she shows no evidence of despising the earthly, for "He does not despise what He has created."

7. W&J remind us that the ME word is *bowke* from the Old English *buc*, usually used for the bodies of animals or slaughtered soldiers—suggesting that Julian intends to emphasize the earthiness.

8. It seems as though Julian is pressing hard in searching for some analogy that can convey her understanding of the ubiquity and the sheer intimacy of God's goodness for human beings. The more typical medieval emphasis on God as a stern judge obviously has no place in her divine cosmology.

9. Here Julian describes God as our "Lover" for the first time. This occurs with some frequency in her writing.

10. Julian surrenders her efforts at analogies and simply admits that no human being can know the inexpressible extent to which God loves us.

11. In the face of the inexplicability of God's love, Julian introduces the Contemplative Way—which would have been deeply familiar to her—in which one simply stands in silent and wordless wonder before the reality of God and God's love.

For the goodness of God is the highest prayer, and it comes down to the lowest part of our need. It vitalizes our soul and brings it to life and makes it grow in grace and virtue.[5] It is nearest us in nature and readiest in grace (for it is the same grace that the soul seeks and ever shall, till we know our God truly who has us all in Himself enclosed).

A man goes upright and the <u>food</u> of his body is sealed as in a purse full fair; and when it is time of his necessity, it is opened and sealed again full honestly.[6]

And that it is He who does this is shown there where He says that He comes down to us to the lowest part of our need.

For He does not despise what He has created, and He does not disdain to serve us even at the simplest duty that is proper to our body in nature, because of the love of our soul which He has made in His own likeness.

For as the body is clad in the clothes, and the flesh in the skin, and the bones in the flesh, and the heart in the <u>breast</u>,[7] so are we, soul and body, clad in the goodness of God and enclosed—yea, and even more intimately, because all these others may waste and wear away, but the goodness of God is ever whole, and nearer to us without any comparison.[8]

For truly our Lover[9] desires that our soul cleave to Him with all its might and that we evermore cleave to His goodness, for of all things that heart can think, this pleases God most and soonest succeeds.

For our soul is so especially beloved by Him that is Highest that it surpasses the knowledge of all creatures (that is to say, there is no creature that is made that can know how much and how sweetly and how tenderly our Creator loves us).[10]

Therefore we can, with His grace and His help, remain in spiritual contemplation, with everlasting wonder at this high, surpassing, inestimable love which Almighty God has for us of His goodness.[11]

12. This is not a license for hedonism or for praying for "whatever we wish," but a way in which our true prayer reflects our intuitive awareness of God's will. Compare Julian's words to those of Jesus: "The Father may give you whatever you ask in my name" (John 15:16), the critical phrase being "in my name."

13. This is Julian's description of the perfect Christian life—"knowing and loving" God until we come to God's perfect presence in heaven—and she further declares that this expression of the Christian life was the purpose for her visions.

14. Julian does not fall into the mystic's trap of forgetting the rest of the world. She knows that the true spiritual life will produce awe, humility, and the love of others.

COMMENTS ON CHAPTER 7

1. The very mention of awe, humility, and love reminds Julian of the Blessed Virgin as an exemplar of these virtues. And notice that in the next few lines Julian describes this thought of the Blessed Virgin as a *spiritual vision*—an intuitive thought—even while she goes on seeing the bleeding of Jesus' head in *bodily sight*. Julian believes that her intuitive insights are as much from God as the "visual" sights she sees in the Showings.

2. The *garland*, of course, is the crown of thorns. The "bodily vision" of the crucifix is as graphic as any in medieval literature, and it was this "rediscovery" of the actual, suffering humanity of Christ that is a hallmark of the spirituality of the age.

And therefore we can ask of our Lover with reverence all that we wish, for our natural wish is to have God and the good wish of God is to have us.[12]

And we can never leave off wishing nor longing until we have Him in fullness of joy, and then can we wish for nothing more, for He wills that we be occupied in knowing and loving until the time that we shall be fulfilled in heaven.[13]

And for this purpose was this lesson of love shown (along with all that follows, as you shall see)—for the strength and the basis of all was shown in the first vision.

For of all things, the beholding and the loving of the Creator makes the soul seem less in its own sight, and most fills it with reverent fear and true humility, with an abundance of love for its fellow Christians.[14]

7

And to teach us this, as I understand it, our Lord God showed Our Lady Saint Mary at the same time (which is to signify the exalted wisdom and truth she had in contemplating her Creator: so great, so high, so mighty, and so good).[1]

This greatness and this nobility of her vision of God filled her with reverent fear, and with this she saw herself so little and so lowly, so simple and so poor, in relation to her Lord God, that this reverent dread filled her with humility.

And thus, for this reason, she was filled full of grace and of all kinds of virtues and surpasses all creatures.

During all the time that He showed this which I have just described in spiritual vision, I was watching the bodily sight of the abundant bleeding of the Head continuing.

The great drops of blood fell down from under the garland like pellets,[2] seeming as if they had come out of the veins; and as they emerged they were brown-red (for the blood was very thick) and in the spreading out they were bright red; and when the blood came to

3. Julian is frustrated in trying to think of an analogy for the "beauty" and the "lifelikeness" of the vision. She does find analogies for the "abundance" and "roundness," but the beautiful lifelikeness has no parallel for her.

4. See Appendix 9, "Pellets, Eaves, and Herring."

5. Now, in her frustration with descriptive language, Julian turns to the mystic's stock-in-trade: the paradox. She will use this figure of speech several times in her book, and notably in her consistent description of Christ as both *courteous* (that is, courtly, elegant, graceful) and *homely* (that is, familiar, ordinary, plain, friendly). This is one way Julian expresses the Incarnation: Jesus is both divine and human, both heavenly and earthy.

6. We must remember that Julian lived in a highly stratified culture. In medieval England, there was literally no one who did not have a "lord"—every person was clearly (and to some degree permanently) slotted into a particular place in society. And the condescension of such a lord in showing "friendship" to his underlings was a rare demonstration of generosity and goodheartedness.

7. This example of the condescension of God is so powerful, given her culture and society, that it is an almost inexpressible joy.

the brows, there the drops vanished; and nevertheless the bleeding continued until many things were seen and understood.

The beauty and the lifelikeness was comparable to nothing except itself.[3]

The abundance was like the drops of water that fall off the eaves of a house after a great shower of rain, which fall so thick that no man can number them with earthly wit.

And because of their roundness, the drops were like the scales of herring as they spread over the forehead.[4]

These three things came to my mind at the time: pellets, because of roundness, in the emerging of the blood; the scales of herring, in the spreading over the forehead, because of the roundness; the drops off the eaves of a house, because of the immeasurable abundance.

This showing was alive and active, and hideous and dreadful, and sweet and lovely.[5]

And of all the sights it was most comfort to me that our God and Lord, who is so worthy of respect and so fearsome, is also so plain and gracious; and this filled me almost full with delight and security of soul.

For the interpretation of this He showed me this clear example: it is the most honor that a solemn king or great lord can do for a poor servant if he is willing to be friendly with him, and, specifically, if he demonstrates it himself, from a full, true intention, and with a glad countenance, both privately and publicly. Then thinks this poor creature thus: "Ah! How could this noble lord give more honor and joy to me than to show me, who am so little, this marvelous friendliness? Truly, it is more joy and pleasure to me than if he gave me great gifts and were himself distant in manner."[6]

This bodily example was shown so mightily that man's heart could be carried away and almost forget itself for joy over this great friendliness.[7]

Thus it fares between our Lord Jesus and ourselves. For truly, it is the most joy that can be, as I see it, that He who is highest and mightiest, noblest and worthiest, is also lowliest and meekest, most friendly and most gracious.

8. One of the major themes in Julian is this admonition that we must have faith in the greatness and goodness of God, even though we may not have the actual experience of it until we come to heaven.

9. How startlingly different this idea is compared to the usual understanding of God as fearful judge and condemner that was common in the Church teaching of her day. To describe God the Father as "gracious and friendly" and to call Jesus "our Brother" is an astounding insight—and this is Julian's first use of the word to describe Jesus.

10. Julian speaks here of the three Theological Virtues: faith, hope, and love.

11. Julian recognizes that others may experience similar revelations as well.

12. In fourteenth-century England, the Creed is often referred to as "the Faith." And Julian is quick to indicate here that what she has been shown in her visions is actually a part (albeit a "secret" part) of the Catholic faith. She is protesting that her insights are not something new, but only a deeper depth of the Church's teachings. In the next paragraph she says, "It is none other than the Faith, neither less nor more." She clearly does not intend any new *teaching*, only new *insights* into the meaning of the traditional teachings.

COMMENTS ON CHAPTER 8

1. See Part Two, section 1, "Julian's Identity," on the erroneous Latin.

And surely and truly this marvelous joy shall be shown us all when we see Him. And this wishes Our Lord: that we believe and trust, enjoy and delight, comfort and solace ourselves, as best we can, with His grace and with His help, until the time that we see that joy truly.[8]

For the greatest fullness of joy that we shall have, as I see it, is the marvelous graciousness and friendliness of the Father who is our Creator, in the Lord Jesus Christ who is our Brother and our Savior.[9]

But no man can be aware of this marvelous friendliness in this life, unless he receives it by special showing from Our Lord, or from a great abundance of grace inwardly given from the Holy Spirit.

But faith and belief with love are worthy to have the reward, and so it is received by grace—for in faith with hope and love, our life is grounded.[10]

The showing (made to whom God wishes[11]) plainly teaches the same, uncovered and explained with many secret details that are parts of our Faith and Belief that it is honorable to know. And when the showing, which is given at one time, is past and hidden, then the Faith keeps it by the grace of the Holy Spirit until our life's end.[12]

And this is the showing—it is none other than the Faith, neither less nor more (as can be seen by our Lord's meaning in the earlier matter) until it comes to the final end.

⁓ 8

As long as I saw this sight of the plenteous bleeding of the head, I could never cease these words: "Benedicite domine!"[1]

In this showing of the bleeding I interpreted six things: the first is the sign of the blessed Passion and the plenteous shedding of His Precious Blood; the second is the Maiden who is His dearworthy Mother; the third is the blessed Godhead that ever was, is and ever shall be, all Power, all Wisdom, all Love; the fourth is everything that He has created (for well I know that heaven and earth and all that

2. Here again Julian the mystic speaks: everything that is good (and the goodness it has) IS GOD. It does not merely "represent" God or "imitate" God, but it IS God. Whenever we encounter goodness in this life, we encounter God. One is reminded of the similar metaphor in 1 John 4:16: "God is love, and those who abide in love abide in God." Goodness in this world is not merely a virtue, but it is God's actual presence in the world God created; it is a "continuing incarnation" of God in the world.

3. "All this. . . ." Julian has taken seven chapters to describe her first vision, confident that the insights she has gathered are as much a part of God's "message" as the bodily sight of Christ's bleeding head itself, and although she no longer saw the vision, the insights she received remained.

4. Unlike some Christian mystics, Julian does not exult merely in the divine vision she has been personally given, but equally in the application and relevance of the vision for all her fellow Christians. It is as though she closed her eyes to see the vision and then opens them to see her fellow Christians.

5. The ME word *doom* means "judgment," so Julian is saying that it seems like Judgment Day for her, because she expects to die.

6. A small but subtle and important note: while Julian usually follows the cultural and linguistic norms and uses the word "man" generically, meaning "human," in seven important instances she uses the phrase "man or woman"—making sure that she speaks of all human beings, not just males.

7. Catholic teaching was that at death each person is judged individually (the "Particular Judgment") and sent to heaven (if one is a saint), to hell (if one is an unredeemable sinner), or to purgatory (if one is good, but not yet perfect). At the end of the world is the General Judgment when bodies of the saints are raised to heaven and purgatory done away with.

8. In SV she calls herself a "wretched worm."

9. Why did Julian record her visions? Here is the answer: so they could be a reassurance for all.

is created is ample and large, fair and good, but the reason why it appeared so little in my vision was because I saw it in the Presence of Him who is the Creator of all things, and to a soul that sees the Creator of everything, all that is created seems very little); the fifth is that He created everything for love and by the same love everything is protected and shall be without end; the sixth is that God is everything that is good, as I see it, and the goodness that everything has, it is He.[2] All this our Lord showed me in the first vision and gave me time and space to contemplate it, and the bodily sight ceased, and the spiritual insight remained in my understanding.[3]

And I waited with reverent fear, rejoicing in what I saw.

And I desired, as much as I dared, to see more, if it were His will (or else the same thing for a longer time).

In all this, I was much moved in love for my fellow Christians—that they could see and know the same that I saw, for I wish it to be a comfort to them—because all this sight was shown universally.[4]

Then I said to those who were around me: "It is <u>Doomsday</u> today for me."[5] (This I said because I expected to have died—for on the day that a man or woman[6] dies, that person experiences the particular judgment as he shall be without end, as I understand it.)[7]

I said this because I wished they would love God the better, in order to remind them that this life is short, as they might see in my example (for in all this time I expected to have died, and that was a wonder to me and sad in part, because it seemed to me that this vision was shown for those who would live).

All that I say concerning myself, I say in the person of all my fellow Christians, for I am taught in the spiritual showing of our Lord God, that He intends it so.

Therefore I beg you all for God's sake, and I advise you for your own benefit, that you believe this vision of a sinner[8] to whom it was shown, and powerfully, wisely, and humbly look to God who of His gracious love and endless goodness wishes to show the vision universally in reassurance for us all.[9]

COMMENTS ON CHAPTER 9

1. Who did she expect her readers would be? This text makes it clear that she is writing for ordinary people—"you who are simple"—and her motive for writing in English is so those who did not know Latin or Norman French could benefit. And she wants her insights and visions to benefit everyone—even those who do not consider themselves especially "good."

2. This phrase, "all mankind that shall be saved," is used thirty-four times in Julian's book and is a certain indicator of what came to be called "predestination." This is NOT, however, the idea of "double predestination" (taught in Julian's day by the heretic John Wycliffe and latterly by John Calvin) in which salvation (of "the elect") or damnation (of "the reprobates") is predetermined by God and is not affected by virtue or sin in a person's life. Julian understands the Catholic teaching of "single predestination" in which God intends *all* people for heaven, but has foreknowledge of who will choose salvation and who will choose damnation. But the use of this phrase by Julian should also be a clear indication that she is NOT a universalist, but believes there are people who will not be in heaven.

3. Julian's almost Johannine commitment to love as God's primary mode is made vividly clear, and its social dimensions are obvious.

4. It is the unity of humanity within God that is the reason for the love of others.

5. There are a number of commentators who like to think of Julian as a kind of crypto-Protestant, slyly disparaging Catholic teaching. That speaks more of the commentator than of Julian, who remains in every sense a true child of the Church.

6. Here are Julian's three "modes" of revelation. She finds it easy to describe the visions ("bodily sight") and her own

◌ 9

I am not good because of this showing, but only if I love God better; and in so much as you love God better, it is more to you than to me. I do not say this to those who are wise, for they know it well, but I say it to you who are simple, for your benefit and comfort, for we are all one in love.

Truly it was not shown to me that God loved me better than the least soul that is in grace, for I am certain that there are many who never had showing nor vision (except from the common teaching of Holy Church) who love God better than I.[1]

If I look individually at myself, I am just nothing; but in general terms I am, I hope, in unity of love with all my fellow Christians.

On this unity is based the lives of all mankind that shall be saved,[2] for God is all that is good, as I see it, and God has created all that is created, and God loves all that He has created, and he who broadly loves all his fellow Christians because of God, he loves all that is.[3]

For in mankind that shall be saved is contained all (that is to say, all that is created and the Creator of all) because in man is God, and in God is all, and he who loves thus, loves all.[4]

And I hope by the grace of God that he who sees it in this way shall be truly taught and mightily comforted if he needs comfort.

I speak of those who shall be saved, because at this time God showed me no other. But in everything I believe as Holy Church believes, preaches, and teaches (for the Faith of Holy Church which I had beforehand believed and, as I hope, by the grace of God, willingly observe in use and custom, remained constantly in my sight), wishing and intending never to accept anything that could be contrary to it.[5]

And with this intent, I watched the showing with all my diligence, because in this whole blessed showing, I saw it as one with that Faith in God's intention.

All this was shown in three parts:[6] that is to say, by bodily sight, and by word formed in my understanding, and by spiritual insight.

(divinely guided) interpretations ("my understanding") but suffers the mystic's universal frustration of being unable fully to put words to the "spiritual insights." And, with true piety, she trusts God to convey the deeper meanings she struggles to teach. This tripartite source of revelation has its roots in Saint Augustine's teaching.

COMMENTS ON CHAPTER 10

1. "The Fifteen Oes" was a very popular fourteenth-century series of prayers addressing the Crucified Christ. Gertrude of Helfta promoted a devotion to the 5,466 wounds of Christ by saying these fifteen prayers daily!

2. The last of these prayers includes the phrase: ". . . Your tender flesh changed color because the liquor of your bowels and the marrow of your bones was dried up."

3. There seems to be no particular historical or devotional explanation for this covering by blood of one half of the face and then the other. C&W suggest that since Julian complains about the darkness in the next line, her sight may have been failing and the colors of the crucifix may have seemed to run together.

4. Julian tells on herself: she wanted something different or something more (in this case, light), but then her own reason corrects her with the assurance that what she has is what God has provided, and if she truly needed more, God would provide it. The point is also made that God's revelation is up to God, not up to us.

5. See Appendix 2, "The Floods in Norwich." And see Isaiah 43:2: "When you pass through water I shall be with you; when you pass through rivers they will not overwhelm you."

6. Another instance of Julian's including "or woman" in her account. The content of the example she offers in no way requires the addition of the female, but she adds it.

(However, the spiritual insight I do not know how nor am I able to show it as openly or as fully as I wish, but I trust in our Lord God Almighty that He shall of His goodness, and because of your love, cause you to receive it more spiritually and more sweetly than I know how or am able to tell it.)

⤳ 10

And after this, I saw with bodily sight on the face of the crucifix which hung before me (on which I gazed constantly) a part of His Passion: contempt, and spitting and defiling and smiting and many distressing pains—more than I can count,[1] and frequent changing of color.[2]

And at the same time I saw how half the face, beginning at the ear, was overspread with dried blood until it was covered up to the middle of the face, and, after that, the other half was covered in the same way, and then it vanished in the first part just as it had come.[3]

This I saw physically, sorrowfully, and obscurely, and I desired more physical light in order to have seen more clearly. But I was answered in my reason: "If God wishes to show thee more, He shall be thy light. Thou needest none but Him."[4] For I saw Him and still sought Him, for we are now so blind and so unwise that we never seek God until He of His goodness shows Himself to us; and when we see anything of Him by grace, then are we moved by the same grace to try with great desire to see Him more perfectly.

And thus I saw Him and I sought Him, and I possessed Him and I lacked Him.

And this is, and should be, our ordinary behavior in this life, as I see it.

At one time my understanding was taken down into the seabed, and there I saw hills and green dales, seeming as if it were overgrown with moss, with seaweed and gravel.[5]

Then I understood this: that even if a man or woman[6] were there under the broad water, if he could have a vision of God there (since God is with a man constantly) he would be safe in body and soul and

7. Julian here presumes to tell her readers what God is like and what God wishes. She is obviously expressing her own convictions, and is not quoting from Scripture or from a vision.

8. Again, Julian's inherent honesty shows itself. She shares with the reader all her own weaknesses and inadequacies—even her own doubts. (See Chapter 70, where she again admits her own doubts about the visions.)

9. See Appendix 4, "The Holy Year." There is, of course, no overt evidence for it (unless the close description in these lines provides it) but it is well within the realm of possibility that Julian may have made a Holy Year pilgrimage to Rome and had actually seen this miraculous Veil with her own eyes. (If the lowborn Margery Kemp could do it, the aristocratic Julian could as well.) If Lady Julian was Julian Erpingham, she would also have heard of Rome from her brother, Sir Thomas Erpingham, who traveled to Prussia, Rome, and the Holy Land with Henry Bolingbroke.

10. "Faith" could properly be translated as "Creed."

11. The ME word translated as "re-creation" is *geynmakyng* or "again-making."

receive no harm and, even more, he would have more solace and more comfort than all this world can tell.

Because He wills that we believe that we experience Him constantly (although we imagine that it is but little) and by this belief He causes us evermore to gain grace, because He wishes to be seen and He wishes to be sought, He wishes to be awaited and He wishes to be trusted.[7]

This second showing was so lowly and so little and so simple that my spirits were in great travail over the sight—mourning, fearful, and yearning—for I was sometimes even in doubt whether it was a showing.[8]

And then at different times our good Lord gave me more insight whereby I understood truly that it was a showing.

It was a shape and image of our foul mortal flesh that our fair, bright, blessed Lord bore for our sins. It made me think of the holy Veronica's Veil of Rome which He has imprinted with His own blessed face (when He was in His cruel Passion, willingly going to His death) and often changing color.[9]

From the brownness and blackness, pitifulness and leanness of this image, many marvel how it could be so, given that He imprinted it with His blessed Face that is the fairness of heaven, the flower of earth, and the fruit of the Maiden's womb. Then how could this image be so discolored and so far from fair?

I desire to say just as I have understood it by the grace of God.

We know in our Faith[10] and believe by the teaching and preaching of Holy Church that the entire blessed Trinity created mankind in His image and to His likeness. In the same sort of way we know that when man fell so deep and so wretchedly by sin, there was no other help to restore man except through Him who created man.

And He that created man for love, by the same love He wished to restore man to the same bliss, and even more.

And just as we were created like the Trinity in our first creation, our Maker wished that we should be like Jesus Christ our Savior, in heaven without end, by the strength of our re-creation.[11]

12. The ME here is *our foule blak dede hame*, literally "our foul, black, dead shelter (or covering)." Julian stretches her language to get as "low" as possible in describing the fallen human state.

13. It was a popular belief that the Incarnation involved God the Son "hiding" inside the humanity of Jesus to fool the Devil into having Him killed (and therefore making possible the Resurrection, which defeated both death and the Devil).

14. See Psalm 45:2 (BCP): "You are the fairest of men. . . ."

15. See Isaiah 53:2: "He had no beauty, no majesty to catch our eyes, no grace to attract us to him."

16. In fact, the Veronica's Veil in Rome did change color until eventually, some witnesses testify, the imprinted face faded out into just a "brown-colored stain."

17. Once again, Julian's new insights seem somewhat detached from the actual vision of the blood-covered face of Christ, and it is not easy for us to make the connection—unless it is through her recognition of what Christ went through in "seeking" us. But the phrase here—"the soul can do no more than seek, suffer, and trust"—may well be the most succinct summary of the holy Christian life in all Christian literature. Note, however, that suffering is never seen by Julian or shown by Christ to be "punishment." In that sense, Julian is radical among her peers. For Julian, suffering is either the result of sin or simply "the way things are." God never inflicts pain or punishment on his people.

18. The "seeking" is the only action the Christian can take (and it pleases God). The "finding" is up to God (and it pleases the soul).

19. This is a simply amazing pastoral perception in Julian's "understanding": that striving is just as morally acceptable as achieving. One is reminded of Jesus' "I am the way . . ." (John 14:6).

Then between these two He was willing (for love and honor of man) to make Himself as much like man in this mortal life (in our foulness and our wretchedness) as man could be without sins.

From this comes what the showing signifies. As I said before, it was the image and likeness of our <u>foul, black, mortal flesh</u>[12] wherein our fair, bright, blessed Lord hid His Godhead.[13] But most surely I dare to say (and we ought to believe) that no man was as fair as He[14] until the time that His fair complexion was changed with toil and sorrow, suffering and dying.[15]

(Of this it is spoken in the eighth revelation where it tells more about the same likeness—and there it says of the Veronica's Veil of Rome, that it moves through different changes of color and expression— sometimes more reassuring and lifelike, and sometimes more pitifully and deathly—as can be seen in the eighth revelation.)[16]

This vision was a teaching for my understanding[17] that the constant seeking of the soul pleases God very much, for the soul can do no more than seek, suffer, and trust, and this is brought about in the soul that has it by the Holy Spirit, but the clarity of finding is by His special grace when it is His will.

The seeking with faith, hope, and love pleases our Lord, and the finding pleases the soul and fills it full of joy.[18]

And thus was I taught for my own understanding that seeking is as good as beholding during the time that He wishes to permit the soul to be in labor.[19]

It is God's will that we seek Him until we behold Him, for by that beholding He shall show us Himself by His special grace when He wishes.

How a soul shall behave itself in beholding Him, He Himself shall teach; and that is most honor to Him and most benefit to the soul and mostly received from humility and virtue with the grace and leading of the Holy Spirit.

A soul that simply makes itself fast to God with true trust—either by seeking or in beholding—that is the most honor that it can do to Him, as I see it.

20. The ME word is *werkyng*, which can mean "action."
21. Once again, Julian directs us to "the teaching of the Holy Church": the goal of one's "seeking" should be to deepen one's understanding of the Church's teachings.
22. Our seeking for God should be (a) active, (b) patient, and (c) faithful.

COMMENTS ON CHAPTER 11

1. W&J maintain that the verb "saw" suggests that this insight ("he is in all things") is part of the revelation.
2. Julian introduces the conundrum that will plague her throughout her book (and that she will never solve): "If God is all good and does everything, how can there be sin?"
3. Julian's protestation that "God does everything" requires an immense faith and trust that the omnipotent God will either positively act in all things or will permit all things for reasons we usually do not understand. So Julian can say that everything that is done is "well done"—an amazing statement from a person who lived through at least three occurrences of the Black Death. Yet it is a supreme act of faith to believe that even in the instance of apparent calamity or catastrophe, God is not merely passive, but will ultimately work His will.

These are two <u>workings</u>[20] which can be seen in this vision: the one is seeking, the other is beholding. The seeking is universal so that every soul can have with His grace (and ought to have) the moral discernment and teaching of the Holy Church.[21]

It is God's will that we have three objects in our seeking: The first is that we seek willingly and diligently, without laziness, as much as possible through His grace, gladly and merrily without unreasonable sadness and useless sorrow. The second is that we await Him steadfastly because of His love, without grumbling or struggling against Him, until our life's end (for it shall last only a while). The third is that we trust in Him mightily in fully certain faith, for it is His will that we know that He shall appear without warning and full of blessing to all His lovers—for His working is secret, but He wishes to be perceived, and His appearing shall be truly without warning, but He wishes to be trusted, because He is most simple and gracious.[22]

Blessed may He be!

⇰ 11

And after this, I saw God in a point (that is to say in my mind), by which vision I understood that He is in all things.[1]

I gazed with deliberation, seeing and knowing in that vision that He does all that is done.[2] I marveled at that sight with a gentle trepidation, and thought: What is sin? (for I saw truly that God does everything no matter how little, and I saw truly that nothing is done by luck or by chance but everything by the foreseeing wisdom of God).[3]

(If it is luck or chance in the sight of man, our blindness and our lack of foresight is the cause, for the things that are in the foreseeing wisdom of God from without beginning [which rightfully and honorably he leads to the best end as they come about] happen to us without warning, ourselves unaware; and thus, by our blindness and our lack of foresight, we say those are luck and chance; but to our Lord God, they are not so—wherefore, it is necessary for me to concede that everything that is done, it is well done, for our

4. In Julian's understanding of God's omnipresence and omnipotence, what "happens" occurs within the province of God's will, which can never be sinful or wrong. Hence, there is some way to see God's active or permissive will in all things.

5. This is an awkward and difficult line. Apparently Julian means that sin is not a deed *of God*. It is interesting, however, that at this point the SV adds the phrase, "Therefore it seemed to me that sin is nothing." This may be related to the statement in the BV (Chapter 13) ". . . I did not see sin, for I believe that it has no kind of substance. . . ." This reflects the common Scholastic teaching that sin is not a "thing in itself" but merely the absence of goodness, and therefore it has no power in and of itself, but only the power we give it.

6. More of Julian's wonderful humility and submission: she decides not to think about this difficult matter, but to leave it up to God to show her what God wants her to know.

7. The ME word *blind* can carry the meaning of "dark" or "obscure." Julian's point here is that God does not judge good and evil on the same basis as humans, and what seems an evil to humans may be a good in God's eyes.

8. See Ecclesiasticus 39:33–34: ". . . all that the Lord has made is good, and he supplies every need as it arises. Let no one say, 'This is less good than that,' for all things prove good at their proper time."

9. It seems impossible that Julian does not have in mind the catastrophe of the plagues that hit England in the fourteenth century—especially when she refers in the previous paragraph to "all that has being in nature." In one sense, she is saying, "We look upon things (like the Plague) as evil, but God may not see them as evil."

Lord God does all [for at this time the action of creatures was not shown, but of our Lord God in the creature].)

He is in the midpoint of everything and He does everything, and I was certain He does no sin.[4]

And here I saw truthfully that sin is no deed,[5] for in all this revelation sin was not shown. And I wished no longer to wonder at this, but I looked to our Lord for what He wished to show.[6]

And thus insofar as could be shown for the present, the rightfulness of God's action was shown to the soul. Rightfulness has two fair qualities: it is right, and it is full; and so are all the actions of our Lord God; and to them is lacking neither the working of mercy nor of grace, for it is all right-full, in which nothing is wanting (and at a different time He made a showing in order for me to see sin nakedly, as I shall say later, where He uses the working of mercy and grace).

This vision was shown to my understanding, for our Lord wished to have the soul turned truly unto the beholding of Him, and generally of all His works (for they are most good and all His judgments are comfortable and gracious, and they bring to great comfort the soul which has turned from paying attention to the blind judgment of man to the fair, gracious judgment of our Lord God).[7]

A man looks upon some deeds as well done and some deeds as evil, but our Lord does not look upon them so; for just as all that has being in nature is of God's creating, so everything that is done is in the character of God's doing.

It is easy to understand that the best deed is well done, but just as well as the best and most exalted deed is done, so well is the least deed done—and all in the character and in the order in which our Lord has it ordained from without beginning.[8] For there is no doer but He.[9]

I saw full certainly that He never changes His purpose in anything, nor ever shall, without end.

There was nothing unknown to Him in His rightful ordering from without beginning. And therefore everything was set in order before anything was created, just as it would stand without end, and no manner of thing shall fall short of that mark.

10. Julian's familiar theme emerges again: God is with humanity, not distant from us. God promises never to "lift my hands from my works." God is not distant or disinterested.

11. Another hint at Julian's humility: she admits that her soul was "tested" in this insight, that God corrected her thinking.

12. The word translated as "appropriate" could well be translated as "proper" or even "necessary."

COMMENTS ON CHAPTER 12

1. The ME words are *in seming of the scorgyng. In seeming* could mean "in the seams" or "in the slashes" or "in the furrows" made by the whipping—a term used by plowmen. (Psalm 129:3, BCP—"The plowmen plowed upon my back.")

2. We are reminded again of the "Fifteen Oes" (see note in Chapter 10), which spoke of the tradition of there having been 5,466 wounds on Christ's body.

3. Julian reminds us that what she is describing is a miraculous vision and not a historical reality. But this sentence is also an evidence of the accuracy of Julian's account of the vision, since it is not "natural" that the blood should thus vanish.

4. Julian says, "it came to my mind," since she still credits her own insights about her visions as divine revelations in themselves.

5. W&R suggest this may refer to a medicine.

He made everything in fullness of goodness, and therefore the Blessed Trinity is always completely pleased with all His works.

And all this He showed most blessedly, meaning this: "See, I am God. See, I am in everything. See, I do everything. See, I never lift my hands from my works, nor ever shall, without end. See, I lead everything to the end I ordained for it from without beginning by the same Power, Wisdom, and Love with which I made it. How would anything be amiss?"[10]

Thus powerfully, wisely, and lovingly was the soul tested in this vision.[11]

Then I saw truthfully that it was appropriate[12] that I needs must assent with great reverence, rejoicing in God.

⁌ 12

After this, as I watched, I saw the body plenteously bleeding (as could be expected[1] from the scourging) in this way: the fair skin was split very deeply into the tender flesh by the harsh beating all over the dear body; so plenteously did the hot blood run out that one could see neither skin nor wound, but, as it were, all blood.[2]

And when it came to the place where it should have fallen down, there it vanished.[3]

Nevertheless, the bleeding continued awhile until it could be seen with careful deliberation.

And this blood looked so plenteous that it seemed to me, if it had been as plenteous in nature and in matter during that time, it would have made the bed all bloody and have overflowed around the outside.

And then it came to my mind[4] that God has made plentiful waters on earth for our assistance and for our bodily comfort because of the tender love He has for us, but it still pleases Him better if we accept most beneficially His blessed Blood to wash us from sin. There is no liquid[5] that is made that it pleases Him so well to give us, for just as it

6. From the verse in Lamentations (1:12) often considered a prophecy of the Crucifixion: "If only you would look and see: is there any agony like mine . . . ?"

7. The *Stimulus Amoris* (a fourteenth-century Franciscan book of devotion): "Behold, his wounds overcome the fiend's power, and burst the gates of hell." This refers to the Harrowing of Hell, by which Christ releases the souls of the just who died before His Incarnation. W&R point to medieval paintings of the Passion with blood dripping from the cross into hell.

8. Julian describes the blood of Christ as washing from sin all creatures who are, have been, or shall be of good will. This reflects on Julian's frequent phrase: ". . . those who shall be saved." Clearly she means to include as saved all who "are of good will."

9. See Hebrews 12:24: ". . . [Jesus'] sprinkled blood has better things to say than the blood of Abel."

10. The "it" is "His dearworthy Blood," which is here personified as "rejoicing in"—Julian's ME word is *enioying*. See Revelation 6:11: "[The martyrs] were each given a white robe, and told to rest a little longer, until the number should be complete of all their brothers in Christ's service who were to be put to death, as they themselves had been." W&R remind of the tradition that the number of saved souls will equal the number of fallen angels, that is, the demons.

COMMENTS ON CHAPTER 13

1. The vision has come, and Julian patiently awaits the insights.

2. The ME word *intellecte* could be accurately translated as "meaning" rather than "comprehension."

3. Here we see Julian's second dimension of revelation: "words formed in my soul."

4. Julian's term *Fiend* is simply another word for "Devil."

is most plentiful, so it is most precious (and that by the virtue of His blessed Godhead).

And the blood is of our own nature, and all beneficently flows over us by the virtue of His precious love. The dearworthy Blood of our Lord Jesus Christ, as truly as it is most precious, so truly it is most plentiful.

Behold and see.[6]

The precious abundance of His dearworthy Blood descended down into hell, and burst their bonds and delivered all that were there who belonged to the court of heaven.[7]

The precious abundance of His dearworthy Blood flows over all earth and is quick to wash all creatures from sin who are of good will, have been, and shall be.[8]

The precious abundance of His dearworthy Blood ascended up into heaven to the blessed Body of our Lord Jesus Christ, and there it is within Him, bleeding and praying for us to the Father[9]—and it is and shall be so as long as it is needed.

And evermore it flows in all heavens rejoicing in the salvation of all mankind that are there and shall be, completing the count that falls short.[10]

⁀ 13

Afterward, before God showed any words,[1] He permitted me to gaze on Him a suitable time—and on all that I had seen and all the <u>comprehension</u>[2] that was in it (as much as the simplicity of the soul could receive it).

Then, without voice or an opening of lips, He formed in my soul these words:[3] "With this the Fiend[4] is overcome." (Our Lord said these words, referring to His Blessed Passion as He showed it before.)

In this our Lord showed that His Passion is the overcoming of the Fiend.

5. Reference particularly to the story of Job in which God gives the Devil permission to tempt Job. (See Job 1:6–12.)

6. This is one of Julian's most radical teachings, because it flies in the face of Holy Scripture's multiple instances referring to God's anger and wrath. It is also a hallmark of Julian's theology of love, opposing the medieval theology that saw God as a fearsome and angry judge. Julian expands on this teaching in Chapter 46.

7. I take the title *the Reprobate* to refer to the Devil, but the word is translated by several scholars as "the reproved" (referring to sinners who oppose God's will).

8. The word *scorn* carries implications of mocking. The Lord refuses to take the Fiend's malice seriously.

9. Julian's laughter comes from seeing the pretentious posturing of the Devil mocked by the Lord. Once again, this is a radical stance for the fourteenth century, in which the Devil was universally feared. (It should also be noted that Julian speaks of others "that were about me"—a strong piece of evidence that she was *not* in her anchorhold at the time of the visions.)

10. There was a strong and ancient oral tradition that Jesus never laughed. In Benedict's Rule, for instance, laughter is strongly censured. (See Umberto Eco's *The Name of the Rose* for a story built primarily on that prohibition of laughter.)

11. God's scorning of the Fiend is a permanent internal state, not as temporary as laughter.

God showed that the Fiend has now the same malice that he had before the Incarnation; and no matter how vigorously nor how constantly he labors, he sees that all salvation's souls escape him gloriously by virtue of Christ's precious Passion.

That is [the Fiend's] sorrow, and most unpleasantly is he brought down, because all that God allows him to do brings us to joy and him to shame and woe and pain.

And he has as much sorrow when God gives him leave to work[5] as when he does not work (and that is because he can never do as much evil as he would like, for his power is all locked in God's hand).

(But in God can be no wrath,[6] as I see it, for our good Lord endlessly has regard for His own honor and for the benefit of all that shall be saved.)

With power and justice He withstands the Reprobate,[7] who because of malice and shrewdness busies himself to conspire and to act against God's will.

Also I saw our Lord scorn the Fiend's malice and totally discount his powerlessness (and He wills that we do so, too).[8]

Because of this sight I laughed mightily,[9] and that made them laugh that were about me, and their laughing was a delight to me.

I thought how I wished that all my fellow Christians had seen as I had seen, and then would they all laugh with me. (Except I saw not Christ laughing;[10] even though I was well aware that it was the sight that He showed which made me laugh, because I understood that we can laugh in comforting ourselves and rejoicing in God, because the Devil is overcome. And when I saw Him scorn the Devil's malice, it was only by a leading of my understanding into our Lord, that is to say, an inward showing of constancy, without alteration of outward expression for, as I see it, constancy is a worthy quality that is in God, which is enduring.)[11]

After this I fell into a soberness and said: "I see three things: amusement, scorn, and seriousness. I see amusement in that the Fiend is overcome. I see scorn in that God scorns him and he shall be scorned. And I see seriousness in that he is overcome by the blissful Passion and

12. Julian suggests that at Judgment Day, the saved will mock and ridicule the Devil just as Christ does; the Devil will not be feared by the saved. The Devil will see that all the pain and trouble he has caused will redound to the salvation of souls.

13. A statement of Julian's clear belief in hell (contrary to many commentators who mistakenly believe her to teach universal salvation).

COMMENTS ON CHAPTER 14

1. Julian tells a classic parable, drawing on familiar biblical themes around feasting: the marriage feast a king gives for his son (Matthew 22); the lord who seats his servants and waits on them (Luke 12:37); and the Prodigal Son (Luke 15:11–32).

2. The lord calls both servants and friends to his banquet: a socially radical departure from the cultural hierarchy of Julian's day.

3. A wonderful demonstration of Julian's homely/courteous paradigm of God's nature. He is "a lord" and he "royally reigns" but does not take a throne, yet is "present" to all his household.

4. The ME word Julian uses is *chere*, which can be translated as "countenance" or "appearance" or even "attitude."

5. Julian begins to hint at one of her major ideas (which will be more fully developed later): that the pain of sin actually brings rewards in heaven rather than blame.

Death of our Lord Jesus Christ which was done in full earnest and with weary labor." (When I said, "He is scorned," I mean that God scorns him—that is to say: because He sees him now as He shall see him without end.)

In this God showed that the Fiend is damned (and this I meant when I said, "He shall be scorned": at Doomsday generally by all who shall be saved—for whose salvation he has great envy).[12] Then he shall see that all the woe and tribulation that he has done to them shall be turned into increase of their joy without end, and all the pain and tribulation to which he would have brought them, shall endlessly go with him to hell.[13]

⌁ 14

After this our good Lord said: "I thank thee for thy labor and especially for thy youth."

[1]And in this showing my understanding was lifted up into heaven where I saw our Lord as a lord in his own house, who has called all his dearworthy servants and friends[2] to a solemn feast. Then I saw the lord take no special high-ranked seat in his own household,[3] but I saw him royally reign throughout his house, and he filled it full of joy and mirth himself, in order endlessly to cheer and comfort his dearworthy friends most plainly and most graciously, with marvelous melody of endless love in his own fair blessed face (which glorious <u>face</u>[4] of the Godhead fills up heavens of joy and bliss).

God showed three degrees of bliss that every soul shall have in heaven who has willingly served God in any degree on earth.

The first is the honor-filled favor of our Lord God which the soul shall receive when it is delivered from pain. This favor is so exalted and so full of honor that it seems to the soul that it fills him completely even if there were nothing more, for it seemed to me that all the pain and labor that could be suffered by all living men could not deserve the honorable gratitude that one man shall have who has willingly served God.[5]

6. It was common in Julian's day for people to put off concerns about sanctity until they were elderly and approaching death. Many made arrangements to enter convents or monasteries in their old age in order to receive divine "credit" for devoting a life to God. Julian here credits those who seek sanctity *in their youth.* (See the first sentence in Chapter 14, above.) Julian herself, of course, experienced her visions and began a Christ-centered life "in youth." (Note: This passage does not occur in the SV, but was added when an older Julian wrote the LV.)
7. Another instance of Julian's specific inclusion of both genders.
8. Julian must be thinking of the parable of the laborers in the vineyard in which the late-comers are paid equal wages with those who labored all day. (See Matthew 20.)

COMMENTS ON CHAPTER 15

1. This is one of the most captivating passages in Julian's book, and one of the most useful for anyone committed to spiritual growth. First, it shows Julian's humility, candor, and willingness to share with her readers her weaknesses and emotions. Second, her words support all who also experience the same spiritual volatility. And third, she points to the stable center of spirituality: "faith, hope, and love but very little in feeling." Julian is clear that "feelings" cannot be the basis of reliable spirituality.
2. Faith is reliable; feelings are not. See Chapter 41: ". . . it is in our feeling, our foolishness, that the cause of our weakness lies. . . ."

The second, that all the blessed creatures that are in heaven shall see that honorable favor, and He makes that man's service known to all that are in heaven. And at this time, this example was shown: a king, if he thanks his servants, it is a great honor to them, and if he makes it known to all the realm, then is the servant's honor much increased.

The third is that as new and as pleasing as it is to receive it at that moment, just so shall it last without end.

And I saw that simply and sweetly was this shown: that the age of every man shall be known in heaven, and shall be rewarded for his willing service and for his time; and especially is the age of those who willingly and freely offer their youth to God excellently rewarded and wonderfully thanked.[6]

But I saw that whenever or at whatever time a man or woman[7] is truly turned to God, for one day's service and in order to fulfill His endless will, that one shall enjoy all these three degrees of bliss.[8]

And the more that the loving soul understands this graciousness of God, the more it prefers to serve Him all the days of its life.

⤝ 15

[1]After this He showed a most excellent spiritual pleasure in my soul: I was completely filled with everlasting certainty, powerfully sustained without any painful fear. This feeling was so joyful and so spiritual that I was wholly in peace, at ease, and in repose, and there was nothing on earth that would have grieved me.

This lasted only awhile, and I was changed and left to myself in such sadness and weariness of my life, and annoyance with myself, that scarcely was I able to have patience to live. There was no comfort nor any ease for me except faith, hope, and love, and these I held in truth (but very little in feeling).[2]

And immediately after this, our Blessed Lord gave me again the comfort and the rest in my soul, in delight and in security so blissful and so powerful that no fear, no sorrow, no bodily pain that could be suffered would have distressed me.

3. A reference to Romans 8:35: "Then what can separate us from the love of Christ?"

4. A conflation of two separate Bible verses: Matthew 14:30 when Peter walked on the water, and then, sinking, "he cried, 'Save me, Lord!' " and Matthew 8:25 (NRSV) when the storm arose and the disciples cried: "Save us Lord! We are perishing!" (This is probably a sign that Julian quoted the Bible from memory.)

5. This is a manifestation of sincere faith that does not depend on constant comfort and ease, but accepts trouble without blaming God, knowing that sometimes it benefits the soul to be "in woe." The phrase in "woe and well" is another instance where I have not translated the ME words because their meaning is clear.

6. The ME has *althowe synne is not ever the cause*, but the ME word *ever* means "always." At least one translator leaves it as "ever," changing the meaning dramatically. This stands in opposition to typical medieval thought: that the absence of grace is the fault of the sinner.

7. The phrase "for it was so sudden" is not in the SV, but was added: more of Julian's humility in explaining her sinlessness not by inherent virtue, but by the "suddenness" of the visions—and being clear that she did not "deserve" the blessed feeling.

8. Julian's counsel is sound and familiar: concentrating on one's pain, sorrow, and trouble brings only depression, and we are bidden to "quickly pass over them." (One of the fragmentary manuscripts adds: "... which is God Almighty, our Lover and Keeper.")

And then the pain showed again to my feeling, and then the joy and the delight, and now the one, and now the other, various times—I suppose about twenty times.

And in the times of joy, I could have said with Saint Paul: "Nothing shall separate me from the love of Christ."[3]

And in the pain I could have said with Peter: "Lord, save me, I perish."[4]

This vision was shown me for my understanding that it is profitable for some souls to feel this way—sometimes to be in comfort, and sometimes to fail and to be left by themselves.

God wants us to know that He protects us equally surely in woe and in well.[5]

But for the benefit of man's soul a man is sometimes left to himself (although sin is not always[6] the cause—for during this time I committed no sin for which I should be left to myself, for it was so sudden[7]).

(Equally, I deserved not to have this blessed feeling.)

But freely our Lord gives when He wishes, and permits us to be in woe sometimes.

And both are one love, for it is God's will that we keep us in this comfort with all our might, because bliss is lasting without end, and pain is passing and shall be brought to nothing for those who shall be saved.

And therefore it is not God's will that we submit to the feeling of pains, in sorrow and mourning because of them, but quickly pass over them and keep ourselves in the endless delight which is God.[8]

COMMENTS ON CHAPTER 16

1. Julian speaks of "seeing" this vision to underline the fact that it is not just her imagination. This is important since the scene is embroidered in detail far beyond the biblical account of the Crucifixion. We are reminded that Julian's visions are not limited to the biblical version.
2. Blue is the color of bruises.
3. The account of the changing of color was a common element in late medieval descriptions of the Passion.
4. The next six paragraphs do not appear in the SV, but were added when the LV was written.
5. The word "lifelike" was used in the fourteenth century to mean simply "healthy."
6. The mention of the cold may have come from Julian's memory of John 18:18, which describes the servants and police at Annas' house as gathered around a brazier to keep warm.
7. The drying of Christ's body seems almost an obsession with Julian. The vision of this drying must have been powerful to her. It is related to the vast loss of blood and also to Christ's exclamation "I am thirsty." See Psalm 143:6 (BCP): ". . . my soul gasps to you like a thirsty land."
8. In the PV, this is one word, *senyght*, meaning "a week." W&J remind us that this is also the number of nights of Julian's illness.

⤳ 16

After this Christ showed a portion of His Passion near His death.[1] I saw His sweet face, and it was dry and bloodless with pale dying and deathly ashen; and after that more pale, grievous, distressing, and then turned more lifeless into blue,[2] and after that more dark-blue, as the flesh changed into more profound death.[3]

His suffering revealed itself to me most distinctly in His blessed face, and especially in His lips, where I saw these four colors (though before those lips were fresh, ruddy, and pleasant to my sight).

This was a sorrowful change to see this profound dying, and also the nose was shriveled together and dried, as I saw it, and the sweet body[4] became brown and black, all changed from the fair lifelike[5] color of Himself into dry dying; because at the time that our Lord and Blessed Savior died upon the rood, there was a dry, sharp wind and wondrous cold, as I see it.[6]

And by the time all the Precious Blood was bled out of the sweet body that could pass from it, yet there remained a moisture in the sweet flesh of Christ, as it was shown.

Bloodlessness and painful drying within and the blowing of wind and cold coming from without met together in the sweet body of Christ.

And these four, two without, and two within, dried the flesh of Christ over the course of time.

And though this pain was bitter and sharp, it was most long-lasting, as I saw it, and it painfully dried up all the living elements of Christ's Flesh.[7]

Thus I saw the sweet Flesh die, apparently part after part, drying with awesome pains.

And as long as any element had life in Christ's flesh, so long He suffered pain.

This long torment seemed to me as if He had been <u>seven nights</u>[8] lifeless, dying, at the point of passing away, suffering the last pain. (And

9. There can be little doubt but that Julian's experience of the Black Death at the age of six and later made her conscious of the appearance of a dead body. Julian also needs to explain that "seven nights" is symbolic, since the actual Crucifixion lasted only a few hours.

COMMENTS ON CHAPTER 17

1. In the midst of the ghastly and graphic description of the body, Julian reminds us that there is more than physical reality in the visions. Here is a verse from the medieval N-Town Mystery Play (which Julian may well have seen):

   So great a thirst did never man take
   As I have, mankind, for thy sake.
   For thirst asunder my lips do crack;
   For dryness they together cleave.

2. Christ's aloneness is emphasized again in the parable in Chapter 51 and once more in Chapter 79.

3. The last words of the passage in LV are these: "And all the other pains because of which I saw that all I can say is too little, for it cannot be told." This passage does not appear in the SV, but was added when the LV was written.

4. BV has *deying*.

5. There are several surviving late medieval portrayals of the Crucifixion that show the Crown of Thorns made like a helmet, covering the entire top of Jesus' head. This may have been how Julian saw it.

where I say it seemed to me as if He had been seven nights lifeless, it means that the sweet body was as discolored, as dry, as shriveled, as deathlike and as piteous as though He had been seven nights lifeless, constantly dying.)[9]

And it seemed to me that the drying of Christ's Flesh was the worst pain, and the last, of His Passion.

17

In this dying was brought to my mind the words of Christ: "I thirst," for I saw in Christ a double thirst: one bodily, another spiritual (which I shall speak of in the thirty-first chapter).[1]

I was reminded of this word because of the bodily thirst which I understood was caused by the lack of moisture, for the blessed flesh and bones were left all alone without blood and moisture.

The blessed body dried all alone[2] a long time, with the twisting of the nails and weight of the body (for I understood[3] that because of the tenderness of the sweet hands and of the sweet feet, and by the large size, cruelty, and hardship of the nails, the wounds grew wider), and the body sagged because of the weight by hanging a long time and the piercing and chafing of the head and the binding of the crown, all parched with dry blood, with the sweet hair and the dry flesh clinging to the thorns, and the thorns to the <u>drying</u>[4] flesh.

And in the beginning while the flesh was fresh and bleeding, the constant piercing of the thorns made the wounds wide.

Furthermore I saw that the sweet skin and the tender flesh, with the hair and the blood, were all raised and loosened above from the bone with the thorns,[5] and gashed in many pieces, and were hanging like a cloth that was sagging as if it would very soon have fallen off because of the weight and looseness while it had natural moisture.

(And that was great sorrow and fear for me, because it seemed to me that I would not for my life have seen it fall.)

6. Julian's visions seem to have taken place in a kind of time lapse in which no matter how graphically realistic the visions are, they apparently do not operate in "real time." Time seems to be "speeded up" during the visions.

7. The ME word is *agyd* in the PV, but *akynned* in BV. Curiously, in the BVMS the word is underlined as though it would have a marginal note, but no such note appears. *Akynned* could possibly mean "burned" or "scorched."

8. There are two contemporary references that refer to Christ's hanging on the cross like a piece of parchment hung out to dry. Since Julian grew up in the parchment-makers' neighborhood of Norwich, this may have been the image she had in mind.

9. One thinks of the reference to Christ's words "I am thirsty" (John 19:28), and the offer of "sour wine."

10. Not for the last time is Julian frustrated in finding words inadequate to express the visions she has seen.

11. Julian is experiencing Christ's own pains because of her spiritual identification with Him.

How it was done, I saw not, but I understood it was with the sharp thorns and the violent and painful setting on of the garland unsparingly and without pity.

This continued awhile, and then it began to change, and I beheld and wondered how it could be.

And then I saw it was because the flesh began to dry and lost a part of the weight that was round about the garland. With this it was surrounded all about, as it were garland upon garland. The garland of the thorns was dyed with the blood, and the other fleshly garland and the head were also the same color—like clotted blood when it is dry.[6]

The skin of the flesh of the face and of the body which showed had small wrinkles, with a tanned color, like a dry board when it is <u>old</u>,[7] and the face was darker than the body.

I saw four kinds of dryings: the first was loss of blood; the second was pain following after; the third was that He was hanging up in the air the way men hang a cloth to dry;[8] the fourth, that His bodily nature demanded fluid and there was no kind of comfort administered to Him in all His woe and distress.[9]

Ah! Cruel and grievous was His pain, but much more cruel and grievous it was when the moisture was lacking and all began to dry, shriveling this way.

These were two pains that showed in the blessed head: the first caused by the drying while it was moist; and the other slow, with shriveling and drying, with blowing of the wind from without that dried Him and pained Him more with cold, more than my heart can think.

And all the other pains, because of which I saw that all I can say is too little, for it cannot be told![10]

That showing of Christ's pains filled me full of pain, because I was well aware that He suffered only once, though He wished to show it me, and fill me with remembrance as I had before desired.

And in all this time of Christ's pains I felt no pain except for Christ's pains.[11]

12. We are reminded of Julian's wish in Chapter 2 to experience the pain of those who watched the Crucifixion: "for I wished to be one of them and to suffer with them."

13. Another moment of unconscious humility in Julian's admission that she regretted asking for the pain. It was no high-minded experience, but a very honest and earthy one.

14. The worst pain of hell is its hopeless despair, for there is no expectation of its being relieved for all eternity, whereas earthly pain can carry at least the hope of relief.

15. Julian is reassured of her love for Christ by the pain she experiences in seeing Him suffer. And perhaps an unconscious reference is made once again to Lamentations 1:12, " . . . is there any agony like mine?"

COMMENTS ON CHAPTER 18

1. Julian has just been reminded of her earlier wish: "I desired a bodily sight wherein I could have more knowledge of the bodily pains of our Savior and of the compassion of Our Lady and of all His true lovers who at that time saw His pains . . ." (Chapter 2), and by her own pain in seeing Jesus suffer, she is reminded of the Blessed Virgin and identifies with her. *Meditations on the Life of Christ*: "[Mary] hung with her Son on the cross and wished to die with him. . . ."

2. Julian's frequent association of "nature" and "grace" is first shown here where Saint Mary is seen as the example of natural mother-love as well as love that is grace-filled. (Consider the greeting of the archangel: "Hail Mary, full of grace.")

3. Julian has had the experience she asked for in Chapter 2.

4. Julian recognizes the ontological union—the "one-ing"—between Christ and his lovers as a reality experienced on earth, not only in heaven.

Then I thought, "I knew but little what pain it was that I asked for,"[12] and like a wretch I repented me, thinking that if I had known what it would be, I would have been loath to have prayed for it, for it seemed to me that my pains went beyond any bodily death.[13]

I thought: "Is any pain in hell like this?" And I was answered in my reason: "Hell is a different pain, for despair is there.[14] But of all pains that lead to salvation, this is the most pain—to see thy Beloved suffer."

How can any pain be more to me than to see Him who is all my life, all my bliss, and all my joy, suffer?

Here I felt most truthfully that I loved Christ so much more than myself that there was no pain that could be suffered like to that sorrow which I had to see Him in pain.[15]

⁐ 18

Here I saw a part of the compassion of Our Lady Saint Mary, for Christ and she were so one-ed in love that the magnitude of her love caused the magnitude of her pain.[1]

In this I saw the essence of natural love, extended by grace,[2] which creatures have for Him, and this natural love was most fulsomely shown in His sweet Mother, and even more, for insomuch as she loved Him more than all others, her pains surpassed all others. For ever the higher, the mightier, the sweeter that the love is, the more sorrow it is to the lover to see that body which is beloved in pain.

And all His disciples and all His true lovers suffered more pains than their own bodily dying, for I am certain, by my own experience,[3] that the least of them loved Him so far above himself that it surpasses all that I can say.

Here I saw a great one-ing between Christ and us, as I understand it, for when He was in pain, we were in pain.[4]

And all created things that could suffer pain suffered with Him (that is to say, all created things that God has made for our service). The

5. See Colossians 1:17, "... all things are held together in him"; Hebrews 1:3, "... he sustains the universe by his word of power"; Romans 8:22, " .. as we know, the whole created universe in all its parts groans as if in the pangs of child-birth." Julian refers, of course, to the Gospel account of the earthquake and eclipse that followed Christ's death (Luke 23:44–45 and Matthew 27:45, 51).

6. Although all suffer when Christ suffers, God continues His protection.

7. See Appendix 7, "Pilate and Dionysius the Areopagite."

8. One is given the impression that at the moment of the death of Christ, all creation "held its breath," lacking, for that moment, the "goodness of God"—based on the Gospel accounts of the darkening of the sun, the earthquake, the opening of the graves, and the tearing of the temple veil at the moment of Christ's death.

9. For this reference, see the ending of Chapter 21.

COMMENTS ON CHAPTER 19

1. Translated as "horror," the descriptive ME word in BV is *uggyng*, with an Anglo-Norman and colloquial root related to *ugly*; in PV the word is "cleaned up" and replaced by the less picturesque *drede*.

2. Julian faces the contemplative's conundrum: shall I turn away from the nearly intolerable suffering earth offers and deny earthly life to turn only to God? Or shall I accept the pain, and know that God is at the other side of suffering? Julian refuses resurrection without crucifixion: she refuses "pure spirituality" without the suffering of earthly life.

3. This "voice" is never identified, but it seems to have come from the demons. Once again, Julian makes no attempt to cloak her weaknesses.

firmament and the earth failed for sorrow in their nature at the time of Christ's dying,[5] for it belongs naturally to their character to know Him for their God in whom all their strength is situated.

When He failed, then it was necessary for them out of nature to fail with Him as much as they could, out of sorrow for His pains. And thus they that were His friends suffered pain for love.

And universally, all—that is to say, they that knew Him not—suffered because of the failing of all manner of comfort, except the mighty hidden protection of God.[6] I mean of two manner of folk, as it can be understood by two persons: the one was Pilate,[7] the other was Saint Denis[7] of France, who was at that time a pagan; for when he saw the wonders and marvels, the sorrows and fears that happened at that time, he said, "Either the world is now at an end, or else He that is Maker of nature is suffering." Wherefore, he did write on an altar: "This is the altar of the unknown God."

God out of His goodness creates the planets and the elements in their nature to work for both the blessed man and the cursed, and at that time [that goodness] was withdrawn from both of them. It was for that reason that even those who knew Him not were in sorrow at that time.[8]

Thus was our Lord Jesus debased because of us, and we all stand in this kind of debasement with Him, and shall do until we come to His bliss, as I shall say later.[9]

19

At this time I wished to look up from the Cross, and I dared not, for I was well aware that while I gazed on the cross I was secure and safe; therefore I would not agree to put my soul in peril, because, aside from the cross, there was no protection from the horror[1] of demons.[2]

Then I had a proposal in my reason (as if it were friendly)[3] which said to me, "Look up to heaven to His Father." And I saw well with the Faith that there was nothing between the cross and heaven that could have distressed me. Either it was necessary for me to look up, or else to answer.

4. W&J suggest that this being "bound" is an erotic image—a dubious opinion given Julian's general avoidance of erotic metaphors.

5. Julian demonstrates the depths of her faith—even in the face of what seems a "friendly" temptation; she will not "bypass" Christ's suffering in order to experience only the joy of heaven. For her, this would mean ignoring the Passion and her union of pain with the suffering Lord, and she knows, intuitively, that the suffering is the way to the safety of salvation; so she continues to embrace the pain, however undesirable it seems at the moment.

6. Again, the colorful ME words in the vernacular are *grutching* and *daming*.

7. Julian begins to sort out the failings of the flesh from the wishes of the soul, and sees that God assigns no blame to the faults of the flesh. This expands eventually to her insight that God views all earthly sin "with pity, not with blame" (see Chapter 82).

8. W&J translate this word as "regret."

9. See 2 Corinthians 4:16–17, "Though our outward humanity is in decay, yet day by day we are inwardly renewed. Our troubles are slight and short-lived, and their outcome is an eternal glory which far outweighs them."

10. Here is Julian's theological cosmology: that the inner spirit of humanity is always good, and (as she says later in Chapter 37) "never consents to evil." For Julian, the breaking of rules or failings of the flesh are not seen by God as true sins. And eventually, the present separation of the earthly and the heavenly will be resolved in perfect union.

I answered inwardly with all the powers of my soul and said, "No, I cannot, for Thou art my heaven." (This I said because I wished not to look up, for I had rather have been in that pain until Doomsday than to have come to heaven otherwise than by Him, for I was well aware that He who bound[4] me so tightly would unbind me when He wished.)

So was I taught to choose Jesus for my heaven, whom I saw only in pain at that time. I desired no other heaven than Jesus, who shall be my bliss when I come there.[5]

And this has ever been a comfort to me: that I chose Jesus for my heaven, by His grace, in all this time of suffering and sorrow. And that had been a learning for me that I should evermore do so, choosing only Jesus for my heaven in well and woe.

And although like a sinner I had been sorry (I said before that if I had been aware what pain it would be, I would have been loath to have asked for it), here saw I truly that it was the <u>grouching and cursing</u>[6] of the flesh without agreement of the soul to which God assigns no blame.[7]

Repenting[8] and willing choice are two opposites which I experienced both at once at the same time; and they are two parts: the one outward, the other inward.

The outward part is our mortal flesh, which is now in pain and woe (and always shall be in this life)—of which I experienced much at this time, and that was the part that repented.

The inward part is an exalted, blissful life which is totally in peace and love, and this was more secretly experienced; and this part is that in which mightily, wisely, and willingly, I chose Jesus for my heaven.[9]

And in this I saw truly that the inward part is master and ruler of the outward, and neither receives orders nor pays heed to the will of the outward, but its whole intention and will is endlessly committed to being one-ed into our Lord Jesus. (That the outward could turn the inward to agreement was not shown to me; but rather that the inward moves the outward by grace, and both shall be united in bliss without end by the power of Christ, this was shown.)[10]

COMMENTS ON CHAPTER 20

1. Julian's attention is recalled to the vision, and she sees Christ taking a long time to die—because his divinity makes his humanity stronger than that of most humans, and because it was important for Christ to experience all possible human pain before dying, so it could not be seen that he spared himself.

2. Julian constantly reiterated the theology of Incarnation: she has been concentrating on the human sufferings of Jesus, but now reminds us (and herself) of the divinity cloaked within that suffering body.

3. After this thorough and graphic discussion of the human pain and suffering of Jesus, she can still call that suffering a "lesser" point, compared with the splendor of the divinity behind the humanity.

4. The "one-ing" between Jesus and his mother (and all others) is so deep that the Lord actually suffers "for her sorrow." The theological clarity shows that Julian understands that while God does not remove our suffering from us, he enters into our suffering with us.

5. The ME words are *no more passibyl*—that is, "no more capable of passion." The traditional theological word is "impassible"—that is, once resurrected and in heaven, Christ no longer experienced any earthly passions.

6. She does so in Chapters 22 and 23.

7. The ME translated as "with great satisfaction" is *wel payeying*, that is, "well paying."

⤳ 20

And thus I saw our Lord Jesus languishing a long time (for the unity of the Godhead gave strength to the manhood out of love to suffer more than all men could suffer).[1] (I mean not only more pain than all men could suffer, but also that He suffered more pain than all men of salvation who ever were from the first beginning until the last day could measure or fully imagine—considering the worthiness of the most exalted, honorable King and the shameful, spiteful, painful death—because He that is most exalted and most worthy was most fully debased and most utterly despised.)

The most significant point that can be seen in the Passion is to comprehend and to understand that He who suffered is God,[2] seeing beyond this two other points which are lesser[3] (the one is what He suffered, and the other for whom He suffered).

In this showing He brought partially to mind the exaltation and nobility of the glorious Godhead, and with that the preciousness and the tenderness of the blessed body (which are both united together) and also the reluctance that is in our nature to suffer pain; for as much as He was most tender and pure, just so He was most strong and mighty to suffer.

And for the sin of every man that shall be saved He suffered. And because of every man's sorrow and desolation and anguish, He saw and grieved out of kindness and love. (Inasmuch as Our Lady grieved for His pains, just so much He suffered grief for her sorrow, and more beyond, inasmuch as the sweet Manhood of Him was more noble in nature.)[4]

As long as He was able to suffer, He suffered for us and grieved for us, and now He is risen and <u>no more able to suffer</u>,[5] yet He suffers with us still (as I shall say later).[6]

And I, gazing upon all this by His grace, saw that the love in Him which He has for our soul was so strong that deliberately He chose the Passion with great desire, and humbly He suffered it with great joy, <u>with great satisfaction</u>.[7]

COMMENTS ON CHAPTER 21

1. Here we have the beginning of a summation of the revelations of the Passion.

2. *Contrition* and *compassion* are the first two wounds Julian sought in Chapter 2.

3. The other two "ways of looking at His blessed Passion" appear in Chapters 22 and 23.

4. This vision (the ninth) is so tremendous and radical that it deserves special notice: Julian cannot be surpassed in the graphic character of her description of the Crucifixion, but she never presses on with the same graphic quality to describe his death. Even in the midst of the Passion—at the moment that death should be shown—Julian is shown deliverance instead. For a fourteenth-century Christian to see that transition is almost impossible to imagine. It counters every medieval tradition, and this vision alone sets Julian apart from her confreres. Having just seen the immeasurable brutality of the sufferings, she is suddenly shown a transformation—and she can actually say, "I was completely happy"! This provides the core optimism of Julian's theology.

5. Julian is given a vision of the heaven that is the immediate result of the Passion. For Julian, this finally makes sense of all human travail and pain, that is, its transformation into bliss and glory.

6. The common expression to describe heaven was to speak of "The Beatific Vision," and here Julian gives true meaning to that phrase: the mere sight of the face of the risen Christ is the joy and bliss of heaven.

The soul that sees it in this way (when it is touched by grace) shall truly see that the pains of Christ's Passion surpass all pains—that is to say, those pains which shall be changed into everlasting surpassing joys by the power of Christ's Passion.

⤺ 21

It is God's will, as I understand it, that we have three ways of looking at His blessed Passion.[1]

The first (which we should view with contrition and compassion)[2] is the cruel pain that He suffered, and that one our Lord showed at this time and gave me power and grace to see it.[3]

And I looked for the departing of His life with all my might and expected to have seen the body entirely dead, but I saw Him not so.

And just at the same time that I thought, by appearance, that His life could no longer last, and the showing of the end properly needed to be near, suddenly, as I gazed upon the same cross, He changed His blessed countenance. The changing of His blessed countenance changed mine, and I was as glad and as merry as possible.[4]

Then brought our Lord merrily to my mind: "Where is now any point to thy pain or to thy distress?" And I was completely happy.

I understood that, in our Lord's meaning, we are now on His cross with Him in our pains and our suffering, dying; and if we willingly remain on the same cross with His help and His grace until the last moment, suddenly He shall change his appearance to us, and we shall be with Him in heaven (between the one and the other there shall be no passage of time) and then shall all be brought to joy.[5]

And so meant He in this showing: "Where is now any point to thy pain or thy distress?"

And we shall be fully blessed.

And here I saw truthfully that if He showed us His most blissful face now, there is no pain on earth nor in any other place that would distress us, but everything would be to us joy and bliss.[6] But because

7. Although the idea of "substitutionary atonement" was almost universal in her day, Julian rises beyond that and comes to understand that the Crucifixion is primarily the means of "one-ing" with Christ in heaven.

8. In the midst of the joy Julian experiences, she can own that the pain we experience is necessary for our salvation and "one-ing" with Christ. Pain itself is redeemed as being part of the entire experience of salvation. Later we will see that Julian constantly equates earthly pain with heavenly reward.

COMMENTS ON CHAPTER 22

1. The ME words translated as "satisfied" are *well apayd*, meaning "have you received adequate payment?"

2. Julian's words of reply are an explosion of joyful and almost inexpressible gratitude.

3. In Catholic teaching, the Risen Lord is no longer able to suffer earthly pain—but in any event, Julian knows that He suffered all the pain possible already, and that the historical Crucifixion can never be repeated.

4. ME has *thre hevyns*.

5. Since she is about to write about the Trinity, Julian slips into the language reminiscent of the Athanasian Creed.

6. The second and third "states of bliss" are described in Chapter 23.

7. Julian is quick to deny any "bodily likeness" of the Father—even though the pictures of the Trinity that show the Father as an old man holding the crucified Christ between his knees and with the Dove hovering above was widely common in her day.

8. Julian is describing the immediate reaction in heaven to the Crucifixion and Resurrection. See Luke 3:22, "You are my beloved Son; in you I delight."

He showed to us an expression of suffering as He bore in this life His cross, therefore we are in distress and labor with Him as our frailty demands.

And the reason why He suffers is because He wishes of His goodness to make us heirs with Him in His bliss.[7]

And for this little pain that we suffer here we shall have an exalted, endless knowledge in God, which we could never have without that pain.[8] The crueler our pains have been with Him on His cross, the more shall our honor be with Him in His Kingdom.

⤳ 22

Then spoke our good Lord Jesus Christ, asking: "Art thou well satisfied[1] that I suffered for thee?"

I said: "Yea, good Lord, thanks be to Thee. Yea, good Lord, blessed mayest Thou be!"[2]

Then said Jesus, our kind Lord: "If thou art satisfied, I am satisfied. It is joy, a bliss, an endless delight to me that ever I suffered the Passion for thee; and if I could suffer more, I would suffer more."[3]

In this experience my understanding was lifted up into heaven, and there I saw three states of bliss,[4] by which sight I was greatly amazed. (And although I say "three states of bliss," and all are in the blessed Manhood of Christ, no one is more, no one is less, no one is higher, no one is lower, but equally alike in bliss.)[5]

With respect to the first state,[6] Christ showed me his Father (in no bodily likeness, but in His quality and in His actions—that is to say, I saw in Christ what the Father is).[7] The action of the Father is this: that He gives recompense to His Son, Jesus Christ. This gift and this recompense is so blessed to Jesus that His Father could have given him no recompense that could have pleased Him better.[8]

The first state—that is, the pleasing of the Father—appeared to me as a heaven, and it was filled with bliss, for the Father is fully pleased with all the deeds that Jesus has done concerning our salvation. Wherefore, we are not only His by His paying for us, but also by the

9. Another transformational insight on Julian's part: we "belong" to Christ not only because he "bought" us by his Crucifixion, but because we have been "given" to Christ by the Father. We are God the Father's gift to His Son. The shattering wonder of this is expressed in the phrase that Julian actually repeats, "We are his crown." This is the "victor's wreath" that stands in contrast to the crown of thorns.

10. Christ's willingness to suffer is so limitless that Julian, in a delightful conceit, declares that she cannot count the number of times He would be willing to die. What Julian is trying to do is to quantify Christ's love for us—and admitting that it cannot be done. (In SV, she suggests that the number would be equal to the number of souls saved—one death for each individual soul's salvation.)

11. See Isaiah 65:17, "See, I am creating new heavens and a new earth!" and 2 Corinthians 5:17, "For anyone united to Christ, there is a new creation; the old order has gone; a new order has already begun."

12. This the promised *second* "way of seeing" the Passion, promised in Chapter 21.

13. This is Julian's adaptation of the familiar words "as it was in the beginning, is now, and will be for ever" that conclude the recitation of the Psalms.

gracious gift of His Father we are His bliss; we are His recompense; we are His honor; we are His crown (and this was a particular wonder and a wholly delightful vision: that we are His crown).[9]

This that I describe is such great bliss to Jesus that He sets at naught all His labor and His hard Passion and His cruel and shameful death. And in these words, "If I could suffer more, I would suffer more," I saw truly that as often as He could die, so often He would, and love would never let Him have rest until He had done it.

And I watched with great diligence in order to know how often He would die if He could, and truly, the number passed my understanding and my wits so far that my reason could not, nor knew how to, contain it or take it in.[10]

And when He had thus often died (or was willing to), still He would set it at naught for love; for He considers everything but little in comparison to His love; for though the sweet Manhood of Christ could suffer but once, the goodness in Him can never cease from offering; every day He is prepared for the same, if it could be; for if He said He would for my love make new heavens and new earth,[11] that were but little in comparison, for this could be done every day if He wished, without any labor; but to die for my love so often that the number passes created reason, that is the most exalted offer that our Lord God could make to man's soul, as I see it.

Then He means this: "How could it then be that I would not do for thy love all that I could? This deed does not distress me since I would for thy love die so often with no regard to my cruel pains."

And here I saw with respect to the second way of seeing[12] in this blessed Passion that the love that made Him suffer surpassed all His pains as far as Heaven is above earth; for the pain was a noble, honorable deed done at one time by the action of love; but the love was without beginning, is now, and shall be without ending.[13]

It was because of this love He said most sweetly these words: "If I could suffer more, I would suffer more." He said not, "If it were necessary to suffer more . . ." for even though it were not necessary, if He could suffer more, He would.

COMMENTS ON CHAPTER 23

1. Here is the third "way of seeing," promised in Chapter 21.
2. The ME is *semys* (BV) or *seming* (PV). W&J mistakenly translate this as "representation" (that is, "seeming"). However, the words actually translate as "furrows" or "seams." We have chosen "slashes" as the results of the scourging of Christ.
3. Julian's recognition is that the final outcome of the brutal suffering of Christ is bliss and joy for Him and for us.
4. The ME word translated as "Rising" in BV is *upriste*, which comes from Old English.

This deed and action concerning our salvation was prepared as well as God could prepare it.

And here I saw a complete bliss in Christ; for His bliss would not have been complete if it could have been done any better than it was done.

⁀ 23

In these three words, "It is a joy, a bliss, and endless delight to me," were shown three states of bliss, in this way: in regard to the joy, I interpret the pleasure of the Father; and in regard to the bliss, the honor of the Son; and in regard to the endless delight, the Holy Spirit. The Father is pleased, the Son is honored, the Holy Spirit delights.

And here I saw this in relation to the third way of seeing His blessed Passion[1]—that is to say, the joy and the bliss that make Him delight in it—for our gracious Lord showed His Passion to me in five ways: of which the first is the bleeding of the head, the second is the discoloring of His blessed face, the third is the plenteous bleeding of the body in the slashes[2] of the scourging, the fourth is the profound drying (these four regard the pains of the Passion as I said before), and the fifth is what was shown in regard to the joy and the bliss of the Passion.

It is God's will that we have true delight with Him in our salvation, and in that He wishes us to be mightily comforted and strengthened, and thus He wills that with His grace our soul be happily engaged, for we are His bliss, for in us He delights without end and so shall we in Him with His grace.[3]

All that He has done for us, and does now, and ever shall do, was never a cost or burden to Him, nor can it be (except only what He did in our manhood, beginning at the sweet incarnation and lasting until the blessed Rising[4] on Easter morning—only that long did the cost and the burden concerning our redemption last in deed—about which deed He rejoices endlessly, as was said before).

5. The exclamatory "Ah" appears only in the PV. It may have been added by the scribe.

6. Julian expresses a simple, orthodox theology of the Incarnation: that the entire Holy Trinity ministers to us all the benefits of the Passion, but that only Christ's *human* aspect suffered on the cross.

7. Julian introduces the idea that salvation is offered as a free gift, and God asks "nothing else from" us in our labor. We never have to "earn" salvation.

8. 2 Corinthians 9:7, "God loves a cheerful giver." C&W remind us that Rosemary Woolf noted that a sermon of Archbishop Pecham (1240–92) speaks of Christ as "a courteous friend expecting no return."

9. "Ever" refers to Chapter 22: "It is joy, a bliss, an endless delight to me that ever I suffered the Passion for thee."

10. Julian recapitulates the three joys of Jesus: He has finished the Passion, this work has brought humanity into heaven, and it has redeemed us from hell.

Ah,[5] Jesus wishes that we take heed to the bliss of our salvation that is in the blessed Trinity and that we desire to have as much spiritual pleasure, with His grace, as was said before. (That is to say, that the pleasure of our salvation be like to the joy that Christ has about our salvation as much as it can be while we are here.)

The whole Trinity acted in the Passion of Christ (ministering an abundance of strengths and plenitude of grace to us by Him) but only the Maiden's son suffered (about which the whole blessed Trinity endlessly rejoices).[6]

This was shown in these words: "Art thou well satisfied?" and by that other word that Christ said, "If thou art satisfied, I am satisfied" (as if He said: "It is joy and delight enough to me, and I ask nothing else from thee for my labor except that I can well satisfy thee").[7]

In this He reminded me of the quality of a glad giver:[8] always a glad giver takes but little heed of the thing that he gives, but all his desire and all his intention is to please him and solace him to whom he gives it, and if the receiver accepts the gift gladly and thankfully, then the gracious giver sets at naught all his cost and all his labor for the joy and delight that he has because he has pleased and solaced him whom he loves.

Plenteously and fully was this shown.

Think also wisely of the magnitude of this word "ever";[9] for in that word was shown an exalted awareness of the love that He has in our salvation, with the manifold joys that result from the Passion of Christ: one joy is that He rejoices that He has done it in deed, and He shall suffer no more; another joy is that He brought us up into heaven and made us to be His crown and endless bliss; another joy is that with the Passion He has redeemed us from endless pains of hell.[10]

COMMENTS ON CHAPTER 24

1. See Appendix 8, "The Wounds of Christ." Up to this point, Julian's attention has been on the *face* of Christ; now His eyes direct her attention to the Wound.

2. Julian was one of the earliest mystics to speak of the Sacred Heart as a symbol of the suffering love of Jesus for humankind—the Sacred Heart symbolizing the love and the cleaving or piercing symbolizing the suffering. The devotion did not become widespread for several hundred years.

3. PV adds here: *as farforth as he wolde that time*—"to the extent that he wished to at that time."

4. Julian admits (and later makes very clear) that there are truths that she learned that cannot be expressed in words. (See Chapter 73 for similar disclaimers.)

5. Julian puts forward the Johannine idea that God's love had no beginning and will have no end—that is, God was love even before He created humankind. (A minor confirmation of the Holy Trinity, since if God was love before Creation, there had to be more than one Person in the Godhead for there to be love.)

6. This is a powerfully appropriate epigram for the crucifix.

7. This is Julian's second use (of five) of the word *Brother* to describe Jesus. Note these lines addressed to St. Mary from a fourteenth-century lyric:

    Thou my suster and my moder
    And thy sone my broder
    Who shulde thenne drede?[129]

8. Julian's exposition of the words "Lo, how I loved thee" tells her that Christ's "pleasure" is not just our *obedience*, but our holiness and our union with Him. (In PV, the word "love" is in the present tense: "Lo, how I love thee.") See 1 Thessalonians 4:3—"This is the will of God, that you should be holy. . . ."

⤳ 24

Then, with a glad expression, our Lord looked into His wounded side and gazed with joy, and with His sweet gazing He directed the understanding of His creature through that same wound into His side within.[1]

There He showed a fair, desirable place, and large enough for all mankind that shall be saved to rest in peace and love.

And with that He brought to mind His dearworthy blood and precious water which He allowed to pour all out for love.

And with the sweet sight He showed His blessed Heart cloven in two.[2]

And with this sweet rejoicing, He showed to my understanding, in part, the blessed Godhead,[3] strengthening the pure soul to understand (in so far as it can be expressed)[4] that this Heart is to signify the endless love that was without beginning, and is, and shall be always.[5]

With this our good Lord said most blissfully, "Lo, how I loved thee"[6] (as if He had said: "My dear one, behold and see the Lord, thy God, who is thy Creator and thine endless Joy; see thine own Brother,[7] thy Savior; my child, behold and see what delight and bliss I have in thy salvation, and for my love, enjoy it now with me").

Also for further understanding this blessed word was said: "Lo, how I loved thee. Behold and see that I loved thee so much before I died for thee that I was willing to die for thee; and that now I have died for thee, and suffered willingly what I can. And now is all my bitter pain and all my cruel labor changed to endless joy and bliss for me and for thee. How should it now be that thou wouldst pray for anything that pleases me, and I would not most gladly grant it thee? For my pleasure is thy holiness and thine endless joy and bliss with Me."[8]

This is the understanding, as simply as I can express it, of this blessed word: "Lo, how I loved thee."

This our good Lord showed in order to make us glad and happy.

COMMENTS ON CHAPTER 25

1. Once again, note that Christ directs Julian's attention with his eyes. Universal in medieval English churches was the Rood Beam (usually at the top of a Rood Screen) at the entrance to the chancel. This carried a carved crucifix ("rood") with Saint Mary on Christ's right side, and St. John on His left. (This is one of those instances where familiar liturgical use subtly impacts Julian's thought.)

2. "Blessed Mother" was not a common appellation for Saint Mary in fourteenth-century England (however common it has become in modern times).

3. C&W remind us of the words the people addressed to Judith: "You are the glory of Jerusalem, the great pride of Israel, the great boast of our people! . . . God has shown his approval. Blessings on you from the Lord Almighty for all time to come!" (Judith 15:9–10).

4. While recognizing the veneration in which we are to hold the Blessed Virgin, in this revelation Christ identifies Mary with Julian in His love: "Do you wish to see in her how thou art loved?" And Christ exalts His Mother "because of thy love." Christ shows His love for all as represented in His love for His Mother.

5. One suspects that Julian is here avoiding the confusion of Christ with His Mother and reasserting that she (Julian) had not asked for "bodily sights."

6. Julian has "seen" the Blessed Virgin now in her several manifestations: at the Annunciation, at the Crucifixion, and at her Crowning as Queen of Heaven.

7. This is a simple explication: it pleases Christ to see His followers delight in His Mother.

25

With this same expression of mirth and joy, our good Lord looked down on His right side and brought to my mind where Our Lady stood at the time of His Passion;[1] and He said, "Dost thou wish to see her?" (And in this sweet word, it was as if He had said: "I know well thou wouldst see my Blessed Mother,[2] for after Myself, she is the highest joy that I could show thee, and the most pleasure and honor to me; and she is most desired to be seen by all my blessed creatures.")[3]

Because of the exalted, wondrous, special love that He has for this sweet Maiden, His Blessed Mother, our Lady Saint Mary, He showed her highly rejoicing (as in view of the intention of these sweet words) as if He said: "Dost thou wish to see how I love her, that thou canst rejoice with me in the love that I have in her and she in me?"

And also for further understanding, this sweet word our Lord God speaks to all mankind that shall be saved (as it were all to one person) as if He said: "Dost thou wish to see in her how thou art loved?[4] Because of thy love I made her so exalted, so noble, and so worthy; and this pleases me, and so do I wish that it pleaseth thee."

For after Himself, she is the most blessed sight. (But from this I am not taught to yearn to see her bodily presence while I am here, but the virtues of her blessed soul—her truth, her wisdom, her love— whereby I can learn to know myself and reverently fear my God.)[5]

And when our Good Lord had shown this and said this word, "Dost thou wish to see her?" I answered and said: "Yea, good Lord, thanks be to Thee; yea, good Lord, if it be Thy will." Often I prayed this and I expected to have seen her in bodily presence, but I saw her not so, but Jesus in that word showed me a spiritual sight of her (in the same way as I had seen her before—little and simple—so He showed her now exalted and noble and glorious and pleasing to Him above all created beings).[6]

And so He wishes that it be known that all those that delight in Him should delight in her and in the delight that He has in her and she in Him.[7]

8. Julian moves even more deeply into the nature of divine love: not only is there unqualified love of God for His creatures, but the love extends to the mutual love among those creatures. See Chapter 61: "He makes us to love all that He loves because of His love."

9. It seems that Julian sees the Virgin Mary as a "prototype" of all Christians (in the Annunciation, when God announces His Presence within her; at the Crucifixion, when she sees and knows his sufferings within herself; and at her Crowning in heaven, when like us, she receives delight, honor, and joy), and so no other person need be shown.

COMMENTS ON CHAPTER 26

1. "Simple and gracious" is the translation of Julian's favorite paradoxical and apparently contradictory adjectives that characterize Jesus. The ME is *homely and curteys* (in the PV)—"homely and courteous"—"both like a member of the family and like a royal courtier at the same time." "Homely" does not carry our modern meaning of "ugly," but of "simple" or "ordinary" or "familiar." And "courteous" does not mean "polite" or "well-mannered," but "regal" and "gracious" and "courtly."

2. This list does not capture the directness of the ME "I it am," and so on. C&W translate: "I am he," and so on. The ME gives grand preeminence to the word "I."

3. In this "I it am" list, Jesus' self-identifying is almost overwhelming in answer to the unasked question: "Who are you?"

For further understanding, He showed this example: as, if a man loves a creature uniquely above all creatures, he would like to make all creatures to love and to delight in that creature which he loves so much.[8]

And in this word that Jesus said, "Dost thou wish to see her?" it seemed to me that it was the most pleasing word He could have given me about her with the spiritual showing that He gave me of her— because our Lord showed me no one person in particular except our Lady Saint Mary[9]—and her He showed three times: the first was as she conceived, the second was as she was in her sorrows beneath the cross, the third was as she is now in delight, honor, and joy.

⤳ 26

After this our Lord showed Himself more glorified, as I see it, than I saw Him before, in which I was taught that our soul shall never rest until it comes to Him knowing that He is the fullness of joy, simple and gracious,[1] blissful and true life.

Our Lord Jesus often said:[2]

"It is I,
it is I;
it is I who am most exalted;
it is I whom thou lovest;
it is I whom thou enjoyest;
it is I whom thou servest;
it is I whom thou yearnst for;
it is I whom thou desirest;
it is I whom thou meanest;
it is I who am all;
it is I whom Holy Church preaches and teaches thee;
it is I who showed myself here to thee."[3]

4. Julian is overwhelmed with Jesus' proclaimed identity, and while she tries fully to explain virtually every *other* revelation, she finds herself silenced by the cosmic power of this collection of simple words.

COMMENTS ON CHAPTER 27

1. Here we are introduced to the main impediment to Julian's full grasp of the mystery: how, since there is a good God, can there be sin? This is a conundrum that is never fully solved for Julian.
2. Julian recognizes the futility of her curiosity, and admits her foolishness.
3. Here we encounter perhaps the most controversial word in Julian's book. The ME is *behovabil* (BV) or *behovely* (PV).
4. Julian sees our inevitable sufferings as purgation of our earthliness, and preparation for our full salvation—a kind of earthly purgatory.

The number of these words surpasses my wit and all my understanding and all my abilities, and it is a most high number, as I see it, because therein these words surpass all that heart can wish and soul can desire.

And therefore the words are not explained here, but every man according to the grace that God gives him in interpreting and loving, receive them in our Lord's meaning.[4]

⁀ 27

After that the Lord brought to my mind the yearning that I had for Him in the past, and I saw that nothing stood in my way except sin (and this I observed universally in us all). And it seemed to me that if sin had not been, we would all have been pure and like to our Lord as He made us, and thus, in my folly, before this time I often wondered why, by the great foreseeing wisdom of God, the beginning of sin was not prevented, for then, it seemed to me, all would have been well.[1]

I ought much to have given up this disturbing wondering, but nevertheless, I made mourning and sorrow about it without reason or discretion.[2]

But Jesus (who in this vision informed me of all that I needed) answered by this word and said:

> "Sin is inevitable,[3]
> but all shall be well,
> and all shall be well,
> and all manner of thing
> shall be well."

In this unadorned word "sin," our Lord brought to my mind generally all that is not good, and the shameful despising and the uttermost tribulation that He bore for us in this life, and His dying, and all the pains and sufferings of all His created things, spiritually and bodily (for we are all in part troubled—and we shall be troubled, following our Master Jesus, until we are completely purged—that is to say, until we are fully stripped of our mortal flesh and of all our inward affections which are not truly good).[4]

5. The ME word is *touch* and carries the sense of a "pat" or a "tap" and suggests a very brief contact. Julian is jumping in quickly with assurance of comfort—a balance with the pain she has just described.

6. Julian writes in ME, *[Sin] hath no maner of substannce...,* but the use of the word *substance* today would be vastly misleading. I follow St. Augustine (in *De Trinitate*) and Denise Baker[130] in using "essence" as a synonym that carries the proper meaning in modern English.

   See Pseudo-Dionysius: "The Divine Names" IV, 19: "Evil is not a being; for if it were, it would not be totally evil.... Evil therefore in itself has neither being, goodness, the capacity to beget, nor the ability to create things which have being and goodness: Evil, then, is neither good nor productive of good. ... However, that which is totally bereft of Good never had, does not have, never shall have, never can have any kind of being at all."

7. There are two ways in which sin is a "pain." First, sinful acts will usually produce painful results, as drunkenness produces a hangover. Second, for a Christian the recognition that one has fallen into sin is a painful realization. And we must realize that Julian is not addressing a modern, unchristian audience.

8. The Lord's words to Julian are to be taken eschatologically— that is, they refer to the end of time.

9. Julian suggests that God pities us for our sin. In Chapter 82 she says that God looks on us sinners "with pity, and not with blame."

10. Another central understanding for Julian: in faith she believes that the conundrum of God's goodness versus the existence of sin is a secret (ME: *privitye*), a mystery that God will finally solve in heaven. Julian recognizes that she cannot comprehend all of God's will, but finally must trust in what she knows to be God's ultimate goodness. "All shall be well" is a proposition she does not understand, but is willing to accept on faith.

And with the beholding of this, with all pains that ever were or ever shall be, I understood the Passion of Christ to represent the greatest pain and even more than that.

And all this pain was shown in one stroke[5] and quickly passed over into comfort (for our good Lord does not wish that the soul be made fearful by this ugly sight).

But I saw not sin; for I believe it has no manner of <u>essence</u>[6] nor any portion of being, nor can it be known except by the pain that is caused by it.[7] And this pain, it is something for a time, as I see it, because it purges and forces us to know ourselves and ask for mercy. But the Passion of our Lord is comfort for us against all this, and so is His blessed will.

And because of the tender love that our good Lord has to all that shall be saved, He comforts quickly and sweetly, meaning thus: "It is true that sin is cause of all this pain,

> but all shall be well,
> and all shall be well,
> and all manner of thing shall be well."[8]

These words were said most tenderly, showing no manner of blame to me nor to any that shall be saved.

Then it would be a great unkindness to blame God for my sin, seeing He does not blame me for sin.[9]

In these same words I saw a marvelous, high secret hidden in God, which <u>secret</u> He shall openly make known to us in heaven. In this <u>secret</u> knowledge we shall truly see the reason why He allowed sin to come, and in this sight we shall endlessly rejoice in our Lord God.[10]

COMMENTS ON CHAPTER 28

1. This poignant analogy—"as men shake a cloth in the wind"—speaks powerfully to the turmoil of the Church in Julian's day. This is one of the subtle references she makes to her own culture. She had seen or known hundreds of priests who died in the epidemics of the Pestilence; she had seen churches looted and burned and an archbishop assassinated during the Peasants' Rebellion; she had seen in Lollardy the emergence of England's first heresy and the execution of a Norfolk Lollard priest; she had watched while her bishop led a shameful and bloody crusade against innocent people in Flanders; and she had seen the papacy split between two (and later three) competing popes. (See Chapter 17 where Julian compares Christ's crucified body to a cloth hung out to dry.)

2. The ME is *rapyd*: W&J remark that the word was already used for sexual assault.

3. Could this be a sympathetic view of the suffering and persecuted Lollards? In any case, it is a justification for suffering and disparagement of Christians.

4. The ME is *I shall al tobreke you*. The verb *breke* means "break," but the addition of the word *al* strengthens the sense and the prefix *to-* is an emphatic. It means "more than." Hence "totally shatter." This is very brutal speech. The Lord promises to *smash* His people because of their "vain affections" and "vicious pride" (as Julian has seen Him do) but then He shall redeem and restore his shattered people by making them "humble and gentle, pure and holy." One is reminded of Psalm 2:9 (BCP), "You shall crush them with an iron rod and shatter them like a piece of pottery."

5. Our doing good to others is brought about by Christ's presence within us, although this mystical and ubiquitous presence of Christ within humanity is little emphasized in most medieval writing.

⁓ 28

Thus I saw how Christ has compassion for us because of sin. And just as I was before filled with pain and compassion for the Passion of Christ, similarly, I was here filled in part with compassion for all my fellow Christians, for that is to say (even though He full well loves the people that shall be saved) that God's servants, Holy Church, shall be shaken in sorrows and anguish and tribulation in this world as men shake a cloth in the wind.[1]

And regarding this our Lord answered in this manner: "A great thing shall I make out of this in heaven, of endless honors, and everlasting joys." Yea, so much so I saw that our Lord rejoices at the tribulations of His servants (with pity and compassion), and upon each person whom He loves (in order to bring him to His bliss), He lays upon them something that is no defect from His point of view, whereby they are disparaged and despised in this world, scorned and abused,[2] and cast out.[3] This He does in order to prevent the harm that they would receive from the pomp and from the pride and from the vainglory of this wretched life, and to make their way ready to come to heaven, and to exalt them in His bliss everlasting without end.

For He says: "I shall totally shatter[4] you because of your vain affections and your vicious pride; and after that I shall gather you together and make you humble and gentle, pure and holy, by one-ing you to myself."

Then I saw that each kind compassion that man has toward his fellow Christian with love, it is Christ in him;[5] that each kind of degradation that He has shown in His Passion, it was shown again here in this compassion in which there were two kinds of applications of our Lord's meaning: the one was the bliss that we are brought to in which He wants us to rejoice; the other is for comfort in our pain, because He wants us to be aware that our pain shall all be transformed into honor and benefit by virtue of His Passion, and that we be aware that we do not suffer alone, but with Him, and that we see Him as our

6. There are two "solutions" to our human suffering: one is that whoever endures will be rewarded with heaven's joys. The second (and typical of Julian) is that the Passion of Christ shows us that we do not endure our sufferings alone, but alongside a suffering Jesus.
7. The wonderful ME word translated as "grumbling" here is *gruching* (BV) or *grugyng* (PV).
8. Our sinful sufferings may cause pain and shame to us, but they do not elicit blame from the Lord, who pities us.

COMMENTS ON CHAPTER 29

1. Julian is still ill at ease about the damage done by sin and presumes to ask for further explanation. This is her great conundrum.
2. Julian has the Lord reminding her that the sin of Adam had "contaminated" all humanity with Original Sin, and, therefore, was the worst sin ever committed. (But Julian's questions seem to suggest that she wonders if this is true.)
3. In her divinely inspired reflections, she is given to realize that Christ's redemption was immeasurably more helpful than Adam's sin had been harmful.
4. It was universally believed in the medieval Church (and shown in paintings of the time) that the first people brought out of hell by Jesus during the Harrowing of Hell—after his death and before his Resurrection—were Adam and Eve. So the Lord gives evidence to Julian's mind that if He can "un-do" the worst sin of Adam, He can easily un-do less major sins.

foundation, and that we see His pains and His tribulation surpass so far all that we can suffer that it cannot be fully comprehended.[6]

And the careful awareness to this intention of His saves us from <u>grumbling</u>[7] and despair when we experience our own pains, as long as we see truly that our sin deserves it, yet His love excuses us, and of His great graciousness He does away with all our blame, and He looks upon us with mercy and pity as children, innocent and not loathsome.[8]

⟿ 29

But in this showing I remained, watching widely, sorrowful and mourning, saying thus to our Lord in my meaning with full great fear: "Ah! Good Lord, how can all be well considering the great damage that has come by sin to Thy creatures?" (And here I desired, as much as I dared, to have some more open explanation with which I could be put at ease in this matter.)[1]

To this our blessed Lord answered most gently, and with most loving expression, and showed that Adam's sin was the most harm that ever was done, or ever shall be done, until the world's end (and also He showed that this is openly acknowledged in all the Holy Church on earth).[2]

Furthermore, He taught that I should observe the Glorious Reparation, for making this reparation is more pleasing to the blessed Godhead and more valuable for man's salvation, without comparison, than ever was the sin of Adam harmful.[3]

Then means our blessed Lord thus in this teaching: that we would take heed to this: "For since I had made well the worst harm, then it is my will that thou knowest from that, that I shall make well everything that is less bad."[4]

COMMENTS ON CHAPTER 30

1. Julian's two sources of truth: the Holy Spirit (in her revelations) and the Holy Church (in its teachings).
2. W&J suggest that this may refer to the King's "privy council" or cabinet.
3. The Lord's secret and future "Great Deed" becomes more and more important to Julian, since it is the only way she can explain the tensions between the goodness of God and human sin. Her point is strengthened here where she declares that out of obedience and reverence we should not even try to speculate on what this "Great Deed" will be.
4. Trusting God and not prying into God's secrets will continue to be a major element of Julian's faith.
5. Here we see a fleeting mention of the nature and function of the Communion of Saints in the Church.

⤚ 30

He gave me understanding in two parts:

The first part is our Savior and our salvation; this blessed part is open and clear and fair and light and plenteous, for all mankind that is of good will and shall be is included in this part; to this we are bound by God and attracted and advised, and taught inwardly by the Holy Spirit and outwardly by Holy Church in the same grace;[1] in this our Lord wishes us to be engaged, rejoicing in Him because He rejoices in us, and the more abundantly we accept this with reverence and humility, the more favor we earn from Him and the more help for ourselves; and thus, we can see and rejoice that our portion is our Lord.

The second part is hidden and sealed from us (that is to say, all except for our salvation), for that is our Lord's secret counsel,[2] and it is proper to the royal authority of God to hold His secret counsel in peace, and it is proper for His servants, out of obedience and reverence, not to wish to know His counsels.[3]

Our Lord has pity and compassion on us because some creatures make themselves so busy about His secrets; and I am certain if we were aware of how much we would please Him and ease ourselves by abandoning that, we would.[4]

The saints that are in heaven wish to know nothing except what our Lord wishes to show them, and also their love and their desire is ruled according to the will of our Lord.

Thus we ought to wish as they do—then shall we not wish nor desire anything except the will of our Lord just as they do, for we are all one in God's purpose.[5] And here was I taught that we should trust and rejoice only in our blessed Savior Jesus, for everything.

COMMENTS ON CHAPTER 31

1. The questions and doubts raised in Chapter 29.
2. This list of four (underlined) verbs is a translator's challenge because of three false cognates that all other translators have missed.

    A. ME *may* = "have the power" or the modern "can" (derived from "might").[131]

    B. ME *can* = "know" from the ME word *cann* = "to know or know how."[132]

    C. ME *wil* = "want" or "wish," not merely a future tense.[133]

    D. ME *shalle* = "definite intention."

    Most curiously: *may* means "can", *can* means "know," and *wil* means "want."
3. See Chapter 73, where Julian deals with our doubts that all shall be well.
4. Julian always relates the Father to power (*ability*), the Son to wisdom (*knowledge*), and the Holy Spirit to love (*wish*). (See Chapter 32.)
5. Julian understands salvation as being one-ed *into* the Trinity, joined as one within the community of the Father, Son, and Holy Spirit. And when that one-ing happens, each shall see from God's own point of view that "all things are well."
6. The ME word is *lufongyng*, and it is so significant in its original form that I decided only to modernize the spelling and not to translate it. This idea of God's "longing" for us is a frequent theme in Julian's work.
7. "And some are to come" was added by Julian in the late LV.
8. Christ's spiritual (ME: *gostly*) thirst is again defined as his desire for humans to be in heaven and share the Beatific Vision.
9. Julian sees salvation as full incorporation *into* Christ that will be achieved when we go to heaven.

⇒ 31

And so our good Lord replied to all the questions and doubts[1] that I could raise, saying most reassuringly: "I <u>have the ability</u> to make everything well, and I <u>have the knowledge</u> to make everything well, and I <u>have the wish</u> to make everything well, and I shall[2] make everything well; and thou shalt see for thyself that all manner of thing shall be well."[3]

Where He says, "I have the ability," I understand as referring to the Father;[4] and where He says, "I have the knowledge," I understand as referring to the Son; and where He says, "I have the wish to," I understand as referring to the Holy Spirit; and where He says "I shall," I understand as referring to the unity of the blessed Trinity (three Persons and one truth); and where He says, "Thou shalt see for thyself," I understand the one-ing of all mankind that shall be saved into the blissful Trinity.[5]

With these five words God wills [that we] be enclosed in rest and in peace; and thus shall the spiritual thirst of Christ have an end, for this is the spiritual thirst of Christ: the love-longing[6] that lasts and ever shall, until we see that sight on Doomsday.

[For of us who shall be saved, and shall be Christ's joy and His bliss, some are still here, and some are to come[7] (and so shall some be until that Day).]

Therefore, this is His thirst: a love-longing[8] to possess us all together wholly within Himself[9] for His joy, as I see it (for we are not now fully as wholly within Him as we shall be then).

10. The words "our Faith" in medieval England often meant literally "our Creed."

11. Julian now expostulates at length on three dimensions of the truth of Christ: His divinity, His humanity, and His headship.

12. Christ en-joys the Passion, that is, submerges it in and converts it into joy.

13. Here we find a subtle mystical suggestion: that Christ is not yet "fully glorified" and will not be so until all members of His (mystical) body that shall be saved have joined Him in heaven. Until then He continues to suffer *in his suffering people.*

14. Reminiscent of the Prayer of Humble Access in the *Book of Common Prayer:* "But thou art the same Lord whose property is always to have mercy."

15. A powerful theological statement: that salvation depends on our "yearning for Christ"—not only in being baptized, not only in "being saved," not only in "having faith," not only in doing "good works," but in *longing for* Christ. This echoes the affective spirituality of St. Bernard and St. Francis, but also suggests that the active agent in a human being's salvation is the will.

For we know in our Faith[10] (and also it was shown in all the revelations) that Christ Jesus is both God and man.[11]

Concerning the Godhead, He is Himself highest joy, and was so from without beginning, and shall be until without end; this endless joy can never be increased nor decreased in itself.

(This was plenteously seen in every showing—and specifically in the twelfth where He says: "It is I who am highest.")

Concerning Christ's manhood, it is known in our Faith, and also shown in the revelation, that He, with the strength of Godhead, for the sake of love, endured pains and sufferings and died in order to bring us to His bliss. And these are the works of Christ's manhood, in which He rejoices.[12]

(And that He showed in the ninth revelation, where He says: "It is a joy, a bliss, an endless delight to me that ever I suffered the Passion for thee.")

And this is the joy of Christ's deeds, and this He means where He said in the same showing that:

we are His joy, we are His recompense,

we are His honor, we are His crown.

Concerning Christ as our Head, He is glorified and beyond suffering, but concerning His Body (in which His members are knit), He is not yet fully glorified nor all beyond suffering; because the same desire and thirst which He had upon the cross (which desire, longing, and thirst, as I see it, was in Him from without beginning), the same desire and thirst has He still, and shall have until the time that the last soul that shall be saved has come up to His bliss.[13]

For as truly as there is a quality in God of compassion and pity,[14] just as truly there is a quality in God of thirst and yearning. And because of the strength of this yearning in Christ, we must yearn also for Him (without which yearning, no soul comes to heaven).[15]

This quality of yearning and thirst comes from the endless goodness of God (just as the quality of pity also comes from His endless goodness), and even though He has both yearning and pity, they are two different qualities, as I see it. In this goodness is based the essence

16. Christ's yearning for us acts almost like a magnet, "drawing us up" to His heavenly presence.

COMMENTS ON CHAPTER 32

1. Julian's emphasis here is on the words "all manner," which she understands to mean that even things that are petty or seemingly unimportant will still be part of God's "making all things well." C&W remind us of the verse: "Are not two sparrows sold for a penny? Yet without your Father's knowledge not one of them can fall to the ground. As for you, even the hairs of your head have all been counted" (Matthew 10:29–30). Even someone of no social standing is still precious to God and will be redeemed.

2. A clear indication that our judgment is not God's judgment, and what we may see as horrendously evil (something like the Black Death—or some notorious evildoer) are not necessarily evil in God's sight.

3. For a person committed to affective spirituality, this affirmation of "reason" by Julian comes as a slight surprise, but she is no sentimentalist, and we are reminded of the words we read later in Chapter 41: "it is in our feeling, our foolishness, that the cause of our weakness lies."

4. Once again we see Julian's Trinity: the Father=Power; the Son=Wisdom; the Holy Spirit=Goodness and Love.

5. Julian's ME words are *take now hede*, a clear parallel to Jesus' frequent words: "Truly, I say to you. . . ." It is Jesus saying, "Listen to this *now*, and at the *end* you will see it fulfilled."

of the spiritual thirst, which lasts in Him as long as we are in need, drawing us up[16] to His bliss.

(All this was seen in the showing forth of His compassion, for that shall cease on Doomsday.)

Thus He has pity and compassion on us, and He has a yearning to possess us, and His wisdom and His love do not permit the End to come until the best possible time.

⌐ 32

One time our good Lord said: "All manner of thing shall be well"; and another time He said: "Thou shalt see for thyself that all manner of thing shall be well"; and from these two sentences the soul recognized several implications:

One was this: that He wishes us to be aware that not only does He take heed to noble and great things, but also to little and small things, to lowly and simple things, both to one and to the other; and so means He in that He says, "All manner of thing shall be well"; for He wills that we be aware that the least little thing shall not be forgotten.[1]

Another understanding is this: that, from our point of view, there are many deeds evilly done and such great harm given that it seems to us that it would be impossible that ever it should come to a good end;[2] and we look upon this, sorrowing and mourning because of it, so that we cannot take our ease in the joyful beholding of God as we would like to do; and the cause is this: that the use of our reason is now so blind, so lowly, and so stupid[3] that we cannot know the exalted, wondrous Wisdom, the Power, and the Goodness of the blessed Trinity.[4] And this is what He means when He says, "Thou shalt see for thyself that all manner of thing shall be well," as if He said, "Pay attention to this now,[5] faithfully and trustingly; and at the last end thou shalt see it in fullness of joy."

And thus, in these same previous five words: "I am able to make everything well, etc." I interpret a mighty comfort about all the deeds of our Lord God that are still to come.

6. The rest of this Chapter and the first five paragraphs of Chapter 33 do not appear in the SV. They are the product of Julian's twenty years of reflection. The apparent contradiction had long been on her mind.

7. Another of Julian's direct comments on the mysterious "Great Deed" that will be done on the Last Day. This is the ultimate expression of faith for Julian, who properly gives up wrestling with the paradox between God's goodness and the existence of sin by recognizing that it is none of her business to understand these matters which are beyond her.

8. Proverbs 30:5—"God's every promise has stood the test." Isaiah 40:8—"the word of our God will endure for ever." Matthew 24:35—"Heaven and earth will pass away, but my words will not pass away."

9. A poignant three words describing the damned as those who "die without love" or "die outside of love" (ME: *oute of cheryte*).

10. Julian accurately describes the teachings of the Church, and she does *not* propose to depart from those teachings, however difficult it is for her to understand hell and damnation. She lists those the Church declares in hell:

   A. The fallen angels (now the demons);

   B. The unbaptized heathens;

   C. Christians who live unchristian lives.

11. "What is impossible for men is possible for God" (Luke 18:27).

12. "Heaven and earth will pass away, but my words will never pass away" (Mark 13:31). "So it is with my word issuing from my mouth; it will not return to me empty without accomplishing my purpose and succeeding in the task for which I sent it" (Isaiah 55:11).

13. Here is Julian's solution to the conundrum: she will remain faithful to the Church's teachings, but will also have faith that the mysterious "Great Deed" will provide a solution.

[6]There is a Deed which the blessed Trinity shall do on the Last Day, as I see it, and what the Deed shall be, and how it shall be done, is unknown to all creatures that are beneath Christ, and shall remain so until when it is done.

The Goodness and the Love of our Lord God wills that we be aware that it shall be done, but His Power and Wisdom by the same Love wishes to keep and hide from us what it shall be and how it shall be done. (And the reason why He wills that we know it in this way is because He wishes us to be more at ease in our soul and more peaceful in love, refraining from paying attention to all temptations that could obstruct us from truth, and rejoicing in Him.)

This is the Great Deed intended by our Lord God from without beginning, treasured and hidden in His blessed breast, known only to Himself, by which Deed He shall make all things well.

For as the blessed Trinity created all things from nothing, just so the same blessed Trinity shall make well all that is not well.[7]

At this insight I marveled greatly, and looked at our Faith, marveling thus: our Faith is based in God's word, and it is part of our Faith that we believe that God's word shall be preserved in all things,[8] and one point of our Faith is that many creatures shall be damned (as were the angels who fell out of heaven because of pride—who are now demons), and many on earth who die outside of the Faith of Holy Church (that is to say, those who are heathen men and also men who have received Christianity but live unchristian lives and so die without love[9]) all these shall be damned to hell without end, as Holy Church teaches me to believe.[10]

Given all this, it seemed to me that it was impossible that all manner of thing would be well as our Lord showed at this time; and in regard to this, I had no other answer in any showing of our Lord God except this: "What is impossible for thee is not impossible for me.[11] I shall preserve my word in all things,[12] and I shall make everything well."

Thus I was taught by the grace of God that I should steadfastly keep myself in the Faith as I had interpreted it before, and also[13] that I should firmly believe that everything shall be well as our Lord showed

COMMENTS ON CHAPTER 33

1. The ME in the PV is *to take prefe of,* meaning "to prove" or "to make trial of." W&J suggest: "to put anything to the test."

2. A reader must take Julian at her word, here. Critics have tried to suggest that Julian includes statements like this only so she won't get in trouble with Church authorities. To my mind, those who believe her to be duplicitous don't know Julian very well.

3. Julian's simple description of the damned: first, "all creatures that are of the Devil's character and who end that way" (excepting those who are converted before death), and then the devastating words, "there is no more mention made of them before God." This suggests that the damned are "forgotten" by God—which theologically would mean that they virtually go out of existence. We are reminded of Psalm 69:30 (BCP)—"Let them be wiped out of the book of the living and not be written among the righteous."

4. This is just as she had asked in Chapter 2.

5. Julian was a woman of her day, and this is precisely what the fourteenth-century Church taught, however appalling it sounds to the modern ear. And it must be remembered that in all her life Julian had never seen or met an "unconverted" Jew, since all Jews were deported from England in 1299.

at the same time; because this is the Great Deed that our Lord shall do, in which Deed He shall preserve His word in everything and He shall make well all that is not well. But what the Deed shall be, and how it shall be done, there is no creature beneath Christ that either knows it or shall know it until it is done (according to the understanding that I received of our Lord's meaning at this time).

⇌ 33

And still in this showing I desired, as far as I dared, that I might have had full view of hell and purgatory. (But it was not my intention to undertake to <u>challenge</u>[1] anything that is part of the Faith—for I believe truthfully that hell and purgatory are for the same purpose that Holy Church teaches—but my intention was that for the sake of learning I might have seen everything that is part of my Faith, whereby I could live more to God's honor and to my benefit.)[2]

But in spite of my desire I learned nothing whatsoever about this (except as it was said before in the fifth showing where I saw that the Devil was reproached by God and endlessly damned, in which showing I interpreted that all creatures that are of the Devil's character in this life and who end that way, there is no more mention made of them before God and all His holy ones[3] than of the Devil, notwithstanding that they are of mankind, whether they have been baptized or not).

Although the revelation of goodness was shown in which little mention of evil was made, yet in it I was not drawn away from any point of the Faith that Holy Church teaches me to believe.

I saw the Passion of Christ in various showings (in the second, in the fifth, and in the eighth showings, as I said before) where I had a partial experience of the sorrow of Our Lady and of His true friends who saw Him in pain,[4] but I did not see as specially described in detail the Jews that did Him to death. Nevertheless, I knew in my Faith that they were accursed and damned without end—except for those that were converted by grace.[5]

6. Future faith in God's deeds depends upon our perceptions of God's past deeds.

7. Julian recognizes the limits God has placed on her ability to know all things—and she accepts that limitation in faith. She even "overstates" the situation in claiming that the more we try to find out God's "secrets," the further we shall be from knowing them.

COMMENTS ON CHAPTER 34

1. Julian is aware that in her revelations she has been shown "secrets" (ME: *privityes*) which are not generally known or believed.

2. And one of the reasons these insights have not been more common is "because of our blindness and ignorance" (ME: *our blyndnes and our onknowyng*).

3. W&J suggest the word "with," meaning "besides" or "as a supplement to"—but "through" seems to fit Julian's repeated statements here about the adequacy of Church teaching.

I was strengthened and taught without exception to keep myself in every detail in the Faith, and in all that I had understood before, hoping that I was in that Faith with the mercy and the grace of God, desiring and praying in my intentions that I might continue therein until my life's end.

It is God's will that we have great regard for all His deeds that He has done, for He wills thereby that we know, trust, and believe all that He shall do,[6] and evermore it is necessary for us to leave off involving ourselves with what the Deed shall be, and desire to be like our brethren who are the saints in heaven who wish absolutely nothing but God's will, then shall we rejoice only in God and be well satisfied both with His hiding and with His showing, for I saw truly in our Lord's meaning that the more we busy ourselves to know His secrets in this or any other thing, the farther shall we be from the knowledge of them.[7]

⇒ 34

Our Lord God showed two kinds of <u>secrecies</u>: one is the Great Secret with all the secret details that are part of it, and these things He wills that we understand are hidden until the time that He will clearly show them to us; the other are the <u>secrets</u> which He Himself showed openly in this revelation, for they are <u>secrets</u> that He wishes to make open and known to us; for He wants us to be aware that it is His will that we know them.[1]

They are secrets to us not only because He wills they be secrets to us, but they are secrets to us because of our <u>blindness and our ignorance</u>.[2]

Concerning those weaknesses He has great pity, and therefore He wishes to make the secrets more open to us Himself, by which we can know Him and love Him and cleave to Him.

For all that is advantageous for us to be aware of and to know, full graciously our good Lord will show us <u>through</u>[3] all the preaching and teaching of Holy Church.

4. In the BV the first phrase is "for it is His Holy Church," but in the PV it is "for He it is, Holy Church." One might recall Jesus' words: "I am the way, the truth, and the life" (John 14:6). This is a dramatic statement of the Church as the mystical body of Christ.

5. God's only revelation to Julian about sin was: "Don't worry about it. All shall be well."

COMMENTS ON CHAPTER 35

1. For the first time, Julian is asking to know the future, and God refuses her desire.

2. In the SV, the phrase is "a certain *person* whom I loved, how it should be with *her*," indicating that this person was female. Curiously, twenty years later, in the LV, it is a certain "creature" and the hope is that the person "would continue in good living." If Julian were Julian Erpingham, as I have suggested, she might be referring to her younger sister Joan (b. 1344). Joan married Sir Edward Wodehouse in 1359.

3. Here we have a mystical insight: by desiring more knowledge than God offered, Julian "hindered" herself.

4. This is a gentle slap on the hand: Julian's temptation was to become a kind of clairvoyant or "wise woman," and God does not respond.

God showed the very great pleasure that He has in all men and women who strongly and humbly and willingly receive the preaching and teaching of Holy Church, for He is Holy Church—

He is the foundation,

He is the essence,

He is the teaching,

He is the teacher,

He is the goal,

He is the reward for which every

natural soul toils.[4]

And this is known and shall be known to every soul to which the Holy Spirit declares it. And I hope truly that He will assist all those who seek in this way, for they seek God.

All this that I have said now, and more that I shall say later, is reassuring against sin; for in the third showing when I saw that God does all that is done, I saw no sin, and then I saw that all is well. And when God showed me as regards sin, then He said: "All shall be well."[5]

⇒ 35

When God Almighty had shown so plentifully and so fully of His goodness, I desired to know of a certain creature that I loved if it would continue[1] in good living (which I hoped by the grace of God was begun).[2]

And in this particular desire, it seemed that I hindered myself, because I was not shown at this time.[3]

And then I was answered in my reason, as it were by a friendly go-between: "Take this generally, and see the graciousness of the Lord God as He reveals it to thee; for it is more honor to God for thee to see Him in all things than in any special thing."[4]

I agreed, and with that I learned that it is more honor to God to understand all things in general than to delight in anything in particular.

5. Julian teaches herself patience: "when it is time, we shall see it." She struggles to leave the initiative for revelation to God.

6. This is very solid theology: all things happen either by God's active or His permissive will, and sometimes what God allows may seem to us "evil."

7. Again Julian expresses the Scholastic understanding that God's attributes are part of His essence: God *is* rightfulness itself.

8. *All* things are brought to a good end—even those things which seem unredeemable to human understanding.

9. Here we have clear evidence that Julian's understanding of predestination is "*single* predestination"—that is, all are predestined for heaven.

10. What seems a jump in subject matter is only a natural process in which consideration of the "preservation" of rightfulness on God's part will require mercy.

11. One is reminded of Job's situation in which the Devil is given permission to tempt Job (Job 1:9–12).

And if I would do wisely following this teaching, not only should I not be joyful for anything in particular, but also not be greatly anxious over any manner of thing, for "All shall be well." The fullness of joy is to behold God in everything.

For by the same blessed Power, Wisdom, and Love by which He created all things, to the same end our good Lord leads those things constantly, and He shall bring Himself to them, and when it is time, we shall see it.[5]

All that our Lord does is rightful, what he allows is honorable, and in these two is included both good and evil.[6]

All that is good our Lord does, and what is evil our Lord tolerates. (I say not that any evil is honorable, but I say the toleration of our Lord God is honorable, whereby His goodness shall be known without end in His marvelous humility and gentleness, by the action of mercy and grace.)

Rightfulness is that thing which is so good that it cannot be better than it is, for God Himself is true rightfulness,[7] and all His works are done rightfully as they are appointed from without beginning by His high Power, His high Wisdom, His high Goodness.

And just as He ordained all for the best, just so He works constantly and leads it to that same end;[8] and He is ever most pleased with Himself and with His works.

The beholding of this blissful accord is most sweet to the soul that sees by grace.

All the souls that shall be saved in heaven without end are created rightful in the sight of God,[9] and by His own goodness, and in this rightfulness we are endlessly and marvelously preserved, more than all other created things.

[10]Mercy is an action that comes from the goodness of God, and it shall remain in action as long as sin is permitted to pursue rightful souls,[11] and when sin has no longer permission to pursue, then shall the action of mercy cease. And then shall all be brought to rightfulness and remain therein without end.

12. To summarize these somewhat confusing paragraphs: God tolerates our falling into sin, but even in that sin we are preserved and protected by God, and eventually by God's mercy we are forgiven and attain heaven.

COMMENTS ON CHAPTER 36

1. "By me" probably means "regarding me," but it is enticing to think that the "deed" is the extension of Julian's writings to our modern world. The underlined text is found only in PV, and "me" in C text is "him."
2. This underlined paragraph occurs only in the PV. If God's deed is the forgiveness of sin, then Julian says her only part in it is to be the sinner who is forgiven.
3. Thomas Aquinas holds that all human souls naturally seek the Good. Julian here holds that a "reverent soul" naturally desires God's will—paradoxically "by grace" (which is usually seen as a dynamic distinct from nature).
4. This reference is *not* to the "Great Deed" that will happen on the Last Day—in that "it shall be begun here" and (later) "it shall last thus in action until the Last Day." It would seem that she may be discussing the function of mercy and the function of grace in the present forgiving of sins.

By His permission we fall, and in His blessed Love with His Power and His Wisdom we are preserved, and by mercy and grace we are raised to many more joys.[12]

And thus in rightfulness and in mercy He wishes to be known and loved now and without end. And the soul that wisely holds onto this in grace, is well pleased with both, and endlessly rejoices.

⁘ 36

Our Lord God showed me that a deed shall be done and He Himself shall do it; <u>and it shall be honorable and marvelous and fruitful, and by me it shall be done,[1] and He Himself shall do it.</u>

<u>And this is the highest joy that the soul recognized: that God Himself shall do it, and I shall do nothing at all except sin, and my sin shall not hinder His goodness from working.</u>[2]

And I saw that the beholding of this is a heavenly joy in a fearful soul which evermore naturally by grace desires God's will.[3]

This deed shall be begun here,[4] and it shall be honorable to God and plentifully beneficial to His lovers on earth, and ever as we come to heaven we shall see it in marvelous joy, and it shall last thus in action until the Last Day, and the honor and the bliss of it shall continue in heaven before God and all His holy ones without end.

In this way was this deed seen and interpreted in our Lord's intention, and the reason He showed it is to cause us to rejoice in Him and all His works.

When I saw His showing continued, I understood that it was shown as a great event which was to come (which God showed that He Himself would do). This deed has these qualities which I mentioned before. This He showed most blissfully, intending that I should accept it wisely, faithfully, and trustingly.

But what this deed would be, that was kept secret from me. And in this I saw that He wills not that we fear to know the things that He shows—He shows them because He wishes us to know them, and by

5. Julian may be reminding herself that one need not fear having God's secrets revealed.

6. The word in ME is *close* or "enclosed." C&W suggest a parallel to official chancery practice in which a letter is recorded as "lettre isealed" or "lettre iopened," meaning (a) the mere receipt of the letter is noted, or (b) the contents of the letter have been noted.

7. A familiar teaching of Julian's—perhaps speaking to her own impatience—that there is much about God, the divine nature, salvation, and other such matters that God has not seen fit to reveal. She counsels patience and faith. (See Ecclesiasticus 3:23—"Do not busy yourself with matters that are beyond you; even what has been shown you is above the grasp of mortals.")

8. Julian may be making the point as she does elsewhere that she merely represents all who shall be saved.

9. ME word is *matter*—"cause" in the sense of "material to work with."

10. This is an extremely difficult line: ME has *turne us to the beholdyng of the reprovyd*, which has several possible translations. *The reprovyd* can mean "the judged," "the Reprobate" (that is, the Devil), "the blamed." It seems that Julian is referring here to her questions about those in purgatory and hell, so I have used "those who have been judged," set in opposition to "those who shall be saved."

11. For this phrase PV has "Let me alone." The sense of our translation (from BV) seems more fitting than the pettish sounding "Let me alone." Once again, Julian is counseled to think less of marginal matters and concentrate on her Lord and His love.

12. This was a radical thought in the fourteenth-century English Church in which concern about salvation, damnation, and purgatory seemed to fill everyone's consciousness. The Lord is telling Julian not to bother herself about those matters, but to concentrate on God alone.

this knowledge He wills that we love Him and delight in Him and endlessly rejoice in Him.[5]

Because of the great love that He has for us, He shows us all that is honorable and beneficial for the present. The things that He wills to have secret now, still of His great goodness, He shows them <u>concealed</u>,[6] in which showing He wills that we believe and recognize that we shall see them truly in His endless bliss.

Then we ought to rejoice in Him both for all that He shows, and for all that He hides;[7] and if we willingly and humbly do this, we shall find therein great ease, and we shall have endless favor from Him for that.

Thus is the interpretation of this word: that it shall be done by me[8] (that is, the general man, this is to say, all that shall be saved). It shall be honorable and marvelous and fruitful, and God Himself shall do it. And this shall be the highest joy that can be, to behold the deed that God Himself shall do, and man shall do absolutely nothing except sin.

Then means our Lord God thus: as if He said: "Behold and see.

Here thou hast <u>cause</u>[9] for humility;

here thou hast cause for love;

here thou hast cause to know thyself;

here thou hast cause to rejoice in me; and because of my love, do rejoice in me, for of all things, with that thou canst most please me."

And as long as we are in this life, whenever we by our folly turn to considering <u>those who have been judged</u>,[10] tenderly our Lord God touches us and blessedly calls us, saying in our soul: "Let me be all thy love,[11] my dearworthy child. Occupy thyself with me, for I am enough for thee, and rejoice in thy Savior and in thy salvation."[12]

13. It has become commonplace for Christian mystics to speak of being "pierced" by an arrow or spear of insight or love. "It" refers to the error of "considering those who have been judged."

14. Presumably, these "poor creatures" are those "who have been judged" as above.

15. This *seems* like the sudden introduction of a new subject, but for Julian this unidentified "second deed" that God has begun to do clearly involves the working of miracles, and God here legitimizes this understanding.

16. Julian predicts that sorrow and tribulation are always precedents of soon-to-come redeeming miracles.

17. Again we see Julian's "code words" for the Holy Trinity: Power, Wisdom, and Goodness.

18. Julian never denies sorrow, suffering, and temptations, but suggests that they are always signs that a miracle is coming.

And I am certain that this is our Lord's action in us. The soul that is pierced with it by grace shall see it and experience it.[13]

And though it is so that this deed be truly understood for the general man, yet it does not exclude the particular; for what our good Lord wishes to do in regard to His poor creatures,[14] is now unknown to me.

This deed and the other I mentioned before, they are not both one, but two different ones. However, this deed shall be done sooner, and that other one shall be when we come to heaven.

And to whom our Lord gives it, this deed can be known here in part, but the Great Deed mentioned before shall neither be known in heaven nor earth until it is done.

[15]Besides this, He gave special understanding and teaching about the working of miracles, thus: "It is known that I have done miracles here before, many and very exalted and astounding, honorable and great; and just as I have done in the past, so I do now constantly, and shall do in the course of time." It is known that before miracles come sorrow and anguish and tribulation; and that is so that we would know our own feebleness and our misfortune that we have fallen into by sin in order to humble us, and cause us to fear God, crying for help and grace.[16]

And great miracles come after that, and they come from the exalted Power, Wisdom, and Goodness of God,[17] showing His strength and the joys of heaven (in so far as that can be in this passing life), and that in order to strengthen our faith and to increase our hope, in love. For that reason it pleases Him to be known and honored in miracles.

Then He means thus: He wills that we be not carried overly low because of sorrows and temptations that befall us,[18] for it has ever been this way before the coming of miracles.

COMMENTS ON CHAPTER 37

1. Another wonderful autobiographical note: Julian forgets about sin in the midst of her ecstatic "gazing upon" God, and God simply waits for her to catch up.
2. Another instance of Julian's recollection of her fellow Christians and her responsibility to share the revelations God gives her.
3. The reminder that she would sin (in the midst of a discussion of those who are judged) makes her a little nervous, but God quickly gives her assurance that he will "keep" her—and her fellow Christians—safely.
4. ME has *godly wil* (in BV) or *godly wille* (in PV). Etymologically "godly" means "god-like," so I have translated it as "divine will." The point is that in each soul there is a "splinter" of divinity, a "spark" (to use Meister Eckhardt's word) of God. And the Christian commitment is to foster that godly will so as to bring it into constant conformity with the will of God.
5. In Chapter 28 Julian wrote:"each kind compassion that man has toward his fellow Christian with love, it is Christ in him." This is the same sentiment: that a "dimension" of God dwells within each human being and makes goodness possible.
6. God's universal love for us is not reserved only for heaven, but exists here and now.
7. Julian gives assurance that even in the midst of sin, God does not separate Himself from us, but it is we in our sin who "fall away from love"—an elegant definition of sin. (See Romans 7:13–25.)

⌒ 37

God reminded me that I would sin; and because of the delight that I had in gazing upon Him, I did not pay heed quickly to that showing. And our Lord most mercifully waited and gave me grace to listen.[1] (And this showing I received particularly to myself, but by all the gracious comfort that follows, as you shall see, I was taught to accept it on behalf of all my fellow Christians—all in general, and nothing in particular.) Though our Lord showed me that I would sin, by "me alone" is meant "all."[2]

And in this I perceived a gentle anxiety, and to this our Lord answered: "I keep thee full safely."[3] This word was said with more love and steadiness and spiritual protection than I know how or am able to tell.

As it was shown that I would sin, in just the same way was the comfort shown—safety and protection for all fellow Christians.

What can make me love my fellow Christians more than to see in God that He loves all that shall be saved as if they were all one soul? For in every soul that shall be saved is a <u>divine will</u>[4] that never consented to sin nor ever shall; just as there is a savage will in the lower part of man which can will no good, so, too, there is a divine will in the higher part of man which will is so good that it can never will evil, but always good, and because of that we are what He loves and endlessly we do what delights Him.[5]

And this our Lord showed in the completeness of love in which we stand in His sight—yea, that He loves us now as well while we are here as He shall when we are there before His blessed face.[6]

So because of the falling away from love on our part, from that is all our difficulty.[7]

COMMENTS ON CHAPTER 38

1. The audience for whom Julian writes is not all humanity, but her fellow Christians who recognize that sin causes spiritual pain and sorrow.
2. God never allows sin to be an impediment to sanctification. And then, to illustrate the point, Julian adds a list of some notable saints who had also been notable sinners.
3. In Julian's day, Mary Magdalene was identified with the sinful woman who washed Jesus' feet (Luke 7:44) and was considered a repentant harlot.
4. Medieval tradition held that after the Resurrection St. Thomas the Apostle went east and established Christian communities in India (which still refer to themselves as "Mar Thoma" ["Father Thomas"] Churches).
5. That is, *repented* and *forgiven* sins become honors.

⮞ 38

Also God showed that sin shall not be shame, but honor to man—for just as for every sin there is a corresponding pain in reality, just so, for every sin, to the same soul is given a blessing by love.[1]

Just as various sins are punished with various pains according to how grievous they are, just so shall they be rewarded with different joys in heaven for their victories after the sins have been painful and sorrowful to the soul on earth.

For the soul that shall come to heaven is so precious to God and the place so honor-filled that the goodness of God never permits the soul that shall finally come there to sin unless those sinners of that sort are to be rewarded and made known in Holy Church on earth and also in heaven without end, and blessedly made good by exceeding honors.[2]

In this vision my understanding was lifted up into heaven; and then God brought cheerfully to my mind David and others in the Old Law with him without number, and in the New Law He brought to my mind first Mary Magdalene,[3] Peter and Paul, and Thomas of India,[4] and Saint John of Beverley, and others also without number, and how they are recognized in the Church on earth along with their sins, and it is to them no shame, but all of the sins have been changed to honor.

Because of that our gracious Lord shows about sins here in part like what it is there in fullness, for there the sign of sin is turned to honor.[5]

In comfort to us because of his familiarity our Lord showed Saint John of Beverley, very exalted, and brought to my mind how he is a neighbor at hand and of our acquaintance. And God called him "Saint John of Beverley" as clearly as we do, and did so with a very glad, sweet expression showing that he is a most exalted saint in heaven in His sight, and a blessed one. With this He made mention that in Saint John's youth and in his tender time of life, he was a dearworthy servant of God, much loving and fearing God, and nevertheless God

6. "Losing time" probably means "losing credits that may have been accumulated"—similar to a convict accumulating "good time."
7. See Appendix 5, "Saint John of Beverley," to explain John of Beverley's inclusion in this list of forgiven sinners. This appendix provides information on what C&W call "a now lost legend." Note that Julian sees the miracles worked at St. John's shrine as evidence that God loves St. John in spite of his having sinned.

COMMENTS ON CHAPTER 39

1. Another instance of Julian's specific inclusion of both genders: "a man and woman." Interestingly (and characteristically) she immediately reverts to literary convention in using the masculine pronouns as generic.
2. Julian sees the process of sacramental confession and absolution as a major function of the Church, and as the one place where forgiveness can be assured.
3. The ME has *domysman* or "judge man," referring to the confessor's responsibility to pass judgment on one's sins. ME documents listing appropriate penances were common.
4. Here we see Julian's short catalog of humiliations that please God: (a) penance, (b) sickness, (c) reproof and despite by the world, and (d) grievances and temptations. This seems to suggest that Julian herself may well have experienced "reproof and despite" by the world—possibly (if she was Julian Erpingham) for having chosen the anchoritic life while she still had children living.

allowed him to fall, mercifully protecting him so that he did not perish nor <u>lose any time</u>.[6] And afterward, God raised him to many times more grace, and by the contrition and humility that He showed in his living, God has given him in heaven manifold joys exceeding what he would have had if he had not fallen. And God shows that this is true on earth by the working of plenteous miracles around Saint John's body constantly.[7]

And all this was to make us glad and cheerful in love.

 # 39

Sin is the harshest scourge that any chosen soul can be struck with. This scourge chastises a man and woman[1] terribly and damages him in his own eyes to such an extent that sometimes he thinks of himself as not worthy except to sink into hell—until contrition seizes him by the touching of the Holy Spirit and changes the bitterness into hopes for God's mercy.

Then his wounds begin to heal and the soul, directed into the life of Holy Church, begins to revive. The Holy Spirit leads him to Confession, willingly to confess his sins, nakedly and honestly, with great sorrow and great shame that he has so befouled the fair image of God.[2]

Then he undertakes Penance for every sin, imposed by his <u>Confessor</u>[3] (which is instructed in Holy Church by the teaching of the Holy Spirit).

And this is one humiliation that much pleases God; and also humbly bearing bodily sickness sent from God; and also sorrow and shame from without, and reproof and despising of the world with all kinds of grievance and temptations which we are thrown into, bodily and spiritually.[4] Most preciously our good Lord protects us when it seems to us that we are nearly forsaken and cast away because of our sin and because we see that we have deserved it. And because of the humility that we gain in these troubles, we are raised very high in God's sight, by His grace.

5. Julian speaks autobiographically as she repeats the "three wounds" she had asked for in Chapter 2: contrition, compassion, and yearning for God.

6. It seems that Julian is describing a nonsacramental absolution from sin: that when the Lord gives this "particular grace" with great contrition one is released from sin without priestly intervention.

7. ME has *medicynes*.

8. ME has *worships* which means "honors." I have translated it as "awards" in the sense that the wounds of sin are made badges of grace.

9. This is an awkward phrase: it means that one will not lose any credit for the troubles he or she has gone through because of sin.

10. Julian does not deny sin, but denies that it impedes God's love for us, and gives great hope to a well-meaning sinner.

11. There is no idea of total depravity here. Julian makes a strong (and almost poetic) point that goodness is "in" us, in our very human nature.

12. Once again, one wonders to what degree this is autobiographical: has Julian experienced enemies who are "terrible and fierce" against her? And one even wonders, has she given them raw material by her own sinning?

Also our Lord visits whom He will with particular grace with so great contrition (also with compassion and true yearning for God)[5] that they are suddenly released from sin and pain and taken up to bliss and made equal with the exalted saints.[6]

By contrition we are made pure,

by compassion we are made ready,

and by true yearning for God we are made worthy.

These are three means, as I understand, by which all souls come to heaven—that is to say, those who have been sinners on earth and shall be saved.

By these <u>remedies</u>[7] it would be fitting for every soul to be healed. And even though the soul is healed, its wounds are seen before God, not as wounds, but as <u>awards</u>.[8] And so contrariwise, as we are punished here with sorrow and with penance, we shall be rewarded in heaven by the gracious love of our Lord God almighty who wills that no one who comes there lose his efforts in any degree,[9] for He considers sin as sorrow and pain for His lovers to whom because of love He allots no blame.

The recompense that we shall receive shall not be trivial, but it shall be exalted, glorious, and full of honor. And in this way shall all shame be transformed to honor and more joy.

Our gracious Lord does not wish His servants to despair because of frequent or grievous falling, because our falling does not prevent Him from loving us.[10]

Peace and love are always in us, existing and working, but we are not always in peace and in love.[11] However, He wills that we take heed in this way—that He is the ground of all our whole life in love, and, furthermore, that He is our everlasting protector and mightily defends us against all our enemies who are most terrible and fierce against us (and our need is so much the more because we give those enemies opportunity by our falling).[12]

COMMENTS ON CHAPTER 40

1. Julian speaks of "friendship" with her Lord twenty-six times in her book. It is part of her understanding Him to be "homely." See John 15:15—"No longer do I call you servants ... I have called you friends."
2. Obviously in the gentle and poetic sense of "inspires us." W&J translate it as "moves."
3. Julian speaks of the classical spiritual "self examen" by which one asks God to reveal one's sins in preparation for confessing them. It also seems clear in all this writing that Julian herself has experienced the elation of having her sins forgiven.
4. God's "anger" for our sin is only our own imagination and projection, for as Julian says later, "God cannot be angry because anger is the opposite of friendship."
5. Julian equates the earthly experience of absolution with the joy of heaven.
6. Here is Julian's affirmative sense of predestination.
7. In ME *swete* does not convey the "preciousness" of the word's nineteenth-century use—it carries more accurately the simple sense of "pleasing."
8. Not only is "yearning for God" one of Julian's "three wounds," but it is the core of her practical spirituality. And here she joins her own yearning for Him with the yearning of Christ to have us one-ed with Him.
9. See Romans 6:1–2—"Shall we persist in sin, so that there may be all the more grace? Certainly not!"

➣ 40

It is a supreme friendship[1] of our gracious Lord that He protects us so tenderly while we are in our sin.

Furthermore, He <u>touches</u>[2] us most secretly and shows us our sin by the sweet light of mercy and grace.[3] But when we see ourselves so foul, then we imagine that God is angry with us for our sin,[4] and then by the Holy Spirit we are guided by contrition to prayer and to the desire to amend our life with all our might, in order to abate the anger of God,[4] until the time that we discover a peace in soul and a quietness in conscience.

Then we hope that God has forgiven us our sins—and it is true.

And then our gracious Lord shows Himself to the soul, all merrily and with glad countenance, with friendly greeting, as if the soul had been in pain and in prison, saying sweetly thus: "My dearly beloved, I am glad thou hast come to me. In all thy woe, I have always been with thee, and now thou seest my loving and we are one-ed in bliss."

In this way are sins forgiven by mercy and grace and our soul honorably received in joy (just as it shall be when it comes to heaven)[5] as often as it comes by the gracious working of the Holy Spirit and the virtue of Christ's Passion.

Here I understand truly that everything is prepared for us by the great goodness of God[6] to such an extent that whenever we are ourselves in peace and love, we are truly safe. But because we cannot have this in fullness while we are here, therefore it is right for us evermore to believe in <u>sweet</u> prayer[7] and in love-filled yearning[8] with our Lord Jesus. He yearns ever to bring us to the fullness of joy (as it was said before where He shows the spiritual thirst).

But now, because of all this spiritual comfort that is spoken of above, if any man or woman is led by folly to say or to think: "If this is true, then it would be good to sin in order to have more reward," or else to place less weight on sin, beware of this leading, for truly, if it comes, it is untrue and from the enemy.[9]

10. It is important to note that while Julian has tended to play down the significance of sin in other places—for example, "Sin hath no essence"—she does not compromise on the terrible pain of sin to the good Christian.

11. PV has *hatheth no helle* but BV has *hath non helle*.

12. Once again, the optimist Julian affirms the goodness of all things—excepting only sin.

13. This recalls the beginning of Chapter 31: "I am able to make everything well, and I know how to make everything well, and I wish to make everything well, and I shall make everything well."

14. This is probably a reference to Christ's redefinition of the Old Testament's Ten Commandments with Christ's "new" commandments to love God, our neighbors, and our enemies.

15. Just as Julian said Christ IS the Church, so here she says He IS "this love." See Chapter 26: "It is I who am all." (See 1 John 4:16b—"God is love.")

16. ME has *nakidly*.

Because the same true love that touches us all by His blessed comfort, that same blessed love teaches us that we should hate sin for the sake of love alone.

And I am certain, from my own experience, that the more every natural soul sees this in the gracious love of our Lord God, the more loath it will be to sin, and the more it will be ashamed.

For if before us were laid all the pains in hell and in purgatory and on earth, death and all the rest, over against sin, we ought rather to choose all that pain than sin, because sin is so vile and so much to be hated, that it cannot be compared to any pain—if that pain is not sin.[10]

To me was shown no more cruel hell than sin, for a natural soul <u>hates</u>[11] <u>no hell</u> except sin, and all is good except sin, and nothing is evil except sin.[12]

And when we direct our attention to love and humility, by the working of mercy and grace, we are made all fair and pure.

As powerful and as wise as God is to save man, also He is just as willing to do so.[13]

Christ Himself is the foundation of all the laws of Christian men, and He taught us to do good against evil.[14]

Here we can see that He is Himself this Love,[15] and He does to us as He teaches us to do, for He wills that we be like Him in wholeness of endless love for ourselves and for our fellow Christians.

No more than His love for us is broken off because of our sin, so no more does He will that our love for ourselves and for our fellow Christians be broken off.

But <u>plainly</u>[16] hate sin and endlessly love the soul as God loves it.

Then would we hate sin just as God hates it, and love the soul just as God loves it, for this word that God said is an endless comfort: "I keep thee full safely."

COMMENTS ON CHAPTER 41

1. "Rightful" is an unusual word that Julian uses with some frequency. Its true and original meaning is "just"—that is, prayer is "just" when it is complete submission to the will of God.

2. Julian would maintain (as she does later) that *all* honest prayer is "heard" by God.

3. Prayer, for Julian, has nothing to do with feeling good or being "fulfilled." It is simply a matter of intentionally recognizing one's union with and dependence on God. For her, prayer is always oriented exclusively toward the will of God, never toward one's own emotional reactions or its "practical" fulfillment.

4. Julian's ME has *I am ground of thi besekyng.* It reminds us of her earlier proposition that when we have compassion on our fellow Christians (Chapter 28), it is Christ within us; so, too, when we pray, it is Christ praying within us.

5. Julian's utter simplicity is very powerful. If it is God who does our praying within us, and if we are submissive to His presence, it follows that we will never pray for something that God is not prepared to give us anyway. Prayer is "unitive," not "productive."

6. Prayer does not produce "results" from God that are any different from what God would do if we did not pray. Our praying does not alter God, but makes us more sensitive to His will. If our prayers seem to be "answered," it is only because those prayers have corresponded with God's will.

7. This is a radical statement for a fourteenth-century Catholic. She proposes that goodness and grace come from God alone, and is not "earned" by our praying.

⌒ 41

After this our Lord showed regarding prayer, and in this showing two applications of our Lord's meaning: one is <u>rightful</u>[1] prayer, the other is sure trust. And yet frequently our trust is not complete, for we are not certain that God hears us, because of our unworthiness (as it seems to us)[2] and because we feel absolutely nothing (for we are frequently as barren and dry after our prayers as we were before).[3]

And thus, in our feeling, our foolishness is the cause of our weakness (for this have I experienced in myself).

And all this brought our Lord suddenly to my mind, and He showed these words and said: "<u>I am the ground of thy praying</u>[4]—first, it is my will that thou have something, and next I make thee to want it, and afterward I cause thee to pray for it. If thou prayest for it, how, then, could it be that thou wouldst not get what thou askest for?"[5]

And thus in the first proposition, with the three that follow, our good Lord shows a powerful encouragement, as can be seen in the above words.

In that first statement, where He says: "if thou prayest for it, etc.," there He shows the very great pleasure and endless reward that He will give us because of our praying.

In the second statement, where He says: "How then, could it be? etc.," this was said as an impossible thing, because it is the most impossible thing that can be that we should pray for mercy and grace and not get it. Because everything that our good Lord causes us to pray for, He himself has already appointed to us from without beginning.[6]

Here can we see, then, that it is not our praying that is the cause of the goodness and grace that He does for us, but God's own characteristic goodness.[7]

And that He showed truthfully in all those sweet words when He says, "I am the ground. . . ."

And our good Lord wills that this be recognized by His lovers on earth, and the more that we recognize this, the more we shall pray (if it is wisely received), and this is our Lord's intention.

8. Jesus is our "advocate and mediator," and in a wonderfully homely and anthropomorphic way, Julian describes Him as passing our prayer on to heaven and storing it up in a "Treasury." Note that Julian apparently bypasses all prayers to the saints and angels. (Matthew 19:21—". . . you will have treasure in heaven.")

9. This is the first hint of a radical idea of Julian's: that humanity was given first to God's Son, and then to the rest of humankind in imitation of and in union with that Son. That union is broken by sin and restored by prayer.

10. The ME has: *Pray inderly thow the thynkyth it savowr the nott.* PV has *interly*, and C&W somewhat lamely suggest it should be translated as "entirely" or "wholeheartedly." Either translation would be consistent with Julian's thought.

11. If prayer is barren or feeble, or if one does not perceive any benefit from it and it seems futile, then one is probably praying properly. How immeasurably distant such an idea is to our modern thoughts about prayer! Prayer, for Julian, is basically a kind of "being," a purposeful aligning of oneself with God.

12. If prayer is as Julian defines it—a constant alignment of one's will with God's—then it does not require words or petitions, and all of life can be a prayer.

13. We are reminded of 1 Thessalonians 5:17—"Pray without ceasing" (NRSV).

14. Both prayer and the virtuous life should be approached "reasonably with good sense." No high-flown ecstasies or emotional peaks.

Praying is a true, gracious, enduring will of the soul, one-ed and made fast to the will of our Lord by the sweet, secret working of the Holy Spirit.

Our Lord Himself, He is the first recipient of our prayer,[8] as I see it, and He accepts it most favorably, and, highly rejoicing, He sends the prayer up above and places it in a Treasury where it shall never perish. It is there before God with all His holy saints, constantly acceptable, always assisting our needs; and when we shall receive our bliss, our prayer shall be given to us as a degree of joy with endless honor-filled favor from Him.

Most glad and happy is our Lord about our prayer, and He watches for it and He wishes to enjoy it, because with His grace it makes us like Himself in character as we are in nature.[9] And this is His blessed will, for He says this:

"Pray inwardly[10]even though it seems to give thee no pleasure, for it is beneficial enough though thou perceivest it not.

"Pray inwardly, though thou sensest nothing, though thou seest nothing, yea, though thou thinkest thou canst achieve nothing,

for in dryness and barrenness,

in sickness and in feebleness,

then is thy prayer completely pleasing to me, though it seems to give thee but little pleasure.[11] And thus all thy living is prayer in my eyes."[12]

Because of the reward and the endless favor that He wishes to give us for it, He desires to have us pray constantly in His sight.[13] God accepts the good intention and the toil of His servants, no matter how we feel, wherefore it pleases Him that we work both in our prayer and in good living by His help and His grace, reasonably with good sense,[14] keeping our strength for Him until we have Him whom we seek in fullness of joy, that is, Jesus.

(He showed this word before in the fifteenth revelation: "Thou shalt have Me for thy reward.")

And thanksgiving is also part of prayer. Thanksgiving is a true, inner awareness, with great reverence and loving awe turning ourselves with

15. It is clear that for Julian only rarely does one give audible voice to one's prayer—only rarely does one break out of silence.
16. The combination should be noted: "by reason and by grace." Although Julian is much affected by the Franciscan traditions of affective prayer, she never excludes *reason* from the process.
17. See Chapter 66 where Julian hallucinates about her room being on fire: "And immediately I betook myself to what our Lord had shown me on that same day. . . and I fled to that as to my comfort."

COMMENTS ON CHAPTER 42

1. Julian reiterates that the source and origin of our prayer is not our own minds or even our own needs, but God-in-us. Romans 8:26—"We do not even know how we ought to pray, but through our inarticulate groans the Spirit himself is pleading for us. . . ."
2. In Chapter 6 Julian calls the *Revelations* "a lesson of love," and both here and in Chapter 79 she speaks of them as "a loving lesson."
3. For Julian, the purpose and goal of *all* Christian life is union with our Lord.
4. The ME word *large* may also mean "broad" or "generous" or "ambitious" (W&J).

all our might toward the actions our good Lord guides us to, rejoicing and thanking Him inwardly.

And sometimes, because of its abundance, thanksgiving breaks out with voice and says: "Good Lord, thanks be to Thee; blessed mayest Thou be!"[15]

And sometimes when the heart is dry and feels nothing (or else by temptation of our Enemy) then the heart is driven by reason and by grace[16] to call upon our Lord with voice, recounting His blessed Passion and His great goodness.[17]

And the strength of our Lord's word is directed into the soul, and enlivens the heart, and introduces it by His grace into true practices, and causes it to pray most blessedly, and truly to delight in our Lord.

That is a most blessed, loving thanksgiving in His sight.

⫷ 42

Our Lord God wishes for us to have true understanding, and especially in three matters related to our prayer.

The first is by whom and how our prayer originates; "by whom" He shows when He says, "I am the ground . . ."; and "how" is by His goodness, for He says, "First, it is my will. . . ."[1]

For the second, in what manner and how we should practice our prayers; and that is that our will be transformed into the will of our Lord, rejoicing; and this He means when He says, "I make thee to will it. . . ."

For the third, that we understand the fruit and the end of our prayer: that is, to be one-ed to and like our Lord in everything. And for this meaning and for this end was all this loving lesson[2] shown; and He wishes to help us, if we will make our prayer just as He says Himself—blessed may He be![3]

This is our Lord's will: that our prayer and our trust be both equally great.[4]

5. If, as Julian believes, prayer is actually a gift of God, and God is its source, then why should one not trust that God will answer the very prayer that He Himself initiated?

6. God is existence itself, and therefore God is present in all things, so God is present even in His own apparent refusal to answer a specific prayer. Paradoxically, the very refusal itself should be seen as an evidence of God's presence and God's action.

7. Julian's wonderful ME for "redemption" is *agen byeing* or our being "bought again" by Christ's Atonement.

8. This is Julian's triumphant proclamation of the essential goodness and immeasurable value of a human being. This is a radical theology for the fourteenth century, when most Christian writers (providing a setup for John Calvin) emphasized humanity's wickedness and depravity.

9. Julian points out the several great goods God has done for us without our praying, and declares that we should, therefore, trust that with our prayers, He will not alter His goodness.

10. The preceding phrases echo phrases from the Creed: "maker of heaven and earth"; "For us and for our salvation he came down from heaven"; "all that is seen and unseen."

11. That is, we must see whatever may be happening at present as God's "deed."

For if we do not trust as much as we pray, we do incomplete honor to our Lord in our prayer, and also we delay and pain ourselves; and the reason is, as I believe, because we do not truly acknowledge that our Lord is the ground on which our prayer grows, and also that we do not recognize that prayer is given us by the grace of His love.[5] For if we knew this, it would make us trust that we would receive, by our Lord's gift, all that we desire.

For I am certain that no man asks mercy and grace with a true intention, unless that mercy and that grace have been first given to him.

But sometime, it comes to our mind that we have prayed a long time, and yet, we believe that we have not received our request. However, because of this we should not be sad, for I am certain, in keeping with our Lord's purpose, that either

we are to await a better time,

or more grace,

or a better gift.

He wills we have true knowledge that in Himself He is Existence itself; and in this knowledge He wills that our understanding be grounded with all our might and all our purpose and all our intention. And on this foundation He wills that we take our place and make our dwelling.[6]

By the gracious light of Himself, He wills that we have understanding of three things that follow:

The first is our noble and excellent creation;

the second, our precious and dearworthy redemption;[7]

the third, everything that He has made beneath us to serve us and which, for love of us, He protects.[8]

What He means is thus, as if He said: "Behold and see that I have done all this before thy prayer, and now thou art and thou prayest to Me."[9]

He intends that it is right for us to know that thus the greatest deeds are done, just as Holy Church teaches.[10] And in contemplating this we ought to pray with gratitude for the deed that is now being done[11]— and that is to pray that He rule us and guide us to His honor in this life, and bring us to His bliss—and for that He has done everything.

12. This is a difficult passage: Julian bids simply that we recognize that everything that happens, God either wills or allows, and that we recognize this in our prayer.

13. This is Julian's second "definition" of prayer, and once again it has a quality of passivity in submission to God's will, yearning always for God and trusting God because of our understanding of Him.

14. It is "by nature" that we long for bliss; it is by God's grace that we trust He will see us through to that bliss eventually.

15. Julian is not a preacher of human perfection. Her simple phrase—"let us do what we can"—is a homely and gentle reassurance.

16. "Our weakness and all our doubtful fears": See her two named sins in Chapter 73: "God showed two kinds of sickness of soul that we have: the one is impatience or sloth; the other is despair or doubtful fear."

What He intends is this: that we understand that He does everything, and that we pray for it. For the one is not enough, for if we pray and do not understand that He does it, it makes us sad and doubtful, and that is not to His honor; and if we understand what He does, and we do not pray, we do not our duty. And that way it cannot be, that is to say, that is not the way He sees it, but rather to understand that He does it and to pray also. In that way is He honored and we are helped.[12]

Everything that our Lord has already appointed to do, it is His will that we pray for that, either in particular or in general. And the joy and the bliss that that is to Him, and the favor and honor that we shall have from that, it surpasses the understanding of all creatures in this life, as I see it.

Prayer is a right understanding of that fullness of joy that is to come, along with true yearning and certain trust.[13] In prayer, the lacking of our bliss (that we are naturally appointed to) naturally makes us to yearn; true understanding and love (with sweet remembrance of our Savior) graciously make us trust.

And thus by nature do we yearn, and by grace do we trust. And in these two actions, our Lord watches us constantly, for it is our duty, and His goodness can assign no less to us.[14]

Therefore, it is proper for us to give our best effort thereto; and when we have done it, then shall we still think that it is nothing—and truly it is nothing.

But let us do what we can, and humbly ask mercy and grace, and all that we fall short we shall find in Him.[15]

This He means where He says: "I am ground of thy praying." And thus in this blessed word, along with the showing, I saw a complete victory against all our weakness and all our doubtful fears.[16]

COMMENTS ON CHAPTER 43

1. This is certainly a quotable verse. See 1 Corinthians 6:17—"anyone who joins himself to the Lord is one with him spiritually."

2. The phrase "restored by grace" is not present in the SV. Either Julian felt it necessary for clarity, or (as C&W suggest) it was added by a scribe who did not understand Julian's concept of the human essence included in the divine essence (see note 3, following).

3. Julian is very clear that our essence (she uses the Scholastic term "substance") is within God's own essence. (See Chapter 54 for a fuller treatment of this concept.)

4. Not only is Jesus our friend, but also we are to be His *partners*.

5. Here we have another statement that our prayer is (or ought to be) in exact conformity with God's will.

6. This is a humorous and almost rustic explanation: that God is "beholden" to us for our good deeds, and is pleased if we ask Him to do what He was going to do anyway. Here we find substantial mystical theology expressed in childlike words.

7. C&W somewhat exaggeratedly suggest that this paragraph has cloaked erotic undertones with references to the Song of Songs—that is a stretch, to say the least. (This paragraph does not appear in the SV.)

8. Julian means that the praying itself is not externally noticeable, but happens secretly and almost unconsciously without being intended (that is, when one is "lost" in contemplation of God, one is unaware of praying).

9. ME has *reverent drede*, which we translate as "awe."

10. At this point SV inserts: "For what time a man's soul is homely with God he needs not to pray but behold reverently what he says. For in all this time that this was showed me I was not stirred to pray, but always to have this well in my mind for comfort: that when we see God, we have what we desire, and then we need not pray."

⤳ 43

Prayer ones the soul to God;[1] for though the soul is ever like God in nature and essence (restored by grace),[2] it is often unlike God in its external state by sin on man's part.[3]

Then is prayer a witness that the soul wills as God wills, and it comforts the conscience and inclines man to grace. In this way He teaches us to pray and mightily to trust that we shall have what we pray for; for He looks upon us in love and wishes to make us partners in His good will and deed,[4] and therefore He moves us to pray for that which it pleases Him to do.[5]

For these prayers and good will (which we have as His gift), He will reward us and give us endless recompense.

(And this was shown in this word: "If thou prayest for it. . . .")

In this word, God showed as great pleasure and as great delight as if He were much beholden to us for every good deed that we do (and yet it is He who does it)—and for the fact that we pray to Him mightily to do everything that pleases Him, as if He said: "How couldst thou please me more than to pray to me mightily, wisely, and willingly to do the thing that I am going to do?"[6]

And thus the soul by prayer comes to agree with God.

When our gracious Lord by His particular grace shows Himself to our soul, we have what we desire, and then we do not see for that time what more we should pray for, but all our purpose with all our might is fixed wholly upon the contemplation of Him.[7]

This is an exalted imperceptible prayer, as I see it,[8] for the whole cause for which we pray is to be one-ed to the vision and the contemplation of Him to whom we pray, marvelously rejoicing with <u>awe</u>[9] and such great sweetness and delight in Him that for the time being we can pray absolutely nothing except as He moves us at the time.[10]

11. ME in PV has *unablynes*.

12. See James 4:8—"Come close to God, and he will draw close to you." And John 6:44—"No one can come to me unless he is drawn by the Father who sent me."

13. This is a textual conundrum: BV has *centered to his wonyng*; PV has *entende to his wonning*; (both seem to mean "dwelling"). WM has *wowying*, which Julia Holloway translates as "wooing."[134] Some consider it a scribal error for *movyng*. Based on this and the sense of the context, I have chosen "prompting."

14. This is Julian's absolute optimism: when we see everything God has done, all we can do is contemplate Him, long to be one-ed with Him, listen to his prompting, and acknowledge his love and goodness.

15. The word "into" is important: our Christian goal is to become utterly one-ed with and enclosed in God, and that happens in this life rarely through momentary intuitive encounters with God when we are "simple" enough to bear it.

16. All five senses are included: seeing, touching, hearing, smelling, and tasting. (For "tasting" ME has *swelowyng*—"swallowing"—with its sacramental implications.)

I am well aware that the more the soul sees of God, the more it desires Him by His grace. But when we do not see Him in this way, then we sense a need and cause to pray—because of our falling short and the unfitness[11] of ourselves for Jesus.

For when the soul is tempted, troubled, and left to itself by its unrest, then it is time to pray to make that soul pliant and obedient to God. (But by no kind of prayer does one make God pliant to oneself, for He is always the same in love.)

Thus I saw that whenever we see needs for which we pray, then our good Lord follows us, helping our desire. And when we by His special grace plainly gaze upon Him, seeing no other, then we need to follow Him and He draws us into Him by love.[12] For I saw and sensed that His marvelous and fulsome goodness completes all our abilities.

Then I saw that His constant working in all manner of things is done so well, so wisely, and so powerfully that it surpasses all our imagining, and all that we can suppose and comprehend. And then we can do nothing more than to gaze at Him and rejoice, with a high mighty desire to be wholly one-ed to Him, and to listen to His prompting,[13] and rejoice in His loving, and delight in His goodness.[14]

Then shall we, with His sweet grace, in our own humble constant prayer, come into Him now in this life by many secret touchings of sweet spiritual sights and experiences, meted out to us as our simplicity can bear it.[15]

And this is wrought, and shall be, by the grace of the Holy Spirit, until at last we shall die in yearning for love.

And then shall we all come into the Lord, knowing ourselves clearly, and possessing God fully, and we being eternally completely hidden in God:

> seeing Him truly
> touching Him fully,
> hearing Him spiritually,
> and delectably smelling Him,
> and sweetly tasting Him.[16]

17. See 1 Corinthians 13:12—"At present we see only puzzling reflections in a mirror, but one day we shall see face to face."
18. Note the distinction between simply "seeing" and "contemplating."
19. Genesis 32:30—"[Jacob] said, 'I have seen God face to face yet my life is spared.'" And Exodus 33:20—"My face you cannot see, for no mortal may see me and live."

COMMENTS ON CHAPTER 44

1. This is a difficult passage; apparently Julian refers to the man "who shall be saved," that is, the good and Christian person, since she uses the Blessed Virgin as an example of what she means.
2. The ME word is *saw*, but it can mean to "see *mentally*" or to "apprehend *by thought*" or "to *understand*" (OED). And since Julian now sets off to explain her understanding, this sense of the word is more accurate.
3. This is another Trinitarian formula: Father=Truth; Son=Wisdom; Holy Spirit=Love (which proceeds from Truth and Wisdom). Again we see Julian's exaltation of humanity, in which the human soul has all the same qualities as the Holy Trinity, except that the Trinity is "uncreated" and the soul is "created."
4. Julian describes the Trinitarian soul: perceiving, contemplating, and loving God.
5. Julian's exaltation of the human does not preclude human humility before the magnificence of God, but is an assurance of God's endlessly protecting love.

Then we shall see God face to face,[17] simply and most fully—the creature that is created shall see and eternally contemplate[18] God who is the Creator. (For no man can see God in this way and live afterward[19]—that is to say, in this mortal life—however, when He of His particular grace wishes to show Himself here, He strengthens the creature beyond itself, and He moderates the showing according to His own will, so that it does good at the time.)

ᔑ 44

God showed frequently in all the revelations that man continually performs His will and His honor everlastingly, without any ceasing.[1]

(And what this action is was shown in the first revelation, and that on a wonderful basis: for it was shown in the operation of the soul of Our Blessed Lady Saint Mary, by truth and wisdom.)

And I hope, by the grace of the Holy Spirit, I shall say what I understood[2] of how this should be.

Truth perceives God, and Wisdom contemplates God, and from these two comes the third, and that is a holy, wonderful delight in God, which is Love. Where Truth and Wisdom are, in truth, there is Love, truly proceeding from them both, and all are of God's creation. For He is eternal supreme Truth, eternal supreme Wisdom, eternal supreme Love uncreated; and man's soul is a created thing in God, which has the same divine qualities except created.[3]

And continually the soul does what it was made for: it perceives God, it contemplates God, and it loves God.[4]

Because of this God rejoices in the creature and the creature in God, endlessly marveling. In this marveling the creature sees his God, his Lord, his Creator, so high, so great, and so good in reference to himself who is created, that scarcely does the creature seem anything at all by himself; but the clarity and the purity of truth and wisdom cause him to see and to recognize that he is created because of love, and in this love God endlessly keeps him.[5]

COMMENTS ON CHAPTER 45

1. This is Julian's unique mystical/theological expression: that a human being's "essence" is always kept *in God*. This springs from her view that God created humanity *first* in His Son—that the Son had human nature, which was then passed on to created humans: Christ's humanity *preceded* earthly humanity and was the model for it. God's creative "idea" of every human being remains in the mind of God. And it is that "essence" of a person that God uses in determining a person's worth.

2. The ME word is *dome*, which can literally mean "judgment," "decision," "decree," or "authority."

3. The ME word is *sensualyte*, but in modern use, the word *sensuality* has heavily negative connotations that the ME word does not have.

4. 1 Corinthians 2:14–15—"An unspiritual person refuses what belongs to the Spirit of God. . . . But a spiritual person can judge the worth of everything." Jesus "corrected" human judgment through His Passion.

5. This is Julian's first declaration that God does not *blame* humans for sin and error. This statement occurs in some form fourteen times in the book. (See especially Chapter 51, where God looks at sinners "with pity and not with blame.")

6. Julian introduces her conundrum in the apparent contradiction between sin and the absence of God's blame.

7. Julian expresses a theological quandary: she knows the Church teaches that she is a sinner, and she can accept that; but the further Church teaching that God would *blame* a sinner for the sin, she cannot understand—because what she knows of God shows no blame or anger at a sinner.

⪓ 45

God judges us based on the essence of our human nature which is always kept constantly within Him, whole and safe without end;[1] and this judgment[2] comes from His rightfulness.

But man judges based on our changeable fleshliness,[3] which seems now one thing, now another, depending on what it picks from among the parts and shows publicly. And this human self-judgment[2] is muddled, for sometimes it is good and gentle, and sometimes it is cruel and oppressive. Insofar as it is good and gentle, it is part of [God's] rightfulness; and insofar as it is cruel and oppressive, our good Lord Jesus reforms it by mercy and grace through the virtue of His Blessed Passion and so brings it into rightfulness also.[4]

And though these two [judgments] are thus reconciled and one-ed, still both shall be acknowledged in heaven without end.

The first judgment is of God's rightfulness, and that proceeds from His high endless love. This is that fair, sweet judgment that was shown in the whole fair revelation in which I saw Him assign to us no kind of blame.[5] And although this was sweet and delightful, yet in the observing of this alone I was unable to be fully comforted, because of the judgment of Holy Church which I had understood before and was constantly in my sight.[6]

And therefore by this Church judgment it seemed to me that it was necessary for me to acknowledge myself as a sinner. And by the same judgment, I acknowledged that sinners are sometimes deserving of blame and anger, but these two things—blame and anger—I could not find in God.

Therefore my deliberation and desire was more than I know or can tell, because God Himself showed the higher judgment at the same time, and therefore it was necessary for me to accept that—but the lower judgment was taught me previously in Holy Church, and therefore I could in no way give up that lower judgment.[7]

8. Julian is truly perplexed, and asks for clarity from God, because she wants to "save" both what she believes God has shown her *and* what the Church teaches.

9. God does *not* clarify the matter for her, regardless of her desire—except in the "example" of the lord and servant which she will tell us in Chapter 51 (which entire chapter was added, by the way, in the LV).

10. When Julian speaks of "our failures" one wonders if she means the failures of the Church of which she is a part. It is more likely she refers to her own inadequacies to understand the conundrum.

COMMENTS ON CHAPTER 46

1. Julian's understanding here is that a human being is the same *kind* of being as God is, and we can only recognize that because of our belief in the true spiritual nature of humanity. God is divine by nature; we are "divine" by grace. This begins Julian's extended definition of human nature.

2. "Our own noble human nature" is the aspect of our being that is like God.

3. *Full* knowledge of our own nature will not come until the end when we will finally fully comprehend our spirituality. See Revelation 21:4b—"There shall be an end to death, and to mourning and crying and pain."

Then this was my desire: that I could see in God in what way the judgment of Holy Church here on earth is true in His sight, and how it is proper for me truly to understand it.[8]

(By this both judgments could be saved, insofar as it would be honorable to God and the morally right way for me.)

To all this I had no other response except an amazing example of a lord and of a servant (as I shall tell later)—and that most mystically.[9]

And yet I remained in my desire (and I will until my life's end) that I could by grace distinguish these two judgments as is proper for me—for all heavenly and all earthly things that belong to heaven, are contained in these two judgments, and the more knowledge and understanding that we have of these two judgments by the gracious guiding of the Holy Spirit, the more we shall see and understand our failures, and ever the more that we see our failings, the more naturally by grace we shall yearn to be filled full of endless joy and bliss, for we are created for that, and the essence of our human nature is now blissful in God, and has been since it was made, and shall be, without end.[10]

⇒ 46

But the passing life that we have here in our fleshliness does not know what our self is, except through our Faith. And when we know and see truly and clearly what our self is, then shall we truly and clearly see and know our Lord God in fullness of joy.[1] And therefore, it is inevitable that the nearer we are to our bliss, the more we shall yearn—and that both by nature and by grace.

We can have knowledge of our self in this life by the continual help and strength of our own transcendent human nature.[2]

In this [self-] knowledge, we can increase and grow by the furthering and aiding of mercy and grace, but we can never fully know our self, until the last point, and at that point this passing life and all manner of pain and woe shall have an end.[3]

4. When we finally understand our own true spiritual nature, we will be able to understand God as well.

5. This is a clear reaffirmation of the teachings of the Church. Julian is not setting up herself or her revelations against that teaching.

6. Having dwelt for a short time on the divine nature of human beings, Julian returns to the issue: as the Church teaches, we must see ourselves as sinners and deserving of God's blame and wrath.

7. The Confession in Morning and Evening Prayer in the BCP (pp. 41–42 and 63): "We have left undone those things which we ought to have done, and we have done those things which we ought not to have done."

8. We "deserve" blame and wrath of God—but Julian cannot admit to any wrath or anger or blame in God—because of God's very nature.

9. If our soul is like God (as Julian believes), then how could God be angry at such a godlike soul that is already one-ed to Himself?

And therefore, it belongs properly to us, both by nature and grace, to yearn and desire with all our might to know our self, and in this full knowledge we shall truly and clearly know our God in fullness of endless joy.[4]

And yet, during all this time from the beginning to the end of the revelation, I had two kinds of observations: the one was of endless continuing love, with a security of protection and blissful salvation (for the whole showing was about this); the other was the common teaching of Holy Church, in which teaching I was previously formed and grounded, and was willingly keeping it in practice and in understanding.[5]

And the beholding of all this did not depart from me, because I was not by the showing moved nor led from the Church teaching in any kind of point, but in the showing I was rather taught to love that teaching, to delight in it, for by it I could (with the help of our Lord and His grace) grow and rise to more heavenly knowledge and nobler loving.[6]

And thus, in all this beholding it seemed to me to be necessary to see and to know that we are sinners, and we do many evils that we ought to stop, and we leave many good deeds undone that we ought to do.[7]

And for this we deserve pain and blame and wrath.[8]

But notwithstanding all this, I saw truthfully that our Lord was never angry, nor ever shall be, for He is God:

He is good,

He is life,

He is truth,

He is love,

He is peace;

and His power, His wisdom, His Love, and His Unity do not allow Him to be angry. (For I saw truly that it is against the character of His Power to be angry, and against the character of His Wisdom, and against the character of His Goodness.)[9]

10. God in not just "good," but God is "goodness" itself. The Scholastics taught that God did not "have" attributes, but "was" those attributes themselves. God is all essence, and has no external characteristics.
11. There is a mystical identity between God and the human soul, with nothing interposing.

COMMENTS ON CHAPTER 47

1. Clearly Julian is speaking of death.
2. There is some possibility that Julian is here referring to the concept of purgatory, which can be seen as bringing about the remission of God's wrath.

God is the goodness that cannot be angry, for He is nothing but goodness.[10]

Our soul is one-ed to Him, who is unchangeable goodness, and between God and our soul is neither anger nor forgiveness, as He sees it. For our soul is so completely one-ed to God by His own goodness, that there can be absolutely nothing at all separating God and soul.[11]

To this understanding the soul was led by love and drawn by power in every showing. That it is thus—and how it is thus—our good Lord showed truly by His great goodness, and also that He wills that we desire to comprehend it (that is to say, insofar as it is proper for His creature to comprehend it).

Everything that this simple soul understood, God wills that it be shown and known, for those things which He wishes to keep secret, He Himself mightily and wisely hides out of love (for I saw in the same showing that much that is secret is hidden which can never be known until the time that God of His goodness has made us worthy to see it).

With this I am well satisfied, awaiting our Lord's will in this high wonder.

And now I yield myself to my mother, Holy Church, as a simple child ought.

⤺ 47

Two objectives belong to our soul by obligation: *one* is that we reverently marvel, the other is that we meekly suffer, ever rejoicing in God. For He wants us to know that we shall in a short time[1] see clearly within Himself all that we desire.

Notwithstanding all this, I beheld and marveled greatly at the mercy and forgiveness of God, for by the teaching that I had beforehand, I understood that the mercy of God was supposed to be the remission of His wrath after the time that we have sinned.[2]

3. But God has never shown her a "remission of His wrath" because He has never shown her any divine wrath at all.

4. Julian begins a consideration of mercy that continues for several chapters.

5. We begin to get just a taste of Julian's understanding of sin: it happens because of human changeability, "frailty," and "ignorance"—not by malicious intent. For Julian sin often seems to be not much more than an unintentional mistake.

6. ME has *tempest*.

7. This sentence describes the fallen sinner in Chapter 51, and it sets forth three qualities contrary to the triple qualities of the Holy Trinity: "impotent" versus Power; "unwise" versus Wisdom; "overwhelmed will" versus Love.

8. This is a radical and unique insight: sin is not *inherent* in human nature, but comes from blinding oneself to God.

9. ME has *steryng*, which C&W curiously consider to be related to "sins of the flesh." (Note: Nowhere does Julian specifically refer to sexual sins.)

10. Our "ordinary experience in this life" is our blindness to God, but Julian reiterates her (Scholastic) conviction that, nonetheless, the soul (of one "who shall be saved") always longs to see God.

11. See Chapter 4: "I conceived truly and powerfully that it was He Himself . . . who showed it to me without any go-between."

12. See Chapter 15: "This vision was shown me . . . that it is advantageous for some souls . . . sometimes to fail and to be left by themselves."

13. See Chapter 8: "And I desired, as much as I dared, to see more, if it were His will. . . ."

14. See Chapter 50: "I could have no rest for fear that His blessed Presence would pass from my sight."

(It seemed to me that to a soul whose intention and desire is to love, the wrath of God would be more severe than any other pain, and therefore I accepted that the remission of His wrath would be one of the principal objectives of His mercy.)

But in spite of anything that I might behold and desire, I could not see this point in the entire showing.[3]

[4]But how I saw and understood concerning the works of mercy, I shall say somewhat, insofar as God wishes to give me grace. I understood thus: man is changeable in this life, and by frailty and by ignorance and lack of cunning,[5] being overcome, he falls into sin. He is impotent and unwise by himself, and also his will is overwhelmed during this time he is in <u>turmoil</u>[6] and in sorrow and woe.[7]

And the cause is blindness,[8] for man sees not God—because if he saw God constantly, he would have no harmful experience, nor <u>disturbance</u>[9] of any kind, nor the distress that is a servant to sin.

This I saw and felt at the same time, and it seemed to me that the sight and the feeling was noble and plenteous and gracious in comparison to what our ordinary experience is in this life,[10] but yet I thought it was only small and lowly in comparison to the great desire that the soul has to see God.

I perceived in me five kinds of activities, which are these:

> rejoicing,
>
> mourning,
>
> desire,
>
> fear,
>
> and certain hope:

"rejoicing" because God gave me understanding and knowledge that it was Himself that I saw;[11]

"mourning," and that was because of failing;[12]

"desire," and that was that I might see Him ever more and more, understanding and acknowledging that we shall never have full rest till we see Him truly and clearly in heaven;[13]

"fear" was because it seemed to me in all that time that that vision would fail and I would be left to myself;[14]

15. Two things alleviate Julian's mourning and fear: (a) she would be protected by God (ME: *kept*), and (b) she would be "brought to His bliss."

16. "We fall back into ourselves" is a particularly poetic expression of sin—especially since Julian has just been talking about our being "in God." Sin is simply being "in ourselves" instead of "in God."

17. As the source of our "contrariness," Julian includes both the "First Sin" (that is, the sin of Eden—original sin) and the sins "of our own contrivance" (that is, actual sins we have committed ourselves).

COMMENTS ON CHAPTER 48

1. Julian understands the ineradicable presence of the Holy Spirit in the human soul. She is still thinking here about the supposed "wrath of God," and recognizes that mercy replaces wrath in God.

"certain hope" was in the endless love, that I saw I would be protected by His mercy and brought to His bliss, and rejoicing in His sight with this certain hope of His merciful protection gave me understanding and comfort, so that mourning and fear were not greatly painful.[15]

And yet in all this I beheld in the showing of God that this kind of understanding of Him cannot be constant in this life—and that for His own honor and for increase of our endless joy. And therefore we are frequently without the sight of Him, and at once we fall back into ourselves,[16] and then we discover no sense of rightness—nothing but the contrariness that is within ourselves (and that from the ancient root of our First Sin with all that follows after from our own contrivance[17]) and in this we are troubled and tempted with a sense of sins and of pains in many different ways, spiritually and bodily, as it is familiar to us in this life.

⤜ 48

But our good Lord, the Holy Spirit (who is endless life dwelling in our soul), full safely keeps us, and makes a peace in the soul, and brings it to rest by grace, and makes it submissive, and reconciles it to God. And this is the mercy and the way in which our Lord constantly leads us as long as we are here in this changeable life.[1]

I saw no wrath except on man's part, and that He forgives in us. For wrath is nothing else but a rebellion from and an opposition to peace and to love, and either it comes from the failure of power or from the failure of wisdom, or from the failure of goodness (which failure is not in God but it is on our part—for we, because of sin and wretchedness, have in us a wrath and a continuing opposition to peace and to love—and that He showed very often in His loving demeanor of compassion and pity).

The basis of mercy is love, and the action of mercy is our protection in love; and this was shown in such manner that I could not conceive of the property of mercy in any other way than as if it were all united

2. For Julian, mercy is the fruit of love; that is, because God is love, God must be merciful, suspending the judgment that springs from wrath.

3. Mercy is God's love in action, protecting us from divine judgment and leading us through trouble by transforming it into good. (See Proverbs 27:6—"The blows a friend gives are well meant. . . .")

4. The presence of trouble in our lives, however, does not mean that God's mercy has been suspended. God must always allow us to use our free will, and as a result God allows us to "fail." And the failure results from our "blindness" to God. Note, also, that God is described as identical with "our life."

5. Even if it seems that God is punishing us by allowing us to fall, God maintains His loving presence with us in the midst of our failing, our falling, and our dying.

6. This is the first hint of Julian's notion of God's motherhood.

7. Julian reconciles the two dimensions of God's actions: mercy from God's (homely) motherhood, and grace from God's (courtly) lordship.

8. This is a continuation of the former idea, showing the dimensions and qualities of mercy, and then the attributes of grace. We see the implications of Julian's notion that God is both homely (mercy) and courtly (grace).

9. Julian demonstrates her literary art, showing that grace acts in the face of our failing, falling, and dying.

10. The word "reward" here carries with it the sense of "award," like a military decoration following a hard battle. In the four-teenth century, it also carried the sense of "recompense."

11. Here we find another reference to one of Julian's central paradoxical notions: that the more we suffer from our own sin on earth, the more we will be rewarded for that suffering in heaven, where we will actually rejoice that we suffered on earth, since the suffering has brought heavenly rewards.

in love. That is to say, mercy is a sweet, gracious working in love mingled with plenteous pity, as I see it.[2]

Mercy works, protecting us, and mercy works transforming everything into good for us.[3]

Mercy, out of love, allows us to fail to a limited extent, and insofar as we fail, insomuch we fall; and insofar as we fall, so much we die; for it is necessary that we die inasmuch as we fall short of the sight and sense of God, who is our life.[4]

Our failing is frightful, our falling is shameful, and our dying is sorrowful; but still in all this, the sweet eye of pity and of love never departs from us, and the working of mercy ceases not.[5]

For I observed the quality of mercy and I observed the quality of grace, which are two kinds of action in one love; mercy is a pity-filled attribute which belongs to Motherhood[6] in tender love, and grace is a dignified attribute which belongs to royal Lordship in the same love.[7]

Mercy works: protecting, tolerating, bringing life, and healing, and all is from the tenderness of love.

And grace works: building up, rewarding, and endlessly transcending what our loving and our labor deserves, spreading out widely and showing the noble, plenteous largess of God's royal Lordship in His marvelous courtesy.[8]

And this is from the abundance of love, for grace transforms our frightful failing into plenteous endless solace, and grace converts our shameful falling into noble, honorable rising, and grace converts our sorrowful dying into holy, blissful life.[9]

I saw full certainly that ever as our contrariness makes pain, shame, and sorrow for us here on earth, just so on the contrary, grace makes solace, honor, and transcendent bliss for us in heaven, exceeding the earthly to such an extent that when we come up and receive the sweet <u>reward</u>[10] which grace has created for us, then we shall thank and bless our Lord, endlessly rejoicing that ever we suffered woe.[11]

12. This is an expansion on her notion of sin/reward: God's mercy to us in our sinning shows us a dimension of that divine love that we might not have known had we not sinned. Here is a suggestion of the familiar idea of the *felix culpa*, the lucky sin—lucky because it shows us God's love that we might not have experienced otherwise.

13. "Abate and consume" may not be quite strong enough words; Julian's ME has *slaken and wasten*. They carry the sense of "unbind and wipe out."

COMMENTS ON CHAPTER 49

1. This is a conceit that takes one's breath away. It even awes Julian herself, who sees it as "a mighty wonder." God cannot forgive, because from His point of view there is no offense to forgive that is not already forgiven. God holds nothing against a sinner. This is an awesome thought in a fourteenth-century culture in which virtually everyone's primary religious effort was to try to earn or buy God's forgiveness.

2. "Look," says Julian in her unpretentious naiveté, "it is all very simple: if God is our friend, how can there be divine anger? It's impossible."

3. This is one of Julian's most powerful and controversial principles, as it plainly conflicts with much of the Old Testament. But she apparently sees no need to justify it since it was given her in her revelations.

4. Julian recognizes that it is the love of God that creates us and gives us life, and if that omnipotent and creative love turned to wrath we would simply cease to exist. (See Acts 17:28—" . . . for in him we live and move, in him we exist.")

5. This is another doubled Trinitarian formula: Power, Wisdom, and Goodness. We were created by the Trinity, and we are protected by the Trinity.

And that shall be because of an attribute of blessed love that we shall discover in God—which we might never have known without woe going before.[12]

And when I saw all this, it was necessary to agree that the mercy of God and the forgiveness is in order to abate and consume our wrath, not His.[13]

ᔧ 49

To the soul this was a mighty wonder (which was continually shown in all showings, and was observed with great diligence) that our Lord God, as far as He is concerned, cannot forgive—because He cannot be angry—it would be impossible.[1]

For this was shown: that our life is all based and rooted in love, and without love we cannot live. And therefore to the soul (which by His special grace sees so obviously the exalted marvelous goodness of God, and that we are endlessly one-ed to Him in love) it is the most impossible thing that can be that God should be angry, for wrath and friendship are two opposites.[2]

He who lays waste and destroys our wrath and makes us humble and gentle, it is essential for us to believe that He is always clothed in that same love, humble and gentle—which is opposite to wrath. I saw full certainly that where our Lord appears, peace comes to pass and wrath has no place.[3]

I saw no kind of wrath in God, neither for a short time nor for long. (For truly, as I see it, if God were to be angry even a hint, we would never have life nor place nor being.)[4] As truly as we have our being from the endless Power of God and from the endless Wisdom, and from the endless Goodness, just as truly we have our protection in the endless Power of God, in the endless Wisdom, and in the endless Goodness.[5]

6. One suspects that Julian is referring subtly to the divided papacy, the Peasants' Rebellion, the Pestilence, and other calamitous events of her time.

7. "Mildness," "humility," kindliness," and "gentleness" are not adjectives commonly applied to God in fourteenth-century England, where God was seen more as a stern taskmaster and judge. The ME word is *buxumhede*, which literally means "flexibility" or "submissiveness." W&J translate it as "obedient."

8. See note 2 above. And see Colossians 3:3—"You died; and now your life lies hidden with Christ in God." (On God's friendship, see Psalm 25:13—"The LORD is a friend to those who fear him" [BCP]; and Wisdom 7:14—"[Wisdom] is an inexhaustible treasure for mortals, and those who profit by it become God's friends . . ."; and James 2:23—"Abraham put his faith in God . . . and he was called 'God's friend.'")

9. The ME word is *treteth*, meaning "treats" or "manages." W&J translate it as "nurtures."

10. Julian equates or defines "salvation" with being "truly in peace and in love."

11. This is a characteristic statement indicating a basically passive view of matters in the world—that we defer to God and God's judgment regarding what happens around us, and that we live peaceably with others. Julian suggests an almost Buddhist acceptance of the present reality and a repudiation of desire for something else.

12. We might well suppose that being made "humble and gentle" was one of Julian's own intentions in becoming an anchorite.

Although we feel miseries, disputes, and strifes in ourselves,[6] yet are we all mercifully enwrapped in the mildness of God and in His humility, in His kindliness, and in His <u>gentleness</u>.[7]

I saw full certainly that all our endless friendship, our place, our life, and our being is in God,[8] because that same endless goodness that keeps us that we perish not when we sin, that same endless goodness continually <u>manages</u>[9] in us a peace against our wrath and our contrary falling, and with a true fear makes us realize our need strongly to seek unto God in order to have forgiveness with a grace-filled desire for our salvation.

We may not be blissfully saved until we are truly in peace and in love, for that is our salvation.[10]

Although we (by the wrath and the contrariness that is in us) are now in tribulation, distress, and woe (as it falls to our blindness and frailty), yet are we securely safe by the merciful protection of God so that we perish not.

But we are not blissfully safe in possessing our endless joy until we are wholly in peace and in love—that is to say, fully gratified with God and with all His works and with all His judgments, and loving and peaceable with ourselves and with our fellow Christians, and with all that God loves,[11] as love pleases. And this God's goodness carries out in us.

Thus I saw that God is our true peace and He is our sure keeper when we are ourselves unpeaceful, and He continually works to bring us into endless peace.

And thus, when we, by the action of mercy and grace, are made humble and gentle, we are completely safe.[12] When it is truly at peace in itself, immediately the soul is one-ed to God, because in Him is found no wrath.

Thus I saw that when we are wholly in peace and in love, we find no contrariness nor any kind of hindrance. And that contrariness which is now in us, our Lord God of His goodness makes most profitable for us, because that contrariness is the cause of our tribulations and all our woe, and our Lord Jesus takes those and sends them up to heaven, and

13. This is another hint of Julian's idea that our pains on earth are made into rewards in heaven. And, as in the next sentence, Julian bewails the inconstancy of our life on earth, making the "unchangeable" life in heaven much to be yearned for.

COMMENTS ON CHAPTER 50

1. "We are often dead"—that is to say, "morally dead" or "hopeless." One is reminded of the Scripture used at funerals: "The souls of the just are in God's hand; no torment will touch them. In the eyes of the foolish they seemed to be dead. . ."(Wisdom 3:1–2). Julian may also be referring to her own symbolic "death" as an enclosed recluse.
2. After Julian's several chapters of meditation on the apparent absence of "deserved" blame for our sin, she comes back to the conundrum in plain words: "How can this be?"
3. Even Julian's literary style becomes more extreme and hyperbolic, showing her deep frustration. We must recognize a distinction between our own sense of *guilt* over sin, and God's refusal to assign *blame* to us.
4. It is as though she were saying, "Oh, Christ, don't go yet, until you show me this one thing!" Of course, she is building up literarily to the explanation that appears in the next chapter.
5. Notice that all of this reflection is going on *while Julian is gazing on the face of the Crucified*.
6. In Chapter 73 Julian will write: "God showed two kinds of sickness of soul that we have: the one is impatience or sloth (for we bear our labor and our pains gloomily); the other is despair or doubtful fear. . . ." Here she admits her own "sickness of soul" by declaring her impatience.

there are they made more sweet and delectable than heart can think or tongue can tell, and when we come there, we shall find them ready, all transformed into truly beautiful and endless honors.[13]

Thus is God our steadfast foundation here, and He shall be our complete bliss and make us unchangeable as He is, when we are there.

⤳ 50

In this mortal life mercy and forgiveness is our way that evermore leads us to grace. By the temptation and the sorrow that we fall into on our part, we are often dead,[1] according to man's judgment on earth, but in the sight of God the soul that shall be saved was never dead and never shall be.

And yet here I wondered and marveled with all the diligence of my soul, meaning thus: "Good Lord, I see Thee who art very truth and I know truly that we sin grievously all day and are much blameworthy; and I can neither relinquish the knowledge of this truth, nor can I see Thee showing to us any manner of blame. How can this be?"[2]

(For I knew by the common teaching of Holy Church and by my own sense that the guilt of our sin continually hangs upon us, from the First Man unto the time that we come up into heaven.)

Then was this a miracle to me: that I saw our Lord God showing to us no more blame than as if we were as pure and as holy as angels are in heaven.[3]

Between these two opposites my reason was greatly troubled by my blindness, and could have no rest for fear that His blessed Presence would pass from my sight and I be left in ignorance of how He looks on us in our sin.[4] (For either it was necessary for me to see in God that sin was all done away, or else it was necessary for me to see in God how He looks at it—whereby I could truly recognize how I [in my turn] ought to look at sin and the manner of our guilt.)

My yearning went on, continually gazing on Him,[5] and yet I could have no patience[6] because of great dread and perplexity, thinking: "If

7. At this point Julian is so distressed that she fears she has crossed the line into impropriety by her impertinence, and in the next lines justifies herself.
8. Could "here" refer to her anchorite's cell?
9. Her justification is that the issue is "a lowly thing" and "ordinary" and her asking is only so she can live a better life.
10. Her frustration has brought her to "inward" weeping, and she even addresses our Lord with an ejaculatory prayer, beginning with the emotional interjection "Ah!" She is now ready for the enormous revelation of her vision of the lord and servant.

COMMENTS ON CHAPTER 51

1. The ME word is *example* (Latin: *exemplum*). This was a word used with great frequency to describe the illustrations offered in sermons—used effectively by the popular itinerant Franciscan preachers.
2. Julian here speaks of two levels of understanding: the overt in "bodily form" and the allegorical "without bodily form"—and both levels are applied to the two persons in the illustration, making a total of four ways of understanding the parable. She begins with a simple recounting of the overt vision.
3. The phrase "sits solemnly in repose and in peace" is the reminder that God is considered to be impassible, that is, without emotions. He is very "courtly," to use Julian's term.

I take it thus—that we are not sinners and not blameworthy—it seems likely I would err and fall short of knowledge of this truth.

"But if it is so that we are sinners and blameworthy, good Lord, how can it then be that I cannot see this verity in Thee, who are my God, my Creator, in whom I desire to see all truths?"[7]

(Three points make me brave to ask this: the first is because it is so lowly a thing [for if it were a lofty thing, I would be terrified]; the second is that it is so ordinary [for if it were special and secret, also I would be terrified]; the third is that it is necessary for me to know it, as it seems to me, if I shall live here[8] [for the sake of the knowledge of good and evil, by which I can, by reason and grace, the more separate the good from the evil, and love goodness and hate evil, as Holy Church teaches].)[9]

I wept[10] inwardly with all my might, searching in God for help, meaning thus: "Ah, Lord Jesus, King of bliss, how shall I be comforted? Who is it that shall teach me and tell me what I need to know, if I cannot at this time see it in Thee?"

51

Then our gracious Lord answered in showing very mysteriously a wonderful <u>illustration</u>[1] of a lord who has a servant, and He gave insight to my understanding of both of them.

(This insight was shown twice in the lord, and the insight was shown twice in the servant; then one part was shown spiritually in bodily form, and the other part was shown more spiritually, without bodily form.)[2]

For the first was thus: I saw two persons in bodily form, that is to say, a lord and a servant; and with this God gave me spiritual understanding.

The lord sits solemnly in repose and in peace;[3] the servant stands near, before his lord reverently, ready to do his lord's will. The lord looks upon his servant most lovingly and sweetly, and humbly he sends him to a certain place to do his will.

4. Julian's point of view concerning sin is that in the case of committed Christians, sins are not entirely intentional. Once one has made a primary choice *for Christ*, the secondary choice *of sin* does not override or invalidate what is primary. Julian's servant *intends* to do good but falls from that good intention.

5. Julian's ME is *comforte*.

6. Sin is a temporary state of "insanity" in which one is blind to God and totally absorbed with oneself.

7. We could add "by himself"; it is God's grace that is needed to recover from sin.

8. Julian has the wonderful perception that a major result of sin is isolation, self-absorption, and the collapse of community.

9. The ME word is *onlothful* meaning, "not loathful," that is, "willing."

10. Julian makes a distinction between the *guilt* felt by the sinner (that is, the seven pains) and the absence of *blame* on God's part. The servant has no wish to *remain* in the "pit" of sin. (Thomas Aquinas taught that a human being was metaphysically incapable of willing to do evil, but could misperceive evil for good, and thus could sin.)

11. See Chapter 28: "Our Lord rejoices at the tribulations of His servants (with pity and compassion)."

The servant not only goes, but he suddenly leaps up and runs in great haste because of his love to do his lord's will. And immediately he falls into a deep pit and receives very great injury. Then he groans and moans and wails and writhes, but he cannot rise up nor help himself in any way.[4]

In all this, the greatest misfortune that I saw him in was the lack of <u>reassurance</u>,[5] for he could not turn his face to look back upon his loving lord (who was very near to him and in whom there is complete reassurance), but like a man who was feeble and witless for the moment,[6] he was intent on his suffering, and waited in woe.

In this woe he endured seven great pains.

The first was the painful bruising that he received in his falling, which was very painful to him.

The second was the sluggishness of his body.

The third was the weakness resulting from these two.

The fourth, that he was deluded in his reason and stunned in his mind to such an extent that he had almost forgotten his own love to do his lord's will.

The fifth was that he could not rise up.[7]

The sixth was a most profound pain to me and that was that he lay alone—I looked all about and watched, and neither far nor near, high nor low, did I see any help for him.[8]

The seventh was that the place in which he lay was a deep, hard, and painful one.

I wondered how this servant could humbly endure there all this woe. And I watched deliberately to see if I could discover any failure in him, or if the lord would allot him any blame, and truly there was none seen—for only his good will and his great desire were the cause of his falling, and he was as <u>willing</u>[9] and as good inwardly as when he stood before his lord ready to do his will.[10]

And in the same way his loving lord constantly watched him most tenderly; and now with a twofold attitude: one outward, most humbly and gently with great compassion and pity[11] (and this was from the first level of the showing); another inward, more spiritual, and this

12. In ME, BV has *resting*; PV has *restoring*.
13. "Honorable and noble restoration" is God's will for His servants. This is the single predestination discussed in Appendix 10, "Predestination and Salvation in Julian."
14. Julian sums up God's twofold reaction to human sin: (a) pity for the pain it causes His faithful servant, and (b) joy for the great gifts He knew His grace would provide the fallen servant.
15. This is one of the most radical of Julian's insights: that our reward in heaven would be *greater* because of our sins and the pain they gave us than it would have been if we had not sinned. This is Julian optimism at its most extreme.
16. For Julian even sin itself can be seen as a promise of God's unwavering and redeeming love.
17. It seems that this was the end of the original revelation, and the following is the product of Julian's twenty years of reflection.
18. ME has *forthledyng*.

was shown with a guiding of my understanding to the lord, and by this guiding, I saw him greatly rejoice, because of the honorable and noble <u>restoration</u>[12] that he wills[13] and shall bring his servant to by his plenteous grace (and this was from that other level of the showing), and now my understanding led back to the first part of the showing, keeping both attitudes in mind.[14]

Then says this gracious lord in his meaning: "Behold, behold, my beloved servant. What harm and distress he has received in my service for my love, yea, and because of his good will! Is it not reasonable that I reward him for his fright and his dread, his injury and his wounds and all his woe? And not only this, but does it not fall to me to give a gift that is to him better and more honorable than his own health would have been?[15] Otherwise it seems to me I would be doing him no favor."

In this an inward, spiritual showing of the lord's meaning settled into my soul, in which I saw that it was fitting and necessary—seeing his great goodness and his own honor—that his dearworthy servant whom he loved so much would be truly and blessedly rewarded without end beyond what he would have been if he had not fallen. Yea, and to such an extent that his falling and all the woe that he had received from it would be transformed into high and surpassing honor and endless bliss.[16]

At this point the showing of this illustration vanished, and our good Lord directed my understanding onward in vision and in showing the rest of the revelations to the end.[17]

But notwithstanding all this <u>diversion</u>,[18] the wonder of the illustration never went from me; for it seemed to me it was given me as an answer to my desire, and yet I could not perceive in it a full interpretation for my comfort at that time.

In the servant (who symbolized Adam, as I shall say) I saw many varied characteristics that could by no means be attributed to the individual Adam.

And so at that time I remained much in ignorance, because the full interpretation of this wondrous illustration was not given me at that

19. Julian's simple and practical way of dealing with one's lack of understanding of matters theological is this: just wait. And God will reveal what we need to know when God wishes to do so. We need not spend much time and energy trying to comprehend everything that comes to our attention.

20. That is, sometime in February 1393. However, Julia Holloway alone transcribes the BV as reading "XV yeres" (fifteen years) rather than "XX yeres" (twenty years).

21. Even decades after the vision, Julian believes she is still receiving "inner teaching" from God.

22. Julian is bidden to look more closely at all the small details and elements of the illustration to seek for hidden meaning. God said, in effect, "Go back to those memories of the vision, and do not be satisfied with the mere outward forms: look for spiritual meanings." (Note: This promotes the classical ancient method of reading the Scriptures allegorically, now applied to Julian's vision.)

23. Julian assents to the prodding of this "inner teaching" and agrees to look more deeply at the details of the vision, to "exegete" the vision's details.

time. In this mysterious illustration the secrets of the revelation are still much hidden, and nevertheless I saw and understood that every showing is full of secrets, and therefore it behooves me now to tell three aspects by which I am somewhat eased.

The first is the beginning of the teaching which I understood in the showing at that original time;

the second is the inner teaching which I have understood in it since then;

the third, all the whole revelation from the beginning to the end (that is to say, concerning this book) which our Lord God of His goodness frequently brings freely to the sight of my understanding.

And these three are so united, as I understand it, that I do not know how to, nor am I able to divide them. From this three-in-one I gain teaching by which I ought to believe and trust in our Lord God: that of the same goodness with which He showed it and for the same purpose, just so of that same goodness and for that same purpose He will explain it to us when that is His will.[19]

Twenty years after the time of the showing (short three months)[20] I received inner teaching,[21] as I shall say: "It is fitting for thee to take heed to all the qualities and conditions that were shown in the illustration even though thou thinkest that they are obscure and uninteresting to thy sight."[22]

I assented willingly with great desire, looking inwardly with deliberation at all the points and aspects that were shown at the previous time, to as great an extent as my wit and understanding would serve—beginning with my looking at the lord and at the servant, and the lord's manner of sitting, and the place that he sat on, and the color of his clothing and the kind of style, and his outward expression, and his nobility and his goodness within; at the servant's manner of standing and the place where and how, at his manner of clothing, the color and the style, at his outward behavior, and at his inward goodness and his willingness.[23]

The lord that sat solemnly in repose and in peace, I interpreted that he is God.

24. The servant is seen to represent Adam (that is, all humankind). See Romans 5:19—". . . as through the disobedience of one man many were made sinners, so through the obedience of one man many will be made righteous."

25. Even in his sin, Adam's *will* was still for God, and God knew that, even though Adam was not aware of it in the midst of sin.

26. It is the loss of perspective (that is, blindness) on the sinner's part that causes the pain and confusion.

27. Julian will later say that we cannot know God unless we know our own soul. (See Chapter 56.)

28. Punishment never comes from God. Just as God cannot be angry, so God cannot punish.

29. In the fourteenth century, the distinctions between the dress of men and women had not yet fully developed. For all people, the basic piece of clothing was the T-shaped tunic. For the poor it was short and skimpy, for the common folk it was calf-length; for the nobility it was ankle length and ample.

30. ME has *blew as asure*, but "azure" in the fourteenth century usually referred either to the precious blue stone (lapis lazuli), or to the blue dome of the heavens, or to the color of the sea. It is also the term used for "blue" in the tincture of formal heraldry. Blue was also the symbol of faithfulness as symbolized by the blue-colored flowers, the "forget-me-nots" (as worn by Sir Gawain).[135]

31. In fourteenth-century writing, brown symbolizes earthiness, warmth, and masculinity. It was originally a noun, meaning "the hide of a deer." It also suggests a weathered face.

32. ME has *a hey ward*, literally "a tall castle or tower." The word "ward" carries the sense of a safe place of refuge. (One is reminded of St. Teresa's "Interior Castle.")

The servant that stood before the lord, I interpreted that he symbol-ized Adam (that is to say, one man was shown at that time, and his falling, to make it thereby to be understood how God looks upon any man and his falling, for in the sight of God all mankind is one man and one man is all mankind).[24]

This man was damaged in his strength, and made completely feeble, and he was stunned in his understanding, for he turned away from the gaze of his lord; but his will was kept wholly in God's sight[25]—for I saw our Lord commend and approve his will (however, he himself was prevented and blinded from the knowledge of this will, and this is great sorrow and painful anguish to him; for he neither sees clearly his loving lord [who is most humble and gentle to him] nor sees truly what he himself is in the sight of that loving lord).[26]

And well I knew, when these two elements—the knowledge of self and the knowledge of our Lord—are wisely and truly perceived, we shall get rest and peace here in part, and the fullness of the bliss of heaven, by His plenteous grace.[27]

(This was a beginning of teaching which I saw at that same time by which I could come to recognize how He looks upon us in our sin. And at that time I saw that pain alone blames and punishes, but our gracious Lord comforts and succors,[28] and He is always of glad disposition to the soul, loving and yearning to bring us to bliss.)

The place that our Lord sat on was humble, on the barren and desert earth, alone in wilderness. His clothing was wide and long, and most befitting as becomes a lord.[29] The color of his clothing was blue as lapis lazuli,[30] most grave and fair. His countenance was merciful; the color of his face was a beautiful brown[31] with well-shaped features. His eyes were dark, most fair and fitting, showing full of loving pity.

And within him was a lofty sanctuary,[32] long and broad, all full of endless heavens. And the loving gaze with which he looked upon his servant constantly (and especially when he fell) it seemed to me could melt our hearts for love, and burst them in two for joy.

This beautiful gazing appeared a fitting mixture that was wondrous to see: one part was compassion and pity, the other was joy and bliss.

33. ME has *cher*, which literally means "face" or "countenance." The reference is to the Beatific Vision promised to those who are saved.

34. It was the universal medieval belief that when Christ "descended into hell" after His death and before his Resurrection, the first person He freed from hell was Adam.

35. Julian gets a little ahead of herself: she doesn't specifically identify the servant with Christ until later in the chapter.

36. Julian would have been familiar with the frequent medieval depiction of the Holy Trinity with the Father as an old, bearded man, holding the crucified Christ between his knees, with the Holy Spirit hovering in the form of a dove. Julian goes on to describe the Lord in very human terms, probably reflecting that familiar depiction of the Trinity.

37. The ME has *cyte*, literally meaning "city," as all other translators have it. But in fourteenth-century England the word "city" was restricted to those settlements that were "see cities" (that is, cities where a bishop had his cathedral throne). The word *cyte* implied an episcopal throne in the settlement so described. Here Julian compares God to a bishop.

38. Human sin made the human soul unfit for the Godhead, but God was so committed to the human soul that He refused to take any substitute dwelling place, and therefore simply sat on the bare earth without a proper throne.

39. The ME has *flamand abowten*, meaning literally "flaming around," and it has confounded most translators. Julia Holloway curiously translates it as "fair gathered about"; C&W equally curiously translate it as "billowing." It should be clear that it has to do with flame-like *color*—the precise meaning of "flamboyant." See also Wisdom 18:24 (NJB)— "For the whole world was on his flowing robe. . . ."

40. God's joy when he sees the fallen servant comes from God's foresight that in the future the Adam/servant will be "restored" and brought to joy.

(The joy and bliss surpassed as far the compassion and pity as heaven is above earth.) The pity was earthly and the bliss was heavenly.

The compassion and the pity of the Father was for the falling of Adam, who is His most beloved creation.

The joy and bliss were for the falling of His dearworthy Son, who is equal with the Father. (The merciful vision of His lovely <u>face</u>[33] filled all earth and descended down with Adam into hell, and with this constant pity Adam was preserved from endless death.[34] And this mercy and pity dwell with mankind until the time we come up into heaven.)[35]

But Man is blinded in this life, and therefore we cannot see our Father God as He is.

So whenever He of His goodness wills to show Himself to Man, He shows Himself humbly as man (notwithstanding that, I understood truly we ought to know and believe that the Father is not man).[36]

And His sitting on the bare earth and desert is to mean this—He made Man's soul to be His own <u>Throne</u>[37] and His dwelling place (which is the most pleasing to Him of all His works), and whenever man had fallen into sorrow and pain he was not wholly fit to serve in that noble position; and therefore our kind Father rather than give Himself any other space, sits upon the earth, awaiting mankind (who are mixed with earth) until whenever by His grace His dearworthy Son had brought again His see into its noble beauty with His harsh labor.[38]

The blueness of His clothing symbolizes His steadfastness.

The brownness of His fair face with the fitting darkness of the eyes was most agreeable to show His holy gravity.

The breadth of His clothing, which was beautiful and <u>flamboyant</u>,[39] symbolizes that He has enclosed within Himself all heavens and all joy and bliss.

(And this was shown in one stroke where I say "my understanding was guided to the Lord." In this guiding I saw Him highly rejoicing because of the honorable restoration that He wills and shall bring His servant to by His plenteous grace.)[40]

41. At this point Julian has so far described the servant as Adam (that is, all humankind). It is quite amazing that she should see an equal and mutual love in both God and humankind.

42. We are reminded that wisdom is the character of the second person of the Trinity.

43. W&J remind us that the lord does not command the servant, but the servant recognizes that he could serve his lord.

44. Julian begins to build the paradoxical identity of the servant both as Adam and also as Christ. Christ's labor of redemption was to be "new."

45. It seems likely that Julian makes reference here to the "treasure hidden in a field" (Matthew 13:44, NRSV).

46. This may be a reference to John 4:32 and 34—"I have food to eat of which you know nothing" and "For me it is meat and drink to do the will of him who sent me until I have finished his work." The food allegory is a challenging (and somewhat forced) one. It is perhaps best understood that the "food" is a gift—the redemption of humankind—given to the Father by the Son through the "labor" of Christ's Passion.

47. Julian shows naiveté in noticing that the lord had no provisions in sight, and no one to serve him food and drink. She is transferring to the vision her own cultural experience of a lord and his servants.

And still I wondered, examining the lord and the servant as I said before. I saw the lord sit solemnly and the servant standing reverently before his lord.

In the servant there is a double meaning: one outward, another inward. Outwardly, he was clad humbly as a workman who was used to hard labor, and he stood very near the lord (not right in front of him, but partly aside on the left). His clothing was a white tunic, thin, old and all soiled, stained with sweat of his body, tight fitting for him and short, as it were only a hand's width below the knee, undecorated, seeming as if it would soon be worn out, about to be turned to rags and torn.

And in this I marveled greatly, thinking: "This is now unfitting clothing for the servant that is so highly loved to stand before so dignified a lord."

But inwardly, in the servant was shown a foundation of love that he had for the lord which was equal to the love that the lord had for him.[41] The wisdom[42] of the servant saw inwardly that there was one thing to do that would be to the honor of the lord.[43] And the servant, for love, having no regard for himself nor for anything that might befall him, hastily leaped up and ran at the bidding of his lord to do that thing which was the lord's will and his honor.

For it seemed by his outward clothing that he had been a regular workman for a long time; but by the insight that I had (both in the lord and in the servant), it seemed that he was new, that is to say, newly beginning to labor—as a servant who had never been sent out before.[44]

There was a treasure in the earth which the lord loved.[45] I marveled and imagined what it could be. And I was answered in my understanding: "It is a <u>food</u> which is lovely and pleasant to the lord."[46]

(For I saw the lord sit as a man, but I saw neither food nor drink wherewith to serve him; that was a wonder. Another wonder was that this solemn lord had no servant but one, and him he sent out.)[47]

I watched, wondering what kind of work it might be that the servant would do.

48. Genesis 3:17—"And to the man [God] said . . . 'on your account the earth will be cursed. You will get your food from it only by labour all the days of your life; it will yield thorns and thistles for you. You will eat of the produce of the field, and only by the sweat of your brow will you win your bread until you return to the earth. . . .' " Remember that the risen Christ is mistaken for a gardener by Mary Magdalene (John 20:15). One is also reminded of a maxim taught by the radical priest John Ball during the Peasants' Rebellion in 1381:

    When Adam delved, and Eve span
    Who was then the gentleman?
    When Adam delved and Eve span,
    Spur if thou wilt speed,
    Where was then the pride of man
    That now so mars his meed?
    [*delved*=dug; *span*=spinned; *meed*=merit; *Eve* in ME was
    pronounced "Eveh"]

49. In these two paragraphs Julian is setting up her recognition of the servant as the Son of the Father. Her questioning "from whence the servant came," since she saw that all life was in the lord, leads directly to her validation of the familiar language of the Nicene Creed: "We believe in one Lord, Jesus Christ, the only Son of God, eternally begotten of the Father, God from God, Light from Light, true God from true God, begotten, not made." In the next paragraph she expresses the answer to her questioning.

50. Finally Julian expresses her central paradox: the servant is both the Son and also (at the same time) Adam/humankind. The absolute identification of Christ with humanity is one of Julian's special teachings. From her point of view, humanity was the Father's gift to His Son even before human beings were created. This is a sensitivity that confronts the intricate conundrum of a "timeless" God and "time-bound" humanity. At the eternal begetting of the Son, He was human, and

Then I understood that he would do the greatest work and hardest toil that is—he would be a gardener;[48]

> digging and ditching,
>
> straining and sweating,
>
> and turning over the earth,
>
> and seeking the depths,
>
> and watering the plants on time.

And in this he would continue his labor and make sweet streams to run, and noble and plenteous fruits to spring, which he would bring before the lord and serve him therewith to his delight.

And he would never return until he had prepared this food all ready as he knew that it delighted the lord, and then he would take this food with the drink, and bear it most honorably before the lord.

And all this time the lord would sit in the same place awaiting his servant whom he sent out.

(I still wondered from whence the servant came, for I saw that the lord had within himself endless life and all kinds of goodness, except that treasure that was on the earth—and that was grounded in the lord in wondrous depth of endless love [but it was not wholly to his honor until this servant had prepared it thus nobly and brought it before him, in the lord's own presence].)

And except for the lord there was nothing but wilderness. And I did not understand all that this illustration meant, and therefore I wondered whence the servant came.[49]

In the servant is included the Second Person in the Trinity, and also in the servant is included Adam, that is to say, all men.[50]

(And therefore, when I say "the Son," it means the Godhead which is equal with the Father, and when I say "the servant," it means Christ's manhood which is true Adam.)

when earthly humanity was created, it was an imitation of the preexisting humanity of the Son. At the Incarnation, the Son was already human, but merely took on the outward form of earthly humanity. Julian's concept is so radical that it is one of the highest mystical insights in the history of Christology. See Romans 8:29 (NJB)—"[God] decided beforehand who were the ones destined to be moulded to the pattern of his Son, so that he should be the eldest of many brothers. . . ."

51. We know that the Son's place was on the Father's right hand, so humanity's place was on the left.

52. This is another reference to the Harrowing of Hell in which Christ brought Adam out of hell after Christ's death and before His Resurrection.

53. This is a final clear statement of the identity of the Son and humanity.

54. The essential goodness of humanity exists because of the "Christ-in-us," and the sin and weakness of humanity comes from our earthly "non-Christ-ness."

55. By entering into our earthliness, Christ has "absorbed" our guilt, and, since we are identified with Him, we are not blamed by God.

By the nearness of the servant is understood the Son, and by the standing on the left side is understood Adam.[51]

The lord is the Father, God.

The servant is the Son, Christ Jesus.

The Holy Spirit is equal Love who is in them both.

When Adam fell, God's Son fell—because of the true union that was made in heaven. God's Son could not be separated from Adam (for by "Adam" I understand "all men").

Adam fell from life to death into the pit of this miserable world and after that into hell.

God's Son fell with Adam into the pit of the womb of the Maiden (who was the fairest daughter of Adam) and that in order to obtain for Adam exemption from guilt in heaven and on earth. And he mightily fetched Adam out of hell.[52]

By the wisdom and goodness that was in the servant is understood God's Son.

By the poor clothing as a workman standing near the left side is understood the manhood of Adam, with all the misfortune and weakness that follow from that—for in all this our Good Lord showed His own Son and Adam as but one man.[53]

The virtue and the goodness that we have is from Jesus Christ, the weakness and the blindness that we have is from Adam—both of which were shown in the servant.[54]

And thus has our good Lord Jesus taken upon Himself all our guilt; and therefore our Father can, and will, no more assign blame to us than to His own Son, dearworthy Christ.[55]

In this way He was the servant before His coming onto the earth, standing ready before the Father intentionally until whatever time the Father would send Him to do that honorable deed by which mankind was brought again into heaven—that is to say, notwithstanding that He is God (equal with the Father as concerns the Godhead) in His foreseeing purpose He was willing to be man to save man by fulfilling His Father's will.

56. Christ's heavenly humanity was linked with earthly humanity in the Incarnation. The perfect humanity of the heavenly Son is tied to the poverty and toil of earthly humanity. W&J quote *Ancrene Wisse* (part 6): "Our old dress is the flesh which we have from Adam our first father."

57. Julian corrects herself: of course, the Son as God already knew the Father's will and when the Incarnation would happen. It is His *humanity* that asks, "How long. . . ."

58. The original meaning of the word *member* was "limb" or "organ" or "part of a body," not merely a person who joined a club.

59. Mark 13:32—"Yet about that day or hour no one knows, not even the angels in heaven, not even the Son; no one but the Father."

60. It can be expressed this way: the only person who "shall be saved" is Jesus, and all others "shall be saved" only because they are part of His mystical body.

61. The "ABC" was a combination spelling primer–prayer book for children that included the basic prayers: the Lord's Prayer, the Hail Mary, and the Creed. Once a child learned his or her letters, the first piece of prose used to teach reading was the Lord's Prayer.

So He stood before His Father as a servant, willingly taking upon Himself all our burden. And then He leaped up wholly ready at the Father's will, and soon He fell most lowly into the Maiden's womb, having no regard for Himself nor for His harsh pains.

The white tunic is His flesh; its thinness is that there was absolutely nothing separating the Godhead and manhood; the tightness of the tunic is poverty; the age is from Adam's wearing it; the staining of sweat, from Adam's toil; the shortness shows the servant's work.[56]

And thus I saw the Son standing, saying in His meaning, "Behold, my dear Father, I stand before Thee in Adam's tunic all ready to jump up and to run. I am willing to be on the earth to do Thine honor when it is Thy will to send me. How long shall I wish for it?"

(Most truly was the Son aware when it was the Father's will and how long He would wish for it—that is to say, from the point of view of His Godhead, for He is the Wisdom of the Father.)[57]

Therefore this meaning was shown in understanding about the manhood of Christ: all mankind that shall be saved by the sweet incarnation and blessed Passion of Christ, all is the manhood of Christ, for He is the Head and we are His members[58] (to which members the day and the time is unknown when every passing woe and sorrow shall have an end, and the everlasting joy and bliss shall be fulfilled—which day and time, all the company of heaven yearns to see).[59]

All who are under heaven who shall come to heaven, their way is by yearning and desire. This desire and yeaning was shown in the servant standing before the lord (or else thus, in the Son's standing before the Father in Adam's tunic), for the yearning and desire of all mankind that shall be saved was manifested in Jesus (for Jesus is all that shall be saved and all that shall be saved is Jesus),[60] and all from the love of God, with obedience, meekness and patience, and virtues that belong to us.

Also in this marvelous illustration I receive a teaching within me (as it were the beginning of an ABC)[61] whereby I can have some understanding of our Lord's meaning, because the secrets of the revelation are hidden in this illustration (notwithstanding that all the showings are full of secrets).

62. Here is Julian's understanding of Christ's emptying Himself of His divine prerogatives in the Incarnation. (In the Greek this is called *kenosis*.) See Philippians 2:6–7—"[Christ] was in the form of God; yet he laid no claim to equality with God, but made himself nothing, assuming the form of a slave. Bearing the human likeness, sharing the human lot, he humbled himself, and was obedient, even to the point of death, death on a cross!"

63. The reference is to Christ's dying words, "Father, into your hands I commit my spirit" (Luke 23:46).

The sitting of the Father symbolizes His Godhead (that is to say, in order to show repose and peace, for in the Godhead can be no toil).

And that He showed Himself as lord symbolizes our manhood.

The standing of the servant symbolizes labor.

That he stands on the side and on the left symbolizes that he was not fully worthy to stand directly before the lord.

His leaping up was the Godhead, and the running was the manhood (for the Godhead leaps from the Father into the Maiden's womb, descending into the taking of our human nature; and in this falling He received great injury; the injury that He received was our flesh in which He also soon had powerful experiences of mortal pains).

By the fact that He stood fearfully before the lord, and not directly so, indicates that His clothing was not respectable enough to stand directly before the lord, and that could not, or would not, be His position while He was a workman.[62] And also He could not sit in repose and peace with the lord until He had won His peace properly with His harsh toil. By the left side symbolizes that the Father left His own Son willingly in the manhood to suffer all man's pains without sparing Him.

By the fact that His tunic was at the point of being turned to rags and torn is understood the stripes and the scourges, the thorns and the nails, the pulling and the dragging, His tender flesh tearing (as I saw to some degree, the flesh was torn from the skull, falling in shreds until the time the bleeding stopped; and then the flesh began to dry again, clinging to the bone).

And by the wallowing and writhing, groaning and moaning, is understood that He could never rise omnipotently from the time that He was fallen into the Maiden's womb until His body was slain and dead, He yielding His soul into the Father's hands along with all mankind for whom He was sent.[63]

And at this point of rising He began first to show His power, for He went into hell, and when He was there He raised up out of the deep Depths the Great Root of Jesse which properly was knit to Him in high heaven.

64. The ME has *medlar*. Julia Holloway translates it as "rainbow." It is possible that Julian was thinking of Joseph's "coat of many colors." It is also possible that Julian is remembering scenes from the mystery plays that were popular in her day, dramatizing the Harrowing of Hell and other "scenes" from the Passion.

65. It is quite amazing that Julian finds the clothing of the risen Christ/servant to be even "fairer and richer" than that of the Father/lord.

66. Julian is visualizing the icon of the Holy Trinity frequently seen in Norwich Cathedral, with the Father as an old man on a large throne.

67. "We are His crown" reminds the reader that we were also His "crown of thorns." See James 1:12 (NRSV)—"Blessed is anyone who endures temptation. Such a one has stood the test and will receive the crown of life that the Lord has promised to those who love him."

68. Julian's wonderful simplicity shows through her concern that sitting "on His Father's right hand" should not be taken literally.

69. Here and below we find the only evidence of "nuptial mysticism" in Julian's writings, although it is almost universal in the writings of other medieval women mystics.

70. The ME has *cyte*. See note 37 above. Note that the "wilderness" is now gone, replaced by the city, which is the human soul, and it is interesting to reflect on the statement here that God "has devoted" the human soul to the Son "out of his endless purpose."

The Body lay in the grave until Easter morning, and from that time on He lay down never more.

Then was rightfully ended the wallowing and the writhing, the groaning and the moaning; and our foul mortal flesh that God's Son took upon Himself (which was Adam's old tunic, tight, bare, and short then by our Savior was made fair, new, white, and bright, and of endless purity, wide and ample, fairer and richer than was then the clothing which I saw on the Father, for that clothing was blue, and Christ's clothing is now of a light, becoming mixture[64] which is so wonderful that I cannot describe it, for it is all of true glory).[65]

No longer does the Lord sit on the ground in wilderness, but now He sits on His noblest throne that He made in heaven most to His pleasure.[66]

No longer stands the Son before the Father as a servant fearfully poorly clad, in part naked, but now He stands before the Father directly, richly clad in blessed ampleness, with a crown upon His Head of precious richness (for it was shown that we are His crown,[67] which crown is the Father's joy, the Son's honor, the Holy Spirit's pleasure, and endless marvelous bliss to all that are in heaven).

Now the Son does not stand before the Father on the left side as a workman, but He sits on His Father's right hand in endless repose and peace.

(But it is not meant that the Son sits on the right hand, side by side, as one man sits by another in this life; for there is no such sitting, as to my sight, in the Trinity for He sits on His Father's right hand, that is to say, in the highest nobility of the Father's joys.)[68]

Now is the Spouse, God's Son, in peace with His beloved Wife, which is Holy Church, the Fair Maiden of endless joy.[69]

Now sits the Son, true God and Man, in repose and peace on His Throne,[70] which His Father has devoted to Him out of His endless purpose, and the Father is in the Son, and the Holy Spirit in the Father and in the Son.

COMMENTS ON CHAPTER 52

1. This is the first clear statement that God is our Mother. In Chapter 46 Julian speaks of the Church as our Mother, and in Chapter 48 she mentions that mercy is part of the character of motherhood, but this is the first clear statement that God is our Mother.
2. PV curiously places the period after "all we who shall be saved."
3. In modern Norfolk, the ME word *medlur* would probably be translated by the popular word "muddle."
4. Again Julian emphasizes the unity between humanity (Adam) and Christ: sometimes we experience the joy of resurrection, and sometimes the misery of falling.
5. This is a reference to our own resurrection: if we die as Adam, we still rise as Christ.
6. Note the distinction between God's actively raising us to joy and passively permitting us to sin.
7. The ME has *in what way we stonden*.
8. Remember that Julian had lived through three onsets of the Black Death when she first wrote this (and knew that many believed the Plague to be a "punishment" from God).

⤳ 52

Thus I saw that God rejoices that He is our Father, God rejoices that He is our Mother,[1] and God rejoices that He is our true Spouse and that our soul is His beloved wife. And Christ rejoices that He is our Brother, and Jesus rejoices that He is our Savior.

These are five high joys, as I understand, in which He wills: that we rejoice, praising Him, thanking Him, loving Him, endlessly blessing Him.[2]

All we who shall be saved, for the period of this life, have in us a wondrous <u>mixture</u>[3] both of well and woe: we have in us our Lord Jesus arisen; we have in us the misery of the misfortune of Adam's falling.[4]

Dying, we are steadfastly protected by Christ, and by His gracious touching we are raised in certain trust of salvation.[5]

And by Adam's falling we are so fragmented in our feeling in differing ways (by sins and by various pains, in which we are made sad and blind as well) that scarcely do we know how to obtain any comfort.

But in our intention we await God and faithfully trust to receive mercy and grace; and this is His own working in us.

Of his goodness He opens the eye of our understanding by which we have insight—sometimes more and sometimes less—as God gives us ability to receive it.

And now we are raised into one, and again we are allowed to fall into the other.[6]

And thus is this mixture so wondrous in us that scarcely do we know about our selves or about our fellow Christians <u>how we hold out</u>,[7] because of the wonderment of these different feelings—except for that same holy assent that we consent to God when we sense Him, truly willing to be with Him with all our heart, with all our soul, and with all our strength.

And then we hate and despise our evil stirrings and all that might be occasion of sin, spiritually and bodily.

And yet nevertheless when this sweetness is hidden, we fall again into blindness, and so into woe and tribulation in diverse ways.[8] But

9. Julian never demands an oversimplified clarity. She is willing to accept that we humans are in a constant "muddle"—up and down, right and wrong, virtuous and sinful, but never forsaken by Christ. Sin, for her, is no impediment to the constant and unending mercy and grace of God.

10. We can see something of the "mechanics" of Julian's reflective thinking, the conclusions she comes to as a result of the revelations.

11. Julian sees *both* humanity and God's Son as concurrently present in the servant figure. It is not a case of the servant figure at some times representing humanity and at some other times representing Christ, but rather they are always identical, although we may think of them separately.

12. This is another reiteration of the idea of the *felix culpa*, the fortunate sin—fortunate because it brought about the Incarnation, the Passion, and the Resurrection, and all the blissful benefits to mankind derived from them. C&W remind us that in Julian's day there was an ongoing controversy between followers of Thomas Aquinas and those of Bonaventure about whether Christ would have come if Adam had not sinned. C&W also quote Walter Hilton's *Scale of Perfection* II, Chapter 4: ". . . [the soul] shall be restored to much more bliss and much higher joy through the great mercy and the endless goodness of God than it would have had if it had never fallen."

13. Here we see a quiet moral implication: that hate is inappropriate when addressed to anything except sin.

14. This is a seemingly shocking idea: that our inability to keep from sinning was part of "God's purpose"—in that His purpose was to give us free will in order to love Him, but also to be able to reject Him, and hence to sin.

then this is our comfort: that we know in our faith that by the strength of Christ, who is our protector, we never consent to sin, but we rail against it, and endure in pain and woe, praying until that time when He shows Himself again to us.

And thus we remain in this muddle all the days of our lives.[9]

But He wills that we trust that He is everlastingly with us, and that in three ways:

He is with us in heaven, true man in His own Person drawing us upward (and that was shown in the spiritual thirst); and He is with us on earth, leading us (and that was shown in the third showing, where I saw God in a point); and He is with us in our soul eternally dwelling, ruling and taking care of us (and that was shown in the sixteenth showing, as I shall say).[10]

Thus in the servant was shown the misfortune and blindness of Adam's falling, and in the servant was also shown the wisdom and goodness of God's Son.[11] In the Lord was shown the compassion and pity for Adam's woe; and in the Lord was also shown the high nobility and the endless honor that mankind has come to by virtue of the Passion and the death of His dearworthy Son.

Therefore He powerfully rejoices in Adam's falling, because of the noble raising and fullness of bliss that mankind has come to, surpassing what we would have had if Adam had not fallen.[12]

And thus in order to see this surpassing nobility, my understanding was led into God at the same time that I saw the servant fall.

And so we have now cause for mourning, for our sin is the cause of Christ's pains;

And we have everlastingly cause for joy, for endless love caused Him to suffer.

Therefore the creature who sees and senses the working of love by grace hates nothing but sin; for of all things, as I see it, love and hate are the most unyielding and most immoderate opposites.[13]

Notwithstanding all this, I saw and understood in our Lord's purpose that we cannot in this life keep ourselves from sin as totally in complete purity as we shall in heaven.[14] But by grace we can well keep us

15. Julian distinguishes between mortal sin (which is overcome with confession, penance, and absolution) and venial sin, which can be overcome by will power aided by grace.

16. This is one of the rare times when Julian actually gives advice and teaching to her readers.

17. Julian does not merely "write off" sin, but requires that we recognize our sin and accuse ourselves of it, knowing when we do so that God will forgive it.

from the sins which would lead us to endless pain (as Holy Church teaches us) and avoid the venial ones, reasonably within our power; and, if at any time we fall by our blindness and our misery, that we can readily arise, knowing the sweet touching of grace, and willingly amend ourselves following the teaching of Holy Church according to the sin's gravity, and go forthwith to God in love.[15]

Neither on the one hand fall overly low, inclining to despair, nor on the other hand be over reckless as if we gave no heed, but humbly acknowledging our weakness, aware that we cannot stand even a twinkling of an eye except by the protection of grace, and reverently cleaving to God, trusting in Him alone.[16]

For one way is God's point of view, and the other way is man's point of view; for it belongs to man humbly to accuse himself, and it belongs to the excellent goodness of our Lord God graciously to forgive man.

These are two parts that were shown in the double attitude in which the lord viewed the falling of his beloved servant.

The one was shown outward, very humbly and gently, with great compassion and pity, and the other of inward endless love.

And just so wills our Lord that we accuse ourselves, willingly and truly seeing and recognizing our falling and all the harms that come therefrom, understanding and being aware that we can never reinstate it, and along with that that we also willingly and truly recognize and acknowledge His everlasting love that He has for us, and His plenteous mercy.[17]

Thus graciously to recognize and acknowledge both together is the gentle self-accusing that our Lord asks of us, and He Himself does it wherever it happens.

This is the lower part of man's life, and it was shown in the outward expression, in which showing I saw two parts:

—the one is the pitiful falling of man,

—the other is the honorable amends that our Lord has made for man.

The other attitude was shown inwardly, and that was more exalted and all the same; for the life and the strength that we have in the lower

18 This is a difficult passage as it begins to introduce Julian's idea of the "lower" and "higher" aspects of humanity: the "lower" being the outward, visible, and physically evident dimension (which the Church addresses) and the "higher" being the inward, spiritual, and metaphysical dimension (which her revelations address). The positive aspects of the "lower," earthly dimension come to us by grace from the love we have rising from our good human nature. C&W seriously mistranslate this as "the substantial love of the self."[136]

19. These two "levels" of the human dimension are not alien to each other, because both the compassion and forgiveness of the "lower" part (the Church's part) and the joy of the "higher" part (God's heavenly part) have their origins in the perfect love of God. The "lower" part is the love/forgiveness we experience on earth and the "higher" part is the love/joy we experience in heaven.

20. PV has *holy dystroyed*; BV has *holy restored*. The latter is senseless.

21. Julian escapes the limitations of time and space by recognizing the unity between the love God shows us on earth and the final love God shows us in heaven.

COMMENTS ON CHAPTER 53

1. It was the common belief of medieval Christians that Adam, since he was unbaptized, had been sent to limbo at his death, and was released by Christ in His Harrowing of Hell before the Resurrection. Limbo (Latin: *limbus*, meaning "hem" or "border") was considered to be the place or state of the unbaptized after death—at the "border" of heaven, but excluded from the Beatific Vision.

2. The conundrum of Chapter 50 is to some degree solved for Julian and not mentioned again until the end of the book in Chapter 82.

part is from the higher, and it comes down to us from the self's natural love by grace.[18]

There is absolutely nothing separating the one and the other, for it is all one love.[19]

This blessed love has now in us a double action:

—for in the lower part are pains and sufferings, compassions and pities, mercies and forgiveness and such other things that are beneficial,

—but in the higher part are none of these, except the same high love and overwhelming joy, in which overwhelming joy all pains are <u>wholly destroyed</u>.[20]

In this our good Lord showed not only our excusing, but also the honorable nobility that He shall bring us to, transforming all our guilt into endless honor.[21]

⟿ 53

I saw that He wishes us to be aware that He does not take the falling of any creature that shall be saved more severely than He took the falling of Adam (who we know was endlessly loved and safely protected in the time of all his need, and now is blissfully restored in high, surpassing joys),[1] for our Lord God is so good, so gentle, and so gracious that He can never assign fault to those in whom He shall ever be blessed and praised.

And in this that I have now said my desire was in part answered, and my great fear somewhat eased by the loving, gracious showing of our Good Lord.[2]

3. The ME has *godly wille*. Since the word *godly* etymologically means "godlike," I have translated it as "divine." This seems to be a controversial teaching, but Julian explains herself carefully later in this chapter.
4. Julian clearly declares that she does not deviate from the teachings of the Church.
5. The divine will is present in human nature because of that nature's actual participation in the Divine Being through its utter union with Christ, a union that sin cannot destroy.
6. The ME has *substance*, but the modern meaning of that word is drastically different from Julian's meaning. The medieval meaning is equivalent to our modern word "essence." Here Julian introduces the idea (which she develops more fully later) that the "essence" of each human being remains in heaven one-ed to God. In nontheological language, we might say that the "idea" of each human being remains in the mind of God since before Creation.
7. Holy Church taught that the Atonement and Redemption were necessary for the forgiveness of human sins, and Julian accepts that proposition.
8. Julian's insight is a kind of "reverse eternity"—that is, an eternity stretching backward "without beginning"—that just as God will love humanity forever in the future, so God has loved humanity since before Creation in His divine "foresight."
9. C&W suggest that Julian may have invented this way of referring to the Second Person of the Trinity.
10. "In [the Son] everything in heaven and on earth was created ...the whole universe has been created through him and for him" (Colossians 1:16).
11. We came out of the humanity of the Son (whose humanity preceded ours); we are now enclosed in the Mystical Body of Christ, the Church; and we shall join Him in perfect union in heaven.

In this showing I saw and understood full certainly that in every soul that shall be saved is a <u>divine will</u>[3] that never consents to sin, nor ever will. This will is so good that it can never will evil, but evermore continually it wills good and does good in the sight of God.

Therefore our Lord wishes that we recognize this in the Faith and the Belief of the Church[4] and specifically and truly that we have all this blessed will whole and safe in our Lord Jesus Christ,[5] for that kind of human nature with which heaven shall be filled ought properly, by God's righteousness, to be so knitted and one-ed to Him that in that human nature is guarded an <u>essence</u>[6] which can never be (nor should be) parted from Him—and that through His own good will in His endless foreseeing purpose.

Notwithstanding this rightful knitting and this eternal one-ing, still the redemption and the buying back of mankind is necessary and beneficial in every instance, since it is done for the same intention and to the same end that Holy Church in our Faith teaches us.[7]

I saw that God never started to love mankind, for just as mankind shall be in endless bliss fulfilling the joy of God as regards His works, just so the same mankind has been, in the foresight of God, known and loved from without beginning in His rightful intention.[8]

By the endless intention and consent of the full agreement of all the Trinity, the <u>Mid-Person</u>[9] wished to be ground and head of this fair human nature,[10] out of Whom we are all come, in Whom we are all enclosed, into Whom we shall all go,[11] in Him finding our full heaven in everlasting joy by the foreseeing purpose of all the blessed Trinity from without beginning.

12. Julian returns all of her thought once again to the Holy Trinity, putting her new insights into the familiar pattern: Goodness=the Holy Spirit; Power=the Father; Wisdom=the Son.

13. In BV the ME word is *slyppe*. Interestingly, "slip" is still a potter's word for a thin fluid mixture of water and clay often used for adding decorations to a completed pot.

14. "The LORD God formed a human being from the dust of the ground and breathed into his nostrils the breath of life" (Genesis 2:7).

15. This simple statement flies in the face of all the popular religious ideas of Julian's day that saw humankind as vastly distant from God and fearful of His judgment.

16. The ME has *our soule is a lif.* The soul has a life of its own and can exist without the body, but the body cannot exist without the soul.

17. One might say that God loved even God's very intention to create humankind.

18. Julian is an "originist"—that is, she sees things as they are at their origins: so she sees humanity as "noble" when in her day humanity would have generally been thought of as sin-ridden and wretched. This is another example of the optimism that is a hallmark of Julian's thought.

19. The sanctity of the human soul comes not just from its own nature, but from its endless union with/in God. And it is always holy, sin notwithstanding.

20. Julian moves beyond the individual soul and its relation to God to recognize the common bond among all human souls, knit not only to God, but to each other.

Before ever He made us, He loved us, and when we were created we loved Him. And this is a love created by the natural essential Goodness of the Holy Spirit, mighty by reason of the Power of the Father, and wise in reminder of the Wisdom of the Son, and thus is man's soul made by God and at the same moment knit to God.[12]

Thus I understand that man's soul is created out of nothing—that is to say it is created, but out of nothing that has been created, like this: when God wished to create man's body, He took the slime[13] of earth (which is material mixed and gathered for all physical creatures) and out of that He created man's body.[14] But for the creating of man's soul, He willed to take absolutely nothing, but He created it.

And thus is the human nature created rightfully one-ed to the Creator—who is Essential Nature Uncreated: that is, God.

And therefore it is that there can, and will be, absolutely nothing separating God and man's soul.[15]

In this endless love man's soul is kept whole as the matter of the Revelations means and shows;

In this endless love we are led and protected by God and never shall be lost, for He wishes us to be aware that our soul has[16] a life which, of His goodness and His grace, shall last in heaven without end, loving Him, thanking Him, praising Him.

And just as we shall exist without end, so too we were treasured in God, and hidden, known, and loved from without beginning.[17]

Wherefore, He wishes us to be aware that the noblest being that ever He made is mankind (and the fullest essence and the highest virtue is the blessed soul of Christ).[18]

Furthermore, He wishes us to be aware that mankind's dearworthy soul was preciously knit to Him in the creation—and this knot is subtle and so powerful that it is one-ed into God. In this one-ing it is made endlessly holy.[19]

Furthermore, He wishes us to be aware that all the souls that shall be saved in heaven without end are knit and one-ed in this one-ing, and made holy in this holiness.[20]

COMMENTS ON CHAPTER 54

1. The identity within the figure of the servant of both the Son and all humanity brings God to give the same love to humanity as He does to His Son. He loves the least soul as much as He loves His Son.

2. Another indication that the "essence" of the human soul is in heaven—because of the union of the human soul with Christ, who is in heaven. See John 17:24—"Father, they are your gift to me; and my desire is that they may be with me where I am, so that they may look upon my glory."

3. Julian addresses this paradox: the human soul was made by God to be His "dwelling place," and concomitantly the soul also dwells within God. There seems to be a hint here of the theology of the Incarnation, in which the Creator of all things is "created" within the womb of the Blessed Virgin Mary. As an early hymn put it: "The Maker is made."

4. Julian speaks metaphorically: the essence of God is the same "kind of being" as the essence of a human being—both pure spirit—but she is careful to point out that there is a difference between God's essence and ours, in that one is uncreated and the other created.

5. This is a difficult passage to translate. The ME of the word translated as "power" is *vertue*. It seems that Julian is saying that strength of faith is a gift that the Holy Spirit "transfers" from our "heavenly essence" into our earthly selves. The ME of "fleshly" is *sensual*, but in common modern use that tends to mean "voluptuous" or "unchaste," whereas its original meaning was simply "involved with the five senses" (akin to our "sensuous"). I have chosen "fleshly" as more accurate. The "fleshly soul" is the spiritual aspect (consciousness) of our earthly selves.

⇀ 54

Because of the great endless love that God has toward all mankind, He makes no distinction in love between the blessed soul of Christ and the least souls that shall be saved.[1]

It is very easy to believe and to trust that the dwelling of the blessed soul of Christ is utterly high in the glorious Godhead, but truly, as I understand in our Lord's meaning, where the blessed soul of Christ is, there is the essence of all the souls that shall be saved by Christ.[2]

We ought greatly to rejoice that God dwells in our soul, and much more highly to rejoice that our soul dwells in God. Our soul is created to be God's dwelling place, and the dwelling place of the soul is God, who is uncreated.

It is an exalted understanding inwardly to see and to know that God, who is our Creator, dwells in our soul, and it is a more exalted understanding inwardly to see and to know that our soul, which is created, dwells in God's in its essence—from which essence, by God, we are what we are.[3]

I saw no distinction between God and our essence, but just as if it were all God, and yet my understanding accepted that our essence is in God—that is to say, that God is God, and our essence is a creation of God.[4]

The all–Powerful truth of the Trinity is our Father, for He created us and keeps us within Him; and the deep Wisdom of the Trinity is our Mother, in whom we are all enclosed; the exalted Goodness of the Trinity is our Lord, and in Him we are enclosed and He in us. We are enclosed in the Father, we are enclosed in the Son, and we are enclosed in the Holy Spirit; and the Father is enclosed in us, and the Son is enclosed in us, and the Holy Spirit is enclosed in us: all Power, all Wisdom, all Goodness, one God, one Lord.

And our faith is a <u>power</u> that comes from our natural essence into our <u>fleshly</u> soul by the Holy Spirit, and within this faith all our virtues come to us (for without that no man may receive virtue).[5]

6. For Julian, "faith" is simply recognizing what is true even if it is invisible (see Hebrews 11:1—"Faith . . . convinces us of realities we do not see").

7. Our virtue comes from Christ's presence. C&W suggest that the passage refers to Holy Baptism. See John 1:12—"But to all who did accept him . . . he gave the right to become children of God."

COMMENTS ON CHAPTER 55

1. In Chapter 52, Julian described Christ as with us in heaven, leading us on earth and keeping us eternally. Now she speaks of these second and third aspects of the relationship. See John 14:6—"I am the way, the truth, and the life. . . ."

2. All baptized Christians are "in Him" and are members of His Mystical Body, the Church.

3. This "double gift-giving" is curious. It may refer to Ephesians 5:25–7—". . . Christ loved the church and gave himself up for it, to consecrate and cleanse it by water and word, so that he might present the church to himself all glorious, with no stain or wrinkle or anything of the sort, but holy and without blemish."

4. This is classical Catholic metaphysics: that the heavenly reality is more deeply "real" than earthly reality, and it is the human's spiritual (rather than earthly) dimension that actually defines humanity.

5. The source of faith is threefold: (1) the love of the good, which is "built in" to each human nature at Creation; (2) the "clear light of reason," when applied in observation of the world around us; (3) the unconscious "recall" we have of God's nature, from the spiritual incorporation of our essence into God before earthly creation.

Faith is nothing else but a right understanding (with true belief and certain trust) of our being—that we are in God, and God in us—which we do not see.⁶ And this virtue of faith (with all others that God has ordained to us coming within it) works great things in us, for Christ's merciful working is in us (and we graciously reconciling to Him through the gifts and the virtues of the Holy Spirit), and this working causes us to be Christ's children and Christian in living.⁷

⌔ 55

Thus Christ is our Way, safely leading us in His laws, and Christ in His Body powerfully bears us up to heaven.¹

I saw that Christ, having in Him all of us who shall be saved by Him,² graciously presents his Father in heaven with us. And this present most thankfully His Father receives and courteously gives it to His Son, Jesus Christ. This gift and deed is joy to the Father and bliss to the Son and delight to the Holy Spirit.³

And of everything that is proper to us, it is most delight to our Lord that we rejoice in this joy which is in the blessed Trinity because of our salvation.

(This was seen in the ninth showing, where it speaks more of this matter.)

Notwithstanding all our feeling, woe or well, God wills that we understand and believe that we exist more truly in heaven than on earth.⁴

Our faith comes from the natural love of our soul, and from the clear light of our reason, and from the steadfast remembrance that we have of God in our first creation.⁵

At the time that our soul is breathed into our body (at which time we are made fleshly) also quickly mercy and grace begin to work, having charge of us and protecting us with pity and love. In this deed the Holy Spirit forms in our faith the hope that we shall come again up to our essence, into the strength of Christ, increased and fulfilled

One recalls Wordsworth's Ode:
The Soul that rises with us, our life's Star,
Hath had elsewhere its setting,
And cometh from afar:
Not in entire forgetfulness,
And not in utter nakedness,
But trailing clouds of glory do we come
From God, who is our home. . . .[137]

6. For Julian, even our fleshliness is not alienated from God, but is also "inhabited" by God. There is no trace of dualism for her.

7. We are reminded that for Julian "City" means "the seat of the bishop."

8. Now we finally see Julian's full metaphysic: The human *essence* is in God in heaven; the fleshly human *body* is on earth; the spiritual human *soul* has been "breathed" into the body but is linked to the heavenly essence. And that fleshly soul is the dwelling place ("City") of God and is the vehicle through which the grace of God enters our lives.

9. There is a spiritual maturation process that Christ initiates in each soul (where He dwells) and that is confirmed by the traditional seven gifts of the Holy Spirit (received in Holy Baptism and Confirmation). We must note that—unlike so many late medieval writers—Julian believes wholeheartedly in the basic goodness of human nature. She does not believe that human nature itself was contaminated by Original Sin.

10. See Romans 8:9–11: "You live by the Spirit, since God's Spirit dwells in you. . . . [I]f Christ is in you, then although the body is dead because of sin, yet the Spirit is your life. . . . Moreover, if the Spirit of him who raised Jesus from the dead dwells in you, then the God who raised Christ Jesus from the dead will also give new life to your mortal bodies through his indwelling Spirit." The "double death" refers to natural death of the body and the death of the soul through sin. Christ was seen as suffering "single death," that is, only

through the Holy Spirit. Thus I understood that the fleshliness is based in nature, in mercy, and in grace, and this basis enables us to receive gifts that lead us to endless life.

For I saw most certainly that our essence is in God, and also I saw that God is in our fleshliness,[6] for at the self-same moment that our soul is made fleshly, at the same moment is the City of God[7] established in our soul from without beginning. Into that City He comes and never shall remove it, for God is never out of the soul in which He dwells blissfully without end.[8]

(This was seen in the sixteenth showing where it says: "The place that Jesus takes in our soul, He shall never remove it.")

All the gifts that God can give to creatures He has given to His Son, Jesus, for us. These gifts He, dwelling in us, has enclosed in Himself until the time that we are grown and matured, our soul with our body and our body with our soul (either of them taking help from the other), until we are brought up in stature as nature works, and then, on the basis of human nature with the action of mercy, the Holy Spirit graciously breathes into us the gifts leading to endless life.[9]

Thus was my understanding led by God to perceive in Him and to understand, to be aware and to know, that our soul is a "created trinity," like to the uncreated blessed Trinity (known and loved from without beginning), and in its creation it is joined to the Creator, as it is aforesaid.

This sight was most sweet and wondrous to behold, peaceable and restful, safe and delightful. And because of the honorable one-ing that was thus brought about by God between the soul and body, it is inevitable that mankind should be brought back from double death.[10] This bringing back could never be until the time that the Second Person in the Trinity had taken the lower part of mankind (He to whom the highest part was one-ed in the first creation), and these two parts were in Christ—the higher and the lower—which is but one soul. In Christ, the higher part was one in peace with God in full joy and bliss; the lower part, which is fleshly, suffered for the salvation of mankind.

natural death of the body. (See St. Augustine's *On the Trinity*, Book 4, and St. Thomas Aquinas's *Summa Theologica*, Book 4.)

11. In Chapter 17 Julian regretted having asked for the experience of the pain of the Passion, but in Chapter 19 when she was tempted to look "past" the Passion into heaven, she refused. Here she tells us that her refusal was because she had "an ethereal feeling and secret inward vision" that there was an "inner life" in the Passion, and that is what she discovered in her later reflections.

COMMENTS ON CHAPTER 56

1. Julian's proposition is that the soul is of the same spiritual nature as God, and in order to "know" the soul, we need to first understand that spiritual nature of God.

2. Julian reiterates her conviction that human nature intuitively seeks knowledge of the Good, that is, God. This was a popular understanding of the Scholastic theologians, who held that all humans by nature will seek the Good, and that sin comes in confusing the Good with the less-than-good.

3. Meister Eckhart wrote: "I am certain, as certain as that I live, that nothing is so near to me as God. God is nearer to me than I am to myself" (Sermon II: "The Nearness of the Kingdom").

4. Since it is by God's creative deed that the heavenly essence and the earthly fleshliness of humankind have been brought together, by the same action of God, they will never be separated (pointing to the creedal belief in the resurrection of the body: the bonding of essence, soul, and body, once having been effected by God, is permanent and eternal).

5. Here is an indication that Julian is not writing a mere stream of consciousness, but is aware of the literary "organization" of her writings. She knows what is ahead.

(These two parts were seen and experienced in the eighth showing, in which my body was filled with the experience and memory of Christ's passion and His death—and furthermore, with this was an ethereal feeling and secret inward vision of the high part that I was shown at that same time [when I could not on account of the intermediary's suggestion look up into heaven], and that was because of the same powerful vision of the inner life, and this inner life is that exalted essence, that precious soul, which is endlessly rejoicing in the Godhead.)[11]

⇒ 56

Thus I saw most surely that it is easier for us to come to the knowledge of God than to know our own soul, for our soul is so profoundly based in God, and so endlessly treasured, that we may not come to the knowledge of it until we first have knowledge of God, who is the Creator to whom our soul is one-ed.[1]

But, nevertheless, I saw that we have by our human nature a fullness of desire wisely and truly to know our own soul, and by this desire we are taught to seek our soul where it is, and that is in God.[2]

Thus by the gracious leading of the Holy Spirit, we must know them both in one, whether we are stirred to know God or our soul. Both stirrings are good and true.

God is nearer to us than our own soul,[3] because He is the foundation on which our soul stands, and He is the means that keeps the essence and the fleshliness together so that they shall never separate.[4] For our soul sits in God in true repose, and our soul stands in God in certain strength, and our soul is naturally rooted in God in endless love. And therefore if we wish to have knowledge of our soul and communion and conversation with it, it behooves us that we search into our Lord God, in whom it is enclosed.

(And of this enclosing I saw and understood more in the sixteenth showing, as I shall say.)[5]

6. This is a difficult passage: Julian is trying to express the absolute mystical union between God and the human being. For Julian there is the spiritual "essence" and the physical "fleshliness," and both are "overlapped" by the soul, which is manifested both spiritually and physically. Moderns might choose to use the word "self" where Julian uses the word "soul."

7. Julian expresses the conviction that the humanity Christ took in the Incarnation was not sloughed off at the Resurrection, but that His humanity continues to "enclose" the risen Christ in heaven (that is, once human, eternally human). And the parallel to that is that our spiritual essence, which was originally heavenly, remains heavenly. For Julian, there is no aspect of humanity that is not united to God.

8. Simply put: our yearning and our present pains are only preparations for the full and complete entry "into" God, that is, into heaven.

9. Julian states the mystical paradox: that we cannot know our own soul until we know God, *and* we cannot know God until we know our own soul—because they are so mystically intertwined that they truly cannot be separated.

10. A "touching" for Julian means an inspiration from God. Here she declares that her understanding is partly from divine inspiration, and partly from application of her own reason.

11. Here is an image of the mercy and grace of God as an overflowing spring, washing over the edges of heaven into our humanity.

12. Our life and existence (that is, our human nature) require the mercy and grace of God in order to be fulfilled. And Julian gives yet another description of the Trinity: we have being from the Father, mercy from the Son, and grace from the Holy Spirit—"three aspects of one goodness."

And regarding our essence, it can rightly be called our soul, and regarding our fleshliness, it, too, can rightly be called our soul (and that is because of the one-ing that it has in God).[6]

The honorable city that our Lord Jesus sits in, it is our fleshliness in which He is enclosed; and our natural essence is enclosed in Jesus with the blessed soul of Christ sitting in repose in the Godhead.[7]

I saw most surely that it is inevitable that we must be in yearning and in penance until the time that we are led so deeply into God that we honestly and truly know our own soul. And truly I saw that into this great divine depth our good Lord Himself leads us in the same love in which He created us, and in the same love that He bought us by mercy and grace by virtue of his blessed Passion.[8]

Notwithstanding all this, we can never come to full knowledge of God until we first know clearly our own soul, for until the time that the soul is in its full powers, we cannot be all fully holy—and that is as soon as our fleshliness (by the virtue of Christ's Passion) is brought up into the essence with all the benefits of our tribulation that our Lord shall cause us to gain by mercy and grace.[9]

I had a partial <u>touching</u>, and it is grounded in nature (that is to say, our reason is based in God, who is essential nature).[10] From this essential nature of God mercy and grace spring and expand into us, accomplishing all things in completing our joy.[11]

These three are our foundations on which we have our being, our growth, and our fulfillment—for in our human nature we have our life and our being, and in mercy and grace we have our growth and our fulfillment. These are three aspects of one goodness, and where one works, all work, in the things which are now proper to us.[12]

God wills that we understand, desiring with all our heart and all our strength to have knowledge of these three more and more until the time that we are fulfilled. For fully to know them and clearly to see them is nothing else but the endless joy and bliss that we shall have in heaven (which God wills we begin here in knowledge of His love). For by our reason alone we cannot benefit, unless we have memory and love with it equally; nor can we be saved only with reference to

13. Julian speaks again of the "created" trinity of the human being: we have our human nature (including our reason), but we also need God's mercy (to forgive our weaknesses) and God's grace (to enable us to live lives in accord with His will).

14. Here we see more of Julian's theological optimism regarding human nature. Unlike her fellow late medieval writers, she sees true human nature as the greatest good, not in the least "depraved."

15. Simply put: God's creation of us as fleshly beings provides us with "greater goods" than we would have had as purely spiritual beings. There was a legend popular in the Middle Ages that the angels were jealous of human beings because humans had free will, and because through Christ's humanity, humans could unite with God in a way angels could not.

COMMENTS ON CHAPTER 57

1. The explication of the "we" in this paragraph demonstrates that Julian did not write the account of her revelations for the general public. Her intended readers are committed Christians: her "even-Christians" and "those who shall be saved." Her understandings and her advice presume a high degree of commitment on the part of her readers.

2. In our fleshliness we "are insufficient" (ME: *we faylyn*) only because we are limited by our body to this world, but in the resurrection of the body, that "insufficiency" will be remedied.

our natural origin that we have in God, unless we have, coming from the same origin, mercy and grace.[13]

From these three acting all together we receive all our goods; the first of which is the good of human nature[14] (for in our first creation God gave to us as many good and even greater goods than we could receive in our spiritual essence alone,[15] but His foreseeing purpose in His endless wisdom willed that we be twofold in our human natures).

⤳ 57

Regarding our essence, He made us so noble and so rich that we constantly work His will and His honor. (When I say "we," it means "men who will be saved";[1] for truly I saw that we are what He loves, and we do what He desires constantly without any ceasing.) And from these great riches and from this high nobility, virtues beyond measure come to our soul when it is knit to our body (in which knitting we are made fleshly).

Thus in our essence we are complete, and in our fleshliness we are <u>insufficient</u>. This insufficiency God will restore and make complete by the action of mercy and grace plenteously flowing into us from His own natural goodness.[2]

So His natural goodness causes mercy and grace to work in us, and the natural goodness that we have from Him enables us to receive that working of mercy and grace.

I saw that our human nature is completely within God. In this human nature He makes diversities flowing out of Him to work His will; nature protects it, and mercy and grace restore and complete it, and of these none shall be lost. For our human nature (which is the higher part) is knit to God in creation; and God is knit to our human nature (which is the lower part) in the taking of our flesh.

3. The Son was human before all others. He was the "pioneer" of humanity, and our humanity is an imitation of His. He did not merely assume humanity at the Incarnation, but He was already "spiritually human" in heaven.

4. This "foreknowledge" of God is the theological reality that generates the idea of predestination.

5. The first good we receive is our creation; the second good is God's gift of mercy and grace; the third gift is our faith (and the Church that enshrines it).

6. Julian reminds us that our faith is not something we ourselves confect, but that it is a gift from God, coming down to us from God through our heavenly essence.

7. The first gift we have from the Church (that is, our faith) is the moral guidance of the commandments, which lets us know both God's "biddings" and "forbiddings."

8. The second gift from the Church is the Seven Sacraments. Each of the sacraments parallels a developmental stage or activity in the natural world (for example, baptism=birth, confirmation=maturity, matrimony=mating, orders=career; unction=sickness and death, communion=feeding the body, penance=cleansing the body.)

9. The third gift is the collection of virtues or strengths that we have from our human nature (by God's mercy) and that are strengthened by God's grace through the Holy Spirit.

Thus in Christ our two natures are united, for the Trinity is encompassed in Christ in whom our higher part is based and rooted, and our lower part the Second Person has taken, which human nature was first assigned to Him.[3]

I saw most certainly that all the works God has done, or ever shall do, were completely known to Him and foreseen from without beginning, and for love He made mankind, and for the same love He Himself was willing to be man.[4]

The next good that we receive[5] is our Faith, in which our benefiting begins; and it comes from the high riches of our natural essence into our fleshly soul; and it is based in us and we in it through the natural goodness of God by the working of mercy and grace.[6]

From Faith come all other goods by which we are guided and saved. The commandments of God come in our Faith (about which we ought to have two kinds of understanding, which are: His bidding to love them and to keep them; the other is that we ought to know His forbiddings in order to hate and to refuse them; for in these two are all our actions contained).[7]

Also in our Faith come the Seven Sacraments (each following the other in order as God has ordained them to us)[8] and all manner of virtues (for the same virtues that we received from our essence, given to us in human nature, by the goodness of God, these same virtues, by the action of mercy, are also given to us in grace, renewed through the Holy Spirit).[9]

These virtues and gifts are treasured for us within Jesus Christ, for at that same time that God knitted Him to our body in the Maiden's womb, He assumed our fleshly soul. In taking this fleshly soul, He, having enclosed us all in Himself, one-ed our fleshly soul to our essence. In this one-ing He was complete humanity, for Christ, having knit unto Himself all men who shall be saved, is Perfect Man.

10. Reminded of Mary by thoughts of the Incarnation, Julian sees the mystic truth that since we are "within" Jesus and Jesus is "within" Mary as her child, so we also are mystically enclosed in Mary (who here is seen as a "type" or symbol of the Church).

11. But Christ's motherhood even supersedes the motherhood of Mary—mystically speaking, Christ is the mystical Mother of Mary, His own natural mother, and of all of us who shall be saved.

12. The ME has *werkeng*. C&W suggest it may carry a horticultural sense of "grafting" or "cultivating."

13. Julian seldom gives spiritual advice to her readers, but here she expresses God's wishes that were shown to her: that we all participate in the "enfolding" process of Christ by giving Him our attention, keeping His laws, desiring His will, and trusting in Him.

COMMENTS ON CHAPTER 58

1. Julian's high orthodoxy: God does not *have* existence as an attribute, but *is* everlasting existence itself. W&J remind us that the last nine chapters began with "And. . . ."

2. By Julian's insight all human beings were spiritually created at once and one-ed to God, and it is that spiritual part of us that constantly delights and has grateful joy in God.

3. It is the bond between the human soul and the divine that opposes sin constantly.

Thus Our Lady is our Mother in whom we are all enclosed, and out of her we are born in Christ (for she who is Mother of our Savior is Mother of all who shall be saved within our Savior).[10]

But our Savior is our true Mother in whom we are endlessly borne and never shall come to birth out of Him.[11]

Plenteously and completely and sweetly was this shown (and it is spoken of in the first showing, where He says that we are all enclosed in Him and He is enclosed in us; and it is spoken of in the sixteenth showing, where it says that He sits in our soul).

It is His delight to reign in our understanding blissfully, and to sit in our soul restfully, and to dwell in our soul endlessly, <u>drawing</u>[12] us all into Him.

In this drawing He wishes that we be His helpers, giving Him all our attention, learning His lesson, keeping His laws, desiring that all be done which He does, honestly trusting in Him—for truly I saw that our essence is in God.[13]

⌒ 58

God, the blessed Trinity (who is everlasting Existence), just as He is endless from without beginning, just so was it in His endless purpose to create mankind.[1]

This fair human nature was first assigned to His own Son, the Second Person.

And when He wished, by full accord of all the Trinity, He created us all at once, and in our creation He knit us and one-ed us to Himself. By this one-ing we are kept as pure and as noble as we were created. By the virtue of the same precious one-ing, we love our Maker and delight Him, praising Him, and thanking Him, and endlessly rejoicing in Him.[2]

And this one-ing is the deed that is done constantly in every soul that shall be saved (which is the divine will in the soul mentioned before).[3]

4. Wisdom in the Old Testament is always considered to be feminine. The identification of the Son with Wisdom automatically identifies Him with the feminine.

5. This is one of the few instances of "spousal mysticism" in Julian. Curiously (and paradoxically), it follows immediately on the preceding paragraph, in which the Son is described as Mother. It occurs again in Chapters 79 and 82.

6. Our "being" (nature) we have from the Creator Father; our spiritual growth (mercy) we have from the Redeemer Son; our fulfillment (grace) we have from the sanctifying Holy Spirit.

7. The Son is our "mother" in essence (that is, He had a human essence before us and shared that human essence with us) and He became our "mother" in flesh (that is, He became our "mother"—our earthly caretaker—at the Incarnation).

Thus in our creation, God All Power is our natural Father, and God All Wisdom is our natural Mother,[4] with the Love and the Goodness of the Holy Spirit—who is all one God, one Lord.

And in the knitting and in the one-ing, He is our most true Spouse, and we are His beloved Wife and His fair Maiden. With this Wife He is never displeased, for He says: "I love thee and thou lovest me, and our love shall never be separated in two."[5]

I beheld the action of all the blessed Trinity. In that sight I saw and understood these three aspects: the aspect of the Fatherhood, the aspect of the Motherhood, and the aspect of the Lordhood, in one God.

In our Father Almighty we have our protection and our bliss as regards our natural essence (which is ours by our creation from without beginning).

And in the Second Person, in understanding and wisdom, we have our protection as regards our fleshliness, our redeeming and our saving, for He is our Mother, Brother, and Savior.

And in our good Lord the Holy Spirit, we have our rewarding and our recompense for our living and our trouble—endlessly surpassing all that we desire, in His amazing courtesy, from His high plenteous grace.

For all our life is in three. In the first, we have our being; and in the second, we have our growing; and in the third, we have our completing.

The first is nature; the second is mercy; the third is grace.[6]

As for the first: I saw and understood that the high Power of the Trinity is our Father, and the deep Wisdom of the Trinity is our Mother, and the great Love of the Trinity is our Lord; and all this we have in our human nature and in our essential creation.

And furthermore, I saw that the Second Person, who is our Mother, in essence that same dearworthy Person has become our Mother in flesh, because we are twofold in God's creation: that is to say, essential and fleshly.[7] Our essence is the higher part, which we have in our Father, God Almighty; and the Second Person of the Trinity is our

8. In the human "trinity" of nature, mercy, and grace, the Father and Son together provide our nature, and the incarnate Son provides the mercy.

9. The function of Christ's Incarnation, Death, and Resurrection is to maintain the unity between our spiritual parts (our essence) and our fleshly parts (our body).

10. ME has *trewth* in BV and *trust* in PV. A second meaning of *trewth* is "faith," and faith is theologically the gift of the Spirit.

11. In the human "trinity" of nature, mercy, and grace, it is the Holy Spirit who provides the grace, in "rewards" and gifts.

12. Christ is the perfect, fulfilled, and integrated complete human.

13. Julian almost piles paradox upon paradox, and mystical contradiction upon mystical contradiction.

Mother in human nature in our essential creation. In Him we are grounded and rooted, and he is our Mother in mercy by taking on our fleshliness.[8]

And thus our Mother does for us various kinds of deeds (in Whom our parts are kept unseparated), for in our Mother Christ, we benefit and grow, and in mercy He redeems and restores us, and, by the virtue of His Passion and His Death and Resurrection, He ones us to our essence.[9] In this way our Mother works in mercy to all His children who are submissive and obedient to Him.

And grace works with mercy, and namely in two aspects, as it was shown (which working belongs to the Third Person, the Holy Spirit). He works, rewarding and giving: "rewarding" is a great gift of <u>faith</u>[10] which the Lord gives to him who has labored; and "giving" is a gracious deed which he does freely of grace, fulfilling and surpassing all that is deserved by creatures.[11]

Thus in our Father, God Almighty, we have our being;

and in our Mother of mercy we have our redeeming and restoring, in whom our parts are one-ed and all made complete man;[12]

and by the rewards and gifts of grace from the Holy Spirit, we are fulfilled.

And our essence is in our Father, God Almighty,

and our essence is in our Mother, God all Wisdom,

and our essence is in our Lord the Holy Spirit, God all Goodness,

for our essence is total in each Person of the Trinity, which is One God.

But our fleshliness is only in the Second Person, Christ Jesus (in whom is the Father and the Holy Spirit), and in Him and by Him we are mightily taken out of hell and out of the misery on earth, and honorably brought up into heaven and full blissfully one-ed to our essence, increased in riches and nobility, by all the virtue of Christ and by the grace and action of the Holy Spirit.[13]

COMMENTS ON CHAPTER 59

1. This is another example of the *felix culpa*—the "fortunate sin." Had goodness never been "opposed" by wickedness, the Incarnation would never have occurred.

2. Not only does God oppose wickedness, but God converts it into goodness; for example, when we have to endure pain and trouble, that is credited to us as virtue.

3. This is the first indication that the actual source of all motherhood is Jesus Christ; it is not that Jesus is like our mothers, but that our mothers are like Jesus.

4. This is another powerful theological statement, that God is "Being itself"; the corollary is that anything with being (that is, that exists) participates in the divine nature. *All* creation, by its very existence, has a dimension of divinity within it.

5. Once again, we see Julian's conviction that our human essence existed in God before time began.

⤳ 59

All this bliss we have by mercy and grace, which kind of bliss we might never have had or known if the quality of goodness which is in God had not been opposed[1]—by which goodness we have this bliss. For wickedness has been permitted to rise in opposition to that goodness, and the goodness of mercy and grace opposed against the wickedness, and transformed all into goodness and into honor for all those that shall be saved, for that is the quality in God which does good against evil.[2]

Thus Jesus Christ, who does good against evil, is our true Mother—we have our being from Him where the basis of motherhood begins,[3] with all the sweet protection of love that accompanies it endlessly.

As truly as God is our Father, so truly God is our Mother.

(And that He showed in all the showings, and particularly in those sweet words where he says:

"It is I"—that is to say,

"It is I: the Power and the Goodness of the Fatherhood.

It is I: the Wisdom of the Motherhood.

It is I: the Light and the Grace that is all blessed Love.

It is I: the Trinity.

It is I: the Unity.

I am the supreme goodness of all manner of things.

I am what causes thee to love.

I am what causes thee to yearn.

It is I: the endless fulfilling of all true desires.")

For the soul is highest, noblest, and worthiest when it is lowest, humblest, and gentlest.

From this essential foundation we have all our virtues and our flesh-liness by the gift of nature and by the help and assistance of mercy and grace, without which we cannot benefit.

Our high Father, God Almighty, who is Being itself,[4] knew us and loved us from before any time,[5] and from this knowledge in His

6. This is the "divine will" in each of us "which never consents to sin." (See Chapter 53.)

7. The ME is *forthspreadyng*. C&W translate it as "everything is penetrated." The sense of the word is meant to suggest that the divine motherhood is ubiquitous and expands itself everywhere without limit.

8. See Ephesians 3:17–19—". . . that through faith Christ may dwell in your hearts in love. With deep roots and firm foundations, may you, in company with all God's people, be strong to grasp what is the breadth and length and height and depth of Christ's love, and to know it, though it is beyond knowledge."

wondrous profound love, by the foreseeing endless agreement of all the Blessed Trinity, He willed that the Second Person should become our Mother, our Brother, and our Savior.

Whereof it follows that as truly as God is our Father, so truly God is our Mother. Our Father wills, our Mother acts, our good Lord the Holy Spirit strengthens.

And therefore it is right for us to love our God in whom we have our being, reverently thanking and praising Him for our creation, powerfully praying to our Mother for mercy and pity, and to our Lord the Holy Spirit for help and grace, for in these three is all our life— nature, mercy, and grace—from which we get humility, gentleness, patience, and pity, and hatred of sin and wickedness (for it is right and proper for the virtuous to hate sin and wickedness).

Thus is Jesus our true Mother in nature, from our first creation, and He is our true Mother in grace by His taking our created human nature.

All the fair deeds and all the sweet natural function of dearworthy motherhood is attached to the Second Person; for in Him we have this divine will[6] whole and safe without end, both in nature and grace, from His own excellent goodness.

I understood three ways of looking at motherhood in God:

the first is the creating of our human nature;

the second is His taking of our human nature (and there commences the motherhood of grace);

the third is motherhood in action (and in that is a great spreading outward,[7] by the same grace, of length and breadth and of height and of depth without end) and all is one love.[8]

COMMENTS ON CHAPTER 60

1. The ME has *our kindly stede wher that we were made*, which means literally "our natural place where we were made," but the motherhood analogy would relate that to being born. Hence "the womb of our human nature," that is, our essence in God. Note that this is done by the action of the Son (mercy) and of the Holy Spirit (grace).

2. What Julian is saying is that even if He is high and lordly as our Creator and our Redeemer, He based his work on His humility in becoming one of us "in the Maiden's womb."

3. In order for His "divine mothering" to be complete, He had to become incarnate so He could be a "mother" to us in our fleshliness as well as in our spirit/essence. W&J put it well: "God was born of a mother in order to become a mother."

4. This phrase occurs only in the PV.

5. Continuing her considerations of the motherhood of Christ, Julian considers Christ's Passion an analogy of His birth pangs in mystically "giving birth" to us and bringing us forth into joy and endless life.

⤳ 60

But now it is appropriate to say a little more about this spreading outward, as I understood it in the meaning of our Lord—how that we are brought back by the Motherhood of mercy and grace into the <u>womb of our human nature</u> where we were created[1] by the Motherhood of natural love, which natural love never leaves us.

Our Mother in human nature, our Mother in grace (because He wished to completely become our Mother in everything), He accepted the foundation of His work most lowly and most mildly in the Maiden's womb.[2]

(And that He showed in the first showing, where He brought that meek Maid before the eye of my understanding in the simple state she was in when she conceived.)

That is to say, our high God, the supreme Wisdom of all, in this lowly womb clothed Himself and enclosed Himself most willingly in our poor flesh, in order that He Himself could do the service and the duty of motherhood in everything.[3]

The mother's serving is most near, most willing, and most certain ("near," because it is most of our nature; "willing," because it is most loving; and "certain,"[4] because it is most true).

This duty no one can do, nor could do, nor ever did do to the fullest, except He alone.

We are aware that all our mothers give us birth only to pain and dying; and what is it but that our true Mother Jesus, He—all love—gives us birth to joy and to endless life. Blessed may He be!

Thus He carries us within Himself in love, and labors until full term so that He could suffer the sharpest throes and the hardest birth pains[5] that ever were or ever shall be, and die at the last.

And when He had finished, and so given us birth to bliss, not even all this could satisfy His wondrous love.

(And that He showed in these high, surpassing words of love: "If I could suffer more, I would suffer more.")

6. Julian now begins to move into the motherhood imagery in earnest—more deeply than any of her predecessors. She has described Christ's "birth pangs" in bringing us to birth; now, she moves on to His feeding of the newborn.

7. Jesus' motherhood does earthly motherhood one better: she provides only her milk, but He provides His body and blood in the sacrament. (Note: Medieval physiology believed that a mother's milk was the transformation of her menstrual blood. Note also the medieval tradition of symbolically identifying Christ with the pelican, who was thought to feed her young with the blood of her own breast.)

8. See Appendix 8, "The Wounds of Christ."

9. This is another expression of Julian's "originist" metaphysics: just as Christ was endowed with human nature before earthly humans were, so, too, Christ is the very font of motherhood itself.

10. It is Christ who "causes" not only the spiritual birth of our essence in the mind of God, but also our physical birth from our own mothers. There may also be a reference here to Christ's own birthing in the Incarnation.

He could die no more, but He would not cease working; therefore, it behooved Him that He feed us (for the dearworthy love of mother-hood has made Him owe us that).[6]

The mother can give her child suck from her milk, but our precious Mother Jesus can feed us with Himself; and He does it most graciously and most tenderly with the Blessed Sacrament, which is the Precious Food of true life.[7]

And with all the sweet Sacraments He supports us most mercifully and graciously.

(And thus meant He in this blessed word where He said: "It is I that Holy Church preaches to thee and teaches to thee"; that is to say, "All the wholeness and life of Sacraments, all the virtue and grace of my Word, all the goodness that is ordained in Holy Church for thee, it is I.")

The mother can lay the child tenderly on her breast, but our tender Mother Jesus can more intimately lead us into His blessed Breast by His sweet open Side, and show therein part of the Godhead and part of the joys of heaven, with spiritual certainty of eternal bliss.[8]

(And that was shown in the tenth showing, giving the same under-standing in this sweet word where He says, "Lo, how I love thee," gazing into His side and rejoicing.)

This fair lovely word "mother" is so sweet and so kind in itself, that it cannot truly be said of anyone nor to anyone except of Him and to Him who is true Mother of life and of all.[9]

To the quality of motherhood belongs natural love, wisdom, and knowledge—and this is God; for though it is true that our bodily birth is but little, lowly, and simple as compared to our spiritual birth, yet it is He who does it within the created mothers by whom it is done.[10]

The kind, loving mother who is aware and knows the need of her child protects the child most tenderly as the nature and state of motherhood wills.

And as the child increases in age, she changes her method but not her love.

11. See Hebrews 12:11—"Discipline, to be sure, is never pleasant; at the time it seems painful, but afterwards those who have been trained by it reap a harvest of a peaceful and upright life."

12. Even our mothers' nurturing of their children is effected by the action of Christ within our mothers. This is consistent with Julian's understanding that whatever good any human being does is actually the result of the presence of Christ within us.

13. The reference here is to the Fourth Commandment to "Honor your father and mother." Julian suggests that this commandment is fulfilled by truly loving God (who is both Father and Mother). See also Matthew 12:50—"Whoever does the will of my heavenly Father is my brother and sister and mother."

And when the child is increased further in age, she permits it to be chastised to break down vices and to cause the child to accept virtues and graces.[11]

This nurturing of the child, with all that is fair and good, our Lord does in the mothers by whom it is done.[12]

Thus He is our Mother in our human nature through the action of grace in the lower part, out of love for the higher part.

And He wishes us to know it; for He wishes to have all our love made fast to Him.

In this I saw that all our debt that we owe by God's bidding to fatherhood and motherhood (because of God's Fatherhood and Motherhood) is fulfilled in true loving of God, which blessed love Christ works in us.[13]

(And this was shown in all the showings and specifically in the high bountiful words where He says: "It is I whom thou lovest.")

⤳ 61

In our spiritual birthing, our Mother uses more tenderness for our protection without any comparison (by as much as our soul is of more value in His sight than the flesh).

> He kindles our understanding,
> He directs our ways,
> He eases our conscience,
> He comforts our soul,
> He lightens our heart,

and He gives us, partially, knowledge and love of His blessed Godhead—along with gracious remembrance of His sweet manhood and His blessed Passion, with gracious wonder at His high, surpassing goodness, and He makes us to love all that He loves because of His love, and to be satisfied with Him and all His works.

If we fall, quickly He raises us by His loving embracing and merciful touching.

COMMENTS ON CHAPTER 61

1. The preceding passage, while it presents solidly orthodox theology, seems to have an autobiographical ring to it: it is as though Julian is not only describing true teaching, but is telling of her own experience of the divine Mother.

2. Julian does not address some sinless, saintly person, but persons (like herself) who have fallen into sin. And after her description of the great gifts of the divine Mother, she quickly explains that there is actually a positive result possible after a fall into sin: it shows us our own weakness and dependency on God, and reinforces our understanding of the unqualified love of God.

3. Here we have an expansion of the above statement: that no amount of sin or trespass on our part can cause God to withdraw His love from us.

4. This is a further expansion of the "benefit" of sinning, in that if we are aware of our sin, we will be more humble, and that humility will itself aid in our salvation.

5. The recognition of our sin may not be present at the moment of sin, but reflection and the self-examen leads us to recognize the sin. Once again, there seems to be a strong autobiographical dimension to her teaching: Julian knows about sinning and recognizing her sin. This not merely an exercise in principles, but a revelation of the actual way it works out in real life.

6. Julian is brought back to the motherhood metaphor in explaining God's permitting us to fall—but never to perish. See John 3:16—"God so loved the world that he gave his only Son, that everyone who has faith in him may not perish but have eternal life." Also see Psalm 27:10 (BCP)—"Though my father and my mother forsake me, the LORD will take me into his care."

7. On those occasions when Julian makes this apostrophe to God, it is almost as though she were emotionally overwhelmed with the sheer wonder of what she has just written.

And when we are thus strengthened by His sweet deed, then we willingly choose Him, by His sweet grace, to be His servants and His lovers everlastingly without end.[1]

After this He permits some of us to fall more severely and more grievously than ever we did before, as it seems to us. And then we believe (we who are not all-wise) that all was naught that we had begun, but it is not so, because it is necessary for us to fall, and it is necessary for us to recognize it. For if we fell not, we would not know how weak and how miserable we are by ourselves—nor also would we so thoroughly know the amazing love of our Creator.[2]

For we shall see truly in heaven without end that we have grievously sinned in this life, and, notwithstanding this, we shall see that we were never lessened in His love, nor were we ever of less value in His sight.

By means of the test of this falling, we shall gain a high, wondrous knowledge of love in God without end. For strong and wondrous is that love which cannot nor will not be broken because of trespass. And this is one understanding of our benefits from falling.[3]

Another is the lowliness and humility that we shall gain by the sight of our falling, for thereby we shall be highly raised in heaven and we might never have come to this raising without that humility.[4]

And therefore it is necessary for us to see our fall, for if we see it not, though we fall, it would not benefit us.

And usually, first we fall, and afterward we see it—and both by the mercy of God.[5]

The mother can allow the child to fall sometimes and to be distressed in various ways for its own benefit, but she can never permit any kind of peril to come to the child, because of her love. But even if our earthly mother could allow her child to perish, our heavenly Mother Jesus cannot allow us that are His children to perish.[6]

He is all Power, all Wisdom, and all Love, and so is none but He. Blessed may He be![7]

8. Julian may be thinking of the efforts of Adam and Even to hide themselves from God after their sin. (See Genesis 3:8.)

9. See Isaiah 66:13—"As a mother comforts her son so shall I myself comfort you."

10. Again, Julian speaks out of her own wisdom and experience that sometimes even serious penance does not bring immediate relief from the guilt of sin because God thinks it is beneficial for us that we mourn "until the best time."

11. Here Julian is probably referring to "Mother Church." This demonstrates a strongly orthodox concept of the communal Catholic Church (as opposed to the Protestant concept of a private individual relationship between the self and God). Even the relative isolation of a contemplative mystic does not abrogate the significance of the ecclesial community.

12. Julian may be referring to the sacraments of Eucharist and baptism (that is, blood and water), but more probably since she has just mentioned the wound in Christ's side (and mentions it again in the next sentence), she is referring to that piercing: "and at once there was a flow of blood and water" (John 19:34).

13. This is the paradox of the Wounded Healer: it is the wounds of Christ that heal our spiritual wounds.

But often when our falling and our misery is shown us, we are so sorely frightened and so greatly ashamed of ourselves that scarcely do we know where we can hide ourselves away.[8]

Then our courteous Mother wills not that we flee away—for Him nothing would be more distasteful—but He wills then that we follow the behavior of a child, for when a child is distressed or afraid, it runs hastily to the mother for help with all its might.[9] So wishes He that we act as a humble child, saying thus: "My kind Mother, my gracious Mother, my dearworthy Mother, have mercy on me. I have made myself foul and unlike to Thee, and I am neither able nor know how to amend it except with Thy secret help and grace."

And if we do not feel ourselves eased very quickly, we may be sure that He is practicing the behavior of a wise Mother, for if He sees that it would be more benefit to us to mourn and weep, out of love He permits it with compassion and pity until the best time.[10]

And He wills that we betake ourselves strongly to the Faith of Holy Church and find there our dearworthy Mother[11] in the solace of true understanding with all the Blessed Communion of Saints. For one particular person can often be broken, as it seems, by himself, but the whole Body of Holy Church is never broken, nor ever shall be, without end.

And therefore a certain thing it is, a good and a gracious thing, to will humbly and strongly to be made fast and one-ed to our Mother, Holy Church, that is, Christ Jesus. For the flood of mercy that is His dearworthy Blood and precious Water is adequate to make us fair and pure.[12]

The blessed Wound of our Savior is open and rejoices to heal us.[13]

The sweet gracious hands of our Mother are already and diligently about us.

For He in all this action practices the duty of a kind nurse who has nothing else to do except to attend to the safety of her child.

It is His function to save us,

it is His honor to do it, and

it is His will that we acknowledge it.

14. See Chapter 37.

COMMENTS ON CHAPTER 62

1. See Chapter 37.
2. This unusual phrase has four possible meanings. The ME has *never to lese time.* (a) This may mean that God will always allow time for contrition and repentance. (b) It may intend to convey the idea that we accumulate "good time" (to use a prison term) in God's mind and that "good time" will not be lost. (c) It may convey the meaning shown in OED of "prosperity" as an early variant meaning for "time" (that is, "never permits us to lose prosperity"). (d) Since OED gives a fourteenth-century use of the word "lose" to mean "waste," the phrase may mean that God's love does not permit us to waste time waiting for His blessings.
3. Here we have a deep and highly mystical series of insights: God *is* goodness; God *is* existence itself; God *is* nature. Julian always recognizes the ubiquity of God in all things, that is, whatever has existence, thereby has a divine dimension to it.
4. The reason God has created the world of nature (that is, allowed all nature to "flow out of Him") is to provide for and assist the salvation of all humankind, and when that salvation is attained, all the world and nature will be "drawn back again into God" and will cease to have external existence.
5. Every created thing shares a part of what the human has totally: being, life, order, senses, affection, reproduction, and so on. Each created thing in the world has some of these qualities, but humanity has them all.
6. Julian is saying that we need not search for truths of God "far out" in nature, but need only turn to Holy Church for those truths.

For He wills that we love Him sweetly and trust in Him humbly and strongly. (And this He showed in these grace-filled words: "I keep thee full safely.")[14]

⌢ 62

At that time[1] He showed our frailty and our failings, our betrayals and our denials, our despisings and our burdens, and all our woes to whatever extent they could befall us in this life, as it seemed to me.

And along with that He showed His blessed Power, His blessed Wisdom, His blessed Love, in which He keeps us in these difficult times just as tenderly and as sweetly for His honor and as surely for our salvation as He does when we are in the most solace and comfort.

To do that He raises us spiritually and nobly into heaven, and transforms all our woe into His honor and our joy without end. His love never permits us to lose opportunity.[2]

And all of this is from the natural goodness of God, by the working of grace.

God is natural in His very being—that is to say, that goodness which is of nature, it is God. He is the ground; He is the essence; He is the same thing as nature; and He is true Father and true Mother of human nature.[3]

All nature that He has caused to flow out of Him to accomplish His will shall be returned and brought again into Him by the salvation of man through the working of grace.[4] For of all natures that He has placed partially in various created things, only in man is all the whole in fullness, in strength, in beauty and in goodness, in majesty and nobility, in all manner of solemnity, of preciousness, and of honor.[5]

Here we can see that we are fully bound to God because of our human nature, and we are also fully bound to God because of grace.

Here we can see that we need not intensely search far away to discover the different species, but only as far as Holy Church[6]—into our Mother's breast (that is to say, into our own soul, where our Lord

7. The truths of God's nature that we find in the Church and in our own souls we find now by faith and our own comprehension, but in heaven we will know them firsthand.

8. This is another example of Julian's intentionally and specifically including both genders: "let no man or woman. . . ."

9. Julian cautions: "Do not think that you have some private or exclusive access to comprehending God's nature, for all we humans share those insights because the humanity of each of us comes from Christ's universal humanity."

COMMENTS ON CHAPTER 63

1. That is to say, "in our union with God in Christ."

2. Again Julian says plainly that human nature in itself is good and any weakness it may develop is overcome by God's grace, and so it is brought back to its original pristine character. Julian's positive appraisal of human nature could not be further from the typical medieval stance (or the Puritan and Calvinist attitudes), which sees human nature as essentially wicked and flawed.

3. Julian is clear that not only is grace divine, but human nature itself has the divine attribute, and that both what we are by God's creation and what we receive from God (grace) after Creation are necessary for salvation.

4. Julian corrects a popular error: that sinning is "natural" to human beings and that virtue is "supernatural." She states that given the divine character of the human being and the grace given by God, it is *sin* that is "unnatural" and "contrary to our true nature."

5. See 1 Peter 1:2—". . . chosen in the foreknowledge of God the Father, by the consecrating work of the Holy Spirit, for obedience to Jesus Christ and sprinkling with his blood."

dwells), and there we shall find everything—now in faith and insight, and afterward, truly in Himself clearly, in bliss.[7]

But let no man or woman[8] take this exclusively to himself, for it is not so—it is universal.[9] For it was our precious Mother Christ for whom this fair human nature was prepared, for the honor and nobility of man's creation, and for the joy and the bliss of man's salvation—just as He understood, knew, and recognized from without beginning.

⌁ 63

Here[1] we can see that we truly have it from our human nature to hate sin, and we truly have it from grace to hate sin—for human nature is all good and fair in itself, and grace was sent out to preserve human nature and to destroy sin and to bring back fair human nature and to the blessed point from whence it came—that is, God—with more nobility and honor by the virtuous working of grace.[2]

For it shall be seen before God by all His holy saints in joy without end that human nature has been tested in the fire of tribulation and no lack, no flaw found in it.

Thus are human nature and grace of one accord—for grace is God just as human nature is God. He is double in His way of working but single in love, and neither of these two works without the other, nor is either separated from the other.[3]

When we, by the mercy of God and with His help, come to harmony with both our human nature and grace, we shall see honestly that sin is truly more vile and more painful than hell, without comparison, for sin is opposite to our fair human nature.

For as truly as sin is impure, just as truly is it unnatural, and thus it is a horrible thing to see for the beloved soul that wishes to be all fair and shining in the sight of God as both human nature and grace direct.[4] But let us not be afraid of this (except insomuch as fear could help us); but humbly let us make our moan to our dearworthy Mother, and He shall all besprinkle us with His Precious Blood[5] and make our souls very pliant and very gentle, and restore us to health

6. By the Incarnation, Christ our Mother brought us back to life spiritually, and by His Death and Passion, he made eternal life available to us.

7. This is a moment of poetic reverie on the complementary nature of our relationship with Christ our Mother.

8. The ME has *presumith not of the selfe.* This is a clear reminder of our dependency on Christ.

9. While human nature is God's creation and therefore good, it is also weak and requires the grace of God. ("Grace" is often theologically defined as "God's life.")

10. Julian reminds us that the familiar promise that "all shall be well" is an eschatological promise, a promise that will be finally fulfilled only in heaven.

11. The paragraph describes the transfer of the source of human happiness from Christ (on earth) to the Father (in heaven). The ME for this phrase is *shal lesten without end, new begynnand.*

12. Julian faces the paradox of our Mother Christ birthing us "out of Himself" and then bringing us back "into Himself" by grace.

most gently in the course of time, in whatever way as it is most honor to Him and most joy to us without end.

He shall never cease this sweet, fair activity, nor pause, until all His dearworthy children are birthed and brought forth.

(And He showed that where He showed the interpretation of spiritual thirst: that is, the love-longing that shall last until Doomsday.)

Thus in our true Mother, Jesus, our life is grounded, in His own foreseeing Wisdom from without beginning, with the high supreme Goodness of the Holy Spirit. In the taking of our human nature He restored life to us, and in His blessed dying upon the cross, He birthed us into endless life.[6] And from that time, and now, and until Doomsday, He feeds us and fosters us just as the high matchless nature of motherhood wills and as the natural need of childhood requires.

Fair and sweet is our heavenly Mother in the eyes of our soul; precious and loving are His grace-filled children in the eyes of our heavenly Mother, with gentleness and humility and all the fair virtues that are proper to children in nature.[7]

Furthermore, by nature the child does not despair of the mother's love; by nature the child <u>does not rely upon itself</u>;[8] by nature the child loves the mother and each one of them the other.

These are the fair virtues (with all others that are like them) with which our heavenly Mother is honored and pleased.

I recognized no state in this life greater in weakness and in the lack of power and intelligence than our childhood, until the time that our grace-filled Mother has brought us up to our Father's bliss.[9] And then truly shall be made known to us His meaning in these sweet words where Christ says: "All shall be well; and thou shalt see for thyself that all manner of thing shall be well."[10]

And then shall the bliss of our Motherhood in Christ be begun anew in the joys of our Father God, and <u>this new beginning shall continue being renewed without end</u>.[11]

Thus I understood that all His blessed children who have been birthed from Him by nature shall be brought back into Him by grace.[12]

COMMENTS ON CHAPTER 64

1. Julian departs from the revelations and slips into an autobiographical memory.
2. Julian reminisces about a previous time when she thought of the Lord as "absent" from human life, and then tells of a comforting inspiration she had from the Lord.
3. This is reminiscent of Philippians 1:21–23—"For to me life is Christ, and death is gain. . . . I am pulled two ways: my own desire is to depart and be with Christ—that is better by far. . . ."
4. The ME has *Sodenly*. One thinks of Matthew 24:50—"then the master will arrive on a day when the servant does not expect him, at a time he has not been told."
5. The Lord remonstrates with Julian's desire to pass from this life by describing the promise He has given of future bliss and joy and challenges her to endure her earthly suffering (which is God's will) for the sake of the final reward.
6. See Colossians 1:11—"In his glorious might may he give you ample strength to meet with fortitude and patience whatever comes . . . "; James 5:7—"You must be patient, my friends, until the Lord comes"; and Psalm 39:5 (BCP)—"LORD, let me know my end and the number of my days, so that I may know how short my life is."

⤳ 64

Before this time, by the gift of God, I had a great yearning and desire to be delivered from this world and from this life, for frequently I beheld the woe that is here, and the well-being and the bliss that exists there.[1]

And even if there had been no pain in this life except the absence of our Lord, it seemed to me that that was sometimes more than I could bear.[2]

And this absence made me mourn and earnestly yearn—and also my own misery, sloth, and weakness—so that I had no delight in living or laboring as it fell to me to do.[3]

To all this our gracious Lord answered for the sake of comfort and patience, and He said these words:

"<u>Without warning</u>[4] thou shalt be taken from all thy pain, from all thy sickness, from all thy distress, and from all thy woe, and thou shalt come up above, and thou shalt have me for thy reward, and thou shalt be filled full of love and bliss, and thou shalt never have any manner of pain, nor any manner of sickness, nor any manner of displeasure, nor any lack of will, but always joy and bliss without end. Why then should it bother thee to suffer awhile, seeing that it is my Will and to my honor?"[5]

In this word, "Without warning thou shalt be taken . . . ," I saw that God rewards man for the patience that he has in awaiting God's will, and for his lifetime (if that man extends his patience over the time of his life) because of not knowing the time of his passing away.[6]

This is a great benefit, for if a man knew the time of his passing, he would not have patience concerning that time.[6]

Also God wills that while the soul is in the body, it [should] seem to itself that it is always at the moment of being taken.

For all this life and this languishing that we have here is only a moment, and when we are taken without warning out of pain into bliss, then the pain shall have been nothing.

7. "And fearsome" appears only in the PV.
8. In this phrase, Julian slips into a colloquial language. ME has *a bolned quave of styngand myre. Bolned* is from *bolnin*, meaning "swollen." *Quave* is an obscure word often translated as "trembling" or "soft" (for example, *quaqmire*), but it also has a common origin with *quarry*, referring to the pile of entrails and offal of a slaughtered deer that is fed to the hunting dogs. "Stinking" reminds us of the raising of the dead Lazarus: John 11:39—"Sir, by now there will be a stench; he has been there four days." Also, in *The Cloud of Unknowing* is the phrase describing a sinner as "filled with a foul, stinking lumpe of him self" (Hodgson, 84). See Appendix 3, "The Pestilence."
9. This is a common medieval image. A fourteenth-century English manuscript shows a man in bed, with a devil and a skeleton at the foot and an angel at the head pulling a tiny child figure out of the dying man's mouth. A similar image appears in the Cluniac Monastery in Moissac, in St. Hildegard's "The Soul and Her Tabernacle," and in the Legenda Aurea.
10. For Julian the repulsive body represents the *great misery* of our mortal flesh, *not* human fleshliness itself.
11. Julian's answer to those who plead for a relief from pain and suffering: it is better to endure the pain until we are wholly taken away from it by death.
12. The promise is above: "Without warning thou shalt be taken. . . ."
13. Revelation 21:4—"There shall be an end to death, and to mourning and crying and pain, for the old order has passed away!"
14. Julian counsels that the endurance of pain can be made less onerous if we concentrate on the rewards that follow death.
15. Julian recalls the condition of the fallen servant in Chapter 51 who in the midst of his pain forgot his lord.

At this time I saw a body lying on the earth which appeared thick and ugly and fearsome,[7] without shape and form, as it were <u>a bloated heap of stinking mire</u>.[8]

And suddenly out of this body sprang a most fair creature, a tiny child, well-shaped and formed, quick and lively, whiter than a lily, which neatly glided up into heaven.[9]

The bloatedness of the body symbolizes the great misery of our mortal flesh, and the tininess of the child symbolizes the clearness and purity of our soul.[10]

And I considered: "With this body remained none of the fairness of the child, nor in this child did there remain any foulness of the body."

It is most blessed for man to be taken from pain, more than for pain to be taken from man;[11] for if pain is taken from us, it can come again. Therefore is it an unequalled comfort and a blessed awareness for a loving soul that we shall be taken from pain, for in this promise[12] I saw a merciful compassion that our Lord has to us in our woe and a gracious promise of pure deliverance, for He wills that we be comforted in surpassing joy.[13]

(And that He showed in these words: "And thou shalt come up above; and thou shalt have me for thy reward; and thou shalt be filled full of joy and bliss.")

It is God's will that we fix the point of our concentration on this blessed sight as often as we can and for as long a time as we can keep ourselves therein with His grace. For this is a blessed contemplation for the soul that is guided by God and very much to its honor for the time that it lasts.[14]

And when we fall again into ourselves by sluggishness and spiritual blindness and the experiencing of spiritual and bodily pains because of our frailty, it is God's will that we recognize that He has not forgotten us.[15]

(And this He means in these words He says for the sake of comfort: "And thou shalt never more have pain, nor any manner of sickness, nor any manner of displeasure, nor lack of will, but ever joy and bliss

16. It is likely that in all these words about enduring suffering, Julian speaks autobiographically—out of her own experience of the pain and suffering she endured in her sickness, and how God took her out of her pain when she contemplated His love and compassion.

COMMENTS ON CHAPTER 65

1. This is another example of Julian's gentle feminism as she specifically includes both genders: "whatever man or woman." And note that it is followed by traditional nongeneric male pronouns.
2. That is to say, the grace to endure suffering in sure knowledge of ultimate bliss. W&J say, "Love chooses those who will love."
3. The use of "we" here has been taken by some as including all humans, but it must be remembered that Julian addresses her words to "those who shall be saved," in other words, committed Christians.
4. Julian's second introduction of the idea of "holy fear" (ME: *holy, curtes drede*), which she will later call "reverent fear." She links this "fear" consistently with humility. (Note: Julian's use of *curtes* [or "courteous"] refers to the civil and gracious nature of a royal court.)
5. ME has *in althing is most desired*.

without end. Why should it bother thee to suffer awhile seeing that it is my will and to my honor?")

It is God's will that we accept His promises and His comfortings as broadly and as powerfully as we can receive them.

And He also wills that we accept our waiting and our distress as lightly as we can take them, and pay no attention to them—for the more lightly we take them, and the less value we place on them for the sake of love, the less pain shall we have in experiencing them, and the more favor and regard will we have because of them.[16]

⟅ 65

Thus I understood that whatever man or woman[1] willingly chooses God in this life for the sake of love, he can be certain that he is loved without end with endless love which creates in him that grace.[2] He wills that we hold on to this trustfully—that we are all in as certain hope of the bliss of heaven while we are here, as we shall be in certainty when we are there.[3] And the more delight and joy that we take in this certainty with reverence and humility, the better it pleases Him, as it was shown.

For, as it was shown, this reverence that I mean is a holy, gracious fear[4] of our Lord, to which humility is knit: and that is that a creature sees the Lord as wondrous great, and the self as wondrous small.

For these virtues are possessed eternally by those beloved of God, and this can be understood and experienced now in some measure by the presence of our Lord when that presence occurs. This presence in every circumstance is most longed for,[5] because it produces wondrous reassurance, in true faith and certain hope by the greatness of love, in fear that is sweet and delightful.

It is God's will that I see myself just as much bound to Him in love as if He had done all that He has done just for me.

And thus should every soul think in regard to His Love: that is to say, the love of God creates in us such a unity that when it is truly understood, no man can separate himself from any other.

6. Although in Chapter 40 Julian speaks of the friendship of our Lord, this is the first time she actually uses the word "Friend" to describe him. She expands on this idea in Chapter 76. We are reminded of Jesus' words to Pilate: "You would have no power over me unless it had been given you from above . . ." (John 19:11, NRSV).

7. Here we have a paradox characteristic of a mystic's understanding: one fears the God whom one loves.

8. This is a pleasing, compassionate dimension to Julian's strong counsel: "as soon as we can. . . ."

9. Julian takes the broadest possible understanding of "God's will," that is, whatever happens is somehow within His will. Her basic idea is that no matter what happens, we are "kept" and protected by God's love, so we need have no fear.

10. Now at the conclusion of Julian's reflections on her revelations, she also credits her own reflections as being divinely inspired ("from the same Spirit").

11. See Part Two, section 5, on the date and time of Julian's visions.

COMMENTS ON CHAPTER 66

1. We recognize the description of the fallen servant from Chapter 51.

And thus ought our soul to understand that God has done just for itself all that He has done.

This He shows in order to make us love Him and fear nothing but Him; for it is His will that we be aware that all the power of the Enemy is held in our Friend's hand.[6]

Therefore the soul that surely recognizes this shall fear nothing except Him whom it loves.[7] All other fears the soul reckons along with passions and bodily sickness and fantasies, and therefore, although we may be in so much pain, woe, and distress that it seems to us that we can think of absolutely nothing except what we are in or what we are experiencing, as soon as we can, we pass lightly over it and we set it at naught.[8]

And why? Because we know God's will that if we know Him and love Him and reverently fear Him, we shall have peace and be in great repose, and all that He does shall be a great pleasure to us.[9]

(And this showed our Lord in these words: "Why should it bother thee to suffer awhile, since it is my will and to my honor?")

Now I have told you of fifteen revelations as God granted to deliver them to my mind, renewed[10] by enlightenings and inspirations (I hope, from the same Spirit who showed them all).

Of these fifteen showings the first began early in the morning, about the hour of four, and they lasted, appearing in a most beautiful order and solemnly, each following the other, until it was three in the afternoon[11] or later.

⬱ 66

After this, the good Lord showed the sixteenth showing on the following night, as I shall say later, and the sixteenth was the conclusion and confirmation of all fifteen.

Except first it behooves me to tell you about my weakness, misery, and blindness.[1]

I have said in the beginning, "And in this all my pain was suddenly taken from me." From this pain I had no grief and no distress as long

2. Julian uses the same words in Chapter 41, where she says that "we are frequently as barren and dry after our prayers as we were before."

3. Note that the revelations themselves do not seem to effect a healing of Julian's illness.

4. ME has *a religious person.* A.I. Doyle writes of the "professional medieval sense of religious (meaning a life by rule)."[138] The noun "religious" means a person under vows in a religious order. Julian's visitor was a monk or friar. It is likely that this person was Julian's confessor or spiritual director.

5. Again, we see an autobiographical element on Julian's part, and one that shows her in a self-accusatory and unattractive light—characteristic of her humility.

6. Interestingly, the SV adds the apparent eyewitness note: "at my bed's foot."

7. C&W remind us that in the SV Julian says the crucifix actually bled, but here she emphasizes that it was a "seeming," not a reality.

8. This is a troublesome phrase: BV has *than saw I no mor therof.* PV has *that sawe no more therof.* SV has *that says na mare therto.* The phrase seems to mean that the visitor took all Julian's words seriously, but she had not taken them equally seriously. Or it could mean that the visitor took Julian's few words seriously even though she had not told him any more of the revelations. W&J translate it as "who knows no more of it than that."

9. This is a further suggestion that the monk or friar may have been Julian's confessor.

10. Julian doubts that a priest would even believe that she was telling the truth if she were to tell of debasing a divine revelation.

11. This is more autobiographical confession and humiliation—and another validation of Julian's sincerity, that is, her willingness to reveal her shame.

12. Julian sees herself as vile and despicable for having demeaned her revelations from God by referring to them as mere

as the fifteen showings lasted one after another, and at the end all was concealed and I saw no more.

And soon I sensed that I would live and linger on, and immediately my sickness came again—first in my head, with a sound and a noise, and without warning all my body was filled full of sickness just as it had been before, and I was so barren and so dry[2] that I had but little comfort.[3]

And as a wretch I moaned gloomily because of the experience of my bodily pains and for the lack of comfort, spiritually and bodily.

Then a <u>member of a religious order</u>[4] came to me and asked how I fared. And I said that I had been raving today,[5] and he laughed aloud and fervently. I said, "The cross that stood before my face,[6] it seemed to me[7] that it bled profusely." And with this word, the person that I spoke to grew all serious and marveled. And immediately I was sore ashamed and amazed at my recklessness, and I thought, "This man takes seriously the least word that I could say <u>even though I told no more of it</u>."[8]

But when I saw that he took it seriously and with such great respect, I grew most greatly ashamed, and I would have been shriven,[9] except at that time I could tell it to no priest, for I thought, "How would a priest believe me when, by saying I raved, I showed myself not to believe our Lord God?"[10] (even though I believed Him truly during the time that I saw Him, and so was then my will and my intention to do so forever without end—but, like a fool, I let it pass from my mind).[11]

Ah, behold me, a <u>wretch</u>![12]

delusions or "raving." The word *wretch* also carried a sense of "sinner." Also note that in PV the wretchedness is put in the past: "Ah, behold how wretched I was."

13. It seems that Julian may have expected a relief from her illness as a result of the revelations, and was disappointed the relief had not come and the illness had reasserted itself.

14. In PV, Chapter 66 ends here and Chapter 67 begins. This suggests that possibly the original text had no chapter divisions.

15. Here we find a fascinating textual contrast: BV has the Fiend's hair *evisid aforn* (that is, "clipped off in front," while PV has *not scoryd afore* (that is, "*not* cut short in front"), and the SV omits the descriptive detail altogether.

16. Julian's dream (vision) of the Devil likely showed characteristics she could have seen in the Mystery Plays' version of the fiends depicted in animal shapes, with paws and/or claws. The unclipped hair and "side-locks" mentioned suggest the archetypal medieval cartoon caricatures of Jews (Leviticus 19:27–28 forbids cutting the hair at the temples or the sides of the beard), although all Jews were expelled from England in 1290. It should also be noted that no matter how hard the Fiend tried to kill Julian, "he could not."

17. It seems important for Julian to differentiate this "dream" from the other revelations that she assures her reader were not mere dreams. A dream was considered less spiritually valid than a waking vision.

18. Wetting the temples with water (or especially with vinegar) was considered a way to bring a fainting person out of a swoon.

19. ME has *comforten*.

20. Fire and the smell of brimstone (burning sulfur) have universally been considered by the Christian tradition as characteristics of hell and evidence of the presence of the Devil.

21. See Chapter 19: "I was well-aware that while I gazed on the cross I was secure and safe. . . ."

This was a great sin, a great unkindness, that I, out of folly, out of feeling a little bodily pain, so stupidly lost for the time the comfort of all this blessed showing of our Lord God.[13]

Here you can see what I am by myself.

But even in this our gracious Lord would not leave me. And I lay still until night, trusting in His mercy, and then I began to sleep.[14]

In my sleep, at the beginning, it seemed that the Fiend fixed on my throat, thrusting forth a face like a young man's very near to my face; and the face was long and wondrous thin. I never saw anything like it.

The color was red like the tile stone when it is new fired, with black spots in it like black holes, fouler than tile stone. His hair was red as rust, <u>clipped off in front</u>,[15] with side locks hanging at the temples. He snarled at me with an evil expression, showing white teeth, and so much that I thought it even more repulsive. He had no fit body nor hands, but with his paws he held me by the throat and would have strangled me, but he could not.[16]

(This horrible showing was given in sleep, as was no other.)[17]

And during all this time, I trusted to be saved and protected by the mercy of God. And our gracious Lord gave me grace to awaken, and scarcely had I any life.

The persons that were with me watched me and wet my temples,[18] and my heart began to <u>relax</u>.[19]

Immediately a little smoke came in the door with a great heat and a foul stench. I said, "Benedicite domine! Everything here is on fire!"

And I imagined that it was a physical fire that would have burnt us all to death.

I asked those who were with me if they sensed any odor. They said no, they smelled none. I said, "Blessed be God!" because then I was well aware that it was the Fiend that had come only to tempt me.[20]

And immediately I betook myself to what our Lord had shown me on that same day, with all the Faith of Holy Church (for I look upon them as both the same), and I fled to that as to my comfort.[21]

22. Finally, in this brief sentence is word of Julian's healing—both physical and spiritual. Her illness has disappeared and her conscience is clear. This is also truly the end of the account of her revelations. There is one more final concluding revelation, but most of the rest of her book is taken up with serious reflections on the implications of the revelations.

COMMENTS ON CHAPTER 67

Note: At this point, the numbering of the chapters begins to differ between BV and PV. We follow the numbering of BV.

1. The ME has *endles world* in BV and *endlesse warde* in PV. A "ward" is a guarded castle or citadel. C&W translate this as "endless citadel"; W&J translate it as "eternal citadel." But it seems that Julian is trying to convey the idea of limitless space within her soul.

2. See Luke 17:21—"The kingdom of God is among you!"

3. "City" again refers to a bishop's see city, where the bishop has his "seat."

4. Man and God are bonded in the Incarnation, and God alone rules and guards.

5. The ME has *couth*. This is a form of the ME verb *can*, which means "to know." Most translators are fooled by this false cognate and translate it as "can" or "is able."

And soon all vanished away, and I was brought to great repose and peace without sickness of body or fear of conscience.[22]

67

And then our Lord opened my spiritual eye and showed me my soul in the midst of my inner self. I saw my soul as large as if it were an <u>endless world</u>[1] and as if it were a blessed kingdom;[2] and by the circumstances I saw in it I understood that it is an honorable City.[3]

In the midst of that <u>City</u> sits[3] our Lord Jesus Christ, true God and true man, a handsome person, and of tall stature, highest bishop, a most honorable Lord. And I saw Him arrayed with great pomp and honor. He sits in the soul calmly upright in peace and repose, and He rules and guards heaven and earth and all that exists.

The Manhood sits with the Godhead in repose, and the Godhead rules and guards without any agent or activity.[4]

And the soul is wholly occupied with the blessed Godhead, who is supreme Power, supreme Wisdom, and supreme Goodness.

The place that Jesus takes in our soul, He will never move it away forever, as I see it, for in us is His most familiar home and His eternal dwelling.

And in this He showed the delight that He has in the creating of man's soul—for as well as the Father had the power to make a creature, and as well as the Son <u>had the knowledge</u>[5] to make a creature, equally well did the Holy Spirit have the wish that many souls be made; and so it was done.

And therefore the blessed Trinity rejoices without end in the creating of man's soul, for He saw from without beginning what would please Him without end. Everything that He has made shows His Lordship.

An understanding was given at the same time by the illustration of a creature that was led to see great nobility and kingdoms belonging to a lord, and when he had seen all the nobility below, then, marveling,

6. The "kingdoms belonging to a lord" symbolize the earth; the "high place where the lord dwells" symbolizes heaven.

7. Julian concludes that the human soul can never find rest in things of the earth, however good or noble they may be. One is reminded of Augustine's apostrophe to God: "You have made us for yourself, and our hearts are restless till they find their rest in you."[139]

8. That is, into the person's essence (which is in God).

9. This is another of Julian's countless expressions of the common (and mystically paradoxical) indwelling of God in the soul and the soul in God.

10. See Revelation 21:23—"The [heavenly] city did not need the sun or the moon to shine on it, for the glory of God gave it light, and its lamp was the Lamb."

11. See Genesis 1:31—"And God saw all that he had made, and it was very good."(Genesis tells us that in his other creations, God "saw that it was good," but after making humans He saw that it was *very* good.)

COMMENTS ON CHAPTER 68

Note: At this point the BV and PV chapter divisions once again concur.

1. This is reminiscent of 2 Corinthians 3:18b—". . . we all see as in a mirror the glory of the Lord, and we are being transformed into his likeness with ever-increasing glory, through the power of the Lord who is the Spirit."

2. Julian describes *seeing* God, but with her "spiritual eyes." (See the beginning of Chapter 67.)

he was moved to go above to the high place where the lord dwells, knowing by reason that his dwelling is in the most honorable place.[6]

And thus I understood truly that our soul can never have rest in things that are beneath itself.[7]

And when it comes above all created things into the self,[8] still it cannot remain in the contemplation of the self, but all its contemplation is blissfully fixed on God, who is the Creator dwelling in the self (for in man's soul is His true dwelling).[9]

The highest light and the brightest shining of the City is the glorious love of our Lord, as I see it.[10]

And what can make us rejoice in God more than to see in Him that He rejoices in us, the highest of all His works?

For I saw in the same showing that if the blessed Trinity could have made man's soul any better, any more beautiful, any nobler than it was made, He would not have been wholly pleased with the creation of man's soul.[11] But because He made man's soul as fair, as good, as precious a creature as He could make it, therefore the Blessed Trinity is wholly pleased without end in the creation of man's soul, and He wills that our hearts be powerfully raised above the depths of the earth and all vain sorrows, and rejoice in Him.

68

This was a delightful sight[1] and a restful showing that is without end, and the contemplation of this while we are here is most pleasant to God and very great help to us. And the soul that thus contemplates it makes itself to be like Him who is contemplated,[1] and ones itself in rest and peace by His grace.

It was a particular joy and bliss to me that I saw[2] Him seated, because the steadiness of sitting suggests endless dwelling.

And He gave me knowledge truthfully that it was He who showed me everything before, for when I had watched this, with time for consideration, then our good Lord revealed words most humbly without voice and without opening of lips, just as He had done before, and

3. Clearly, God's "voice" does not involve *spoken* words, but conveyed the ideas to Julian inwardly. Here is God's reaffirmation of the validity of the revelations in the face of Julian's shameful doubts in Chapter 66. The phrase "thou shalt not be overcome" becomes almost a motif for Julian below.

4. Julian is relieved by the divine affirmation here that the revelations were, indeed, from the Lord.

5. Even though Julian is the one who "saw" the sight and "heard" the words, she makes it clear that they are intended for all committed Christians.

6. God's keeping of His people does not mean they will not suffer. "All shall be well" does not mean there will be no pain or turmoil, but that one can survive the temptations, the trouble, and the distress through trust in God's care.

7. Julian provides the optimistic and brief summation of the "Christian Way," and it has its roots in trust that "in well and woe" God will not allow Christians to be overcome. It should be noted that throughout her book, Julian considers all her own insights to be part of the revelations from God.

COMMENTS ON CHAPTER 69

1. The ME word is *besy*, and in the fourteenth century it carried the sense of "uneasy" or "full-of-care." (See OED, 6.)

2. W&J wisely suggest that Julian considers that the demons may be having an argument about her eternal destiny.

said most sweetly: "Be well aware that it was no raving that thou sawest today, but accept it, and believe it, and keep thyself in it, and comfort thyself with it, and trust thyself to it, and thou shalt not be overcome."[3]

These last words were said to teach true certainty that it is our Lord Jesus who showed me everything.[4]

And just as in the first word that our good Lord revealed, referring to His blessed Passion: "With this is the Devil overcome"—just so He said in this last word with completely true faithfulness, referring to us all: "Thou shalt not be overcome."

And all this teaching and this true comfort is universal for all my fellow Christians as was said before—and this is God's will.[5]

These words: "Thou shall not be overcome," were said very sharply and very powerfully, for certainty and comfort against all tribulations that can come.

He said not, "Thou shalt not be tempted; thou shalt not be troubled; thou shalt not be distressed," but He said, "Thou shalt not be overcome."[6]

God wills that we take heed to these words, and that we be very strong in certain trust, in well and in woe, for as He loves and delights in us, so He wills that we love Him and delight in Him and strongly trust in Him; and all shall be well.[7]

And, soon after, all was concealed, and I saw no more.

ᕲ 69

After this the Fiend came again with his heat and with his stink, and made me most <u>anxious</u>.[1] The stink was so vile and so painful, and the physical heat was fearful and troublesome also.

Also I heard a physical chattering as if it had been from two bodies, and both, it seemed to me, chattered at one time as if they were holding a parliament with a great business;[2] and all was soft muttering, since I understood nothing that they said. All this was to move me to

3. In her entire book Julian mentions only two sins specifically: despair and impatience. (See Chapter 73.)

4. The ME word is *bedes*, coming from the word *bidden*, meaning "commanded" (that is, we are commanded to pray). Eventually, it came to refer to prayer *beads*, but the rosary as we know it had not yet been developed in Julian's day, although an early fifteenth-century portrait shows a large seven-bead rosary with a cross at the end, hanging from the waist.[140]

5. We recall Margery Kempe's evaluation of Julian: "for the anchoress was expert in such things and could give good counsel." And here Julian applies her own skills in counseling to herself.

6. Julian presents a perfect summary of the cataphatic mode of contemplative prayer: using the crucifix as a center of attention for the eyes, reciting prayers and the Creed with the lips, and cleaving spiritually to God with the mind. (Note: Julian uses the word *heart* twenty-four times in her book, and it never carries the modern meaning of the "seat of emotion." For Julian the *heart* is virtually equivalent to the *mind* as the seat of the will and the intellect. In fourteenth-century England, the *bowels* were considered to be the seat of the emotions—especially feelings of pity and compassion.)

7. Julian teaches herself: "Learn from this: you must keep in the Faith the way you did here if you want to avoid sin in the future."

8. ME has the words *prime day*. This is a reference to the monastic Office of Prime that was recited at about 6 AM.

9. In Chapter 13 the Lord scorns the Devil, and Julian has learned that is the way to deal with the Fiend: to scorn and despise him.

10. This passage has been included because it seems important in helping us comprehend Julian's primary understanding of sin as "nothingness."

despair,[3] as I thought, seeming to me that they ridiculed the saying of prayers (as when prayers[4] are said coarsely with the mouth, without the devout intention and wise effort which we owe to God in our prayers).

Our Lord God gave me grace powerfully to trust in Him, and to comfort my soul with physical speech as I would have done to another person who had been troubled.[5] (It seemed to me that their carryings-on could not be agreeable to any physical activity of mine.)

My physical eye I fixed upon the same cross where I had been in comfort before that time, my tongue I occupied with speaking of Christ's Passion and reciting the Faith of Holy Church, and my heart I made fast to God with all my trust and with all my might.[6]

And I thought to myself, saying: "Thou hast now a great duty to keep thyself in the Faith in order that thou shouldst not be seized by the Enemy; if thou wouldst now from this time onward be as busy to keep thyself from sin, this would be a good and a most excellent occupation," for it seemed that if I were truly safe from sin, I would be completely safe from all the fiends of hell and the enemies of my soul.[7]

And so he occupied me all that night, and in the day until it was about six in the morning.[8] And immediately they were all gone, all passed away, and they left nothing but the odor; and that still lasted awhile.

I scorned that Fiend, and so was I delivered from him by the virtue of Christ's Passion, for with that is the Fiend overcome, as our Lord Jesus Christ said before.[9]

[Note: At this point the earlier Short Version (the Amherst Manuscript) includes a long apostrophe to sin that is not present in either BV or PV. The passage follows:[10]

> Ah, wretched sin. What are you? You are nothing. For when I saw that God is everything, I saw you not. And when I saw that God has made everything, I saw you not. And when I saw that God does everything that is done, both small and great, I saw you not.

11. These are critical (and difficult) words. The ME has *endeleslye confownded*, and most use the English cognates and translate that as "endlessly confounded." But *confownded* also carries the meanings of "overcome," "conquered," or "destroyed." Since the words are set as a parallel to "brought to nothing," "destroyed" seems the most appropriate translation. The implications of this can be great, since it suggests that the way in which "all shall be well" is the (painless) divine *de-creation* of hell and its sinful inhabitants, so that they simply no longer exist. Julian left this bit of radical eschatology out of her later Long Version—probably for fear of being declared a heretic. (See Psalm 73:27–28, [BCP]—"Truly, those who forsake you will perish; you destroy all who are unfaithful. But it is good for me to be near God; I have made the Lord God my refuge.")

12. Julian's ME word is *wretchedness*.

13. The "First Sin" is the original sin of Adam and Eve.

14. Julian sees human passions as a source of weakness and sin. See Chapter 41: "it is in our feeling, our foolishness, that the cause of our weakness lies."

15. Julian's understanding of sin is that it is a matter of the will, that is, of human free choice. And she discounts "minor" sins that come from human frailty and ignorance as long as one's primary will chooses God. This refers to the "divine will" in each of us "that never consented to sin nor ever shall" (Chapter 37).

16. BV has the word *by* here, but it is obviously a scribal error since with it the sentence is meaningless.

And when I saw our Lord Jesus sitting in our soul so honorably and [saw Him] love and like and rule and care for all that He has made, I saw you not. Thus I am certain that you are nothing and all those who love you and like you and follow you and are intentionally near to you, I am certain they shall be brought to nothing with you and <u>eternally destroyed</u>.[11] God shield us all from you! So be it, for God's love. What <u>sinfulness</u>[12] is I will say as I am taught by the showing of God: sinfulness is everything that is not good: the spiritual blindness that we fell into in the First Sin,[13] and all that follows from that misery—passions and pains,[14] spiritual or bodily, and all that is on earth or in any other place which is not good.

And then from this can be asked: "What are we?" And I answer to this: "If all that is not good were separated from us, we would be good. When sinfulness is separated from us, God and the soul are all one, and God and man are all one."

Does everything on earth bind us [to God]? I answer and say: "Insofar as it helps us, it is good, and insofar as it shall perish it is sinfulness, and insofar as man sets his heart on it otherwise than in this way, it is sin. And for the time that a man or woman loves sin (if there be any such), he is in pain that surpasses all pains. And when he loves not sin, but hates it and loves God, all is well; and he that truly does this, though he sin sometimes through frailty or ignorance, in his will he does not fall because he will mightily rise again and behold God whom he loves in all his will.[15] God has made them to be loved, even[16] him or her that has been a sinner. And always He loves [us] and always He longs to have our love. And when we mightily and wisely love Jesus, we are in peace.]

COMMENTS ON CHAPTER 70

1. Julian's spiritual maturity: she recognizes that the visions will not continue or be repeated, but she also knows that their messages will be "preserved" not in further ecstasies, but in her personal trust and in the faith of the Church.
2. Some medieval mystics were given "tokens" of their visions—like St. Francis's stigmata or Catherine of Siena's gold ring—but Julian declares there was no "proof" given except her own faith.
3. Julian restates her now-firm faith that the revelations were from the Lord—contrary to the doubts she had expressed when she said she had "raved" (in Chapter 66).
4. This is quoted from Chapter 68.
5. This is a reference to Chapter 66.
6. This is perhaps Julian's way of speaking of the fifteen to twenty years of reflection and memory she had expended on the original revelations.
7. The ME is *seest*, one meaning of which is "understand."
8. See Chapter 68.
9. "Our" and "us," not "my" or "me." It should be noted that Julian now includes her readers (as well as herself) in Jesus' six instructions.
10. In this current discussion, Julian's word "faith" refers to personal faith and trust rather than the faith of the Church as previously.

⤳ 70

In all this blessed showing, our good Lord gave me understanding that the vision would pass[1] (which blessed showing the Faith preserves with His own good will and His grace) for He left with me neither sign nor token by which I could know this,[2] but He left me His own blessed word in true understanding, bidding me most powerfully that I should believe it. And so I do. Blessed may He be!

I believe that He is our Savior who showed it, and that it is the Faith that He showed.[3]

And therefore I believe it, rejoicing; and to it I am bound by all His own intention, with these next words that follow: "Keep thyself therein and comfort thyself with it and trust thyself to it."[4]

Thus I am bound to maintain it in my Faith.

For on the same day that it was shown, as soon as the vision was passed, like a wretch I forsook it and openly said that I had raved.[5]

Then our Lord Jesus of His mercy would not let the vision perish, but He showed it all again within my soul,[6] with more fullness, with the blessed light of His precious Love, saying these words most strongly and most humbly:

"Know it with certainty now that it was no raving that thou sawest this day."

As if He had said: "Because the vision was passed from thee, thou didst let it go and knew not how to preserve it; but know it now, that is to say, now that thou dost <u>understand</u>[7] it."

This was said not only for that particular time, but also to fix it there upon the foundation of my faith where He says immediately following: "But accept it, believe it, and keep thyself in it and comfort thyself with it and trust thyself to it; and thou shalt not be overcome."[8]

In those six words that follow where He says, "accept it . . . ," His intention is truly to make this fast in our heart, for He wills that it dwell with us[9] in faith[10] until our life's end, and afterward in fullness of joy, willing that we always have certain trust in His blessed promises, knowing His goodness.

11. Again, Julian repeats a justification for humanity's troubles and temptations. She never suggests that life will be "easy" for herself and her fellow Christians.

COMMENTS ON CHAPTER 71

1. W&J remind us that this is the single time this word is applied to humanity, rather than to God.
2. God expects us to "keep a good face on it" even if we don't "feel" like it.
3. We are to keep a loving outward demeanor in the hope that God will help to interiorize the love-longing.
4. The ME word used throughout the *Revelations* is *chere*. It means literally "face," but also caries the sense of "countenance" or "attitude." In the remaining paragraphs of this chapter, it carries the sense of Jesus' approach to us or His manifestation of Himself to us in three ways.

For our faith is opposed in various ways by our own blindness and by our spiritual Enemy, within and without, and therefore our Precious Lover helps us with spiritual insight and true teaching in equally various ways, within and without, by which we can know Him.

And therefore in whatever manner He teaches us, He wills that we perceive Him wisely, receive Him sweetly, and keep ourselves in Him full of faith—for beyond the Faith is no goodness kept in this life, as I see it, and below the Faith is no health for souls, but in the Faith there the Lord wills that we maintain ourselves.

For we must by His goodness and His own action maintain ourselves in the Faith, and by His permitting it, we are tested in the Faith by spiritual opposition and made strong.

If our faith had no opposition, it would deserve no reward, as far as the understanding I have of all our Lord's meaning.[11]

⁀ 71

Glad and merry and sweet is the blessed loving face our Lord [turns] to our souls; for He sees us always living in love-longing[1] [for Him], and He wills that our soul be of glad expression to Him in order to give Him his reward.[2]

And thus I hope with His grace that He has—and shall even more—draw in our outer expression to the inner demeanor and make us all at one with Him and each of us with the other, in the true lasting joy that is Jesus.[3]

I understand three kinds of expressions[4] from our Lord.

The first is the face of Passion as He showed it while He was here in this life, dying. (Though this sight is mournful and sorrowful, yet it is also glad and merry, for He is God.)

The second kind of face is pity and sympathy and compassion; and this He shows to all His lovers who have need of His mercy, with certainty of saving.

5. The ME is *meddelyng*—a characteristic Norfolk collo-quialism.

COMMENTS ON CHAPTER 72

1. In these last chapters, it seems that Julian is "cleaning up" loose ends, since they include a collection of clarifications about issues that need explaining. The issue here is the way in which those who commit mortal sin can be saved. "Mortal sin" (ME: *synne deedly*) is serious sin that has the capability of condemning one to hell if it is not confessed and absolved.
2. Notice that Julian again equates sin with pain—that is, it is pain for the committed Christian who recognizes his or her sin.
3. "For that time" is an important qualification for Julian, because she is about to make the point that sin is mortal "for only a short time."

The third is the full blessed face as it shall be without end; and this was continued most often and longest.

And thus in the time of our pain and our woe, He shows us the face of His Passion and of His cross, helping us to bear it by His own blessed strength.

And in the time of our sinning, He shows us the face of compassion and pity, mightily protecting us and defending against all our enemies.

(And these two are the usual faces that He shows to us in this life; with them mixing⁵ the third.)

And this third is His blessed face, partially like what it will be in heaven. And that face is a gracious inspiration and sweet enlightening of the spiritual life by which we are saved in certain faith, hope and love, with contrition and devotion and also with contemplation and all manner of true solace and sweet comforts.

The blessed face of our Lord God accomplishes that inspiring and enlightening in us by grace.

⤳ 72

But now it behooves me to tell how I saw <u>mortal sin</u> in those creatures who shall not die because of sin, but live in the joy of God without end.¹

I saw that two opposites should never be together in one place. The greatest opposites that exist are the highest bliss and the deepest pain.² The highest bliss that exists is to have God in the radiance of endless life, seeing Him truly, experiencing Him sweetly, all peacefully enjoying Him in fullness of joy. (And thus was the blessed face of our Lord shown, but only partially.)

In this showing I saw that sin is most opposite to this, to such an extent that as long as we are mixed up with any part of sin, we shall never see clearly the blessed face of our Lord. And the more horrible and the more grievous our sins are, the deeper distance are we from this blessed sight for that time.³

4. Although we may consider sin to be "mortal" (that is, deadly), God does not see us as "dead."

5. There are two important ideas here: the first is that God wants us with Him and is willing to do almost anything to accomplish that. Second, that our union with God is part of our very human nature itself, aided by God's grace.

6. "The grace of loving" is a central theme for Julian. God's grace shows itself in God's loving us, and if we receive that grace we, too, become loving.

7. The heart "thinks," it does not "feel." Julian's use of the word corresponds more closely to our understanding of "mind."

Therefore it seems to us frequently that we are in peril of death, in some part of hell, because of the sorrow and pain that the sin is for us. And thus we are deadened for the time from the very sight of our blessed life.

But in all this I saw truthfully that we are not dead[4] in the sight of God, nor does He ever pass away from us, but He shall never enjoy His full bliss in us until we enjoy our full bliss in Him, truly seeing His fair, blessed face, for we are ordained to that in nature, and get to it by grace.[5]

Thus I saw how sin is mortal for only a short time in the blessed creature of endless life.

And ever the more clearly that the soul sees this blessed Face by grace of loving,[6] the more it yearns to see it in fullness; for notwithstanding that our Lord God dwells in us, and is here with us, and calls us and enfolds us for tender love so that He can never leave us, and is nearer to us than tongue can tell or heart can think,[7] yet we can never cease moaning nor weeping nor yearning until the time when we look at Him clearly in His blessed face; for in that precious, blessed sight there can remain no woe nor any lack of well-being.

In this I saw cause for mirth and cause for mourning:

—cause for mirth because our Lord our Creator is so near to us and within us, and we in Him, by the faithfulness of His great goodness in protecting us;

—cause for mourning because our spiritual eye is so blind and we are so borne down by the burden of our mortal flesh and the darkness of sin that we cannot look our Lord God clearly in His fair blessed face.

No, and because of this darkness, scarcely can we even believe and trust His great love and His faithful protection of us.

That is why I say that we can never cease mourning nor weeping.

This "weeping" does not wholly signify pouring out of tears by our physical eyes, but also intends more spiritual interpretation, for the natural desire of our soul to see His face is so great and so immeasurable that if all the splendor that ever God made in heaven and on

8. It seems important to Julian that she qualify her speaking of "tears." W&J remind us that in his *Incendium Amoris*, Richard Rolle argues that "tears and weeping are for new converts and beginners." However, with her "approval" of Margery Kempe's spirituality, Julian does not entirely discount the spiritual value of the "gift of tears."

9. This is from Chapter 26.

10. Julian summarizes her understanding of God's purposes behind His revelations to her: to know God, to know ourselves as God created us, and to know ourselves as sinners.

COMMENTS ON CHAPTER 73

1. Julian continues to "sum up" significant aspects of the revelations. She certifies the accuracy of her account of the visions and the words she "heard" from the Lord, but admits the inadequacy of her efforts to convey fully the mystical insights she had in her reflections.

2. It is significant that the only two sins mentioned specifically are impatience/sloth and despair/fear. Both sins are failures of faith, suggesting the unwillingness of human beings to depend on God's love and to trust God even in the midst of trouble. It is important that we see that these two sins are not "ordinary immorality"—neither of them is among the Ten Commandments or other usual catalogs of sin. They are sins against faith and trust—sins of "being" rather than "doing." These two sins are morally foundational and both underlie and "precede" the more ordinary sins of action.

earth were given to us for our solace, but we saw not the fair, blessed face of Himself, still we would not cease from mourning nor from spiritual weeping (that is to say, out of painful yearning) until the time we truly see the fair, blessed face of our Creator.[8]

And if we were in all the pain that heart can think and tongue can tell, if we could at that time see His fair, blessed face, all this pain would not bother us. Thus is this blessed sight the end of all manner of pain to the loving soul, and the fulfillment of all manner of joy and bliss.

(And that He showed in the high, wondrous words where He said, "I am He who is highest; I am He who is lowest; I am He who is all.")[9]

It is proper for us to have three kinds of knowledge:

the first is that we know our Lord God;

the second is that we know ourselves, what we are by Him in nature and grace;

the third that we know humbly what we ourselves are as regards our sin and our weakness.

And the whole showing was given for these three, as I understand it.[10]

⁀ 73

All this blessed teaching of our Lord God was shown in three parts: that is to say, by bodily sight, and by word formed in my understanding, and by spiritual insight.

As for the bodily sight, I have told it as I saw as truly as I can; and as for the words, I have spoken them just as our Lord showed them to me; and as for the spiritual insight, I have said somewhat, but I can never fully relate it, and therefore I am moved to say more about this insight (as God wills to give me grace).[1]

God showed two kinds of sickness of soul that we have:

—the one is impatience or sloth (for we bear our labor and our pains gloomily);

—the other is despair or doubtful fear (as I shall say later).[2]

3. Notice Julian's pronouns: she begins to speak of "them" and ends speaking of "us."

4. Julian holds up the patience of the suffering Lord as the model antidote for our sins of impatience. This "imitation of Christ" was a frequent approach to sanctity among fourteenth-century spiritual writers.

5. If we remember the extraordinary experience of trouble, pain, social catastrophe, and religious upheaval of Julian's fourteenth century, we can see the importance of her counsel to "bear our pains."

6. The ME is *onknoweing of love*, a poignant description of the cause of sin.

7. Julian reprises her Trinitarian teachings and indicates that Christians have a tendency to overlook the presence and power of the Holy Spirit. This had particular applicability for the fourteenth century, when most Christians relied solely on the "mechanics" of the Church for salvation and paid little attention to the personal union with God that Julian encourages.

8. For Julian the obsession with the self and its sins makes the recognition of God's love more difficult.

9. The scrupulous fixation on one's sins passes for humility, but it is, in fact, a sin against God's love. If one cannot see beyond one's sins, one is blinded to the ever-present forgiving love of God. The fourteenth-century norm would have been to see God primarily as a judge only too eager to pass a verdict against sinners, but Julian asks her readers to see God as Love.

In general, He showed sin with which everyone is involved, but in particular He showed none but these two sins. And these two are those which most trouble and tempt us (according to what our Lord showed me), from which He wills that we be put right.

(I speak of such men and women who because of God's love hate sin and dispose themselves to do God's will; then by our spiritual blindness and our bodily gloom, we are most inclined to these sins, and therefore, it is God's will that they be known and then we shall refuse them as we do other sins.)[3]

For help against this, full humbly our Lord showed the patience that He had in His cruel Passion, and also the rejoicing and the delight that He has from that Passion because of love.[4]

And this showed by example that we should gladly and wisely bear our pains, for that is greatly pleasing to Him and endless benefit for us.[5]

And the cause why we are troubled with these sins is because of our ignorance of Love,[6] for though the three Persons in the Trinity are all equal in themselves, the soul received most understanding in Love; yes, and He wills that in everything we have our contemplation and our enjoyment in Love.

To this knowledge we are most blind; for some of us believe that God is all Power and is able to do all, and that He is all Wisdom and knows how to do all, but that He is all Love and will to do all, there we stop.[7]

This ignorance is that which most hinders God's lovers, as I see it, for when we begin to hate sin and amend ourselves by the command of Holy Church, still there persists a fear that hinders us, because of paying attention to ourselves and the sins we have done in the past[8] (and some of us because of our present everyday sins), for we keep not our covenants nor maintain the purity in which our Lord places us, but we fall frequently in so much misery that it is shame to see it. And the recognition of this makes us so sorry and so sorrowful that scarcely do we know how to find any comfort. And this fear we mistake sometimes for humility,[9] but this is a shameful blindness and a weakness.

10. The fearsome Power of the Father and the formidable Wisdom of the Son are both subordinated to the unfailing Love of the Holy Spirit. If we have repented and made amends for our sins, there is no reason for sadness or fear.

COMMENTS ON CHAPTER 74

1. In this catalog of fears Julian speaks of those that assail a good Christian. The "attack" in the first fear is the assault of the demons, which one fears because of spiritual weakness and the possibility that one will be defeated by the demons.
2. This is the fear of punishment after death for sins committed—fear of judgment and the pains of hell.
3. 1 Corinthians 15:34—"Wake up, be sober, and stop sinning. . . ."
4. "Spiritual enemies" refers to the demons of hell. At this point, the SV inserts the words "the fire of Purgatory," which Julian obviously intended to omit in the later LV.
5. This is the frightening doubt and disbelief about the reliability of God's forgiveness: the handmaid of despair.
6. "Reverent fear" can probably best be thought of as "awe" and "wonder" at the magnificence of God, and is linked here with love (which makes the awe/fear seem less formidable).

And we do not know to despise it as we do another sin which we recognize (which comes through lack of true judgment) and it is against truth, for of all the properties of the blessed Trinity, it is God's will that we have most confidence and delight in Love.

For Love makes Power and Wisdom wholly submissive to us; for just as by the graciousness of God He forgives our sin after the time that we repent, just so He wills that we forgive our own sin in regard to our unreasonable sorrow and our doubtful fears.[10]

74

I understand four kinds of fear.

One is the fear of attack that comes to a man suddenly because of his own weakness.[1] This fear does good, because it helps to purge man (as does bodily sickness or such other pain which is not sin), for all such pains help man if they are patiently taken.

The second is fear of pain,[2] by which a man is stirred and awakened from the sleep of sin;[3] for man that is hard asleep in sin is not able, for the time, to perceive the gentle comfort of the Holy Spirit until he has understanding of this fear of pain, of bodily death, and of spiritual enemies.[4] And this fear stirs us to seek the comfort and mercy of God; and thus this fear helps us as an entry place, and enables us to have contrition by the blessed inspiration of the Holy Spirit.

The third is doubtful fear.[5] Doubtful fear, insofar as it draws us to despair, God wills to have transformed in us into love by true acknowledgment of Love; that is to say, that the bitterness of doubt be turned into the sweetness of natural love by grace; for it can never please our Lord that His servants doubt His Goodness.

The fourth is reverent fear, for there is no fear in us that fully pleases God except reverent fear; and this is most gentle, for the more of it one has, the less it is felt because of the sweetness of love.[6]

Love and fear are brothers; and they are rooted in us by the Goodness of our Creator, and they shall never be taken from us without end.

7. Here Julian makes one last reference to the divine motherhood.
8. SV has "false."
9. The ME has *homely*.
10. Just as God is familiar (*homely*) and gracious (*courteous*) with us, so we are to be familiar (*intimate*) and gracious with God.

We have it from our human nature to love and we have it from grace to love; and we have it from human nature to fear and we have it from grace to fear.

It is part of the Lordship and of the Fatherhood to be feared, as it is part of the Goodness to be loved; and it is as proper for us who are His servants and His children to fear Him for His Lordship and His Fatherhood, as it is proper for us to love Him for His Goodness.

And although this reverent fear and love are not separated, yet they are not both the same, but they are two in character and in operation (but neither of them can be had without the other).

Therefore I am certain that he who loves, fears—even though he feels it only a little.

All fears other than reverent fear that are offered to us, although they come under the pretense of holiness, yet are not as true; and by this can they be known apart: that fear which makes us quickly to flee from all that is not good and fall onto our Lord's breast as the child into the mother's arms,[7] with all our intention and with all our mind acknowledging our weakness and our great need, recognizing His everlasting Goodness and His blessed Love, seeking only Him for salvation, cleaving to Him with certain trust—the fear which brings us into this process is natural, merciful, good, and true. And all that opposes this, either it is wrong, or it is mixed up with wrong.

Then this is the remedy—to know them both and refuse the wrong.[8]

For the natural benefit that we have in this life from fear (by the merciful action of the Holy Spirit) that same benefit will be in heaven before God, noble, gracious, and totally delightful.

And thus we shall in love be intimate[9] and near to God, and we shall in fear be noble and gracious to God; and both equally.[10]

We desire of our Lord God to fear Him reverently and to love Him humbly and to trust Him mightily; for when we fear Him reverently and love Him humbly, our trust is never in vain; for the more that we trust—and the more strongly that we trust—the more we please and honor our Lord in whom we trust. If we lack this reverent fear

11. This is reminiscent of the passage in Chapter 10: "the soul can do no more than seek, suffer, and trust."

12. Here Julian recognizes that the virtues of reverent fear and humble love are gifts to the soul from God the Creator, not something accomplished by humanity without God's grace.

COMMENTS ON CHAPTER 75

1. Pity, love, and yearning are the acts of God in relation to humanity.

2. See Chapter 31: "this is His thirst: a love-longing to possess us all together wholly within Himself for His bliss, as I see it." The "whole of mankind" refers to "those who shall be saved."

3. "Draw" both in the sense of "attract" and in the sense of "haul up water from a well" (OED). The image of God hauling the faithful departed up and "drinking" them into Himself is a rare conceit as Julian reaches for another way to describe the "one-ing" with God.

4. The "yearning" is mutual: both God's "thirst" for us and our "yearning" for God.

5. The ME has *fulfilled*, which carries the meaning of "completed"—probably another reference to the resurrection of the body, which those in heaven will not receive until the Last Day, when we will all be "completed" (that is, body and soul reunited).

6. Julian refers to the resurrection of the body that is to happen on Judgment Day at the end of the world.

and humble love (as God forbid we should), our trust shall soon be misdirected for that period of time.[11]

Therefore we much need to beseech our Lord for grace that we may have this reverent fear and humble love as His gift, in heart and in deed—for without this no man can please God.[12]

〜 75

I saw that God can do all that we need; and these three which I shall say we need:

> love,
>
> yearning,
>
> and pity.

Pity in love protects us in the time of our need, and yearning in the same draws us into heaven.[1]

For the thirst of God is to have the whole of mankind within Himself;[2] in this thirst, He has <u>drawn</u>[3] and drunken His Holy Souls who are now in bliss; and, gathering in His living members, He continually draws and drinks, and still He thirsts and yearns.

I saw three kinds of yearning in God (and all for one purpose), of which we have the same in us (and of the same strength and for the same purpose).[4]

The first is that He yearns to teach us to know Him and to love Him forever, since that is suitable and advantageous to us.

The second is that He yearns to have us up into His bliss as souls are when they are taken out of pain into heaven.

The third is to fill us with bliss; and that shall be <u>completed</u>[5] on the Last Day to last forever.

For I saw (as it is known in our Faith) that the pain and sorrow shall be ended for all that shall be saved. And not only shall we receive the same bliss that souls have had in heaven before, but also we shall receive a new bliss, which shall be abundantly flowing out of God into us and completing us.[6]

7. See 1 Corinthians 2:9—"Scripture speaks of 'things beyond our seeing, things beyond our imagining, all prepared by God for those who love him.' "

8. See Colossians 2:2–3—"God's secret, which is Christ himself, in whom lie hidden all the treasures of wisdom and knowledge."

9. Julian distinguishes between God's active will ("everything He has done") and God's permissive will ("all things that He has permitted"). God's purposes in allowing all our earthly pains and troubles will finally be seen clearly.

10. Julian erupts in ecstatic fervor as she attempts to quantify the glory, majesty, and awe of the experience of heaven. And although the pillars of heaven "tremble and quake" at the force of humanity's awe, Julian would also remember Psalm 75:2–3 (BCP): "I will appoint a time," says God; "I will judge with equity. Though the earth and all its inhabitants are quaking, I will make its pillars fast."

11. These words remind one of Julian's vision of the hazel nut (Chapter 5).

12. Heaven is often described as the Beatific Vision.

13. Julian has transformed Judgment Day from the traditional and commonly understood terrifying experience into an outbreak of joy and exultation, and she validates her own account as a way God wishes us to be aware of this.

14. One is reminded of the quaking of the earth at the death of Jesus on the cross (see Chapter 18 and Matthew 27:51), but at the end of the world, when the lovers of Christ shall tremble, it will be for wonder and "for abundance of joy."

These are the good things that He has prepared to give us from without beginning.[7]

These good things are treasured and hidden in Himself, for until that time, a created being is not strong or worthy enough to receive them.[8]

In this we shall see truly the reason for everything He has done, and, even more, we shall see the reason for all things that He has permitted.[9]

And the bliss and the fulfillment shall be so deep and so high that out of wonder and amazement all created beings shall have for God so great a reverent fear (surpassing what has been seen and felt before) that the pillars of heaven shall tremble and quake.[10]

But this kind of trembling and fear shall have no pain—rather it is part of the noble majesty of God to be seen this way by His creatures, fearfully trembling and quaking for abundance of joy, endlessly marveling at the greatness of God the Creator, and at the smallness of all that is made,[11] for the sight of this makes the creature wondrous humble and subdued.

Wherefore God wills (and it is also proper to us both in nature and grace) that we be aware and know of this experience, desiring this sight[12] and this work, for it leads us in the right way and preserves us in true life and ones us to God.[13]

God is as great as He is good; and as much as it is part of His Goodness to be loved, equally much it is part of His Greatness to be feared; for this reverent fear is the fair courtliness that is in heaven before God's face.

And just as much as He shall then be known and loved far more than He is now, to the same extent He shall be feared far more than He is now.

Therefore it is inevitable that all heaven and earth shall tremble and quake when the pillars shall tremble and quake.[14]

COMMENTS ON CHAPTER 76

1. Julian specifically disavows any knowledge of the state of souls other than those that fear God: "those who shall be saved."

2. Curiously, PV has *helles synne*, perhaps suggesting that the Christian soul should hate present earthly sin more than the "permanent" sin of hell, because that would merely be the fear of punishment.

3. The word of the Church in Julian's day would be that virtuous behavior came from fear. Julian transforms that into the loathing of sin itself—more than fear of the punishments of hell—a sophisticated theological point. (W&J point out that this is the first of four chapters mainly concerned with sin.)

4. This is a poignant exposition of the admonition not to judge others. (See Matthew 7:1 and Luke 6:37.)

5. The only circumstance when a Christian should be concerned with another's sins is if that person shares his or her contrition with us, and then we are to show compassion and pray for that person. (Note: W&J remind us that Julian's stance is unusual in that fourteenth-century reformers called for Christians to reproach other sinners for their sin.) Also note that "contrition," "compassion," and "longing for God" are the same three "wounds" Julian asked for herself before her revelations.

6. See Chapter 39.

7. This is possibly a reference to Jesus' comment (John 15:14), "You are my friends, if you do what I command you," but it is also a reiteration of Jesus' "homeliness."

⌁ 76

I speak but little of reverent fear, for I hope it can be understood in this previous matter, but I am well aware that our Lord showed me no souls except those that fear Him.[1]

I am also well aware that the soul that truly accepts the teaching of the Holy Spirit, hates sin more for its vileness and horribleness than it does all the pain that is in hell. For the soul that beholds the good nature of our Lord Jesus, hates not hell, but sin,[2] as I see it.[3]

And therefore it is God's will that we recognize sin, and pray diligently and labor willingly, and seek teaching humbly, so that we do not fall blindly into sin; and if we fall, that we rise quickly (for it is the worst pain that the soul can have to turn from God any time there is sin).

When other men's sins come to mind, the soul that wishes to be in repose shall flee from that as from the pain of hell, searching in God for remedy for help against it, for the beholding of other men's sins makes, as it were, a thick mist before the eye of the soul, and we cannot for the time see the fairness of God[4] (unless we can behold another's sins with contrition with him, with compassion on him, and with holy desire to God for him, for without this it troubles and tempts and hinders the soul that beholds those sins).[5]

(This I understood in the showing about compassion.)[6]

In this blessed showing of our Lord, I have an understanding of two opposites:

—the one is the most wisdom that any creature can do in this life;

—the other is the most folly.

The wisdom is for a creature to act following the will and counsel of his highest supreme Friend.[7] This blessed Friend is Jesus; and it is His will and His counsel that we bind ourselves with Him and fix ourselves intimately to Him ever more in whatever state we are. For whether we are filthy or pure, we are always the same in His love. For well or for woe, He wills that we never flee from Him.

8. Here we find one of the rare places where Julian distinguishes between "ordinary" Christians, and one who has given himself or herself particularly to contemplation—such as an anchorite. This is a subtle autobiographical moment: Julian knows from her contemplative experience the temptation to sloth.

COMMENTS ON CHAPTER 77

1. This is a radical spirituality: even great distress over sin is caused by the Devil and is against God's will, and actually gives power to the forces of evil. We are called to hate our sins, but not to despair over them.
2. We are cautioned not to lose hope because of our sins, but to turn instead to the Lord in the midst of our sinning.
3. One is reminded of the medieval tradition that the fallen angels fell because they were jealous of humankind when God's Son became a human being, rather than an angel.
4. This refers to our Lord's scorning of the Fiend and Julian's laughter in Chapter 13.

However, because of our changeability within ourselves we fall frequently into sin. Then we have this [temptation] by the guidance of our Enemy, through our own folly and blindness; for they say thus: "You are well aware that you are a wretch, a sinner, and also untrue; for you do not keep the covenant: you promise our Lord frequently that you will do better, and immediately afterward, you fall into the same—especially sloth, into the wasting of time." (For that is the beginning of sin, as I see it, and especially to the creatures who have given themselves to serve our Lord with inner contemplation of His blessed goodness).[8] And this makes us fearful to appear before our gracious Lord.

Then it is our Enemy who will set us back with his false fear concerning our sinfulness because of the pain with which he threatens us. It is his intention to make us so gloomy and so weary in this that we would forget the fair, blessed beholding of our everlasting Friend.

⌒ 77

Our good Lord showed the enmity of the Fiend, by which I understood that everything that is in opposition to love and to peace, it is the Fiend and of his party.[1]

We both must fall because of our weakness and our folly; and we must rise to more joy because of the mercy and grace of the Holy Spirit.[2]

And if our enemy wins anything from us by our falling (for it is his delight), he loses manyfold more in our rising by love and humility. This glorious rising is such great sorrow and pain to him, for, because of the hatred that he has for our soul, he burns continually in envy.[3] And all this sorrow that he wishes to make us have, it shall turn upon himself.

And it was because of this that our Lord scorned him; and this made me laugh mightily.[4]

5. ME has *and*; however, the sense is that while God has the ability and knowledge to punish, God also has the love that will make the punishment gentle.

6. Julian says, in effect, "We should not punish ourselves for our sin (as the Fiend wishes) but trust in God's chastening of us that will come about gently within everyday reality."

7. Julian's breadth of vision sees the ordinary pains and troubles of our lives as the penance God chooses to give us, rather than the "assigned" or "intentional" penances we are told (or choose) to undertake. There are no flagellations or pilgrimages or hair shirts for Julian. This also puts our daily burdens in perspective as part of God's permissive will.

8. See Chapters 18 and 28.

9. Julian's caution against excessive self-flagellation over sin has a solemn basis in reality: "No matter what you do, you will have woe, so you needn't overly beat yourself."

10. Julian answers the question: "What about all the pains and troubles we have?" She advises that we accept our everyday woes as penance, and that acceptance will make the toleration of our woes a benefit for us.

11. The ME has *This place is prison*, and there are some commentators who mistakenly suggest that "this place" and "this life" refer to Julian's recluse status. It is clear from what precedes and follows that that is not the meaning.

This, then, is the remedy: that we be aware of our sinfulness and flee to our Lord, for ever the more quickly we do so, the more advantageous it is for us to be near Him.

And this is what we say in our intention: "I know well I have deserved an evil pain, but our Lord is all Power and can punish me mightily, and He is all Wisdom and knows how to punish me with reason, but[5] He is all Goodness and loves me tenderly."

And in this awareness it is necessary that we remain, for it is a loving humility of a sinful soul (wrought by the mercy and grace of the Holy Spirit) when we will willingly and gladly accept the scourging and chastening that our Lord Himself wishes to give us. (And the chastening shall be wholly tender and very gentle if we will only consider ourselves pleased with Him and with all His works.)[6]

For the penance that man takes upon himself was not shown to me—that is to say, it was not shown in particular—but it was shown particularly and highly and with full lovely demeanor that we shall humbly and patiently bear and suffer the penance that God Himself gives us, with remembrance of His blessed Passion. For when we have remembrance of His blessed Passion, with pity and love, then we suffer with Him as His friends did who saw it.[7]

(And this was shown in the thirteenth showing, near the beginning, where it speaks of pity.)[8]

For He says, "Accuse not thyself overly much, questioning if thy tribulation and thy woe is all because of thy sinfulness; for it is not my will that thou be gloomy or sorrowful undiscerningly; for I tell thee, whatsoever thou doest, thou shalt have woe.[9] And therefore I will that thou wisely recognize thy penance which thou art in constantly, and that thou dost humbly accept it for thy penance, and thou shalt then truly understand that all thy living is beneficial penance."[10]

This earth is imprisonment,[11] and this life is penance, and in the remedy He wills that we rejoice: the remedy is that our Lord is with us, guarding us and leading us into the fullness of joy—for it is an endless joy to us in our Lord's purpose that He that shall be our bliss

12. See Chapter 19.
13. See Psalm 73:28 (BCP)—"But it is good for me to be near God; I have made the Lord God my refuge."
14. Or, "carelessly." We are not to take the Lord's familiarity for granted and forget his sovereign lordship. Modern readers might well remember that the word "Lord" would have meant something quite different to a fourteenth-century Englishwoman than it does to us. Literally every person in medieval England (except the king) had a "lord" over him or her with the powers of judgment and life or death.
15. It would be possible to sum up late medieval spirituality as the imitation of Christ—in suffering and in virtue. Indeed the single most popular book was Thomas á Kempis's *Imitation of Christ*.
16. It is interesting to note how in these last chapters Julian's "I" and "me" have changed almost entirely to "we" and "us" as her words become more and more didactic.

COMMENTS ON CHAPTER 78

1. The Lord never leads us to recognize our sins without the accompanying assurance of God's merciful forgiveness for those sins. If we saw our sins as unforgiven or unforgivable, we would be led to despair.

when we are there, He is our protector while we are here. Our way, and our heaven is true love and certain trust.

(He gave understanding of this in all the showings, and particularly in the showing of His Passion where he caused me mightily to choose Him for my heaven.)¹²

If we flee to our Lord, we shall be comforted; if we touch Him we shall be made pure; if we cleave to Him we shall be secure and safe from all manner of peril;¹³ for our gracious Lord wills that we be as friendly with Him as heart can think or soul can desire. But beware that we take not so <u>recklessly</u>¹⁴ this friendliness that we forsake courtesy; for while our Lord Himself is supreme friendliness, He is also as courtly as He is friendly, for He is true courtesy.

And the blessed creatures that shall be in heaven with Him without end, He wishes to have them like Himself in all things, for to be like our Lord perfectly, that is our true salvation and our complete bliss.¹⁵

And if we do not know how we shall do all this, let us desire it from our Lord and He shall teach us, for that is His own delight and His honor.¹⁶

Blessed may He be!

⤳ 78

Our Lord of His mercy shows us our sin and our weakness by the sweet gracious light of Himself, for our sin is so vile and so horrible that He of His courtesy will not show it to us except by the light of His grace and mercy.¹

It is His will that we have knowledge concerning four things:

—the first is that He is our ground from whom we have all our life and our being;

—the second, that he protects us mightily and mercifully at the time we are in our sin and among all our enemies who are most fierce against us (and so much the more are we in greater peril because we give the enemy occasion for that and know not our own need);

2. These are the affirmations of the "four things": (1) human nature is created by God and is good in itself; (2) after creating us, God protects us even when we are in sin and are not even aware that we need protection; (3) God helps us to recognize our sins; and (4) God waits patiently for us to reject our sin and turn to Him.

3. These three uses of the word "break" (this one and those that appear in the second and third following paragraphs) remind one of Chapter 28: "I shall totally shatter you because of your vain affections and your vicious pride. . . ."

4. By showing us our lesser sins in the light of His forgiveness, out of our shame God saves us from falling into more serious sins.

5. These verbs are in the passive voice: that is, it is God who breaks us away from sin, heals us, and ones us to Himself, while we (to use Julian's own phrase) "do nothing but sin." (See Chapter 82.)

6. This is one of Julian's characteristics: God's promises are not for the select few only, but for all who are trying to be good Christians. In her usual simple humility, she includes herself at the bottom of the list of sinners.

7. This is evidence of Julian's beautiful and almost naive simplicity: when she was not paying attention, God simply stopped adding anything new and waited until she could listen. This may refer to the many years of reflection she spent after the original revelations.

8. High-flown theology and contemplative spirituality have no reliable validity unless we also build the virtue of humility by constantly remembering our sins and weaknesses. Once again, this is possibly an autobiographical note: as in the preceding paragraph, it is likely that Julian had experienced the contemplative heights and knew the danger of forgetting her weaknesses.

—the third is how graciously He protects us and lets us know when we go amiss;

—the fourth is how steadfastly He waits for us and does not change His demeanor, for He wills that we be transformed and one-ed to Him in love as He is to us.[2]

Thus by this grace-filled knowledge we can see our sin beneficially without despair (for truly we need to see it) and by that sight we shall be made ashamed of ourselves, and our pride and presumption shall be <u>broken down</u>.[3]

It truly behooves us to see that by ourselves we are just nothing but sin and wretchedness. And thus by the sight of the less which our Lord shows us, the more which we do not see is diminished, for He of His courtesy adjusts the sight to us (for it is so vile and so horrible that we would not endure to see it as it is).[4]

And by this humble knowledge thus, through contrition and grace, we shall be <u>broken</u>[3] away from all things that are not our Lord, and then shall our blessed Savior perfectly heal us and one us to Himself.[5]

This <u>breaking</u>[3] and this healing our Lord means with reference to all mankind, for he who is highest and nearest to God, he can see himself sinful and needy along with me, and I who am the least and the lowest of those that shall be saved, I can be comforted along with him that is highest. So has our Lord one-ed us together in love.[6]

When He showed me that I would sin, because of the joy that I had in beholding Him, I did not readily pay attention to that showing, and our courteous Lord stopped then, and would not teach me further until He gave me grace and the will to pay attention.[7]

From this I was taught that although we are nobly lifted up into contemplation by the particular gift of our Lord, yet it is necessary for us along with that to have knowledge and awareness of our sin and our weakness. Without this knowledge we cannot have true humility, and without this humility we cannot be saved.[8]

9. The only way we can have clear knowledge of our sins is by God's merciful and grace-filled intervention.

COMMENTS ON CHAPTER 79

1. Julian admits her original partial blindness in applying the Lord's teachings to herself. Her long years of reflection gave her greater insight.
2. See Chapter 76: "When other men's sins come to mind, the soul that wishes to be in repose shall flee from that as from the pain of hell. . . ."
3. Julian is suggesting that what might be scrupulosity about her own sins had no support from God. See Chapter 77: "Accuse not thyself overly much. . . ."

And also I saw that we cannot get this knowledge from ourselves, nor from any of our spiritual enemies, for they do not will us very much good (for if it were by their will, we should not see our sin until our ending day).

Then we are much beholden to God that He will Himself out of love show our sin and weakness to us in time out of mercy and grace.[9]

⇍ 79

Also I had in this showing more understanding—when He showed me that I would sin, I applied it simply to my own individual self, for I was not otherwise stirred at that time,[1] but by the high gracious comfort of our Lord which followed afterward, I saw that His meaning was for all mankind—that is to say, all mankind which is sinful and shall be until the Last Day (of which group I am a member, as I hope, by the mercy of God)—for the blessed comfort that I saw is large enough for us all.

And here I was taught that I ought to see my own sin, and not other men's sins (unless it could be for the comfort and help of my fellow Christians).[2]

Also in this same showing where I saw that I would sin, I was taught to be cautious of my own uncertainty, for I am not aware of how I shall fall, nor do I know the measure nor the greatness of my sin. (For I fearfully wished to have known that, but to that I received no answer.)[3]

Also our gracious Lord, at the same time, showed me most certainly and powerfully the endlessness and the unchangeability of His love.

And also, by His great goodness and His grace inwardly guarding, that His love and that of our souls shall never be separated in two, without end.

Thus in this fear I have cause for humility that saves me from presumption; and in the blessed showing of love I have cause for true comfort and joy that saves me from despair.

4. "All this friendly showing" refers to the revelations, affirming that Julian intends her revelations to be a teaching for her readers.

5. Julian cautions that anything we see or hear that does not recognize the universality and unchangeability of God's love is not from God.

6. On the other hand, one must not take God's constant love for granted and relax vigilance against sin. See Chapter 40: "If this is true, then it would be good to sin in order to have more reward, or else to place less weight on sin; beware of this leading, for truly, if it comes, it is untrue and from the enemy."

7. This is Julian's constant theme: God longs for us as much as (or more than) we long for God; and God's "homeliness" is emphasized by His willingness to "wait for us constantly, sorrowing and mourning until we come."

COMMENTS ON CHAPTER 80

1. This is Julian's triad for God's gifts that aid, protect, and save us: human reason, teachings of the Church, and the inspiration of the Holy Spirit. It is interesting that Julian does not refer to Holy Scripture as a separate item. Julian often credits her own reason as an instrument of God's revelations.

All this friendly showing of our gracious Lord is a loving lesson and a sweet, gracious teaching from Himself in the comforting of our soul.[4]

For He wills that we know, by His sweetness and familiar loving, that all that we see or sense, within or without, which is in opposition to this is from the Enemy and not from God[5]—such as this: if we are moved to be more heedless of our living or the keeping of our hearts because we have knowledge of this plenteous love, then we need greatly to beware, for this inclination, if it comes, is untrue and we ought greatly to hate it, for none of it has any similarity to God's will.[6]

When we are fallen because of frailty or blindness, then our gracious Lord inspires us, stirs us, and calls us, and then He wills that we see our wretchedness and humbly let it be acknowledged. But He does not wish us to remain thus, nor does He will that we busy ourselves greatly about accusing ourselves, nor does He will that we be full of misery about ourselves; for He wills that we quickly attend to Him; for He stands all alone and waits for us constantly, sorrowing and mourning until we come, and hastens to take us to Himself;[7] for we are His joy and His delight, and He is our cure and our life. (Though I say that He stands all alone, I leave out speaking of the Blessed Company of heaven, and speak of His function and His working here on earth, in respect to the circumstances of the showing.)

⇌ 80

By three things man is grounded in this life, and by these three God is honored and we are aided, protected, and saved.

The first is the use of man's natural reason;

the second is the common teaching of Holy Church;

the third is the inner grace-filled working of the Holy Spirit;

and these three are all from one God.[1]

God is the ground of our natural reason; and God is the teaching of Holy Church; and God is the Holy Spirit.

2. See the ending paragraphs of Chapter 51: "in this marvelous illustration I receive a teaching within me (as it were the beginning of an ABC) whereby I can have some understanding of our Lord's meaning. . . ."

3. ME has *now the last end*—Julian refers to the present age as the "last end." See the phrase in the Eucharistic Prayer B: "For in these last days you sent him to be incarnate . . ." (BCP, p. 368).

4. Julian has been reflecting on the Lord's "aloneness"; she remembers the Church's teachings about angels who are present in heaven, but she says the revelations did not show her anything about the angels. Then she reiterates that nothing is needed but God.

5. This is a fascinating passage: Julian declares that our own "sorrowing and mourning" and longing for oneness with God is actually Christ's own longing within us.

All are different gifts that He wills that we have great regard for and pay attention to, for these work in us constantly all together, and these are important things.

He wishes us to have knowledge of these things here as it were in an ABC[2]—that is to say, that we have a little knowledge [here], of which we shall have fullness in heaven, and that is to advance us.

We acknowledge in our Faith that God alone took our human nature and none but He;

and, furthermore, that Christ alone did all the works that are part of our salvation, and none but He;

and just so He alone acts now in this last age[3]—that is to say, He dwells here with us and rules us and governs us in this life, and brings us to His bliss.

And this shall He do as long as any soul is on earth who shall come to heaven—to such an extent that if there were no such soul but one, He would be with that one all alone until He had brought it up to his bliss.

I believe and understand the ministration of angels as the priests relate it,[4] but it was not shown to me, for He Himself is nearest and humblest, highest and lowest, and does all; and not only all that we need, but also He does all that is honorable for our joy in heaven.

Where I say that He awaits us, sorrowing and mourning, it means that all the true feeling that we have in ourselves in contrition and compassion, and all the sorrowing and mourning because we are not one-ed with our Lord, and all such which is beneficial, it is Christ in us.[5]

And though some of us sense it seldom, it passes never from Christ until the time that He has brought us out of all our woe.

For love never allows Him to be without pity. And whenever we fall into sin and give up the remembrance of Him and the protection of our own soul, then Christ alone takes care of the responsibility of us.

And thus He stands sorrowing and mourning.

Then it is proper for us, for the sake of reverence and kindness, to turn ourselves quickly to our Lord and not leave Him alone. He is here alone with us all—that is to say, only for us is He here.

6. This is a complicated insight: the Lord is with and within us, and if we pay no attention to His presence within us or alienate ourselves from that presence, we leave Him "alone"—while He, on the other hand, never leaves us "alone," but is always with and within us, constantly forgiving, tenderly refusing to blame us, guarding and offering Himself to us and for us.

COMMENTS ON CHAPTER 81

1. "His creature" is Julian (see the first line in Chapter 2). This phrase appears only in PV.
2. See Chapter 11.
3. C&W recount that a "pilgrimage" was a frequent analogy for human life in the world.
4. The "resting place" is contrasted to the "pilgrimage."
5. Again, the ME word *cyte* was meant to describe the see city of a bishop, where the bishop had his cathedral and throne.
6. Recall Chapter 77: "All this living is penance." See the beginning of the *Ancrene Wisse*: "All that you ever endure is penance and tough penance, my dear sisters, all the good that ever you do, all that you suffer, is your martyrdom. . . ." This is Julian's view of the pain of earthly life: that it is penance for our sins.

And whenever I am alienated from Him by sin, despair, or sloth, then I allow my Lord to stand alone, inasmuch as He is in me—and so it goes with all of us who are sinners.

But though it is true that we act this way frequently, His goodness never allows us to be alone, but He is constantly with us, and He tenderly excuses us, and always shields us from blame in His sight.[6]

⤺ 81

Our good Lord showed Himself to His creature[1] in various ways, both in heaven and in earth, but I saw Him adopt no resting place except in man's soul.

He showed Himself on earth in the sweet Incarnation and in His blessed Passion.

And in other ways He showed Himself on earth where I say: "I saw God in a point."[2]

And in other ways He showed Himself on earth thus, as it were on pilgrimage;[3] that is to say, He is here with us, leading us, and shall be until the time He has brought us all to His bliss in heaven.

He showed Himself reigning at different times, as I said before, but primarily in man's soul. He has adopted His resting place[4] there and His honorable <u>City</u>,[5] out of which honorable throne He shall never rise nor move away without end.

Wondrous and splendid is the place where our Lord dwells.

Therefore He wills that we pay attention to His grace-filled inspiration, more rejoicing in his undivided love than sorrowing in our frequent fallings.

For it is the most honor to Him of anything that we can do that we live in our penance gladly and merrily because of His love, for He looks upon us so tenderly that He sees all our living here to be penance.

The natural yearning in us for Him is a lasting penance in us, which penance He produces in us and mercifully He helps us to bear it.[6]

7. Fulfilled: "completed," "made whole," "filled full."
8. ME has *overpassing*.

COMMENTS ON CHAPTER 82

1. Here is a clear core of Julian's teachings about sin: one makes a true life commitment to the Lord, and in spite of that major choice for God, one can still slip into sin—but the counsel the Lord gives is not to be "much bothered" by such sins.

2. This is a reference to the parable of the lord and servant in Chapter 51. Julian is realistic in recognizing that *no one* in this life lives without guilt and sin, and that the Lord pities us for our falls into sin. But the guilt we feel from sin is our problem: the Lord, for His part, does not blame us for being sinners.

3. These last two paragraphs sum up the process of sin and virtue: God loves us; we sin. God helps us see the sin; we regret and mourn our sins. We then turn to God's mercy: God delights to forgive us, and this pleases Him.

4. The words are those of the Lord.

His love makes Him to yearn,

His wisdom and His truth with His rightfulness make Him to put up with us here, and this is the way He wants to look at it in us.

For this life is our natural penance and the highest, as I see it, for this penance never goes from us until the time that we are fulfilled,[7] when we shall have Him for our reward.

And therefore He wills that we fix our hearts on the <u>transition</u>[8]— that is to say, from the pain that we feel into the bliss that we trust.

⇒ 82

But here our gracious Lord showed the sorrowing and the mourning of the soul, meaning thus: "I am well aware that thou livest for my love, merrily and gladly suffering all the penance that can come to thee, but inasmuch as thou dost not live without sin, therefore thou art sad and sorrowful, and even if thou couldst live without sin, thou wouldst still suffer for the sake of my love all the woe, all the tribulation and distress that could come to thee.

"And that is true.

"But be not much bothered by sin that comes to thee against thy will."[1]

Here I understood that the lord looks upon the servant with pity and not with blame, for this passing life does not require that we live wholly without guilt and sin.[2]

He loves us endlessly, and we sin habitually, and He shows the sin to us most gently; and then we sorrow and mourn prudently, turning ourselves to the contemplation of His mercy, cleaving to His love and goodness, seeing that He is our medicine, aware that we do nothing but sin.

Thus by the humility that we get from the sight of our sin, faithfully knowing His everlasting love, thanking and praising Him, we please Him:[3]

"I love thee and thou lovest me; and our love shall never be divided in two, and for thy benefit, I suffer."[4]

5. This is a direct quote from Chapter 37.

6. The revelations are also called a "lesson of love" in Chapter 6. The use of this language makes it clear that Julian understands her revelations to be to some extent didactic.

7. Here we find a caution: anything that does not lead to a yearning for God or a rejoicing in God has its origin in the Devil and his minions.

8. This sentence is one of Julian's core teachings: that God's love is not dependent on our constant virtue.

9. We take our sinful fallings far more seriously than God does.

10. Julian recognizes the value of critical self-judgment in the case of sins, but suggests that it is more important to know that God does not blame us for those sins, and does not withhold His unchanging love just because we sin.

COMMENTS ON CHAPTER 83

1. The ME has *in parte*, which C&W link to The *New English Dictionary*'s meaning "a part of this matter."

2. See Chapters 26 and 59.

(And all this was shown in spiritual understanding, He saying these words: "I keep thee full safely.")[5]

By the great desire that I saw in our blessed Lord that we should live in this way (that is to say, in yearning and rejoicing, as all this lesson of love[6] shows), by this desire I understood that all that is opposed to this is not from Him, but from enmity,[7] and He wills that we know it by the sweet gracious light of this natural love.

If there is any such one alive on earth who is constantly kept from falling, I know it not, for it was not shown me.

But this was shown: that whether in falling or in rising we are ever preciously protected in one love.[8] In the sight of God we do not fall; in the sight of self, we do not stand—and both of these are true as I see it, but the way our Lord God sees it is the highest truth.[9]

Then are we much bound to God because He wills in this life to show us this high truth.

And I understood that while we are in this life, it is most helpful to us that we see both of these at once; for the higher point of view keeps us in spiritual solace and true rejoicing in God, and the other, that is, the lower point of view, keeps us in fear and makes us ashamed of ourselves. But our good Lord wills always that we see ourselves more from the point of view of the higher (but not give up knowledge of the lower) until the time that we are brought up above, where we shall have our Lord Jesus for our reward, and will be filled full of joy and bliss without end.[10]

⟡ 83

I had <u>in this matter</u>[1] inspiration, vision, and sense of three properties of God of which the strength and outcome of the whole revelation consists (and they were seen in every showing, and most particularly in the twelfth, where it was often said, "I am He").[2]

3. ME has *homlihede* or "homeliness."

4. ME has *kyndhede*. In ME, *kynde* usually is translated "nature" or "being"; in this case, however, where it is in parallel with "familiarity" and "courtesy" it is more accurate to choose the translation of "kindness."

5. Julian subtly associates life, love, and light with the Holy Trinity, united in one "Goodness."

6. Here we find a surprisingly zealous elevation of reason to the highest place in human nature. In the rest of this chapter Julian links reason and faith—both as part of the light.

7. This is perhaps an autobiographical hint: the revelations came to Julian in the night.

8. This chapter is filed with life/light/love imagery reminiscent of the Gospel of John: "In him was life, and that life was the light of mankind. The light shines in the darkness, and the darkness has never mastered it. . . . The true light which gives light to everyone was even then coming into the world" (John 1:4, 9).

9. Julian has referred to sin as "blindness"; she now describes heaven (that is, "the end of woe") as full vision and clear sight.

10. This is another affirmation of the Holy Trinity as the source of the light of faith.

11. Here we find an actual identification of "our Faith" with "God, our Endless Day." This chapter break seems unusual in that the subject matter continues directly into the next chapter—perhaps the scribe simply needed a rest!

The properties are these:
    life,
    love,
    and light.
In life is wondrous <u>familiarity</u>,[3]
and in love is gentle courtesy,
and in light is endless <u>kindness</u>.[4]

These three properties were seen in one Goodness,[5] to which Goodness my reason wished to be one-ed and to cleave to it with all my might.

I beheld with reverent fear (and greatly marveling at the sight and the feeling of the sweet harmony) that our reason is in God, understanding that it is the highest gift that we have received, and that is grounded in human nature.[6]

Our Faith is a light, naturally coming from our Endless Day—that is our Father, God; in this light our Mother, Christ, and our good Lord the Holy Spirit lead us in this passing life.

This light is meted out prudently, faithfully remaining with us as we need it in the night.[7]

The light is the cause of our life; the night is the cause of our pain and of all our woe, on account of which woe we earn endless reward and favor from God, for we, with mercy and grace, willingly acknowledge and believe our light, walking in it wisely and mightily.[8]

And at the end of woe, suddenly our eye shall be opened and in clarity of sight our light shall be full.[9] This light is God our Creator and the Holy Spirit in Christ Jesus our Savior.[10]

Thus I saw and understood that our Faith is our light in our night; and the light is God, our Endless Day.[11]

COMMENTS ON CHAPTER 84

1. Julian expounds: the light is there, but our vision is temporarily limited here on earth. But that is acceptable because by love we know in our faith that the day will come when we will finally see it all clearly.
2. See Chapter 14.
3. This is Julian's absolute identification of love with God (uncreated), with the human soul (created), and with human virtue (given). Love is totally pervasive for Julian in defining God, humanity, and Christian living. Love is everything that is good.
4. Human virtue is the one-ing and identification of oneself with God and God's will. Recall St. Bernard's levels of love in *On Loving God*: to love God for one's own sake; to love God for God's sake; to love God because He is God; and to love self for God's sake.

COMMENTS ON CHAPTER 85

1. Julian is now in the process of drawing together all the teachings of her revelations. Even in the midst of our struggles, we are not forsaken by God, who rejoices even in our foolishness and blindness.

✍ 84

This light is love, and the meting out of this light is done for us beneficially by the wisdom of God, for neither is the light so bright that we can see clearly our blessed Day, nor is it completely barred from us, but it is such a light in which we live rewardingly with toil, earning the endless honor-filled favor of God.[1]

(And this was seen in the sixth showing where He said, "I thank thee for thy service and thy labor.")[2]

Thus love keeps us in faith and hope; and faith and hope lead us to love.

And at the end all shall be love.

I had three kinds of understandings on this light of love:

> the first is love uncreated;
> the second is love created;
> the third is love given.

Love uncreated is God;

love created is our soul in God;

love given is virtue[3]—and that is the grace-filled gift of action, in which we love God for Himself, and ourselves in God, and all that God loves, for God's sake.[4]

✍ 85

I marveled greatly at this vision, for notwithstanding our foolish living and our blindness here, yet endlessly our gracious Lord looks upon us in this struggle, rejoicing.[1]

And of all things, we can please Him best by wisely and truly believing that, and rejoicing with Him and in Him.

For as truly as we shall be in the bliss of God without end, praising Him and thanking Him, just as truly we have been in the foresight of God loved and known in His endless purpose from without beginning.

2. This is Julian's insightful conversion of what can be called a "reverse eternity," as she extends back into the situation before creation the same divine love that will be experienced in the future eternity of heaven. God's love, therefore, has the same "preexistent" quality usually attributed to the Incarnation itself. (See Chapter 53.)

3. Julian does not demonstrate any of the dread of Judgment Day so universal in the Church of her day. This is a clear reference to what Julian speaks of as God's "Great Deed" in Chapter 32.

4. This is Julian's final summary of the faith that whatever happens, whatever events occur, God's will is involved; and regardless of the sufferings or discomfort, God remains in charge. In heaven we will each understand how what we had viewed as misery or distress on earth was part of God's will for our own well-being.

COMMENTS ON CHAPTER 86

1. W&J remind us: this sentence passes the responsibility for living out the revelations from Julian to her readers.

2. The soul of contemplative prayer for Julian is summarized: thanking, trusting, and rejoicing.

3. See Chapter 41.

4. God's heavenly treasure is humanity. Recall Chapter 51: "There was a treasure in the earth which the lord loved. . . ."

5. Presumably, this last revelation of "the Lord's meaning" happened in 1388–89.

In this love without beginning He made us, and in the same love He protects us and never allows us to receive harm by which our bliss might be lessened.[2]

Therefore when the judgment is given and we are all brought up above, then shall we clearly see in God the secrets that are now hidden from us.[3]

Then shall none of us be moved to say in any way: "Lord, if it had been thus-and-so, then it would have been all well"; but we shall say in all one voice: "Lord, blessed mayest Thou be! Because it is as it is, it is well. And now we see truly that everything is done as was Thine ordinance before anything was made."[4]

⇍ 86

This book is begun by God's gift and His grace, but it is not yet performed, as I see it.[1]

For the sake of love let us all pray together with God's working—thanking, trusting, rejoicing, for thus would our good Lord be prayed to[2] (as is the understanding that I received in all His own meaning, and in the sweet words where He says most merrily, "I am the basis of thy praying").[3]

Truly I saw and understood in our Lord's meaning that He showed [this love] because He wished to have it known more than it is, and in this knowledge He will give us grace to love Him and cleave to Him.

For He beholds His heavenly treasure[4] with such great love on earth that He wills to give us more light and solace in heavenly joy by drawing our hearts from the sorrow and darkness which we are in.

For the time that it was shown, I desired frequently to know what our Lord's meaning was. And fifteen years after[5] (and more) I was answered in spiritual understanding, saying thus: "Wouldst thou know thy Lord's meaning in this thing?"

6. This final spiritual communication of the Lord to Julian is the summation of the entire set of revelations, and it holds promise for the future that if one "keeps oneself" in God's love, more and more of it will be revealed. (Could this not be Julian Erpingham's last wish for herself, as she prepares to enter the anchorhold at St. Julian's Church, to "keep herself in that love"?)

7. This is a reaffirmation of the preexistence of God's love (see note 2 in Chapter 85).

"Be well aware:

    love was His meaning.

  Who showed it thee? Love.

  What showed He thee? Love.

  Why did He show it thee? For love.

"Keep thyself in that love and thou shalt know and see more of the same, but thou shalt never see nor know any other thing therein without end."[6]

Thus was I taught that love was our Lord's meaning. And I saw full certainly in this and in all the showings, that before God made us, He loved us, and this love was never slackened nor ever shall be.

In this love He has done all His works, and in this love He has made all things beneficial to us, and in this love our life is everlasting.

In our creation we had a beginning, but the love in which He created us was in Him from without beginning, and in this love we have our beginning.[7]

And all this we shall see in God without end, which may Jesus grant us. Amen.

Here ends the book of revelations of Julian, anchorite of Norwich, upon whose soul may God have mercy.

Attributed to the seventeenth-century scribe

Thus ends the revelation of love of the Blessed Trinity showed by our Savior Christ Jesus for our endless comfort and solace, and also to rejoice in Him in this passing journey of life. Amen, Jesus, Amen.

I pray Almighty God that this book does not come into the hands of anyone except those who are His faithful lovers, and those that will submit themselves to the Faith of Holy Church and obey the wholesome interpretation and teaching of the men who are of virtuous life, settled age, and profound learning, for this revelation is high theology and high wisdom, wherefore it cannot survive with him who is slave to sin and to the Devil. And beware that thou not accept one thing after thine own inclination and preference and omit another, for that is the situation of an heretic. But accept each thing with the other and truly understand that all is in agreement with Holy Scripture and grounded in the same, and that Jesus our true love, light and truth, shall show this wisdom and Himself to all pure souls who with humility ask constantly. And thou to whom this book shall come, thank our Savior Christ Jesus highly and heartily that He made these showings and revelations for thee and to thee, out of His endless love, mercy, and goodness, to be a safe guide and conduct to everlasting bliss for thee and for us—which may Jesus grant us. Amen.

Here ends the sublime and wonderful Revelations
of the unutterable love of God in Jesus Christ,
vouchsafed to a dear lover of His and in
her to all His dear friends and
lovers, whose hearts, like
hers, do flame in the
love of our
dearest
Jesu.

PART
FOUR

APPENDICES

1
JULIAN'S CRUCIFIX

In AD 692, the Council of Constantinople ordered the use of crucifixes (that is, the showing of Jesus as a human being on the cross), rather than only ornamental crosses.

After that, the earliest representation we have shows Jesus as a fully robed priest or king, wearing the *colobium* (a flowing, sleeveless tunic extending nearly to the ankles) and standing *in front of the cross*, not fastened to it in any way, with eyes open, head erect, and showing no agony.

In the ninth century, the *colobium* was replaced by a *perizoma* (a short "skirt" reaching from waist to knees). The Christ figure sometimes had his eyes closed, but was still obviously not in pain.

It was not until the Ottonian period (c. AD 1000) that a significant change began to take place in the representations of the crucifix: the actual nearly nude figure of Jesus appeared. But the figure was stiff and more iconic than natural. And the figure seemed merely to be resting against the cross, although it was a "four-nail" crucifix, with the feet next to each other and a nail in each. (It is interesting that Pope Innocent III formally declared that "there were four nails in our Lord's passion, through his hands and feet.") This was the classic Romanesque crucifix.

By the twelfth century, the representations began to be somewhat more naturalistic. By 1160 the face began to appear to be alive and looking straight forward, and the body remained formally tranquil against the cross. In the early thirteenth century, St. Bonaventure even spoke of "Christ sleeping on the Cross."[141]

By the late thirteenth century, many crucifixes held a body that was quite apparently dead and wounded—a "three-nail" crucifix in which the feet were placed on top of each other and secured by a single nail. The eyes were closed for the first time, and by the end of that century, the head was dropped to the chest and the crucifix showed a clearly dead body, usually slightly twisted in an inverted "S" shape. A crown of thorns appeared for the first time. By 1260 there were also representations in which the corpus was fully naked (as was certainly true in the original crucifixion).

By the fourteenth century—Julian's century—there were representations of the crucifix that became almost vulgar in their depictions of suffering, with the body grossly twisted, wounds overtly bleeding, and crown of thorns painfully present. In such representations as that of the *Kappelkreuz* at the Cathedral of Köln (Cologne), the body on the cross had become little more than a ghastly, agonized scarecrow; similarly, in the drawing of a crucifix in the Schnütgen Museum (also in Köln), (as Carolyn Bynam puts it,) "Christ has become [nothing but] a bloody smear."[142]

It is likely that the crucifix shown to Julian by her "curate" had a graphically suffering corpus. It is *possible* that, since the formal Romanesque crucifix would have been more familiar to Julian, the added graphic detail of the agonized Christ may have been further impetus for her to see the naturalistic Christ figure "come alive."[143]

Gradually the ideal Christian life came to be seen as *nudus nudum Christum sequere*—"nakedly to follow the naked Christ." Thomas à Kempis's *The Imitation of Christ* became the most widely read book in all of Europe. Identification with ("one-ing" with) Christ—especially in Christ's sufferings—became the be-all and end-all, the goal of virtually all Christian ascetics.

And in Christian devotional writing at the same time, the virtue of *compassion*—"feeling with"—began to replace the ancient virtue of *mercy* at the top of the list of Christian virtues.

⤚ 2
THE FLOODS IN NORWICH

In Chapter 10, Julian writes:

> At one time my understanding was taken down into the sea-
> bed, and there I saw hills and green dales, seeming as if it were
> overgrown with moss, with seaweed and gravel.
>
> Then I understood this: that even if a man or woman were
> there under the broad water, if he could have a vision of God
> there (since God is with a man constantly) he would be safe in
> body and soul and receive no harm and, even more, he would
> have more solace and more comfort than all this world can tell.

It always seemed curious to me that suddenly, in the midst of a discussion of how inconstant is our awareness of God's presence, Julian
would bring in an *exemplum* concerning someone *under the broade
watyr*. It seemed to be a complete non sequitur. It was only when I
connected her words *broade watyr* to the Norwich Broads that it began
to make sense.[144] And my intuition was confirmed when I found an
obscure pamphlet written by Norwich's famous seventeenth-century
son Sir Thomas Browne (physician, theologian, archaeologist, and
naturalist), entitled "Notes on the Natural History of Norwich,"[145]
in which Browne refers to the Norwich marshlands as "broads" four
times (once as "the Great Broads") and as "broad waters" three times.
It turns out that the earliest date on which some variant of the word
"broads" was used to describe the marshlands was 1315.[146] All of this
assured me as far as is reasonably possible that Julian's peculiar use of
the words *the broad watyr* was more than a merely generic reference
to the sea.

By the end of the thirteenth century, the harvesting of peat had
been so thoroughgoing that the shallow marshes had been dug out to
the depths of eight to ten feet, and these peat pits filled with water,
producing what finally became the more than 3,000 acres of marsh-
land surrounding Norwich on the north and west, cut through with

125 miles of running rivers and streams and in the present day called "The Broads." At that time, a shallow fjord extended from the North Sea deep into eastern England as far as Norwich.

At the turn of the fourteenth century there was a spectacular continent-wide decline of temperature (which has come to be called "The Little Ice Age").[147] In 1315–17 extremely heavy rains caused flooding across Norfolk that inundated harvests, vineyards, and seeds in the ground with terrible consequences. In the second half of the century, England experienced wetter than usual summers for thirty years, but the Black Plague of 1348–49 became so crushing a disaster that it actually pushed the deaths from famine into the background.[148]

However, in 1362 Norfolk faced what had been recurring cataclysms in earlier centuries, natural disasters that continued to occur at more or less one-hundred-year intervals into the twentieth century: the Great Floods.

Matthew Paris chronicled a severe storm and sea flooding in October 1250. "More than 300 houses and several churches were flooded by the violence of the mounting sea."[149]

W.A. Dutt describes a thirteenth-century flooding of the Broads:

> On Jan 8th 1287, the sea in dense darkness, began to be agitated by the violence of the wind, and in its agitation burst through its accustomed limits, occupying towns, fields, and other places adjacent to the coast, and inundating parts which no age in past times had recorded to have been covered by sea water. It suffocated and drowned men and women sleeping in their beds, with infants in their cradles and all kinds of cattle. It tore up houses from their foundations and all they contained and carried them away and threw them into the sea.[150]

Those floods of 1287 were perhaps the most publicized, and they were also recorded in John of Oxnead's chronicles. Bartholomew of Cotton recorded that in Yarmouth one hundred men were drowned, the priory wall was laid flat, and the flood reached the height of the high altar.[151] Swinden wrote: "The sea flowed into St. Nicholas Church four feet [deep] and a great part of the town was underwater."[152]

Later, in 1343 forty people were drowned in the Wensum River in Conesford (near St. Julian's Church) when their boat was caught in the flood and overturned. There are accounts of coffins and corpses floated up out of graves by the floodwaters.

When Julian would have been twenty, "the worst storms in the memory of man" occurred. Storm surges of thirty feet above ordinary level were reported, with as much as fifteen feet of water covering many of the low-lying parts of Norwich. The winds reached almost one hundred miles per hour, and the Norwich Cathedral spire was blown down.[153] There is an account of one man who climbed a tree in Norwich during the storm to escape the flood waters and was stranded there for three days before he was rescued.

As one modern historian has put it:

> Seven centuries ago, the North Sea washed coastlines very different from those of today. For instance, a now-vanished shallow estuary extended deep into East Anglia, making Norwich and Ely important ports. . . . The same infiltrating creeks made the surrounding low-lying coastlines vulnerable to unpredictable storm surges, which would sweep up the narrow defiles and flood the land on either side, forcing entire villages to evacuate or drowning them almost without warning. We can imagine the scene, repeated so many times over the generations. Huge waves of muddy water attacked the shore, spray blowing horizontally into the dark mist masking the ground. The relentless ocean cascaded up beaches and into narrow inlets, devouring everything before it. Thatched farmhouses tumbled end-for-end in the waves; pigs and cattle rolled like dice across inundated fields. Bedraggled families clung to one another in trees or on rooftops until the boiling waters swept them away. The only sound was the shrieking wind, which drowned out everything—the growl of shifting gravel beaches, the desperate cries of drowning victims, the groaning branches of trees lashed by the gale. When the sky cleared, the sun shone on an enormous muddy lake as far as the eye could see, a desolate landscape devoid of human life.[154]

In England, 20,000 cattle and at least 3,000 sheep were lost.[155]

Further, after Margery Kempe visited Julian in around 1413, she recounts Julian's words of advice to her:

> He that is evyrmor dowtyng is lyke to the flood of the see, the whech is mevyd and born abowte wyth the wynd, and that man is not lyche to receyven the gyftys of God.[156] (He that is evermore doubting is like to the flood of the sea, which is moved and borne about with the wind, and that man is not likely to receive the gifts of God.)

With this information, we can begin to understand that Julian's reference to fear and destruction "under the broade watyr" was no mere general and nonspecific allusion to the oceans, but to a Norwich flood catastrophe permanently impressed on her memory, and on the memories of all of her Norwich readers.

⇝ 3
THE PESTILENCE ("THE BLACK DEATH")

"The effects of [the Black Death] changed Europe profoundly, perhaps more so than any other series of events. For this reason alone, the Black Death should be ranked as the greatest biological-environmental event in history, and one of the major turning points of Western Civilization."[157]

F.A. Gasquet called it "the end of the Middle Ages."[158] The Rand Corporation ranked the Black Death as one of the three worst catastrophes in the history of the world.[159] The loss of life in England during the plague years meant that there would not be a numerical recovery of population to pre-plague levels for over 300 years.[160] Scholars generally agree that the origins of the plague (the bacterium *Yersinis pestis*) came from the fleas of affected shipborne black rats that transferred to humans when their rat hosts died.[161]

What was locally called "the Pestilence"[162] was a combination of bubonic, pneumonic, and septicemial plague,[163] and of all England's regions the most severely afflicted was East Anglia.[164] Because of its location, it received the contagion from Europe through its heavy trade with the Continent (probably bubonic plague) as well as over-land from London and Bristol (probably pneumonic plague), and these multiple sources may well have meant that unlike much of England, Norfolk was infected with more than one strain of the disease. In fact, some scholars believe that it was ships from East Anglia that actually carried the pestilence to Norway.

The Norwich antiquarian Francis Blomefield claimed that during the year of January 1348 to January 1349, there were 57,374 plague deaths out of a population of 70,000 in the county of Norfolk (82 percent)—not including monks and friars. In Norwich proper it is estimated that over 7,000 out of an estimated 12,000 died. And in that year there were 863 formal installations of new parish clergy to replace those who died. Due to the plague deaths of clergy, there was such a shortage of priests that on October 13, 1348, Pope Clement VI issued a bull at the request of William Bateman, Bishop of Norwich, allow-ing candidates for priesthood to be ordained at the age of twenty-one, rather than twenty-four as had previously been the case.[165] Several bishops gave notice that, in the absence of a priest, deathbed confes-sions could be made to a lay person ("even to a woman") because so few priests had survived the plague.[166] Recent scholarship has adjusted the probable percentage of plague mortality considerably upward to 50 to 60 percent of Europe's population, and Norwich percentages would be much higher.[167]

The pestilence then struck Norwich again in 1361 when it killed 23 percent of the population. The victims were mostly children under the age of ten who had not developed immunity from the previous epidemic. And it struck again in 1369 when it claimed another 13 percent and in 1375 when 13 percent died.[168] And still two more hit in 1383 and 1387. The plague in England was not completely overcome until the seventeenth century.

Julian would have been six years old during the first plague and forty-five years old during the last one. It is entirely possible that she may have contracted the plague when young and survived with immunity. If a sufferer did not succumb to exhaustion, heart failure, or internal hemorrhage, convalescence could begin after eight to ten days.

There seems little question that when Julian writes in her Chapter 64: "At this time I saw a body lying on the earth which appeared thick and ugly and fearsome, without shape and form, as it were a bloated heap of stinking mire"—it was not a literary exercise, but a recollection of what must have been a common sight in the streets of Norwich during the years of the Pestilence. And the fact that the Pestilence struck East Anglia when Julian was six, again when she was nineteen, and again when she was twenty-seven, thirty-three, forty-one, and forty-five, would mean that much of her life must have been framed and formed by these pandemics.

4
THE HOLY YEAR
AND THE VERNICLE

On February 22 in the year 1300, the notorious Pope Boniface VIII published the Bull *Antiquorum fida relatio,* in which he spoke somewhat vaguely about supposed past precedents, and then announced "great remissions and indulgences for sins" which could be earned "by visiting the city of Rome and the venerable basilica of the Prince of the Apostles." Then he specified that during that millennial year he offered "not only full and copious, but the most full, pardon of all their sins" for pilgrims who would fulfill certain conditions: (1) they must be truly penitent and confess their sins, and (2) they must visit the two Roman basilicas of St. Peter and St. Paul at least once a day—if they lived in Rome, for thirty days—or, if they were pilgrims from elsewhere, fifteen days. It is said that over two million pilgrims visited Rome in that year, and many were actually trampled to death in the crowds. One eyewitness wrote that the sacristans in the major basilicas had to spend "night and day . . . with rakes in hand as they harvested . . . [the monetary offerings] without end."[169]

Pope Boniface had intended that such Jubilee years should be celebrated only once in a hundred years, but some time before the middle of the fourteenth century, proposals (including petitions from St. Birgitta of Sweden and the poet Petrarch) were made to Pope Clement VI (then residing at Avignon), to shorten this one-hundred-year term on the grounds that the average span of human life was so short that unless the respite were shortened, there would be many who would be born and die between the Jubilee Years. Clement agreed, and in 1350 the next Holy Year of Jubilee was held. So, the second Jubilee or "Holy Year" was celebrated in 1350 and again in 1390, 1423, 1450 (when Pope Paul II decided on a twenty-five-year hiatus), 1475, and on into modern times every twenty-five years.

The Holy Year was initiated by the unbricking (with a silver hammer) and the opening of a sealed door in each of the four basilicas. (These particular doors were sealed and walled up with brick during the hiatus between Holy Years.) The ceremonies also included exposition of the revered sacred relic that came to be known as "Veronica's Veil" or (as Julian calls it) "The Vernicle." There is some confusion in its early years about whether this relic was originally the napkin that had covered Christ's face in the tomb (John 20:7) or the cloth that the legendary St. Veronica used to wipe Jesus' face during the way of the Cross. It may have started out as the former, but when it came to be called the *vera ikon* (that is, "the true image"), the name of "Veronica" (from *vera ikon*) was attached to it, and ever since, it was claimed to be her veil, revealing the miraculously imprinted face of Christ on it.[170] In the Holy Year of Jubilee, it was exposed for pilgrims every Friday. In 1297, by the order of Pope Boniface VIII, the image was brought to St. Peter's. On the occasion of the first Holy Year in 1300, the Veil was publicly displayed and became one of the *Mirabilia Urbis* ("The Wonders of the City") for the pilgrims who visited Rome.

Numerous descriptions by pilgrims noted the veil's fine material—"so fine that a breeze could pass through"—with an image on both its sides of a still living person with eyes wide open, a face full of suffering and with evident blood spots. From historical records, we can learn that the image on the veil gradually faded over the years, so it is likely that a pilgrim who might have seen it both in 1350 and again in 1390 would have seen a change in its coloration.

So, Julian would at least have heard reports from pilgrims who went from Norwich to Rome in the Holy Year(s), and these would have been brought easily to mind when she attempted to describe the face of the Crucified in her Showings. In fact, it is known that Sir Thomas Erpingham visited Rome when on pilgrimage to the Holy Land with Bolingbroke in 1391. If Julian was his sister, he could have been the source of her information about the Vernicle. Although there is no objective evidence of it, it is also *possible* that Julian herself could have been one of the two million pilgrims who traveled to Rome in 1390.

ᔐ 5
SAINT JOHN OF BEVERLEY

When Julian speaks of God's forgiveness for sins, she lists some holy people as examples of those who sinned and yet became saints. In Chapter 38 she lists the following: "Mary Magdalen, Peter and Paul, and Thomas and Jude and Saint John of Beverley, and others also without number, and how they are recognized in the Church on earth along with their sins. . . ."

The comments on St. John of Beverley's life given by Julian have been a puzzle to Julian scholars for years. We know who John of Beverley was, and even though he is no longer a "popular" saint, the historical facts of his life are readily available. However, up to this point no one has been able to discover any biographical or hagiographical references to his falling and rising that seem so central to Julian's use of him as an example.

In the early 1990s, Dr. Alan R. Deighton, Professor of German and Director of the Centre for Medieval Studies at the University of Hull, made the revolutionary discovery of a chapbook in Dutch entitled *Historie van Jan van Beverley*, printed in Brussels circa 1512. Here is a summary of the story in English, which he has graciously provided:

> There once lived in England a rich and powerful man, the Earl of Beverley. A widower, he has been left two children—a son named Jan and a daughter, Colette. On reaching manhood and acquiring a knowledge of Good and Evil, Jan decides to reject and escape the blandishments of this world. His father is upset at this loss of an heir but cannot change the mind of his son, who prays for his father and then departs to live a hermit's life in a cell in a wood. There he receives a visit from his sister, to whom he explains his decision. She thanks him and leaves, promising to visit him more often.
>
> The Devil then appears to Jan in the form of an angel, telling him that to avoid eternal damnation for having prided himself on his piety, he must commit one of three sins: drunkenness, unchastity, or murder. Jan chooses drunkenness, thinking it to be the least of the three evils. At the next visit of his sister, he asks her to bring some wine, which she does, staying with him while he drinks it lest evil befall him. Thoroughly drunk, he rapes and then murders her, burying the body to hide the evidence. Sober again, he repents and decides to make confession to the pope in Rome rather than despair. Having heard his [anonymous] confession, the pope is unable to fix a suitable penance and advises the unrecognized sinner to go to England and seek the advice of the pious hermit Jan van Beverley.
>
> At home again, Jan decides [as a penance] to walk only on all fours, drink [only] water, and eat grass like an animal, and not utter a word until a child is born who at the age of one day will tell him that God has forgiven him.
>
> Seven years pass. Jan's father has died and a new earl has been chosen. To celebrate the birth of his child, the earl goes hunting. Some hunters find Jan, whom they take to be a new species of wild animal. He is captured and taken to the earl's court, where

the newborn child absolves him, upon which the Bishop *[sic]* of Canterbury is brought to Beverley to hear Jan's confession.

Jan then returns to Colette's grave, opens it to discover his sister still alive and describing the joys of paradise which she has been experiencing in the company of angels since her murder. They go off together praising God and in search of the Bishop in order to receive the holy Sacrament.[171]

Dr. Deighton has shown that this legend involves the conflation of two hagiographic traditions: (1) The hermit who is called upon by the Devil to commit one of three sins, chooses what is apparently the least harmful, and as a result, commits all three; and (2) the "hairy anchorite" who, as penance for a serious sin, lives for some years like animal, and is finally absolved by a newborn child.[172]

These legends have many analogues from the thirteenth century onward in French, Italian, and German, and the "John" is variously identified as John of Beverley, John the Baptist, Jehan Paulus, and even John Chrysostom.

This is not the place to go into great detail regarding the various texts and manuscripts of the story,[173] but there are two pieces of external evidence that seem to support Deighton's contention:

(1) A series of marginal illustrations in a British Library manuscript[174] of the *Decretals* of Gregory IX and the *Glossa Ordinaria*, which dates from the early fourteenth century, probably written in Italy for French use, but illuminated in England. The illumination sidebars show a series of pictures of a hermit seated in a thatched wooden hut, confronted by the devil, then drinking while a woman holds a flagon. The next picture shows the hermit lying on top of the woman. The hermit apparently kills a miller who has witnessed the fornication, and then sets out on a journey to a bishop before whom he kneels. He is then shown in penance on all fours, and eventually upright, led by a tonsured figure with a crozier in his right hand away from the hermit's hut.[175]

(2) A wall painting in the church of St. Hubert, Idsworth, Hampshire, UK (discovered in 1864), which seems to recount stories of two

"Johns." The top tier shows a figure being led away by two others, a dancing woman, an incarcerated figure, and a feast with a king and queen and other guests passing a platter on which rests a human head—quite obviously, this is the story of the arrest and beheading of John the Baptist. The second tier of the painting, however, shows a hunting scene, where hunters confront a creature on all fours that has a human face and human limbs, but seems to be covered with hair—known among scholars as the story of "the hairy anchorite." It seems entirely possible that with a "confusion of Johns," the lower tier pictures the penance of St. John of Beverly, possibly mistaken here for John the Baptist.[176]

Suffice it to say that the legend of Saint John of Beverley as recounted in the Dutch chapbook apparently fits with Julian's description, but what is it doing in Dutch? In the late Middle Ages exchange and trade between Norwich and Flanders was extensive. Norwich was a wool staple, meaning that all exported wool went through Norwich to Flanders. There were many Flemish residents in Norwich—mostly cloth workers, weaver, dyers, and so on. And we know that relations were so close between the two that Flanders was even Norwich's primary source of the Pestilence on 1348–49. So it is not at all unlikely that a hagiographical legend could pass from East Anglia to Flanders via Norwich.

I believe one can safely say that it was *some* version of this legend that Julian had in mind when she chose to make Saint John of Beverley an example of God's forgiving mercy.

⪻ 6
GOD IN A POINT

Dame Julian begins her eleventh chapter with these words: "And after this, I saw God in a point (that is to say in my mind), by which vision I understood that He is in all things."

The exact meaning or origin of this vision is controversial. There are those who claim it must have referred to the mathematical concept of a "point," but the likelihood of Julian knowing such refined geometry is slight. I also do not think that "point," in this case, is meant as "an instant of time." My research has led to what seem some more likely sources in the work of Pseudo-Dionysius[177] (c. 500) and that of Robert Grosseteste (c. 1175–1253). Pseudo-Dionysius was the inspiration for the famous and anonymous fourteenth-century *Cloud of Unknowing*, and Grosseteste was the most famous master at Oxford in his time.[178]

DIONYSIUS THE AREOPAGITE
(PSEUDO-DIONYSIUS)

In his treatise *The Divine Names*, Dionysius wrote: "Now this is unified and one and common to the whole of divinity: that the entire wholeness is participated in by each of those who participate in it; none participates in only a part. It is rather like the case of the circle. The *center point* of the circle is shared by the surrounding radii."[179] And, "All the radii of a circle are brought together in the unity of the center, which contains all the straight lines brought together within itself. These are linked one to another because of this *single point of origin* and they are completely unified at this center"[180] (emphasis mine). Given his wide popularity in England in the late Middle Ages, Julian would have known at least some the work of Pseudo-Dionysius; indeed, she speaks of him as "Saint Denis of France" in Chapter 18. And his thinking about God's being the "point" of the universe may well have been in her mind when she wrote.

ROBERT GROSSETESTE

About Grosseteste, Austin Lane Poole wrote:

> [His] conception of the nature of fundamental physical substance was a peculiar one . . . ; he maintained that the fundamental physical substance was a fundamental "light" *(lux)*, not identical with, but manifesting itself in, visible light. In a short treatise, "*De Luce*," he described how in the beginning God created formless matter and *a point of this fundamental light*; this propagated itself in a sphere and produced the dimensions of space, and then, by a complicated series of changes and interactions, the heavenly spheres, the earth, and all the substances and creatures on it.[181]

Grosseteste himself wrote:

> The first corporeal form which some call corporeity is in my opinion light. For light of its very nature diffuses itself in every direction in such a way that *a point of light* will produce instantaneously a sphere of light of any size whatsoever, unless some opaque object stands in the way. Now the extension of matter in three dimensions is a necessary concomitant of corporeity, and this despite the fact that both corporeity and matter are in themselves simple substances lacking all dimension.[182] (my emphasis)

From another slightly different point of view, another scholar wrote:

> Later in the same chapter . . . Julian's claim that God is "at the center of everything" . . . suggests a space within the created world where the Creator resides. . . . Likewise, in the case of seeing "God in a point," Julian suggests a space in which she, a human being, can locate God, the divinity . . . as a point of access to the divine.[183]

As with Pseudo-Dionysius, Julian likely had read the works of Robert Grosseteste, or had heard them spoken of or preached. In support of this position we are reminded that Julian also uses the image of "light" throughout her writing, referring to Christ Himself as the light in Chapters 59, 67, 78, and notably in Chapter 83: "The light is the cause of our life. . . ." Following Grosseteste's idea of the point being the origin of all Creation, Carmen Davis imaginatively suggests that Julian's vision of "God in a pointe" may well be a description of the created universe at the moment before the Big Bang.[184]

⤵ 7
PILATE AND
DIONYSIUS THE AREOPAGITE

Julian's *Revelations*, Chapter 18, describe the worldwide suffering that occurred at the time of Christ's death on the cross:

> [U]niversally, all—that is to say, they that knew Him not—suffered because of the failing of all manner of comfort, except the mighty hidden protection of God. I mean of two manner of folk, as it can be understood by two persons: the one was Pilate, the other was Saint Denis of France, who was at that time a pagan. . . .

She speaks of two specific people who suffered: Pilate and Saint Denis. This requires two explanations.

PILATE

A medieval tradition (virtually forgotten today) held that Pilate "paid a price" for his condemnation of Jesus. Especially in the East, Christian folklore gradually exonerated Pilate based on the Johannine tradition (John 18:28–19:16), which made Pilate an unwilling participant who tried his best to protect and free Jesus. Part of the early tradition saw Pilate as a good man. Tertullian thought that he was a Christian at heart, and says Pilate wrote a letter to the emperor describing the trial and portraying Jesus in a positive light.[185] The author of the *Didascalia Apostolorum* declares that Pilate did not in fact consent to the deeds of the Jews.[186] And Augustine of Hippo classified Pilate among the prophets in Sermon 201. Even the historian Eusebius wrote that Pilate felt remorse for the execution of Jesus and committed suicide.[187] In the second-century *Gospel of Peter*, Jesus is condemned by *Herod*, not by Pilate.

In the Abyssinian and Coptic Orthodox Churches, it was believed that Jesus appeared to Pilate after the Resurrection and blessed him for his role in the trial. In some traditions, Pilate is said to have been exiled or killed, or to have committed suicide out of remorse, and he is venerated as a saint with his feast day on June 15 (in Ethiopia on June 19). The Eastern Orthodox Churches venerate his wife, Claudia Procula, as a saint with a feast day on October 27.

The medieval Western Church, however, was strongly impacted by the anecdotes in Jacobus de Voragine's *Golden Legend* (ca. 1260) that tell of Pilate's wicked early life (including at least two individual murders) and his punishments after the Crucifixion. The story, which is based, the author tells us, on the *Historica Scholastica* of Peter Comestor, is that Tiberius, the Roman Emperor, was seriously ill, and had heard of a miraculous healer [Jesus] in Palestine. He sent his envoy Volusian to Palestine to instruct Pilate to send Jesus to Rome. Since Jesus was already crucified, Pilate was frightened and asked for ten days' grace. During that time, Volusian happened to meet Veronica, who explained that Jesus was dead, but that she had wanted a picture painted of Jesus, and on the way to the painter with the cloth, she had met Jesus, who simply pressed the cloth to his face and left an image on it. She assured Volusian that the Emperor would be healed by gazing on the miraculous image. She accompanied Volusian to Rome, and the Emperor's health was restored.

Angry with Pilate for having allowed the death of Jesus, Tiberias brought Pilate to Rome. However, Pilate had brought Jesus' seamless robe, and when he wore it before the Emperor, Tiberius' anger disappeared. When the Emperor learned of the trick, he had Pilate stripped and then condemned him to a shameful death. Pilate chose, rather, to commit suicide.

His body was thrown into the Tiber River, but the river flooded and terrible storms occurred. So the body of Pilate was retrieved and transported to Gaul, where it was thrown into the Rhone River at Vienne. Similar flooding and storms occurred, so eventually Pilate's body was buried in a small lake on Mount Pilatus (originally "Pileatus" meaning "cloud-capped") near Lausanne, where, it is said, the body rises on every Good Friday, sits on the bank, and tries to wash its hands.

A further development of legends concerning Pilate's suffering for his part in Christ's crucifixion appears in some of the mystery plays that Julian would have seen. In *The Ordinalia* (preserved in a Cornish version), basically the same story is told, with the addition that Tiberius' disease is described as leprosy, and Pilate's body is buried in an earthen grave twice, and twice the earth refuses the body, forcing it out of the grave. Then at Veronica's suggestion, the body is placed in an iron box and cast into the Tiber. However, a passing traveler goes to wash his hands in the Tiber and dies. It turns out that anyone who tries to cross the river or sails a boat upon it dies. So, again at Veronica's suggestion, the body is taken up and pushed out to sea in an unmanned boat. Lucifer, Satan, and Beelzebub then capture the body on a rock in the ocean, and take it to hell for torture.

Julian would have known these stories, and when she speaks of Pilate's "suffering," she is referring to at least one of these apocryphal tales.

DIONYSIUS

To understand Julian's reference to "Saint Denis of France," considerable background information is needed. There are *seven* major figures in church history named Dionysius. Three of them concern us here:

1. There is *Dionysius* the Areopagite referred to in the Acts of the Apostles. The tradition is that after he was converted by St. Paul he became the first bishop of Athens. (The story of his conversion is recounted in Acts 17:22–23, 32–34.)

2. There is Saint *Denis* of Paris ("Denis" or "Denys" is the French translation of "Dionysius"), who is the patron saint of France. According to the tradition, he was one of the first seven missionary bishops sent to convert Gaul and became the first bishop of Paris and a martyr (c. AD 250).

3. There is the anonymous sixth-century mystical theologian, probably a Syrian monk, who wrote under the *pseudonym* of "*Dionysius* the Areopagite." He was, therefore, originally identified with the Dionysius referred to in Acts. That identification gave apparent *apostolic* authority to his writings, and his ideas eventually became the keystone of Western mystical theology. (Aquinas quotes him 1,700 times; Bonaventure calls him "the prince of mystics.") *The Cloud of Unknowing* from Julian's fourteenth century is virtually a translation of some of these writings.

Until well into the sixteenth century it was believed that all these three men named "Dionysius" were *one and the same person*. So, when Julian wrote of "St. Denis of France," she believed (as did everyone at that time) that he was the same man as the Athenian Dionysius who was converted from paganism by St. Paul.

In his *Ecclesiastical History* (III, iv), Eusebius quotes the early Christian historian Hegisippus in saying that Dionysius the Areopagite was a student in Hierapolis in Egypt around the year AD 32–33 (that is, the time of Jesus' death on the cross) when he and a Stoic friend, Apollophanes, experienced an eclipse of the sun during the full moon. In his seventh letter (to Polycarp) he wrote that at the time of the eclipse, his friend Apollophanes had said: "It is a sign that some change is taking place in things divine."

Around 850 in a "Chronography" written by Georgius Syncellus, it is added (from an unknown source) that Dionysius' *response* to

Apollophanes at the time of the eclipse had been, "Either the God of nature is suffering or the fabric of the world is being dissolved." In 1278, when the Roman Breviary was compiled by the Franciscan Friar Haymo for Pope Nicholas III, October 9 was appointed as the feast of St. Denis of France, and Syncellus's account of Dionysius' words upon seeing the eclipse was included in the readings for that day. This was taken as pagan witness to the truth of St. Mark's words about Jesus' crucifixion: "At midday a darkness fell over the whole land, which lasted till three in the afternoon . . ." (Mark 15:33).

Thus it was that Julian had either read or heard this account of Dionysius (St. Denis), the supposed pagan convert of St. Paul, in the Breviary Readings, and had remembered his reputed words—although reversing the clauses when she came to write them down.

The story of Dionysius raising the "altar to the unknown God" Julian must also have found in the legends that a rose from the *Historia Scholastica* of Peter Comestor: "It is said that in Athens at that time there was a flourishing *studium*, and when the philosophers enquired into the cause of the darkness and were unable to discover it, Denis the Areopagite said that the god of nature was suffering. And they made an altar and wrote on it: 'To the unknown God.' "[188]

8
THE WOUNDS OF CHRIST

In Chapter 24 of *Revelations*, Mother Julian writes: "Then, with a glad expression, our Lord looked into His wounded side and gazed with joy, and with His sweet gazing He directed the understanding of His creature through that same wound into His side within. . . ."

The palpably anatomical dimensions of Julian's descriptions of the wounds of Christ in several places in her writing can be a bit daunting for contemporary readers, who are likely to think them extreme and perhaps not in the best taste, but they represent a vital element in the spirituality of the late Middle Ages. Some medieval writers' devotion to the wounds of Christ was so extreme that they determined that including the scourging, crowning with thorns, smiting with a "reed," bruises from carrying the cross, and the nails, Christ had received a total of 5,480 wounds.

A fine contemporaneous example of Julian's vision of the wound in Christ's side as a dwelling and resting place for "all mankind" and a venue for "viewing" the "blessed heart cloven in two" is the familiar and much-loved prayer *Anima Christi*. Here is John Henry Newman's rhymed translation (emphasis mine):

> Soul of Christ be my sanctification;
> Body of Christ, be my salvation;
> Blood of Christ's side, fill all my veins;
> Water of Christ's side, wash out my stains;
> Passion of Christ, my comfort be,
> O Good Jesus, listen to me.
> *Within, Thy wounds I fain would hide,*
> *Never to be parted from Thy side.*
> Guard me should the foe assail me,
> Call me when my life shall fail me.
> Bid me come to Thee above
> With Thy saints to sing Thy love,
> World without end. Amen.[189]

The prayer has often been erroneously ascribed to St. Ignatius Loyola because it was a great favorite of his and was included in his *Spiritual Exercises*, but it is actually very much older. Scholars agree that it appears to date from the early fourteenth century.[190] Julian would have known it.

A near contemporary of Julian's, Thomas à Kempis (c. 1380–1471), in his *Imitation of Christ* wrote:

> If you can not soar up as high as Christ sitting on his throne, behold him hanging on his cross. *Rest in Christ's Passion and live willingly in his holy wounds.* You will gain marvelous strength and comfort in adversities. You will not care that men despise you.

. . . Had we but, with Thomas, put our fingers into the print of his nails and thrust our hands into his side! If we had but known ourselves his sufferings in a deep and serious consideration and tasted the astonishing greatness of his love, the joys and miseries of life would soon become indifferent to us.[191] (emphasis mine)

St. Augustine refers to the wound in Christ's side as the door to the ark:

The Ark is without doubt a figure of the city of God wandering in this world, that is to say, the Church which is saved by means of the wood, on which hung the mediator of God and men, the man Christ Jesus. . . . And the door it received in its side is surely the wound made in the side of the Crucified when pierced by the lance, by which those enter who come to Him.[192]

The Venerable Bede (c. 673–735) wrote:

It was [Christ's] right side that the soldier opened, according to the belief of Holy Church. Here also the Evangelist makes use of an apt word, when he says not "struck," or "wounded," but "opened," that is, the door in the midst of His side, through which the way to heaven might be opened to us.[193]

Professor Miri Rubin of the University of London describes an illustration in a fourteenth-century prayer book:

In an image from a late fourteenth-century English prayer book (c. 1380) *we see the wound on Christ's side as the centre of attention*, while around it are other paraphernalia relating to Christ's death, not least among them the instruments which pierced His flesh, like so many surgical tools. Similar attention to torture and unmaking, to the painful and protracted death is evident in this image, with the wound of the side, the nails, the flails, pincers and markings on Christ's body. . . .[194] (emphasis mine)

In the long prayer/poem "The Fifteen Oes" (which Eamon Duffy calls "the most distinctive and probably the most popular of all prayers in late medieval England"[195]), one verse reads:

> O Jesus, most profound abyss of mercy; I beseech you by the depth of your wounds, which pierced your flesh to the heart and very marrow of your bones, draw me out from the depths of sin into which I have sunk, and *hide me deep in the holes of your wounds* from the face of your anger, Lord, until the judgement is past.[196] (emphasis mine)

And the author of *Ancrene Wisse* advises his anchoresses to "flee into his wounds . . . [c]reep into them with your thought . . . and bloody your heart with his precious blood."[197]

It should be clear from these few examples (of dozens available) that however bizarre it may seem today, Julian's image of entering the wound in Christ's side was a conceit common for spiritual writers in her day. Indeed, Julian's own image may not have been original to her. As one author put it, the fourteenth century was the age when "the Passion became the chief concern of the Christian soul."[198] In fact, there was one circulated woodblock print of the wounds of Christ for which Pope Pius IX gave an indulgence of 32,755 years of pardon for anyone who before the image recited five Paters, five Aves, and a Creed.[199]

Further, the image was continued among pious writers and hymnists (including Protestants) well into the nineteenth century. As an example consider the hymn: "Rock of ages / Cleft for me / Let me hide myself in thee ..."), or an eighteenth-century branch of Moravian spirituality called the *seitenhohlchen*, or "little side hole," whose followers were described as those "who feel at home in the Sidehole and crawl in deep."[200]

⌐ 9
PELLETS, EAVES, AND HERRING

In Chapter 7, Mother Julian offers most "homely" and ordinary similes for the falling of drops of Christ's blood in her vision of the crucified Jesus. She compares the drops of blood to "pellets," to water falling from the eaves of a building, and to herring scales. Exactly what Julian meant by "pellets" may be uncertain. Because guns had begun to be used in the late thirteenth century, the ammunition (often small stones) was called "pellets"—but it is far more likely that Julian uses the word in reference to a quantity of flour.

"Flour" came in three forms in Julian's day: (a) "Meal" was the fine-milled grain (like our modern flour). (b) "Groats" were any cereal grain with the hulls of the individual ears of grain removed. (c) And "pellets" were small round balls of the meal made from any cereal or even from dried and milled potatoes (from very small up to the size of apples).

When we think of Julian's comparison of drops of blood to water falling from the eaves of a house, we must remember that in the fourteenth century, except for elegant buildings such as cathedrals, which had lead roofs, the majority of buildings had *thatched* roofs. The thatch on these roofs "lifts" and loosens somewhat during rain, so it channels the water between the reeds of thatch to produce drops or trickles of water rather than sheets of water such as might flow off a modern roof.

And Julian's comparing the drops of blood covering Jesus' fore-head as scales of herring is an extremely "homely" image. The city of Yarmouth was constructed on a built-up bar of sand and silt at the coastal mouth of the Yare River, into which Norwich's Wensum River flowed. Even in Julian's day, Yarmouth was the largest herring fishery in the world, at one time involving almost a thousand boats. Herring was a staple of the medieval diet. It was of particular value to the medieval world because it was almost the only staple that could be easily preserved by salting or smoking. Herring was so important to Norfolk that in 1904 the Norfolk County Council had a new coat of arms approved in which the shield was held, on the left, by the traditional lion guardant and, on the right, by a herring with a lion's head. Julian's simple use of the "herring scales" simile was based on a great deal of personal experience she had had with herrings.

≈ 10
PREDESTINATION
AND SALVATION IN JULIAN

Julian uses some form of the phrase "those who shall be saved" thirty-seven times in the Long Version of her *Revelations*. This is a problematic phrase that on the surface seems to suggest that Julian followed a narrow concept of predestination: some souls are predestined for heaven and some are predestined to hell, and neither has any choice in the matter. (This concept is commonly called "double predestination.") However, the issue is more complicated than that.

The issue of predestination came to the fore in the late fourth- and early fifth-century work of Augustine of Hippo. And the major problem had to do with the tensions between God's timelessness and our own earthly immersion in time. If, after all, God has immediate and constant knowledge of earthly past, present, and future at once, logically, then, God knows a priori who will ultimately be saved and who will not. Therefore, it would seem that human free will is compromised, and that one's ultimate salvation is already predetermined by God's foreknowledge.

In his early writings, Augustine affirmed that all human beings were predestined *to heaven* because God's predestinating grace was granted universally to all human souls in which dwelled the desire to pursue salvation. (This concept is commonly called "single predestination.") However, when the English monk Pelagius began in the early fifth century to teach that salvation was achieved *not* by a specific infusion of grace, but by an act of inborn human free will, Augustine's concepts began to change. He wrestled with St. Paul's words:

> For those whom [God] foreknew, he also predestined to be conformed to the image of his Son, in order that he might be the firstborn within a large family. And those whom he predestined he also called, and those whom he called he also justified, and those whom he justified he also glorified. (Romans 8:29–30, NRSV)

As a result of his later thinking (that is, after 396), Augustine began to move toward a more deterministic point of view, teaching that it required an act of God for the "corrupted" human will even to *desire* salvation. Tied as this was to Augustine's belief in the fall of man, his concept was that original sin (virtually an invention of Augustine) had so corrupted humankind that while any individual human could *know* what God's will was, that human was deprived of the ability to *desire to do* God's will. It therefore required a specific infusion of God's grace for a person to *want* to follow the will of God, and this infused grace worked in the human heart to stir up that desire. While Augustine's ideas in this matter have influenced other thinkers (perhaps most notably John Calvin), his position has never been officially accepted by the Church.

When Julian speaks of "those who shall be saved," she excludes some from heavenly salvation (with apparent considerable reluctance):

> . . . one point of our Faith is that many creatures shall be damned (as were the angels who fell out of heaven because of pride—who are now demons), and many on earth who die outside of the Faith of Holy Church (that is to say, those who are heathen men[201] and also men who have received Christianity but live unchristian lives and so die without love): all these shall be damned to hell without end, as Holy Church teaches me to believe. (Chapter 32)

and

I did not see as specially described in detail the Jews that did Him to death. Nevertheless, I knew in my Faith that they were accursed and damned without end—except for those that were converted by grace.[202] (Chapter 33)

With the exclusion of these particular people, Julian considers her *audience* to be her "fellow Christians," *all* of whom "shall be saved." Therefore, it can be said that Julian held the very orthodox doctrine of "single predestination": that all souls are predestined for heaven, but they are free to reject that predestination.[203]

The matter was probably most clearly and succinctly expressed by an obscure article on "The Motherhood of God" by Paula S. Datsko Barker,[204] in which she wrote:

> Julian's resolution of the problem of sin presupposes a doctrine of election. She firmly believes in providence and predestination. . . . She limits her assurances of eternal bliss specifically to "alle that shalle be savyd," yet *she appears to include all humanity in that elect group.* "I saw that this menying was for the generalle man, that is to sey alle man, which is synfulle and shall be in to the last day. . . ." But one cannot conclude that she is proposing a doctrine of universal salvation. Since she sees in her visions none but those who will be saved, it may have been her belief that *any who are not to be saved were, like evil itself, simply non-existent from an eternal perspective.* Indeed, she states that although she saw nothing of the damned in the showings, she continued to believe the Church's teachings on hell, purgatory and the damnation of the Jews. . . . Thus she concedes the presence of some persons in the temporal realm who will not be saved. (emphasis mine)

It has become trendy in our day to declare Julian a universalist who held that heavenly salvation is guaranteed to *all* humanity—since how could it be that ultimately "all shall be well" if there are people eternally deprived of heaven? Those who hold this view argue that the "Great Deed" that God will do at the end must be the salvation of all, including the reprobates in hell. The problem with this position is that it directly opposes the teachings of the Church to which Julian repeatedly commits herself.

Barker, however, hinted at what I believe to be the solution to the conundrum: that the "Great Deed" that God will do *may* simply be the "de-creation" of hell, that is, the moving of hell and its inhabitants into what Barker calls "non-existence from an eternal perspective." The free choice of sin-and-hell over virtue-and-heaven is, after all, a choice of "unreality" over Reality, a choice of "nonbeing" over Being, a choice of non-essence over Essence Himself. And, since human beings have no *right* to existence (either on earth or in heaven) but only receive existence itself as a gift from God, the loving God may, then, ultimately give to those "damned" persons exactly what they have chosen: nonexistence. And then all *shall* be well.

Or it might be wise to settle for the philosopher Wittgenstein's celebrated conclusion to his *Tractatus*: "Whereof we cannot speak, thereof we must be silent."

⮎ 11
GOD AS MOTHER

Julian's unapologetic treatment of Christ as Mother is, without doubt, the finest and most sophisticated treatment of that subject in *all of* Christian literature. It is only our contemporary ignorance of the classic Christian mystics and theologians that leads us to think of this as a "new idea" for Julian. It is a venerable tradition supported by Adam of Perseigne, Aelred, Albert the Great, Anselm, Aquinas, Augustine, Bernard of Cluny, Bonaventure, Bridget of Sweden, Catherine of Siena, Clement of Alexandria, Dante, William Flete, Gilbert of Hoyland, Guerric of Igny, Guigo II the Carthusian, Helinand of Froidmont, Isaac of Stella, Margery Kempe, Peter Lombard, Ludolph of Saxony, Marguerite of Oingt, Mechtild of Magdeburg, Richard Rolle, William of St. Thierry, the *Ancrene Wisse*, the *Stimulus Amoris*, and Holy Scripture itself.[205]

It is not surprising that Julian should present this idea as unexceptional. But we do a great injustice to Mother Julian if we assign to her any modern "feminist" motivations in the declaration of Christ's motherhood. Julian's tradition comes from her identification of the Second Person of the Trinity with the traditional character of Wisdom—interpreted in all the Judeo-Christian tradition as the Divine Feminine—and her understanding of the identity between "Mother Church" and the Mystical Body of Christ. For Julian, Christ *is* the Church, and the Church is the Mother. Christ *is* Wisdom, and Wisdom is the feminine.

And Julian does most modernists one better by a simple grammatical structure: she never uses anything but *masculine* pronouns in referring to Christ, so we have such wonderfully mystical and grammatically paradoxical statements of androgyny as "Our Mother Jesus, He. . . ." This approach maintains the balance far better than declaring for a "female Jesus." However, Julian does not hesitate to be graphic about her mystical symbolism, and at one point declares: "He carries us within Himself in love, and labors full term. . . ."[206]

And Julian goes even a step further in that she never characterizes Christ as "like our mother," but the direct opposite—she describes motherhood (as she describes humanity itself) as preexisting in Christ. Our mothers and what we call "mother-love" are only emanations and imitations of Christ's own eternal and timeless motherhood. Christ is the proto-Mother, and earthly motherhood (like all other earthly virtues) is merely an imitation and reflection of Him. Julian goes so far as to say that it is even Christ who actually does our birthing when our natural mothers give us birth.[207] Motherhood, Julian would say, is not a characteristic of womankind that Christ shares, but a characteristic of Christ that women share, and she declares that our natural responsibility to fatherhood and motherhood has its origin in the fatherhood and motherhood of God, and that responsibility is met by loving the Father/Mother God.[208]

ᔿ 12
BEHOVABIL[209]

The most challenging Middle English word in Julian's writings is the word variously written as *behovabil* (in the British Version), *behouely* (in the Paris Version), or *behouelye* (in the Amherst Version). Since Julian wrote in Chapter 27 that "Synne is behovabil . . .," it seems that she intended that the word define sin, or at least, that it describe some aspect or feature of sin. But what exactly was that definition or feature?

The experts vary widely in their decisions:

(1) Marion Glasscoe defines it in the most recent glossary: "behovabil *adj.* expedient, appropriate."[210]

(2) Colledge and Walsh define it in their glossary: "behouelye . . . adj.; 'necessary' (OE behoflic)."[211]

(3) Hugh Greeson defines it in his glossary for the British Version in Julia Holloway's book: "behovabil *adj.* helpful . . . [OE to behofe]."[212]

(4) Fernand Mossé has: "behovelich *adj.* necessary. [*Behovely*]."[213]

(5) Stratmann/Bradley have: "bi-hoflz, adj., = *M.L.G.* behovig, *M.H.G.* behuofec *(egenus);* ? profitable. . . ."[214]

(6) In her own translation, Julia Holloway translates the word as "needful."[215]

(7) The exhaustive *Middle English Dictionary*[216] has the two following entries:

   bihoveable adj. Also behuf-. [From noun.] Helpful, useful, beneficial; convenient; appropriate. c. 1400.

and

   behoveli adj. Also beheflic, bihulik [OE behoflic & beheflic (cp. Also behefe).] (a) Useful, profitable, beneficial, good (for sth. or sb.); (b) suitable, fit; proper, appropriate; (c) requisite, necessary; ~ at nede.

I have struggled with that word in my translation since the 1980s.

My decision has been that the word carried the general import of "necessary," but *only* in the philosophical sense, that is, "rising from the nature of the thing"—which gives the sentence this connotation: "by its very nature, sin will happen—it is inevitable." Some of the other translations add interesting variations in possible meaning: "appropriate" suggests that sin is predictable and fitting, given human weakness; "profitable" or "beneficial" carry the suggestion of the *felix culpa* ("lucky sin"), that is, that without sin, the redemption of Christ would not have happened.

In his short (but exhaustive) study of the word, Denys Turner writes:

> In short, "behovely" means to Julian much the same as what *conveniens* means to Thomas Aquinas and Bonaventure. So, when Julian says that "sin is behovely" what she means is that sin is *conveniens*; and she means it in a sense which Thomas and Bonaventure would have understood, which is . . . roughly this: that it "fits," it is "just so" and that there is something it fits with.[217]

In my opinion, then, what Julian means to say in using this word is that all human beings are sinners, and that sin cannot be entirely avoided by human beings. But even this inevitable sin does not impede God in the working out of His will—so that in spite of this *inevitable* sin, "all shall be well."

13
THE *STABAT MATER*

The Latin original of the familiar hymn "Stabat Mater" addressed to the Blessed Virgin Mary contains twenty intricately rhymed verses. Its composer is uncertain, but most scholars favor Pope Innocent III (d. 1216). In our day, there are some sixty English translations. For our purposes, it is enough to know that it was widely popular in Julian's day, and she would certainly have known it.

The hymn rhapsodizes on the sufferings of the Blessed Mother as she witnessed the Crucifixion, and the poet pleads time and again to be allowed to share in those sufferings. Here are some verses with my unrhymed rough translation:

9
Eia Mater, fons amoris
Me sentire vim doloris
Fac, ut tecum lugeam.

Come Mother! fount of love!
Let me feel the weight of your sorrow.
Make it that I may mourn with you.

10
Fac, ut ardeat cor meum
in amando Christum Deum
ut sibi complaceam.

Make my heart so burn
In loving Christ God
That to him I may be acceptable.

13
Fac me tecum, pie, flere,
Crucifixo condolere,
Donec ego vixero.

Make me weep with you, holy one,
And feel the pain of the Crucified
As long as I have life.

14
Iuxta crucem tecum stare
Et me tibi sociare
In planctu desidero.

To stand with you by the cross
And to be your companion
In mourning is what I long for.

16
Fac, ut portem Christi mortem
Passionis fac consortem
Et plagas recolere.

Make it so that bearing the death of Christ
I may have share in the Passion,
And relive his wounds once more.

The theme of the hymn is the appeal to share in the sufferings of Christ and his Blessed Mother, and this theme was a part of the late medieval cult of the Sorrows of the Virgin.

14
THE HOLY TRINITY

From one point of view, Julian's theme throughout her *Revelations* is a spiritual comprehension of the divine reality of the Holy Trinity and the mystical manifestations and implications of that divinity. So central is the doctrine of the Trinity to Julian that the builders of the present Shrine Chapel at St. Julian's Church included two etched glass insets in the leaded glass windows of the chapel. One illustrates Julian on her sick bed, with the crucifix before her. The other is a version of the familiar late medieval icon of the Holy Trinity, showing God the Father as an aged and bearded king seated on a throne, suspending between his knees a crucifix that holds the body of Jesus (God the Son), with a dove (the Holy Spirit) descending above his head.

Further, the Norwich Cathedral, which Julian would have known well, was formally dedicated as "The Cathedral of the Holy and Undivided Trinity." The thirteenth-century seal of the cathedral carries this peculiar legend: *+EST MICHI NUMEN IDEM TRIBUS UNI LAUS HONOR IDEM ET BENDICO GREGI FAMULATUR QUI MICHI REGI.* Translated, this means: "The same divine will is to me [that is, Christ] as to the three [that is, the Holy Trinity], the praise and honor of one is the same [that is, it passes to all three]; and I bless the flock that serves me as king" (my translation). In fact, Julian almost echoed the meaning of these words when she wrote in Chapter 4: "for whenever Jesus appears, the blessed Trinity is understood."

One of Julian's most powerful presentations is her recurring metaphor of the Trinity: Father=Power, Son=Wisdom, Holy Spirit=Love (or Goodness). This insight into the nature of the persons of the Trinity is neither original nor unique with Julian; it has biblical origins,[218] and it appears in the works of Maximus the Confessor (580–662),[219] Pseudo-Dionysius the Areopagite,[220] Saint Bonaventure (1217–74),[221] and Saint Thomas Aquinas.[222] It was even present in rabbinical teachings,[223] and was picked up in the Augsburg Confessions of Martin Luther,[224] in the writings of Dr. Samuel Johnson,[225] William Penn,[226] and even Lord Byron.[227] And it appears in the first of the "Articles of Religion" in the Church of England's *Book of Common Prayer*[228] and in the Roman Catholic Catechism of 1951.[229] However, Julian makes more central use of it than any of these other authors.

The Father-as-Power is manifested primarily in (a) begetting the Son, (b) creating the universe (Julian's "making"), (c) maintaining the universe (Julian's "keeping"), and (d) resurrecting Jesus and "all who shall be saved."

The Son-as-Wisdom is manifested in (a) the Incarnation (Julian's "into the pit of the womb of the Maiden"), and (b) the Passion/Redemption (Julian's "again-buying"), but most significantly (c) in Julian's recognition of "Jesus as Mother."[230]

The Holy Spirit-as-Love/Goodness is manifested in the continuing demonstration of divine love for fallen humanity, in the teachings of the Spirit-guided Church, and in the sacraments.

One of Julian's greatest insights regarding the Trinity is its parallel manifestation in the nature of human beings. In Chapter 55, Julian writes: "Thus was my understanding led by God to perceive in Him and to understand, to be aware and to know, that our soul is a 'created trinity,' like to the uncreated blessed Trinity . . . and in its creation it is joined to the Creator as it is aforesaid." The classical human "trinity" has been memory, understanding, and will. Julian's insight springs from and further clarifies her understanding of the absolute union between God and humanity: that while she recognizes the distinction between the "uncreated" (that is, God) and the "created" (that is, humanity), she maintains that, nevertheless, humanity is—in its creation and by its very nature—metaphysically one-ed with God, a one-ing that is finally perfected and made eternal in the bliss of heaven.

⌒ NOTES

1. Quoted by The Most Rev. Rowan Williams, in turn quoted by Ron Rosenbaum on "The Slate Book Club," *Slate Online Magazine,* September 20, 2006.
2. Thomas Merton, *Seeds of Destruction* (New York: Farrar, Strauss, 1964), 274–75.
3. Cover comment on Watson and Jenkins, *The Writings of Julian of Norwich* (University Park, PA: Pennsylvania State University Press, 2006).
4. *Encyclopedia Britannica*, Eleventh Edition.
5. John 12:47.
6. Thomas Merton, *Conjectures of a Guilty Bystander* (Garden City, NY: Doubleday, 1966), 192. Emphasis mine.
7. Chapter 49.
8. Chapter 27.
9. Chapter 11.
10. Chapter 37. Julian's own Middle English calls this presence *a godly wille.*
11. Chapter 6.
12. Chapter 32.
13. Chapter 33: ". . . the more we busy ourselves to know His secrets in this or any other thing, the farther we shall be from the knowledge of them."
14. Chapter 41.
15. Chapter 41.
16. Chapter 41.
17. *Meditations on the Life of Christ* was composed at the end of the thirteenth century. In the fourteenth century *seven* separate English translations were made—of these, over 200 manuscript copies survive. (See Denise Despres, *Ghostly Sights: Visual Meditation in Late-Medieval Literature* [Norman, OK: Pilgrim Books, 1989], 35.)
18. Pseudo-Bonaventure, *Meditations on the Life of Christ: An Illustrated Manuscript of the Fourteenth Century*, eds. Isa Ragusa and

Rosalie B. Green, trans. Isa Ragusa (Princeton, NJ: Princeton University Press, 1961), 178.

19. Henry Suso, *The Exemplar, with Two German Sermons* (Mahwah, NJ: Paulist Press, 1989), 219.

20. Francis Blomefield, *History and Antiquities of the County of Norfolk*, Vol. 10, pub. 1805.

21. Henry Collins, ed., *Revelations of Divine Love, shewed to a devout Anchoress, by name Mother Julian of Norwich* (London: Thomas Richardson & Sons, 1877).

22. Thomas Dudley Fosbrooke, *British Monachism or Manners and Customs of the Monks and Nuns of England* (London: M.A. Nattali, 1843).

23. "It was customary to give the title 'Lady' or 'Dame' to a recluse of gentle birth. The fact that it was attached to the author of her *Revelations*, prepared by an unknown scribe, indicates quite plainly her station by birth." Rufus M. Jones, *The Flowering of Mysticism* (New York: Macmillan, 1938), 224, n.18.

24. Francis Blomefield, *An Essay Towards a Topographical History of the County of Norfolk* (London: William Buemer, 1805–1810 [originally published 1739–75]).

25. It seems possible that the duel may have involved a property dispute since the Erpingham, Hauteyn, and Colesby properties in Norfolk abutted each other.

26. It is interesting that the motto on the Phelip coat of arms was *Pro aris et focis*, "For our altars and our homes," demonstrating an obvious devoutly Christian orientation.

27. Primary sources of genealogical information: Blomefield, *An Essay*; John Burke, *A General and Heraldic Dictionary of the Peerages of England* (Oxford: Oxford University Press, 1831); and Thomas Christopher Banks, *The Dormant or Extinct Baronage of England* (London: T. Bensley, 1808); plus countless Internet genealogical collections.

28. A noble Italian who accompanied the Ambassador of Venice to England wrote in his account of life in England: "[E]veryone,

however rich he may be, sends away his children into the houses of others, whilst he, in return, receives those of strangers into his own. And on inquiring their reason for this severity, they answered that they did it in order that their children might learn better manners" (Charlotte Sneyd, tr., *A Relation or Rather a True Account of the Island of England* [London: Camden Society, 1847]). Fostering was also described as a way of giving "friendly hostages" to seal bonds between aristocratic families.

29. It should be noted that Julian's "last" revelation happened fifteen years after the original revelations (that is, 1388–89, the time of her second husband's death). There is no internal evidence that she wrote *as an anchorite*; in fact, the famous rule for anchoresses states that a recluse should "regard any vision [she] may see . . . as mere delusion, for it is nothing but [the Devil's] guile" (*Ancrene Wisse*, 130; see note 32). And as a Suffolk noblewoman, Julian would have had access to a scribe—even a family chaplain.

30. Blomefield declares, "*In 1393*, Lady Julian, the anchoress here, was a strict recluse, and had two servants to attend her *in her old age*. This woman was in these days esteemed one of the greatest holiness" (emphasis mine). Julian's second husband had close political connections with the Duke of Gloucester, and it is likely that she fostered her sons to the Duke of Gloucester. This possibility is supported by three facts: (1) young John's first short-lived marriage was with Isabel Harcourt, from a leading Gloucestershire family; (2) the widowed John went to France in 1415 in the retinue of John Burgh of Gloucester and died of dysentery at Harfleur; and (3) his brother William fought in the retinue of the Duke of Gloucester at Agincourt.

31. A childless widow (as Julian was after her first marriage)— considered in law a *feme sole*—typically received at least half of her husband's estate; if there were children (as in her second marriage), she would receive the return of her dowry and at least a third of the estate. Moreover, "eminent canonical authority strongly deprecated remarriage of widows, discouraged them from doing

416 | The Complete Julian

so, hinted pointedly that remarriage signified shameless placency to the voluptuous enticements of sexual passion, and lauded, sometimes in quite extravagant terms, the virtue of women who spurned remarriage in order to cultivate in widowhood a second career of consecrated chastity" (James A. Brundage, "Widows and Remarriage . . ." in, *Wife and Widow in Medieval England,* Sue Sheridan Walker, ed. [Ann Arbor, MI: University of Michigan Press, 1993], 17).

32. Anne Savage, tr., *Anchoritic Spirituality: Ancrene Wisse and Associated Works* (Mahwah, NJ: Paulist Press, 1991), 130.

33. There are several legacies related to the anchorhold at St. Julian's Church, notably none before 1393: see Article 3, "Testimonial Evidence of Julian's Existence," page 30.

34. John Erpingham's house actually stood in the geographical parish of St. Peter Parmentergate (neighbor to St. Julian's parish). However, in the 1390s there was already a College of twenty Secular Canons living in a house in St. Peter's churchyard and using the church as their chapel, so there would have been no place for an anchorite there. Hence, Julian's choice to establish her cell at the neighboring church—St. Julian's.

35. Harris Nicholas, *Testamenta Vetusta* (London: Nicholas & Son, 1826).

36. The Paris MS has the correct *Benedicite Dominus* in both chapters 4 and 8: possibly corrected by the nuns who copied it? And Cressy's seventeenth-century printed version of Julian's book unaccountably has *Dominis.* However, we know of several fourteenth-century Englishwomen whose last name was some form of "schoolmistress" and some with their occupation listed as *magistra scolarum* ("mistress of scholars") or *doctrix puellarum* ("teacher of girls"), so Julian *may* have had secular schooling under such a schoolmistress. (See N. Orme, "What Did Medieval Schools Do For Us?" *History Today,* June 2006.)

37. Department of English, University of Bristol, UK.

38. It could be argued against Julian's own wealth that donations and legacies to her were not necessary for her support. However,

such legacies were left primarily for the spiritual benefit *of the donor*, not for the necessities of the recipient.

39. Robert H. Flood, *A Description of St. Julian's Church, Norwich and an Account of Dame Julian's Connection With It* (Norwich: Wherry Press, n.d.).

40. Julia Bolton Holloway, *Julian of Norwich: Showing of Love* (Collegeville, MN: Liturgical Press, 2003), viii, xii.

41. Edmund Colledge and James Walsh, *Julian of Norwich: Showings* (Mahwah, NJ: Paulist Press, 1978), 19–20.

42. Denys Turner, " 'Sin is Behovely' in Julian of Norwich's *Revelations of Divine Love*," *Modern Theology* 20, (July: 2004).

43. Wolfgang Riehle, *The Middle English Mystics* Bernard Standring, trans., (London: Routledge & Kegan Paul, 1981), 29.

44. Anna Marie Reynolds, ed., *A Shewing of God's Love* (London: Sheed & Ward, 1958), xvii.

45. M. Diane F. Kranz, *The Life and Text of Julian of Norwich: The Poetics of Enclosure* (New York: Peter Lang, 1997), 10.

46. A.C. Spearing, *Julian of Norwich: Revelations of Divine Love*, Elisabeth Spearing, trans., (London: Penguin, 1998), ix.

47. Grace M. Jantzen, *Julian of Norwich: Mystic and Theologian* (Mahwah, NJ: Paulist Press, 2000), 16.

48. Watson and Jenkins, *The Writings of Julian of Norwich*, 7.

49. Marion Glasscoe, ed., *Julian of Norwich: A Revelation of Love* (Exeter, UK: University of Exeter Press, 1993), xviii.

50. Blomefield wrote, "For many ages this nunnery was a school or place of education for the young ladies of the chief families of the diocese of Norwich, who boarded with and were educated by the nuns." But Blomefield does not mention (and apparently did not know) that that school existed only in the fifteenth century.

51. Edward II's queen, Isabella, for instance, could read, but could not write (see Alison Weir, *Queen Isabella* [New York: Ballantine, 2005], 11). "Latin 'made you officially literate,' but few lay folk (even aristocrats) knew it. French was common language for

great families" (Norman Cantor, *The Meaning of the Middle Ages* [Boston: Allyn & Bacon, 1973]).

52. However, note that Wycliffe's English Bible was available to Julian. See Article 9, "Julian's Bible," page 52.

53. In a culture like Julian's where printed matter was rare, people's memories were far better developed and reliable than in our present culture.

54. Source: Norwich Consistory Court, Harsyk f. 194^v [Reed] (cited in Norman Tanner, *The Church in Late Medieval Norwich 1370– 1532* (Toronto, ON, Canada: Pontifical Institute of Mediaeval Studies, 1984).

55. Source: Thomas Edmund; Register of Thomas Arundel I, f. 540^d 19 May [Emund]. (Lambeth Palace Library), (cited in Tanner). Aylsham (modern spelling) was situated directly next to the villages of (1) Erpingham (the Erpingham family estate and in whose church Julian Erpingham's father was interred), (2) Oxnead (in the holding of Julian Erpingham's first husband, Roger Hauteyn), (3) Colby (the holding of John de Coleby who killed Roger Hauteyn), and (4) Ingham (where the killing took place). It would be likely, therefore, that the clerical testator, Thomas Emund, had been a personal friend of Julian Erpingham, and her family and his legacy to her may have been a result of that friendship. Otherwise, it seems unusual (thought not impossible) that a resident of Aylsham would bequeath a legacy to a Norwich anchorite.

56. Source: *The Book of Margery Kempe*, trans. Barry Windeatt, (London: Penguin Classics, 2000).

57. Source: E.F. Jacob, *The Register of Henry Chichele, Archbishop of Canterbury, 1414–1443* (Oxford, UK: Clarendon Press, 1938), ii, fols. 170v–171 (cited in C&W).

58. Source: Jacob, *The Register of Henry Chichele*, ii, fol. 95 (cited in C&W).

59. Source: Norwich Consistory Court, 86, Surflete (cited in Glasscoe).

60. Jacob, *The Register of Henry Chichele,* II:381.

61. Jacob, *The Register of Henry Chichele,* II:600.

62. Cited in Ann K. Warren, *Anchorites and Their Patrons in Medieval England* (Berkeley: University of California Press, 1986), 283–85. Also in Jacob, *The Register of Henry Chichele.*

63. Note Julian's own *Revelations,* Chapter 51: "He made Man's soul to be His own City and His dwelling place. . ." and Chapter 52: "He is with us in our soul eternally dwelling. . . ." And Chapter 54: ". . . We ought highly to rejoice that God dwells in our soul. . . ." However, it seems impossible to discover a specific reference in Scripture to which Julian refers here.

64. Margery Kempe, *The Book of Margery Kempe,* ed. Lynn Staley (Kalamazoo, MI: Medieval Institute Publications, 1996), Bk I, Pt I. My translation.

65. "The note of reassurance was struck at the very outset of the *Ordo Visitandi,* . . . The priest was directed to hold up before the face of the dying person the image of the Crucifix 'that in that image they may adore their redeemer and have in mind his passion, which he endured for their sins.' . . . This was the standard opening of the service of visitation, and many texts devised to guide the clergy in their deathbed ministrations do little more than elaborate it. . . . 'Put alle thi trust in his passion and in his deth, and thenke onli theron, and non other thing. With his deth medil the and wrappe the therinne . . . and have the crosse to fore the, and sai thus;—I wot wel thou art nought my God, but thou art imagened aftir him, and makest me have more mind of him after who thou art imagened. Lord fader of hevene, the deth of oure lord Jhu Crist, thi sone, wiche is here imagened, I set betwene the and my evil dedis, and the desert of Jhu Crist I offre for that I shuld have deservid, and have nought.'" (Eamon Duffy, *The Stripping of the Altars* [New Haven: Yale University Press, 1992], 314–15).

66. Clocks were rare in England in Julian's day, present in only three or four cathedrals—one of which was Norwich's (although that

original clock was apparently inside the building for the use of the monks, had no face, and was not visible to the public).

67. See C&W, *Showings*, 631. Note: refers to the Middle English *Dialogue of St. Anselm and of our Lady* where we are told that the eclipse on Good Friday ". . . duryd iij houris, vu to the houre of none, that ys to vndurstond iij of clok aftyr noonn."

68. "Particularly remarkable is the shift of the word 'none' meaning the ninth hour, or mid-afternoon, to the meaning midday (noon in the modern sense). This occurred in English by 1300 but is scarcely visible by our period [that is, 1075–1225]. Even as late as the last quarter of the thirteenth century it still made sense to talk of Christ's three hours on the cross extending from 'midday' to 'noon.' " (Robert Bartlett, *England Under the Norman and Angevin Kings: 1075–1225* [Oxford, UK: Clarendon Press, 2000], 834.)

69. See Nicholas Whyte, "Hours and Unequal Hours," a dissertation toward an MPhil degree at Clare College, Cambridge, at <http://explorers.whyte.com/hours.htm>.

70. There were anchorholds in England of no more than a *very* ascetic 12 square feet (3' x 4' or 2' x 6'); others we know of were 6'8" x 4'4" and 8' x 8', and one is on record as being 29' by 24'. Julian's cell seems to have been of about average size.

71. R.H. Flood, *A Description of St. Julian's Church, Norwich, and an Account of Dame Julian's Connection With It* (Norwich: Wherry Press, 1936), says the nave roof was tiled and the chancel roof was thatched.

72. In large houses and castles, the seldom-changed floor rushes often hid food scraps, dog feces, and vermin; Julian's cell was certainly not as foul.

73. A "squint" window (sometimes called a "hagioscope") was usually a cone-shaped opening through the wall of the church, wide on the outside and narrow on the inside (so one could see through it fairly easily and light could come in, but no one could climb through it). There are some surviving early Saxon squint windows in the north wall of St. Julian's. Sometimes the squint

was in the shape of two narrow slots in the shape of a cross. (The present window between the Julian Shrine Chapel and the church is modern, but the bottom of it may have been part of the original squint.)

74. The familiar altar tabernacle for the reserved sacrament had not been invented in fourteenth-century England. The sacrament was reserved in a pyx hanging over the altar on a pulley arrangement.

75. Ordinarily a fourteenth-century layperson in England would receive Holy Communion only once a year—at Easter—and only after making a Confession. It was characteristic for holy anchorites and nuns, on the other hand, to receive Communion at least on fifteen Holy Days during the year (also after Confession). In 1413 Margery Kempe received special permission from Archbishop Arundel to receive Communion weekly.

76. A caution was given in *Ancrene Wisse* that there be *two* servants, so that if one had gone to market, the anchorite would never be left wholly alone.

77. Usually the unpaid servant girl(s) lived there; less frequently they slept elsewhere. In many cases, the lay sister had a recognized claim to the anchorhold to live there as an anchorite herself when the woman she served died.

78. Only one record survives that gives proper measurements for an anchorhold window: 21" x 21".

79. At present, there is only a churchyard there, but early medieval maps show a small lane (called "Freway" or "Horn's Lane") leading directly to the south side of St. Julian's Church where Julian's cell was (and where the main door to the church was before it was moved to the north side).

80. Many modern accounts portray the anchorite as watching the changing seasons through the window or looking at the face of the visitors. Neither would have happened.

81. None of these variations is likely for Julian's cell. An old photograph that the author has seen (now sadly lost) showed

a just-visible roofline mark on the church wall where Julian's cell would have been. The original anchorhold was apparently considerably enlarged at a later date so that the priest's door at St. Julian's (characteristically on the south wall of a church chancel) had to be moved to the north wall. There is other evidence that at a later time there were two male anchorites sharing the cell at St. Julian's. (It should be noted that in a 1821 reconstruction of a medieval map of monasteries in Norwich [R. Taylor, *Index Monasticus*] an "Anchorage" is shown as a separate building west of St. Julian's church.)

82. In the 1362 *Vision of Piers Plowman*, Langland refers to "a chamber with a chimney."

83. The Benedictine monastery at Norwich Cathedral alone burned 200,000 bales of peat a year. There was also a strong local tradition that no fire was to be lit for heat after Easter Day.

84. A cresset light was a deep saucer or bowl or funnel made of stone or pottery that held oil or wax. There was usually a handle on one side and an indented lip on the other to receive a wick.

85. Since beeswax was the only wax available and was extremely expensive, the rush light was the most common lighting: a short length of rush was dipped in wax or tallow, and attached by a clip to a specially designed holder.

86. Some medieval beds were strung with ropes, but see Julian's Chapter 12: "And this blood looked so plenteous that it seemed to me, if it had been as plenteous in nature and in matter during that time, it would have made the bed all bloody and have *overflowed around the outside*."

87. This assumes that Julian could write—not always true for a woman. Most highborn women would have learned to *read*, but reading and writing did not automatically go together.

88. An anchorite would be obligated to recite at least some form of the Monastic Offices, and books, being entirely handwritten and on parchment or vellum, were hugely expensive. Even small monastery libraries might own only a half-dozen books or so.

However, over 800 Books of Hours have survived in England, so there is a reasonable probability that Julian may have owned one. (Next to St. Julian's parish is the parish St. Peter Parmentergate [a "parmenter" is a maker of parchment, and "gate" is the Danish word for "street" or "way"], so Julian grew up near a community of parchment makers. Paper was not made commercially in England until the 1450s.)

89. Notice that in her Chapter 51, Julian's Adam/Poor Man wore a tunic "tight fitting for him and short, as it were but a hand's width below the knee, undecorated."

90. Dorothy Hartley, *Lost Country Life* (New York: Pantheon, 1979), 136.

91. During the late fourteenth century, *secular* shoes (called "crakows") became very long and pointed. Edward III decreed 2 inch points as maximum, but under Richard II some were as long as 18 inches.

92. The *Ancrene Wisse* said: "wear no haircloth, not hedgehog skins; and do not beat yourselves therewith, nor with a scourge of leather thongs, nor leaded; and do not with holly nor with briars cause yourselves to bleed without leave of your confessor."

93. Michael Gore, "Sin Will Be No Shame," *Spiritual Life*, Fall 2000.

94. England's famed roast beef was seldom known in the fourteenth century. Except in royal or noble palaces, most beef came from old, nonproducing milk cows and was served in pottage or stew.

95. Much based on Samuel Pegge, *The Forme of Cury: Compiled by the Master-Cooks of Richard II: 1390.*

96. *Ancrene Wisse.*

97. Quoted in Hartley, 124–25.

98. However, one unusually large anchorhold (for a priest, of course) was recorded as including a wooden bathtub.

99. William Langland, *Piers Plowman*, trans. J.F. Goodrich (London: Harmondsworth, 1966), 18, quoted in J.M. Theilmann, "The Regulation of Public Health in Late Medieval England" in *The Age of Richard II*, ed. James L. Gillespie (Stroud, Gloucestershire, UK: Sutton, 1997).

100. In some larger anchorholds, a crypt or coffin was actually part of the furnishings: it was included to remind the anchorite of the transient nature of earthly life. *Ancrene Wisse* recommends that anchoresses should "each day scrape up the earth of their graves, in which they will rot."

101. Alban Butler, *The Lives of the Fathers, Martyrs, and Other Principal Saints* (Baltimore: John Murphy & Co., 1873), 152. In later years, several abridged editions of this four-volume work appeared, called simply *Butler's Lives of the Saints*.

102. Like a number of French-born English monarchs, Henry II was born in 1133 in Le Mans, France. He was crowned King of England at Westminster Abbey in 1154 and was buried in Fontrevault Abbey in his native France. If Butler is accurate here, it would suggest that St. Julian's was rebuilt and dedicated in the early twelfth century.

103. Francis Blomefield, *History and Antiquities of the County of Norfolk*, Vol. 4, 80.

104. The ruins of St. Edward's were still visible in the early eighteenth century, but have disappeared completely in modern times.

105. Flood, *A Description of St. Julian's Church,* 4.

106. Claude J.W. Messent, *The Monastic Remains of Norfolk & Suffolk* (Norwich: H.W. Hunt, 1934), 54.

107. <http://www.origins.org.uk/genuki/NFK/places/n/norwich/church/built.shtml>

108. Carrow Priory also held lands, rents, and tithes in some seventy-four other parishes in Norfolk and Suffolk, and the Prioress erected her "town house" directly across the lane from St. Julian's Church.

109. The extract is from *Plunkett's History of Norwich* and is used with the permission of George A. F. Plunkett. <http://www.the-plunketts.freeserve.co.uk/KingStreet.htm> Note: The Rev. Canon Michael McLean (then Rector of St. Julian's) maintains the font was actually installed there ca. 1978.

110. Barbara Tuchman, *A Distant Mirror: The Calamitous Fourteenth Century* (New York: Random House, 1978).

111. It was Clement V who, intimidated by King Philip IV of France, falsely charged the Knights Templar with heresy, immorality, and other abuses and dissolved their Order.

112. Gregory XI was the pope who formally condemned the writings of the English heretic John Wycliffe.

113. Because the seventy years of absence from Rome corresponded to the seventy years of Israel's captivity in Babylon, the time was referred to by Petrarch as the "Babylonian Captivity of the Papacy."

114. Among other things, he made twenty-six new cardinals in one day, effectively overwhelming the votes of his enemies in the College of Cardinals, and sold off Church properties to raise funds for an army.

115. Urban not only excommunicated Clement, but declared him the Antichrist.

116. Urban apparently died from a fall from his mule, but not without rumors of poisoning.

117. *Revelations*, Chapter 2. (It should be noted that "cowde" refers to a *past* time, that is, when she experienced the Showings, she *was* [at that time] unable to write—suggesting that at a later time she may have learned Latin [and writing?].)

118. Alister McGrath, *In the Beginning: The Story of the King James Bible and How It Changed a Nation, a Language, and a Culture* (New York: Doubleday, 2001), 33.

119. Frederic Madden and Josiah Forshall, eds., *The Holy Bible ... in the Earliest English Versions Made from the Latin Vulgate by John Wycliffe and his Followers* (Oxford, UK: Oxford University Press, 1850).
Francis Aidan Gasquet, *The Old English Bible and Other Essays* (Port Washington, NY: Kennikat Press, 1969), 102 seq. (This book was first published in 1897.)

120. John Eadie, *The English Bible: An External and Critical History of the Various English Translations of Scripture*, Vol. 1 (London: Macmillan, 1876), 89.

121. Anne Hudson, *The First Compete English Bible* <http://www.tyndale.org/TSJ/2/hudson.html>

122. Richard Rex, *The Lollards*, Palgrave imprint (Hampshire, UK: St. Martin's Press, 2002), 75.

123. Benson Bobrick, *Wide as the Waters: The Story of the English Bible and the Revolution It Inspired* (New York: Simon & Schuster, 2001), 137.

124. S. L. Ollard & Gordon Crosse, eds., *A Dictionary of English Church History* (London: A.R. Gordon Mowbray & Co., 1912), 658.

125. Bobrick, 51.

126. Wycliffe called anchoritic life "the cursed spirit of falsehood." Rex, 108.

127. Rex, 123.

128. Of course, if Julian *were* Julian Phelip (née Erpingham) she would certainly have been wealthy enough to have afforded such a Bible. We also know that rules of the Austin Friary specifically allowed the loaning out of a library book as long as a duplicate remained in the library.

129. M.S. Luria and R.L. Hoffman, ed., *Middle English Lyrics* (New York: W.W. Norton, 1974), 173.

130. Denise Baker, "The Image of God: Contrasting Configurations in Julian of Norwich's *Showings* and Walter Hilton's *Scale of Perfection*," in Sandra J. McEntire, ed., *Julian of Norwich: A Book of Essays*, Garland Medieval Casebooks, vol. 21 (New York: Garland, 1998), 162..

131. See Fernand Mossé, *A Handbook of Middle English,* trans. James Walker (Baltimore: Johns Hopkins University Press, 1968) and OED for "May [2]."

132. See F.H. Stratmann (Bradley, Henry, rev. ed.), *A Middle-English Dictionary, etc.* (Oxford, UK: Oxford University Press, 1995) for the verb *can*.

133. See Stratmann for the verb *willen*.

134. Julia Bolton Holloway, *Julian of Norwich: Showing of Love*.

135. Elizabeth A. Hoff, "A Re-Hearing of 'Sir Gawain and the Green Knight'" in *Essays in Medieval Studies*, (Chicage, Illinois Medieval Association. <http://www.luc.edu/publications/medieval/vol2/2ch5.html>.

136. Colledge and Walsh, *Showings*, 282.

137. From Wordsworth's "Ode: Intimations of Immorality from Recollections of Early Childhood" published in *Poems in Two Volumes* (1807).

138. A.I. Doyle, York Manuscripts Conference, (University of York, UK, July 1991).

139. St. Augustine, *Confessions* I, 1.

140. See Eithne Wilkins, *The Rose Garden Game: A Tradition of Beads and Flowers* (New York: Herder & Herder, 1969).

141. Bonaventure: *Lignum Vitae*, Fr. VIII, 30.

142. Caroline Bynum, "Violent Imagery in Medieval Piety," Lecture for German Historical Institute, 2001.

143. A small bronze crucifix, gilded and enameled, from the late fourteenth or early fifteenth century was discovered beneath the floor of St. Crouch, Norwich, in 1838, apparently hidden from the Puritan iconoclasts.

144. J. Wentworth Day, *Norwich and the Broads* (London: B.T. Batsworth, 1953).

145. Sir Thomas Browne, "Sir Thomas Browne's Norfolk": extracts from the writings of Sir Thomas Browne relating to the natural history and archeology of Norfolk in the seventeenth century (Dereham, Norfolk, UK: The Larks Press, 1989). I am indebted to Mr. James Eason of the University of Chicago for the discovery and location of this obscure pamphlet.

146. J.M. Lambert, et al, *The Making of the Broads* (London: Royal Geographic Society, 1960).

147. Lambert, *The Making of the Broads*.

148. Lambert, *The Making of the Broads*, 16.

149. Henry Ellis, ed., *Chronica Johannis de Oxenedes* (London: Longman, Brown, Green, Longmans and Roberts, 1859).

150. W. A. Dutt, *The Norfolk Broads* (London: Methuen, 1905).

151. Bartholomaei de Cotton, *Historia Anglicana* (London: Longman, Green, 1859).

152. H. Swinden, *The History and Antiquities of the Ancient Burgh of Great Yarmouth* (Norwich, UK: John Crouse, 1772).

153. "About Norfolk Weather" <http://www.about-norfolk.com> (9/8/03).

154. Brian Fagan, *The Little Ice Age: How Climate Made History 1300–1850* (New York: Basic Books, 2001), 62–63.

155. Godfrey Chatfield, "The High Tides of Lincolnshire" <http://www.sjs.sd83.bc.ca/museum/thepast/geog/hightide> (03/26/04).

156. Staley, ed., *The Book of Margery Kempe*.

157. Robert S. Gottfried, *The Black Death: Natural and Human Disaster in Medieval Europe* (New York: The Free Press, 1983), 163.

158. F. A. Gasquet, *The Great Pestilence* (London: Marshall, Hamilton & Kent, 1893).

159. Jack Hirshleifer, "Disaster and Recovery: The Black Death in Western Europe" (The Rand Corporation, RM-4700-TAB [February 1966]). Note: This study was undertaken for the U.S. Department of Defense to anticipate possible results of nuclear attack.

160. Richard Fletcher, *The Barbarian Conversion: From Paganism to Christianity* (New York: Henry Holt, 1997), 483.

161. The only city in Europe to avoid the epidemic was Milan. When three households were affected, the city fathers bricked up the windows and doors, sealing the victims inside . . . with their rats.

162. It was not called "the Black Death" until many years later, probably because the blood vessels burst and the skin turned blackish. Some suggest, however, that this term is a mistranslation of the Latin *atra mors*, *atra* meaning "fierce" or "terrible" as well as "black."

163. Twentieth-century archaeology in Scotland and the work of two scholars, Twigg and Herlihy, suggest that it may have involved anthrax poisoning as well. Herlihy has also suggested that it was a form of "galloping tuberculosis." (David Herlihy, *The Black Death and the Transformation of the West* [Cambridge, MA: Harvard University Press, 1997].)

164. Robert Gottfried, *Epidemic Disease in Fifteenth Century England* (New Brunswick, NJ: Rutgers University Press, 1978), 142–50.

165. Blomefield, *An Essay Towards a Topographical History of the County of Norfolk,* Vol. 3 (1739).

166. Herlihy, *The Black Death and the Transformation of the West*, 42.

167. Ole J. Benedictow, *The Black Death 1346–1353: The Complete History* (Woodbridge, Suffolk, UK: Boydell Press, 2005). Benedictow sets the total at 50 million (out of 80 million) in all Europe.

168. Emmanuel Le Roy Ladurie, *Times of Feast, Times of Famine: A History of Climate Since the Year 1000,* trans. Barbara Bray (New York: Farrar, Straus & Giroux, 1971), 16.

169. Thomas Cahill, *Pope John XXIII* (New York: Penguin/Viking, 2002), 41.

170. In her book *The Dolorous Passion of Our Lord Jesus Christ,* Sr. Anne Catherine Emmerich (1774–1824) wrote: "Seraphia was the name of the brave woman who thus dared to confront the enraged multitude; she was the wife of Sirach, one of the councilors belonging to the Temple." (This is the same book used by Mel Gibson in his film *The Passion of the Christ.*) Also, in the apocryphal fourth-century "Acts (or "Gospel") of Pilate," "Veronica" is the name given to the woman with a flow of blood (Matthew 9:20).

171. See Alan Deighton, "Julian of Norwich's Knowledge of the Life of St. John of Beverley," Oxford University Press, Notes and Queries, Vol. 238 [New Series, Vol. 40], no. 4, December 1993, 441ff.

172. Deighton, "Julian of Norwich's Knowledge of the Life of St. John of Beverley," 442–43.

173. For thorough textual analyses, see Alan Deighton, "The Sins of Saint John of Beverley: The Case of the Dutch 'volksboek' *Jan van Beverley*," *Leuvense Bijdragen* 82 (1993). Note that the mixture of poetry and prose in one text suggests its origin in a theatrical (perhaps a miracle) play.

174. British Library Ms Royal 10 E IV, commencing on fol. 113v.

175. *Leuvense Bijdragen*, 237–38.

176. Alan Deighton, "The Literary Context of the Wall-Painting at Idsworth, Hampshire," *The Antiquaries Journal*, 1993, Vol. 73; seq. Also see "The Church of St. Hubert, Idsworth, Hampshire" at <http://www.hull.ac.uk/Hull/GR_Web/Idsworth.htm>.

177. In the Middle Ages, he was believed to have been the Athenian Areopagite converted by Paul in Acts 17:34 but has since been identified as probably a fifth- or sixth-century Syrian. He was the author of several works, including *Celestial Hierarchy*, *Ecclesiastical Hierarchy*, and *Divine Names*.

178. In 1235 he was made Bishop of Lincoln (England's largest diocese at the time). He witnessed the confirmation of the Magna Carta in 1236, attended the Council of Lyons in 1245, and preached in Rome in 1250. That his work was known in Julian's Norwich is confirmed by the 1481 will of a Norwich gentlewoman, whose legacies to a convent of Franciscan Sisters includes the work of Grosseteste.

179. Colm Luibheid, trans., "The Divine Names," II, 5, in *Pseudo-Dionysius: The Complete Works* (Mahwah, NJ: Paulist Press, 1987).

180. Luibheid, trans., "The Divine Names," v. 6.

181. Austin Lane Poole, ed., *Medieval England*, v. II (London: Oxford, 1958), 587–88.

182. Robert Grosseteste, *On Light,* trans. Clare Riedl (Milwaukee, WI: Marquette University Press, 1978).

183. Cynthea Masson, "The Point of Coincidence: Rhetoric and the Apophatic in Julian of Norwich's Showings" in *Julian of Norwich: A Book of Essays,* ed. Sandra J. McEntire, (New York: Garland Publishing, 1998), 162–64.

184. Carmen Bendan Davis, "'God In a Poynt': What Julian of Norwich Knew About Modern Science" in Proceedings of Peaceworks: 3rd Triennial Conference of Women Scholars of Religion & Theology, Australian Catholic University, 2004.

185. Tertullian, *Apologeticum*.

186. *Didascalia Apostolorum*, V.19.4.

187. Eusebius, *History of the Church*, II.7.1.

188. *Historia Scholastica*, Chapter 75.

189. From a letter to Mr. G.T. Edwards, 29 January 1890, in Wilfrid Ward, *The Life of John Henry Cardinal Newman, etc.*, v. 2 (London: Longmans, Green, 1912).

190. "It appears in British Museum MS. Harl. 1269, f.158 (AD 1370); in a prayer book of Cardinal Peter of Luxembourg (d. 1387) preserved at Avignon; and on an inscription of Moorish workmanship on the gates of the Alcazar in Seville (c. 1364)." F.L. Cross & E.A. Livingstone, *The Oxford Dictionary of the Christian Church* (Oxford, UK: Oxford University Press, 1988), 58.

191. *Imitatio Christi*, Bk. II/1, 1425.

192. *De Civitate Dei*, XV, 26: *PL* 41, 472.

193. *De Templo Salamonis*, VIII: *PL* 91, 753.

194. Miri Rubin, "Historical Perspectives on the Art of Dying in Europe," lecture delivered at King's College, London, 11 October 2002.

195. Duffy, *The Stripping of the Altars*, 249.

196. Quoted in Duffy, *The Stripping of the Altars*, 251.

197. Ancrene Wisse, in *Anchoritic Spirituality*, trans. Savage §155.

198. Emile Mâle, *Religious Art in France: the Late Middle Ages* (Princeton, NJ: Princeton University Press, 1986).

199. Duffy, *The Stripping of the Altars*, 239.

200. Gillian Lindt Gollin, *Moravians in Two Worlds: A Study of Changing Communities* (New York: Columbia University Press, 1967).

201. "Heathen men" for Julian would have meant the Muslim Saracens.

202. It is sad for us, of course, but Julian was a woman of her day, and she followed the general belief that the Jews "that did Him to death" were "Christ killers" and were universally damned.

203. See J.P.H. Clark, "Predestination in Christ According to Julian of Norwich," *The Downside Review*, v. 100, No. 339, April 1982, 79–91.

204. Paula S. Datsko Barker, "The Motherhood of God in Julian of Norwich's Theology," *The Downside Review*, v. 100, No. 341, October 1982, 290–304. (At this writing, Baker is Associate Professor of Historical Theology at Seabury-Western Theological Seminary.)

205. Caroline Walker Bynum, *Jesus as Mother* (Berkeley: University of California Press, 1984), 140.

206. Fr. John-Julian, OJN, *A Lesson of Love: The Revelations of Julian of Norwich* (Bloomington, IN: iUniverse, 2003), Chapter 60.

207. Fr. John-Julian, OJN, *A Lesson of Love*, Chapter 60:"...though it is true that our bodily birth is but little, lowly, and simple compared to our spiritual birth, yet it is He who does it within the created mothers by whom it is done."

208. Fr. John-Julian, OJN, *A Lesson of Love*, Chapter 60:"...all our debt that we owe by God's bidding to fatherhood and motherhood, because of God's Fatherhood and Motherhood is fulfilled in the loving of God. . . ."

209. The author is especially grateful for the invaluable assistance of Dr. Hoyt Greeson, retired Professor of English at Laurentian University, Sudbury, Ontario, in analyzing the word *behovabil*.

210. Glasscoe, ed., *Julian of Norwich*, 144.

211. Edmund Colledge, OSA, and James Walsh, SJ, eds., *A Book of Showings to the Anchoress Julian of Norwich, Part Two* (Toronto, ON, Canada: Pontifical Institute of Medieval Studies,1978), 750.

212. Sister Anna Maria Reynolds, CP, and Julia Bolton Holloway, eds., *Julian of Norwich: Showing of Love: Extant Texts and Translation* (Firenze [Florence], Italy: Sismel, 2001), 644. Note: In considerable correspondence between us, Dr. Greeson now suspects

that in his glossary definition he may have accepted MED too uncritically.

213. Mossé, *A Handbook of Middle English*, 427.

214. Stratmann, *A Middle-English Dictionary,* 62.

215. Holloway, *Julian of Norwich*.

216. *The Middle English Dictionary* (Ann Arbor, MI: University of Michigan Press, 2001).

217. Denys Turner, " 'Sin is Behovely,' " 409.

218. "Christ [is] the power of God and the wisdom of God" (1 Corinthians 1:24); "Christ Jesus . . . became for us wisdom from God" (1 Corinthians 1:30).

219. *Capita de caritate* 3.25 (tr. Berthold Maximos) says that God gave humans power, wisdom, and goodness so humans could be the image of God's own power, wisdom, and goodness. Also see Ian A. McFarland, "Developing an Apophatic Christocentrism: Lessons from St. Maximus the Confessor" in *Theology Today* 60/2 (2003), 200–14.

220. *Divine Names*, Chapter 7.

221. "The Supreme power, wisdom, and benevolence of the Creator shine forth in created things in so far as the bodily senses inform the interior senses": Bonaventure, *Itinerarium mentis in Deum*, trans. and ed. Philotheus Boehneer (New York: Saint Bonaventure University Press,1956), 45.

222. "Charity [love] and goodness are especially attributed to the Holy Ghost, as power is to the Father and wisdom to the Son": Aquinas II-II, Q. xiv.

223. See Deeana C. Klepper, *The Insight of Unbelievers: Nicholas of Lyra and Christian Reading of Jewish Text in the Later Middle Ages*, p. 93, where the plural name of God (*Elohim*) was explained by the rabbis as derived from God's qualities of power, wisdom, and love. (Noted by Julia Holloway at <http://www.umilta.net/judaism.html>.)

224. *Augsburg Confession,* Article 1, "Of God."

225. Samuel Johnson, "The Rambler," David Greene, ed., in *The Major Works*, Oxford World's Classics (Oxford, UK, Oxford University Press, 1984), #32, 1750.

226. In his introduction to George Fox's Journal.

227. "Fame, wisdom, love, and power were mine . . ." from George Gordon, Lord Byron, "The Hebrew Melodies."

228. "There is but one living and true God, everlasting, without body, parts, or passions; of infinite power, wisdom, and goodness; the Maker, and Preserver of all things both visible and invisible."

229. "The moral law presupposes the rational order, established among creatures for their good and to serve their final end, by the power, wisdom, and goodness of the Creator" (Catechism 1951).

230. Biblically and doctrinally among Christians the personification of "Wisdom" has always been feminine, in some instances to such a degree that Wisdom is characterized as the feminine aspect of God. "What pre-Christian Judaism said of Wisdom and Philo also of the Logos, Paul and the others say of Jesus. The role that Proverbs, ben Sira, etc. ascribe to Wisdom, these earliest Christians ascribe to Jesus." (James D.G. Dunn, *Christology in the Making* [Grand Rapids, MI: Eerdmans, 2005], 167.)

☞ SOURCES AND RECOMMENDED READING

1. JULIAN TEXTS AND TRANSLATIONS

Baker, Denise Nowakowski. *The Showings of Julian of Norwich*. New York: W.W. Norton, 2004.

Beer, Frances. *Julian of Norwich: Revelations of Divine Love: The Motherhood of God*. Cambridge, UK: D.S. Brewer, 1998.

Chambers, P. Franklin. *Juliana of Norwich*. London: Victor Gollanz, Ltd., 1955.

Colledge, Edmund, and James Walsh, translators and editors. *Julian of Norwich: Showings*. Mahwah, NJ: Paulist Press, 1978.

———. *A Book of Showings to the Anchoress Julian of Norwich*, Vols. 1 and 2. Toronto, ON, Canada: Pontifical Institute of Medieval Studies, 1978.

Crampton, Georgia Ronan. *Shewings of Julian of Norwich*. Kalamazoo, MI: Medieval Institute Publications, 1994.

Del Mastro, M.L., translator. *The Revelation of Divine Love in Sixteen Showings Made to Dame Julian*. Liguori, MO: Triumph Books, 1994.

Glasscoe, Marion, editor. *Julian of Norwich: A Revelation of Love*. Exeter, UK: University of Exeter Press, 1986 (and 1993).

Hartford, Dundas, editor and translator. *Comfortable Words For Christ's Lovers*. London: H.R. Allenson, Ltd., 1911.

Holloway, Julia Bolton. *Julian of Norwich: Showing of Love*. Collegeville, MN: Liturgical Press, 2003.

Huddleston, Dom Roger, OSB. *Revelations of Divine Love*. London: Burns Oates, 1927, 1952.

John-Julian, OJN, Fr., translator and editor. *A Lesson of Love: The Revelations of Julian of Norwich*. New York: Walker, 1989. Second edition, Lincoln, NE: iUniverse, 2003.

Milton, Ralph. *The Essence of Julian: A Paraphrase of Julian of Norwich's Revelations of Divine Love.* Kelonah, BC, Canada: Northstone, 2002.

Reynolds, Anna Maria, editor. *A Shewing of God's Love.* London: Sheed & Ward, 1958.

Reynolds, Anna Maria, and Julia Bolton Holloway. *Julian of Norwich: Showing of Love: Extant Texts and Translation.* Florence, Italy: Sismel–Edizioni del Galluzzo, 2001.

Skinner, John, translator. *Julian of Norwich: Revelation of Love.* New York: Doubleday/Image, 1997.

Spearing, Elizabeth, translator. *The Revelations of Divine Love.* London: Penguin Books, Ltd., 1998.

Upjohn, Sheila. *All Shall Be Well: Revelations of Divine Love of Julian of Norwich.* London: Darton, Longman & Todd, 1992.

Walsh, James, translator. *The Revelations of Divine Love of Julian of Norwich.* London: Burns & Oates, 1961.

Warrack, Grace, editor. *Revelations of Divine Love: A Version from the MS in the British Museum.* London: Methuen, 1901.

Watson, Nicholas, and Jacqueline Jenkins. *The Writings of Julian of Norwich: A Vision Showed to a Devout Woman and A Revelation of Love.* University Park, PA: Pennsylvania State University Press, 2006.

Wolters, Clifton, editor. *Revelations of Divine Love.* London: Penguin Books, 1966 (1974).

2. Background on Julian of Norwich

Aers, David and Lynn Staley. *The Powers of the Holy: Religion, Politics and Gender in Late Medieval Culture.* University Park, PA: Pennsylvania State University Press, 1996.

Ambrose, Tinsley. *Neighbour Kind and Known: Spirituality of Julian of Norwich.* Dublin, Ireland: Columba Press, 1997.

Anderson, Derek N. *Julian of Norwich's Nonviolent Account of Salvation.* Chicago: Loyola University Chicago, 2005.

Barker, Paula S. Datsko. "The Motherhood of God in Julian of Norwich's Theology." *Downside Review*, 100 (Oct. 1982), 290–304.

Bartlett, Anne Clark, and Thomas Bestul, editors. *Cultures of Piety*. Ithaca, NY: Cornell University Press, 1999.

Buber, Martin. *Ecstatic Confessions: The Heart of Mysticism*. Translated by Esther Cameron. Edited by Paul Mendes-Flohr. Syracuse, NY: Syracuse University Press, 1996.

Bynum, Caroline Walker. *Fragmentation and Redemption: Essays on Gender and the Human Body in Medieval Religions*. New York: Zone Books, 1992.

Colledge, Eric, editor. *The Medieval Mystics of England*. New York: Charles Scribners, 1961.

Delumeau, Jean. *History of Paradise: The Garden of Eden in Myth and Tradition*. Translated by Matthew O'Connell. New York: Continuum, 1995.

Duffy, Eamon. *The Stripping of the Altars: Traditional Religion in England c. 1400–c. 1580*. New Haven, CT: Yale University Press, 1992.

Dupré, Louis, and James A. Wiseman, editors. *Light from Light: An Anthology of Christian Mysticism*. Mahwah, NJ: Paulist Press, 1988.

Furlong, Monica. *Visions and Longing: Medieval Women Mystics*. Boston: Shambala, 1996.

Gatta, Julian. *Three Spiritual Directors for our Time: Julian of Norwich, the Cloud of Unknowing, Walter Hilton*. Cambridge, MA: Cowley, 1987.

Glasscoe, Marion, editor. *The Medieval Mystical Tradition in England*. Exeter, UK: University of Exeter Press, 1980.

Glasscoe, Marion. *English Medieval Mystics: Games of Faith*. London: Longman, 1933.

Grant, Patrick. *Spiritual Discourse and the Meaning of Persons*. New York: St. Martin's, 1994.

Hodgson, Geraldine E. *English Mystics*. London: Mowbray, 1922.

Inge, William Ralph. *Studies of Eight Mystics*. London: John Murray, 1901.

Jones, E.A., editor. *The Medieval Mystical Tradition in England.* Papers read at Charney Manor, July 2004. Woodbridge, Suffolk, UK: Boydell & Brewer, 2004.

Jones, Rufus M. *The Flowering of Mysticism: The Friends of God in the Fourteenth Century.* New York: Macmillan, 1939.

Luria, M.S., and R.L. Hoffman, editors. *Middle English Lyrics.* New York: W.W. Norton, 1974.

Knowlton, Sr. Mary Arthur. *The Influence of Richard Rolle and of Julian of Norwich on the Middle English Lyrics.* The Hague, Netherlands: Mouton & Co., NV, 1973.

Mahan, Susan M. Thrift. "The Christian Anthropology of Julian of Norwich." PhD dissertation, Marquette University, 1998.

Marzac-Holland, Nicole. *Three Norfolk Mystics: Richelde de Faverches in Walsingham, Julian, Recluse in Norwich, Margery Kempe in Lynn.* Norfolk, UK: Isaacson, 1983.

Morton, James, translator. *The Ancren Riwle: A Treatise on the Rules and Duties of Monastic Life.* New York: AMS Press, 1968.

Nolan, Edward Peter. *Cry Out and Write: Feminine Poetics of Revelation.* New York: Continuum, 1994.

Nuth, Joan M. *God's Lovers in an Age of Anxiety: The Medieval English Mystics.* Maryknoll, NY: Orbis Books, 2001.

Pepler, Conrad, OP. *The English Religious Heritage.* St. Louis, MO: Herder, 1958.

Person, Henry Axel. *Cambridge Middle English Lyrics.* Seattle: University of Washington Press, 1953.

Riehle, Wolfgang. *The Middle English Mystics.* Edited by Bernard Standring. London: Routledge & Kegan Paul, 1977.

Watson, Nicholas. "Censorship and Cultural Change in Late-Medieval England: Vernacular Theology, the Oxford Translation Debate, and Arundel's Constitutions of 1409." *Speculum* 70 (1995), 822–64.

Windeatt, Barry, editor. *English Mystics of the Middle Ages.* Cambridge, UK: Cambridge University Press, 1994.

3. JULIAN OF NORWICH

Abbot, Christopher. *Julian of Norwich: Autobiography and Theology.* Cambridge, UK: D.S. Brewer, 1999.

Allchin, A.M. *Julian of Norwich.* Oxford, UK: Fairacres Publications, 1973.

Allchin, A.M., et al. *Julian of Norwich: Four Studies to Commemorate the Sixth Centenary of the Revelations of Divine Love.* Fairacres, Oxford, UK: SLG Press, 1975 (1976).

Baker, Denise Nowakowski. *Julian of Norwich's Showings: From Vision to Book.* Princeton, NJ: Princeton University Press, 1994.

Bradley, Ritamary. *Julian's Way: Practical Comments on Julian of Norwich.* San Francisco: Harper Collins, 1992.

Busshart, Helen. "Christ as Feminine in Julian of Norwich in the Light of the Psychology of C.G. Jung." PhD dissertation, Fordham University, 1985.

Calderwood, Robert H. *Julian's Challenge.* New York: Vantage, 1995.

Cooper, Austin, OMI. *Julian of Norwich: Reflections on Selected Texts.* Mystic, CT: Twenty-Third Publications, 1988.

Cranston, Pamela Lee. *Love Was His Meaning: An Introduction to Julian of Norwich.* Cincinnati, OH: Forward Movement, 2002.

Daffern, Adrian. *The Cross and Julian of Norwich.* Cambridge, UK: Grove Bks, Ltd, 1993.

Hemmel, Jennifer P. *God Is Our Mother: Julian of Norwich and the Medieval Christian Divinity.* Lewiston, NY: Edwin Mellen Press, 1999.

Hide, Kerrie. *Gifted Origins to Graced Fulfillment: The Soteriology of Julian of Norwich.* Collegeville, MN: Liturgical Press, 2001.

Hildesley, C. Hugh. *Journeying with Julian.* Harrisburg, PA: Morehouse, 1993.

Holloway, Julia Bolton. *The Julian Library Portfolio.* Florence, Italy: Julian Library Project, 1996.

Israel, Martin. *Revelations of Julian of Norwich.* N. Louth, Lincs., UK: Churches' Fellowship for Psychical & Spiritual Studies, 2000.

Jantzen, Grace. *Julian of Norwich: Mystic and Theologian.* Mahwah, NJ: Paulist Press, 2000.

Krantz, M. Diane F. *The Life and Text of Julian of Norwich: The Poetics of Enclosure.* New York: Peter Lang, 1997.

Leach, Kenneth, and Sr. Benedicta, SLG. *Julian Reconsidered.* Fairacres, Oxford, UK: SLG Press, 1988.

Llewelyn, Robert. *All Shall Be Well: The Spirituality of Julian of Norwich for Today.* Mahwah, NJ: Paulist Press, 1985.

———. *Enfolded in Love.* London: Darton, Longman & Todd, 2004.

———. *In Love Enclosed.* London: Darton, Longman & Todd, 1985.

———. *Love Bade Me Welcome.* London: Darton, Longman & Todd, 1984.

———. *With Pity Not With Blame: The Spirituality of Julian of Norwich and the Cloud of Unknowing for Today.* London: Darton, Longman & Todd, 1982.

Llewelyn, Robert, editor. *Julian: Woman of Our Day.* Mystic, CT: Twenty-Third Publications, 1987.

Long, Thomas L. "Julian of Norwich's 'Christ as Mother' and Medieval Constructions of Gender." Paper given at Madison Conference on English Studies, James Madison University, March 18, 1995.

Mary Paul, SLG, Sister. *All Shall Be Well: Julian of Norwich and the Compassion of God.* Fairacres, Oxford, UK: SLG Press, 1976.

McEntire, Sandra J., editor. *Julian of Norwich: A Book of Essays.* New York: Garland, 1998.

McGill, Kevin. *Julian of Norwich: Visionary or Mystic?* New York: Routledge, 2005.

Mountney, John Michael. *Sin Shall Be Glory as Revealed by Julian of Norwich.* London: Darton, Longman & Todd, 1992.

Nuth, Joan M. *Wisdom's Daughter: The Theology of Julian of Norwich.* New York: Crossroad, 1991.

Obbard, Elizabeth. *Introducing Julian: Woman of Norwich.* Hyde Park, NY: New City Press, 1995.

———. *Medieval Women Mystics: Gertrude the Great, Angela of Foligno, Birgitta of Sweden, Julian of Norwich.* Peabody, MA: New City Press, 2002.

Okulam, Frodo. *The Julian Mystique: Her Life and Teachings*. Mystic, CT: Twenty-Third Publications, 1998.

Palliser, Margaret Ann. *Christ, Our Mother of Mercy: Divine Mercy and Compassion in the Theology of the "Shewings" of Julian of Norwich*. Berlin, Germany: Walter de Gruyter, 1992.

Pelphrey, Brant. *Christ our Mother: Julian of Norwich*. Collegeville, MN: Michael Glazier Books (an imprint of Liturgical Press), 1989.

———. *Love Was His Meaning: The Theology and Mysticism of Julian of Norwich*. Salzburg, Austria: Institut für Anglistik und Amerikanistik, Universität Salzburg, 1982.

Roman, Christopher. *Domestic Mysticism in Margery Kempe and Dame Julian of Norwich: The Transformation of Christian Spirituality in the Late Middle Ages*. Lewiston, NY: Edwin Mellen Press, 2005.

Sayer, Frank Dale, editor. *Julian and Her Norwich: Commemorative Essays and Handbook to the Exhibition 'Revelations of Divine Love'*. Norwich, UK: 1973 Celebration Committee, 1973.

Thorne, Brian. *Julian of Norwich: Counsellor for Our Age*. London: Guild of Pastoral Psychology, 1999.

Tinsley, Ambrose, OSB. *A Neighbour Kind and Known: The Spirituality of Julian of Norwich*. Dublin, Ireland: Columba Press, 1997.

Underhill, Evelyn. *Julian of Norwich*. Whitefish; MT: Kessinger Publishing, 2005.

Upjohn, Sheila. *In Search of Julian of Norwich*. London: Darton, Longman & Todd, 1991; and New York: Morehouse, 2007.

———. *Why Julian Now: A Voyage of Discovery*. London: Darton, Longman & Todd, 1989.

Vinge, Patricia Mary. *An Understanding of Love According to the Anchoress Julian of Norwich*. Salzburg, Austria: Institut für Anglistik und Amerikanistik, Universität Salzburg, 1983.

Watkin, E.I. *On Julian of Norwich, and in Defence of Margery Kempe*. Exeter, UK: University of Exeter Press, 1979.

Watson, Nicholas. "The Composition of Julian of Norwich's *Revelation of Love*." *Speculum* 68 (1993), 637–83.

4. Julian's Cell and Monastic Habits

Baker, Timothy. *Medieval London*. New York: Praeger, 1970.

Clay, Rotha Mary. *The Hermits and Anchorites of England*. London: Methuen, 1914.

Du Boulay, F.R.H. *An Age of Ambition: English Society in the Late Middle Ages*. New York: Viking, 1970.

Duffy, Eamon. *Marking the Hours: English People and Their Prayers, 1240–1570*. New Haven, CT: Yale University Press, 2006.

Fosbrooke, Thomas Dudley. *British Monachism or Manners and Customs of the Monks and Nuns of England....* London: M. A. Nattali, 1843.

Hartley, Dorothy. *Lost Country Life*. New York: Pantheon, 1979.

Keen, M.H. *England in the Later Middle Ages*. London: Methuen & Co., 1973.

Pegge, Samuel. *The Forme of Cury: A Roll of Ancient English Cookery* [Compiled by the Master-Cooks of Richard II in 1390]. London, 1780. Available as an eBook from several Internet sites.

Steele, Francesca M. *Anchoresses of the West*. London: Sands & Co., 1903.

Tolkien, J.R.R., editor. *The English Text of the Ancrene Riwle: Ancrene Wisse, Edited from the Corpus Christi College Cambridge MS 402*. EETS #249. London: Oxford University Press, 1962.

Warren, Ann K. *Anchorites and Their Patrons in Medieval England*. Berkeley, CA: University of Calfornia Press, 1985.

5. Julian and Margery Kempe

Atkinson, Clarissa W. *Mystic and Pilgrim: The Book and the Word of Margery Kempe*. Ithaca, NY: Cornell University Press, 1983.

Gallyon, Margaret. *Margery Kempe of Lynn and Medieval England*. Norwich, UK: Canterbury Press, 1995.

Kempe, Margery. *The Book of Margery Kempe*. Translated and edited by John Skinner. New York: Doubleday, 1998.

————. *The Book of Margery Kempe*. Edited by Lynn Staley. Kalamazoo, MI: Medieval Institute Publications, 1996.

————. *The Book of Margery Kempe: The Autobiography of the Madwoman of God*. Translated by Tony D. Triggs. Chicago: Triumph Books, 1995.

McEntire, Sandra J. *Margery Kempe: A Book of Essays*. New York: Garland, 1992.

Stone, Robert Karl. *Middle English Prose Style: Margery Kempe and Julian of Norwich*. The Hague, Netherlands: Mouton, 1970.

Undset, Sigrid. "Margery Kempe of Lynn." *The Atlantic*, August 1939.

6. HISTORY OF JULIAN'S RELIGIOUS ERA

Blackburn, Bonnie and Lefranc Holford-Strevens. *The Oxford Companion to the Year*. Oxford, UK: Oxford University Press, 1999.

Flood, Robert H. *A Description of St. Julian's, Norwich, and an Account of Dame Julian's connection with it*. Norwich, UK: The Wherry Press, n.d.

Fowler, David C. *The Bible in Middle English Literature*. Seattle: University of Washington Press, 1984.

McKisack, May. *The Fourteenth Century 1307–1399*. Oxford, UK: Oxford University Press, 1959.

Messent, Claude J.W. *The Monastic Remains of Norfolk & Suffolk*. Norwich, UK: H.W. Hunt, 1934.

Orme, Nicholas. *Medieval Children*. New Haven: Yale University Press, 2001.

Parker, Robert C. *The Whilton Dispute 1264–1380: A Social-Legal Study of Dispute Settlements*. Princeton, NJ: Princeton University Press, 1984.

Simmons, Thomas Frederick, editor. *The Lay Folks Mass Book*. EETS. London: N. Trübner & Co., 1879.

Tanner, Norman P. *The Church in Late Medieval Norwich 1379–1532*. Toronto, ON, Canada: Pontifical Institute of Medieval Studies, 1984.

Walker, Sue Sheridan. *Wife and Widow in Medieval England*. Ann Arbor, MI: University of Michigan Press, 1993.

Wallace, David. *The Cambridge History of Medieval English Literature*. Cambridge, UK: Cambridge University Press, 1999.

Watson, Nicholas. *Anchoritic Spirituality: Ancrene Wisse and Associated Works*. Mahwah, NJ: Paulist Press, 1991.

7. The Religious Milieu of the Fourteenth Century

Kieckhefer, Richard. *Unquiet Souls: Fourteenth Century Saints and Their Religious Milieu*. Chicago: University of Chicago Press, 1984.

LeVert, Laurelle. "'Crucifye hem, Crucifye hem': The Subject and Affective Response in Middle English Passion Narratives." In Essays in Medieval Studies, vol. 14. *Popular Piety: Prayer, Devotion, and Cult*, edited by Allen J. Frantzen. Chicago: Illinois Medieval Association, 1997. <http://www.illinoismedieval.org/ems/emsv14.html> (12/05/05).

Sargent, Michael G., editor. *Nicholas Love's Mirror of the Blessed Life of Jesus Christ*. New York: Garland, 1992.

Tauler, John. *Meditations on the Life and Passion of our Lord Jesus Christ*. Translated by an anonymous secular priest. London: Thomas Baker, 1889.

———.*Meditations on the Life and Passion of our Lord Jesus Christ* Translated by A.P.J. Cruickshank. London: Burns, Oates & Washbourne, 1925.

8. Julian's Bible

Blunt, J.H. *A Plain Account of the English Bible*. Quoted in F.A. Gasquet. *The Old English Bible and Other Essays* (see entry on Gasquet, below).

Bobrick, Benson. *Wide as the Waters: The Story of the English Bible and the Revolution It Inspired*. New York: Penguin, 2002.

De Hamel, Christopher. *The Book: A History of the Bible*. London: Phaidon, 2001.

Deanesly, Margaret. *The Significance of the Lollard Bible*. The Ethel M. Wood lecture delivered before the University of London on 12 March 1951. London: The Athlone Press, 1951.

Eadie, John. *The English Bible*. New York: Macmillan, 1876.

Fowler, David C. *The Bible in Middle English Literature*. Seattle: University of Washington Press, 1984.

Gasquet, F.A. *The Old English Bible and Other Essays*. Port Washington, NY: Kennikat Press, 1969. (Originally published London: John C. Nimmo, 1897.)

Heaton, W.J. *Our Own English Bible: Its Translators and Their Work*. London: Francis Griffiths, 1913.

Madden and Forshall. *The Holy Bible...Made from the Latin Vulgate by John Wycliffe and His Followers*. Oxford, UK: Oxford University Press, 1850.

McFarlane, K.B. *John Wycliffe and the Beginnings of English Nonconformity*. London: English Universities Press, 1952.

McGrath, Alister. *In the Beginning: The Story of the King James Bible and How It Changed a Nation, a Language, and a Culture*. New York: Doubleday, 2001.

Ollard, S.L., and Gordon Crosse. *A Dictionary of English Church History*. Oxford, UK: Mowbray, 1912.

Orne, Nicholas. "What Did Medieval Schools Do For Us?" *History Today*. Vol. 56.6, June 2006.

Paues, Anna C. *A Fourteenth Century English Biblical Version*. Cambridge, UK: Cambridge University Press, 1904.

Pollard, Alfred W. *Records of the English Bible*. London: Oxford University Press, 1911.

Rex, Richard. *The Lollards*. Hampshire, UK: Palgrave imprint—St. Martin's Press, 2002.

Robinson, H. Wheeler. *The Bible in Its Ancient and English Versions*. Oxford, UK: Clarendon Press, 1940.

9. THE PAPACY IN JULIAN'S TIME

Gail, Marzieh. *The Three Popes: An Account of the Great Schism*. New York: Simon & Schuster, 1969.

Holmes, George, editor. *The Oxford History of Medieval Europe*. Oxford, UK: Oxford University Press, 1988.

Kaminsky, Howard. "The Great Schism." In *The New Cambridge Medieval History*. Vol. 6. Cambridge, UK: Cambridge University Press, 2000.

Logan, F. Donald. *A History of the Church in the Middle Ages*. London: Routledge, 2002.

Mulder, William. "Pope Urban VI." *The Catholic Encyclopedia*. Vol. 15. New York: Robert Appleton Co, 1912.

Oakley, Francis. *The Western Church in the Late Middle Ages*. Ithaca, NY: Cornell University Press, 1985.

Salembier, Louis. "Western Schism." In *The Catholic Encyclopedia*. Vol. 13. New York: Robert Appleton Co., 1912.

Smith, John Holland. *The Great Schism: 1378*. New York: Harris & Hamilton, 1970.

Tuchman, Barbara. *A Distant Mirror*. New York: Ballantine, 1978.

Ullman, Walter. *The Origins of the Great Schism: A Study in Fourteenth Century Ecclesiastical History*. London: Burns, Oates & Washburne, 1948.

10. JULIAN'S CHURCH BUILDING

Cautley, H. Munro. *Norfolk Churches*. Norwich, UK: Boydell Press, 1979.

Cox, J. Charles. *County Churches: Norfolk*. London: George Allen & Co Ltd, 1911.

Goode, W. J. *East Anglian Round Towers and Their Churches*. Lowestoft, UK: Friends of the Round Tower Churches Society, 1982.

Mee, Arthur. *The King's England—Norfolk*. Revised and edited by Andrew Stephenon. London: Hodder & Stoughton, 1972.

Messent, Claude W.J. *Parish Churches Of Norfolk & Norwich*. London: H. W. Hunt, 1936.

———. *The Round Towers to English Parish Churches*. London: Fletcher & Son Ltd, 1958.

Pevsner, Nikolaus. *Buildings Of England—North East Norfolk & Norwich*. London: Penguin, 1979.

11. THE NORWICH FLOODS

Day, J. Wentworth. *Norwich and the Broads.* London: B.T. Batsworth, 1953.

Dutt, William A. *The Norfolk Broads.* London: Methuen, 1905.

12. THE PESTILENCE ("THE BLACK DEATH")

Fagan, Brian. *The Little Ice Age: How Climate Made History 1300–1850.* New York: Basic Books, 2000. 81ff.

Hatcher, J. *Plague, Population and the English Economy 1348–1530.* London: Basingstroke, 1977.

Mettler, Cecilia, and Fred A. Mettler. *History of Medicine.* Pittsburgh, PA: Blakiston Co., 1847.

Ranger, Terrence, and Paul Slack, editors. *Epidemics and Ideas.* Cambridge, UK: Cambridge University Press, 1995.

Williman, Daniel, editor. *The Black Death: The Impact of the Fourteenth-century Plague.* Binghamton, NY: Center for Medieval and Early Renaissance Studies, 1982.

13. ABOUT PILATE

Clough, W.O., translator and editor. *Gesta Pilati: or the Reports, Letters and Acts of Pontius Pilate.* Indianapolis: Robert Douglas, 1887.

Comestor, Peter. *Historica Scholastica.* In *Patrilogiae Latinae,* 1631.

De Voragine, Jacobus. *The Golden Legend, v. 1.* Princeton, NJ: Princeton University Press, 1993.

Elliott, J.K. *The Apocryphal New Testament.* Oxford, UK: Clarendon Press, 1993.

James, M.R. *Apocrypha Anecdota.* Cambridge, UK: Cambridge University Press, 1893.

Kolve, V.A. *The Play Called Corpus Christi.* Stanford, CA: Stanford University Press, 1966.

Meredith, Peter, and Stanley Kahrl, editors. *The N-Town Plays: A Facsimile of British Library MS Cotton Vespasian D VIII*. Leeds, UK: University of Leeds, 1977.

Richardson, Patricia. *Scholarly Pursuits: The Lively Legends of Pontius Pilate*. (Comments on a dissertation by Kateryna Rudnytzky.) Chapel Hill, NC: University of North Carolina Press, 1995.

Spector, Stephen, editor. *The N-Town Play: Cotton MS Vespasian D 8*. EETS. Oxford, UK: Oxford University Press, 1991.

Stalker, J. *Trial and Death of Jesus Christ*. London: G.H. Doran, 1894.

14. ABOUT DENIS OF FRANCE

Brockway, Alan. http://www.abrock.com/Greece-Turkey/godunknown.html. (04/19/05).

Carrier, Richard C. "Cultural History of the Lunar and Solar Eclipse in the Early Roman Empire." MA essay for Columbia University History Department, 1998.

Carrier, Richard C. "Thallus: an Analysis" (1999). http://www.infidels.org/library/ modern/richard_carrier/thallus.html (02/17/05).

———. "Why I Don't Buy the Resurrection Story." Lecture to Yale College Humanists and Secularists, 10/26/2000. http://home.freeuk.com/jesusmyth/lecture.htm (02/17/05).

Guerin, Msgr. Paul. *Les Petits Bollandistes: Vies des Saints*. Paris: Bloud & Barral, 1865.

Luibheid, Colm, translator. *Pseudo-Dionysius: The Complete Works*. Mahwah, NJ: Paulist Press, 1987.

Newton, Robert. *Ancient Astronomical Observations and the Accelerations of the Earth and Moon*. Baltimore: Johns Hopkins, 1970.

Stearns, W.N. *Fragments from Graeco-Jewish Writers*. Chicago: University of Chicago Press, 1908.

15. DEVOTIONAL READING BASED ON JULIAN

Chelsea, Robert. *All Will Be Well*. Notre Dame, IN: Ave Marie Press, 1995.

Colledge, Edmund, and James Walsh. *The Life of the Soul: The Wisdom of Julian of Norwich*. Mahwah NJ: Paulist Press, 1996.

Durka, Gloria. *Praying with Julian of Norwich*. Winona, MN: St. Mary's Press, 1989.

Forbes, F.A., editor. *Meditations on the Litany of the Sacred Heat of Jesus Culled from the Writings of Juliana of Norwich*. London: Burns Oates & Washbourne, 1857.

Furness, Jean. *Love Is His Meaning: Meditations on Julian of Norwich*. Essex, UK: McCrimmons, 1993.

Furlong, Monica, editor. *The Wisdom of Julian of Norwich*. Grand Rapids, MI: W.B. Eerdmans, 1996.

Hazard, David. *I Promise You a Crown: A 40-Day Journey in the Company of Julian of Norwich*. Minneapolis: Bethany House, 1995.

Llewelyn, Robert. *Circles of Silence: Explorations in Prayer with Julian Meetings*. London: Darton, Longman & Todd, 2002.

———. *The Fountain Within*. London: Darton, Longman & Todd, 1989.

Manton, Karen. *The Gift of Julian of Norwich*. Notre Dame, IN: Ave Maria Press, 2005.

Obbard, Elizabeth Ruth. *See How I Love You: Meditations on the Way of the Cross with Julian of Norwich*. Norwich, UK: Canterbury, 1996.

Roberts, Roger L. *Revelations of Divine Love: Julian of Norwich*. Treasures of Spiritual Classics. London: Mowbray, 1981.

Roker, Penny, RSM. *Homely Love: Prayers and Reflections Using the Words of Julian of Norwich*. Norwich, UK: Canterbury, 2006.

Searle, Pamela, editor. *Julian of Norwich: Masters of Prayer*. London: Church House Publishing, 1984.

Sherley-Price, Leo. *Lent with Mother Julian*. London: Mowbray, 1962.

Skinner, Richard. *In the Stillness: A Sequence of Poems Based on Julian of Norwich*. Exeter, Devonshire, UK: Dilettante Pubs., 1990.

Upjohn, Sheila, and Irene Ogden, illustrator. *Stations of the Cross: A Devotion Using the* Revelations of Divine Love *of Julian of Norwich*. Norwich, UK: Friends of Julian of Norwich, 2001.

16. NOVELS AND PLAYS ABOUT JULIAN

Janda, James. *Julian: A Play Based on the Life of Julian of Norwich*. New York: Vineyard/Seabury Press, 1984.

Little, Mary F. *Julian's Cat: The Imagining History of a Cat of Destiny*. Wilton, CT: Morehouse, 1989.

Milton, Ralph. *Julian's Cell: The Earthy Story of Julian of Norwich*. Kelonah, B.C., Canada: Woodlake Books, 2002/3.

Pantaleo, Jack. *Mother Julian and the Gentle Vampire*. Roseville, CA: Dry Bones Press, 2000.

Seton, Anya. *Katherine*. Boston: Houghton Mifflin, 1954.

Upjohn, Sheila. *Mind Out of Time: A Play about Julian of Norwich*. Norwich, UK: Julian Shrine Publications, 1979.

17. DICTIONARIES AND LINGUISTIC REFERENCES

Greeson, Hoyt (Glossarist). In *Julian of Norwich: Showing of Love: Extant Texts and Translation,* edited by Anna Maria Reynolds and Julia Bolton Holloway. Florence, Italy: Sismel-Edizioni del Galluzzo, 2001.

Horobin, Simon, and Jeremy Smith, *An Introduction to Middle English*. Edinburgh, UK: Edinburgh University Press, 2002.

Lewis, Robert E., editor in chief. *The Middle English Dictionary*. Ann Arbor, MI: University of Michigan Press, 2006. [http://quod.lib.umich.edu/m/med/]

Mayhew, A.L., and Walter W. Skeat. *A Concise Dictionary of Middle English from A.D. 1150 to 1580*. n.p., 1888. [http://www.gutenberg.org/etext/10625]

Mossé, Fernand. *A Handbook of Middle English*. Edited by James A. Walker. Baltimore: John Hopkins University Press, 1952 (1968).

Stratmann, Francis Henry. *A Middle English Dictionary*. Edited by Henry Bradley. Oxford, UK: Oxford University Press, 1891 (1995).

Weiner, E.S.C., and J.A. Simpson, editors. *The Compact Edition of the Oxford English Dictionary*. Oxford, UK: Oxford University Press, 1971.

DISCOVER MORE PARACLETE GIANTS

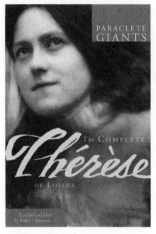

THE COMPLETE THÉRÈSE OF LISIEUX

ISBN: 978-1-55725-670-6
420 pages, $24.99

The most comprehensive introduction to
St. Thérèse available today, including:

- Her classic *The Story of a Soul*, complete
  and unabridged
- Rarely seen, her sisters' description of her
  final days
- A poignant collection of ancedotes about
  Thérèse recounted after her death
- Prayers, letters, and poems, including the poem
  that inspired the name "Little Flower"
- Appendices, engravings, and rare photographs.

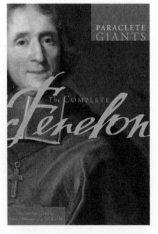

THE COMPLETE FÉNELON

ISBN: 978-1-55725-607-2
338 pages, $24.95

The writings of François Fénelon have never been
as accessible as they are now in *The Complete Fénelon*,
which includes more than one hundred of his letters
and meditations. Also translated here into English for
the first time are Fénelon's reflections on the seasons
and holidays of the Christian year.

Available from most booksellers or through Paraclete Press:
www.paracletepress.com; 1–800–451–5006.
Try your local bookstore first.